MW00522839

'Who better to shed light on the complex and much mi of the practice of diplomacy than Johan Verbeke, who subsequent service as the Special Representative of the U... ... ... period as Belgium's ambassador in London provide a solid foundation for this valuable book? He understands and explains why diplomacy is not, and cannot be, a matter of drawing up blueprints, but rather of adapting to events and attempting to shape their handling. And he explains too why diplomacy is as essential as ever in this digital age with which diplomats have to come to terms.'

David Hannay, *former UK Permanent Representative to the EU and UN, and former member of Kofi Annan's High Level Panel on Threats, Challenges and Change*

'By focusing on "diplomacy in practice", Johan Verbeke offers a much-needed reality check: what can diplomacy do, and how to ensure that it is successful? But also, what can diplomacy not do, what are its limits? A highly successful national and UN diplomat himself, his sharp analysis goes straight to the heart of the matter.'

Sven Biscop, *Director of Programs at Egmont – the Royal Institute for International Relations in Brussels and Professor at Ghent University*

'Johan Verbeke's *Diplomacy in Practice* strikes by its novel approach to an old subject. Coming from a great practitioner with a solid academic background, the book not only offers an understanding of what diplomacy as a practice really comes down to, but also invites the reader to critically reflect on it. For that the book's interdisciplinary approach proves invaluable. There is clarity and boldness of thought in this book and that is what makes it indispensable reading for students of diplomacy and professional diplomats alike.'

Peter Piot, *Special Advisor to the EU Commission President, former Director of the London School of Hygiene and Tropical Medicine and former Executive Director of UNAIDS*

'The publication of Johan Verbeke's *Diplomacy in Practice* could not be better timed. The art, as much as the practice of diplomacy, has appeared to be slipping to the margins of international politics, as parliaments, non-state actors, business leaders and prime ministers competed over the domestic impacts of globalisation. But China's rise, America's decline, Russia's determination to regain its status, and the emergence of new regional powers have together brought diplomacy back to the centre of statecraft for large, small and mid-sized countries alike. In this book, Verbeke provides both a conceptual framework and a set of practical guideposts for the practice of modern diplomacy, thereby ensuring that a new generation of diplomats, policymakers and analysts can benefit from the insights of one of Europe's most seasoned and thoughtful diplomats.'

Robin Niblett, *Director and Chief Executive of Chatham House*

'This book by my former Chief of Staff is timely. The new era of great power competition we are entering in will need a lot of diplomacy: producing the right analysis, formulating and finetuning the politician's decisions, doing the after-care. Johan Verbeke is overly humble to limit himself to a practitioner. His broad knowledge of history and context make him a scholar drenched in practice.'

Karel De Gucht, *former Belgian Minister of Foreign Affairs and EU Trade Commissioner*

'Stripped of smoke and mirrors, away from pomp and circumstance, this book gives a clear toolkit for the daily practice of diplomacy in the 21st century.'

Stefan Dercon, *Professor of Economic Policy, University of Oxford, UK*

Diplomacy in Practice

This book informs students about the practice of modern diplomacy while simultaneously inviting them to critically reflect on it.

The work introduces the world of diplomacy from a practitioner's point of view. Rather than listening to what diplomats say they do, the book looks at what they actually do. Diplomacy is thus approached through the lenses of its manifold practices: from political analysis to policy-shaping, from conflict prevention over conflict-management to conflict-resolution. However, the book not only aims at informing or instructing but also, and primarily, wants its readers to critically reflect on diplomacy. It reviews received ideas by posing questions such as: what does 'preventive diplomacy' really mean?; what is the place of 'transparency' in diplomatic practice?; why is the relationship between 'law and diplomacy' ambiguous?; how come that our leaders have such a difficult time in credibly defending 'human rights'?; and why is conducting an 'ethical foreign policy' a mission impossible? To tackle these and other questions, the book uses the tools of contemporary academic disciplines, such as behavioural economics, game theory, social psychology, argumentation theory, and practical logic, among others. This interdisciplinary approach brings fresh perspective to a field of study that has long remained self-contained.

This book will be of great interest to students of diplomacy, foreign policy, and International Relations, as well as those seeking a career in diplomacy and existing diplomatic practitioners and international analysts.

Johan Verbeke is a visiting professor at the Universities of Brussels (VUB) and Lille (UCL, France) and a Senior Fellow of Egmont – the Royal Institute for International Relations in Brussels. He has been a diplomat for 35 years, ending his career as Ambassador in Washington. He was the Chief Adviser to two Ministers of Foreign Affairs and a Special Representative of the UN Secretary General.

Diplomacy in Practice

A Critical Approach

Johan Verbeke

Routledge
Taylor & Francis Group

LONDON AND NEW YORK

Cover Image: Qketel., El hombre (The man), 2019, H 20x W14 cm, Watercolor, paper.
Copyright and photo credits: Quentin Ketelaers
Collection: Artist collection. Location: Brussels

First published 2023
by Routledge
4 Park Square, Milton Park, Abingdon, Oxon OX14 4RN

and by Routledge
605 Third Avenue, New York, NY 10158

Routledge is an imprint of the Taylor & Francis Group, an informa business

© 2023 Johan Verbeke

The right of Johan Verbeke to be identified as author of this work has been asserted in accordance with sections 77 and 78 of the Copyright, Designs and Patents Act 1988.

British Library Cataloguing-in-Publication Data
A catalogue record for this book is available from the British Library

Library of Congress Cataloging-in-Publication Data
A catalog record has been requested for this book

ISBN: 978-1-032-28716-4 (hbk)
ISBN: 978-1-032-28708-9 (pbk)
ISBN: 978-1-003-29818-2 (ebk)

DOI: 10.4324/9781003298182

Typeset in Times New Roman
by Newgen Publishing UK

Contents

Boxes

Tables

Abbreviations

ABM	Anti-Ballistic Missile Treaty
ASEAN	Association of Southeast Asian Nations
AU	African Union
BRICS	Brazil, Russia, India, China, South Africa
CAR	Central African Republic
CFSP	Common Foreign and Security Policy
COP	Conference of the Parties
CSCE	Conference on Security and Cooperation in Europe
CTBT	Comprehensive Nuclear Test Ban Treaty
DCM	Deputy Chief of Mission
DRC	Democratic Republic of Congo
ECOWAS	Economic Community of West African States
EEZ	Exclusive Economic Zone
EU	European Union
G-7	group of 7
G-20	group of 20
G-77	group of 77
HR	Human Rights
IAEA	International Atomic Energy Agency
ICC	International Criminal Court
IL	international law
IMF	International Monetary Fund
IMO	International Maritime Organisation
IR	international relations
ISIS	Islamic State of Iraq and the Levant
JCPOA	Joint Comprehensive Plan of Action
MFAs	Ministries of Foreign Affairs
MONUSCO	United Nations Organisation Stabilization Mission in Congo
NAM	Non-Aligned Movement
NATO	North Atlantic Treaty Organisation
NFU	No First Use
NGO	non-governmental organisation
NPT	Nuclear Non-Proliferation Treaty
SDG	Sustainable Development Goals
OECD	Organisation for Economic Cooperation and Development
OSCE	Organisation for Security and Cooperation in Europe

P5	The five permanent members of the United Nations Security Council
PKO	Peacekeeping operation
PLO	Palestine Liberation Organisation
PR	Permanent Representative
R2P	Responsibility to Protect
ROL	Rule of Law
SALT	Strategic Arms Limitation Talks
START	Strategic Arms Reduction Treaty
TPP	Trans-Pacific Partnership
UN	United Nations
UNAMA	United Nations Mission in Afghanistan
UNAMI	United Nations Assistance Mission for Iraq
UNCTAD	United Nations Conference on Trade and Development
UNDP	United Nations Development Programme
UNESCO	United Nations Educational, Scientific and Cultural Organisation
UNFICYP	United Nations Force in Cyprus
UNICEF	United Nations Children's Fund
UNPROFOR	United Nations Protection Force in Former Yugoslavia
UNSC	United Nations Security Council
UNSG	United Nations Secretary General
US	United States
USSR	Union of Soviet Socialist Republics
WHO	World Health Organisation
WMD	Weapons of mass destruction
WTO	World Trade Organisation

Preface

Origins. This book has grown out of the lectures I gave at institutions and universities during my last diplomatic postings in London and Washington. I particularly enjoyed meeting with those clever students at the London School of Economics, Georgetown University, or Johns Hopkins, to name just these few. Reaching out, speaking, and lecturing to a wider audience is part of a diplomat's job. It is called 'public diplomacy', and I liked it. Upon finishing my last diplomatic assignment as ambassador in Washington, came retirement – obligatory retirement. But I was lucky. I was offered positions as visiting professor both at the Free University of Brussels and the Catholic University of Lille (France), where I teach master classes in 'Modern Diplomacy' and 'Diplomacy in Practice'. Lecturing thus turned into teaching. The fragmented landscape of the former had to be reshaped into something more structured and systematic. That, however, on itself, did not mean that the teaching material had to be written out as a book. But then came Covid-19. Teaching 'at distance' through virtual media is no substitute for physical interaction with debate and Q&A. The students needed and deserved some written material supporting and complementing what I told them through that abstract medium. It started with a few chapters and ended up as an entire course book.

Covid-19. Covid-19's confinement policy helped. In fact, for me Covid-19 constituted what psychologists call a '*liminal moment*', one where you experience a transition from one state to another. Liminality can be frightening, as Covid-19 certainly is, but it can also offer a chance to reflect, reboot, and reshape. Indeed, there is an entire industry of personal coaching that is dedicated to using 'liminal space' to reboot careers. I did not need such coaching. Covid-19 did it for me. It ripped me out of my 'normal'. I decided to turn my *course* on diplomacy into a *book*.

Book or course. Is what you have before you a university-level textbook aimed at instructing students or is it an accessible book for the enlightenment *and* enjoyment of a larger public? Do we really have to decide on such either/or question? Why not both? 'Course' and 'book' do not seem to be incompatible categories. Perhaps they may even be mutually reinforcing. Why then not go for the hybrid course-book, a book in which you simultaneously *learn about* diplomacy while being invited to critically *reflect on* it. True enough, this book is primarily based on the lifelong day-to-day practice of diplomacy as I have experienced it. But that experiencing never forbade me to critically reflect on what I was doing. Indeed, I often found that it was this reflection that gave depth to the practice and that made diplomacy a worthwhile enterprise. Remember Socrates: 'The unexamined life is not worth living'.

Practitioner versus academic. The book you have before you aims to contribute to bridging the supposed divide between the academic and the non-academic, as if these were two separate realms. Recently I came across a defensive statement made by a non-academic: 'Scholars may vehemently protest, but I am a practitioner'. Such outcries rest on the false dichotomy that you are either a scholar or a practitioner and that you cannot be both. I am not an academic, but I have always had a keen interest for what academia had to tell me. Conversely, I know a lot of first-rate academics who would never ignore, let alone despise what the *mere* practitioner of his field of study is making of it in his daily dealings. Practice-based research and research-inspired practice need not lay that far apart. In fact, they should coincide. That is what the 'revolving doors'–principle in the American recruitment system for State Department officials is all about. Civil servants and academics simply switch jobs.

Which brings me to another, related point. The methodological approach of diplomacy in this book is a pragmatic one: diplomacy is what diplomats do. Put differently: to know what diplomacy is, look at diplomatic practice. That, however, does not mean that the *study* of diplomacy is itself a practice. Such study requires reflecting on what diplomatic practice is, and such reflection is primarily a theoretical endeavour. Hence, the paradox that may puzzle some readers but should not. There is nothing contradictory in studying a practice from a theoretical perspective. Indeed, there is no alternative to doing so.

Finally, and before moving on to questions regarding the form in which this book was written, a short note. Researchers are often too eager to pursue striking results (and editors too prone to approve of them) hoping to impress on their readership. I have avoided falling into this trap by sticking to sobriety in language and rigour in analysis. Impressing readers has not been my aim. For that I am too wary of high-conviction views and too circumspect of exaggerations and dramatisations.

On form. In this book with its hybrid character inviting the reader to simultaneously *learn about* and critically *reflect on* diplomacy, I have endeavoured to spurn obscurity as much as possible and offer clarity instead, both in thought and language. My words may leave many of you unconvinced, sometimes even repelled but never, I hope, mystified. I no doubt am sometimes clearly wrong, but when this is so I hope to be always wrong clearly. That is why I have made use of two typographical devices that help fix ideas. One is the use of **bold** type to highlight concepts that play an important role in the story, the other is the use of *italics* whenever we meet a thought or idea that is central to the understanding of what is being explained. A word also on the use of 'we' and 'I'. I do not wish to claim great originality in this book. For that I am too befriended with Umberto Eco who once said that 'books are made only on or around other books'. Much of what I tell in this book is what I learned from others and can be considered 'shared' knowledge: that is the 'we'-part of the book. But there are of course pages in this book where I differ with what others have said or where I proffer personal views, with which many may disagree; for those obviously I assume full responsibility – they constitute the 'I' – part of the book.

Acknowledgements. Ideas do not come out of thin air. As far as this book is concerned, they obviously came out of my own diplomatic practice but certainly no less the practice of some great masters in diplomacy: Nick Burns, William Burns, Abba Eban, Gérard Errera, Philippe de Schoutheete, David Hannay, Emir Jones-Perry, John Sawers, and Frans Van Daele. The general ideas in this book rely on various intellectual disciplines that have always fascinated me (logic and argumentation, decision and game theory, behavioural economics). Of this, the select bibliography will give you a hint. The ideas in this book also show the influence of colleagues, students, and friends. I wish to thank them for the time and energy they spent in reviewing parts of earlier versions of this book, for their insights and comments and above all for encouraging me in pursuing my work: Thomas Antoine, Arthur Barbé, Sven Biscop, Jan Grauls, Andy Jackson, Marcus Leroy, Alexander Mattelaer, Annick Paternoster, Caroline Piret, Bruno Van der Pluijm, Peter Van Kemseke. A warm thank you also to my wife Catherine for her support throughout the process. Let me finally thank my editor at Routledge, Andrew Humphrys, for his advice and patience.

Introduction

Diplomacy is what diplomats do

In this introduction, we will briefly sketch our **methodological approach** to the study of diplomacy. The approach is somewhat idiosyncratic. But we trust that we can convince our readers of its interest and plausibility. Our approach is a pragmatic and realist one, sober and down-to-earth, and above all critical.

I.1 The Socratic fallacy

Most treatises on diplomacy start out with the grand question: 'What is Diplomacy'. Then follows the high-end elegant classical definition given by the 19th century British diplomat Ernest Satow who defined diplomacy as 'the application of intelligence and tact to the conduct of official relations between independent states', or the one given by his 20th century successor Harold Nicolson: 'Diplomacy is the management of relations between independent states by the process of negotiations'. Less elevated and somewhat more metaphorical is Robin Hobb's definition of 'Diplomacy (as) the velvet glove that cloaks the fist of power'. Are such definitions helpful? People crave for the certainty offered by definitions. But the sense of certainty offered by them is often illusory. 'What-questions' are misleading as they lead to reductive, partial, and uninformative answers. Question: 'What is Man?' Answer: 'Man is a rational animal' (Aristotle). Any wiser? There is no such thing as the 'essence' of Man (with capital M), or for that matter of Diplomacy (with capital D). That is why the lofty definitions of diplomacy have so often been supplemented if not ridiculed by low-end joking definitions such as the one given by Wynn Catlin: 'Diplomacy is the art of saying "nice doggie" until you can find a rock', or the one given by Winston Churchill: 'Diplomacy is the art of telling people to go to hell in such a way that they ask for directions' (FLETCHER, 2017, p. 95).

One must resist this essentialist tendency known as the Socratic fallacy. One must learn to accept that diplomacy means different things to different people at different times and that diplomacy can be approached in different ways:

- Some go for a *descriptive* approach to diplomacy and focus on *diplomatic history* not simply as the study of the past for its own sake, but to critically use it as a way of illuminating the present. Henry Kissinger and his classic *Diplomacy* (KISSINGER, 1994) stand out here as the eminent example of such '*applied history*' approach. More recent examples are Joseph Siracusa's compact *Diplomacy* (SIRACUSA, 2010) and Robert Cooper's *The Ambassadors* (COOPER, 2021).

DOI: 10.4324/9781003298182-1

- Others stress the **normative** side of diplomacy, linking it to international law, human rights, the Rule of Law, and sometimes global ethics. A good example is David Amstrong's *International Law and International Relations* (AMSTRONG et al., 2012).
- Still others put the emphasis on the **theoretical** underpinnings of diplomacy through a rigorous *analytical and conceptual* approach of international relations. Good examples are Knud Jörgensen's *International Relations Theory* (JÖRGENSEN, 2010) and James der Derian's *On Diplomacy* (DER DERIAN, 1987).

One could go on: there are *International Security* studies and studies in *Human Security*, *Geopolitics*, *Geo-economics*, and *Global Governance*. All of them have a direct bearing on diplomacy, but diplomacy does not reduce to any of them.

I.2 The Practice Turn

Primarily, diplomacy is not a study, it is a practice. Diplomacy is what diplomats do. We will approach diplomacy pragmatically through the lens of its manifold practices. We are interested in the question 'how does it work' rather than 'what is it really'. Our motto: 'if you want to understand something, observe it in action'. By focusing on what the practicing diplomat actually does, we zoom in on the quotidian unfolding of diplomatic work, from political analysis to policy-shaping, from problem-solving to negotiation and communication. We analyse the ongoing **diplomatic practices** that, put together, constitute the 'big picture' that is variously but only partially described by the different approaches mentioned in the preceding paragraph. Our claim is *not* that by putting diplomatic practice centre stage we offer a universal, grand theory or totalising synthesis of everything diplomatic. We are not interested in 'system'-building. Ours is a sober and prosaic approach aimed at rediscovering the fundamentals of the craft: smart policy judgement, communication and negotiation skills, a feel for the foreign countries where diplomats serve (called 'rational empathy') and above all a sense of limitation. As William Burns, the former US Deputy Secretary of State and current CIA boss, puts it: 'Diplomacy may be one of the world's oldest professions, but it's also one of the most misunderstood. It's mostly a quiet endeavour, less swaggering than unrelenting, oftentimes operating in backchannels, out of sight and out of mind' (BURNS, 2019).

The Practice Turn that we here operate is not unique. It has been variously applied to other fields. Lawyers will be familiar with Legal Realism, an approach that leads to a definition of legal concepts and rules in terms of judicial decisions: law is what judges actually make it to be, not what the statutes or legal codes abstractly say it is; law-in-action rather than law-in-books (COHEN, 1937). Similar approaches have been applied to science. Let me quote an authority in the field, Gerald Holton, who in his *Introduction to Concepts and Theories in Physical Science* writes: 'When you ask, "What is science?" you are in effect asking, "What do scientists now do at their desks and in their laboratories?"' (HOLTON, 1973, p. 173); just looking at their final product, the well-elaborated scientific theory would be quite misleading. The Practice Turn has now even entered the study of mathematics, where a 'dissolution strategy' powered by a 'widespread scepticism towards establishing the certainty of mathematical methods' has led to a redirection of its attention to 'mathematical practice' (OLIVERI, 2010, p. 89, see also FERREIROS, 2016).

I.3 Deflating diplomacy

Somehow, diplomacy must come **back to basics**. Diplomacy has for too long been clouded in a halo of intangibility, secrecy, superiority, pedantry, and pomposity. And for long diplomats, infused with an unshakeable sense of self-importance, have been pleased in entertaining that image. That is a stereotype, of course, but there remains something to it and we had better be on our guards. We will focus on the common sense diplomat, the diplomat-at-work, two feet on earth. Rather than looking at what diplomats, when asked, might *say they do*, we will simply be looking at what they ***actually are doing***, their practice. With such approach we will see that diplomacy is more about such prosaic things as damage control, troubleshooting, bargaining, and fixing, than it is about 'securing the peaceful coexistence of sovereign independent States' and 'promoting friendly relations between them' (as stipulated in Article 3 of the 1961 *Vienna Convention on Diplomatic Relations*). When at 29, Machiavelli entered politics (indeed diplomacy) as First Secretary to the Florentine Republic's Chancery, a good friend of his father, Bartolomeo Scala, told him he was now going to descend to 'the cloaca of the people', the messy things of real politics and diplomacy.

Diplomacy needs a **reality check**. A way to proceed is to look at the diplomat's hidden vocabulary, including its euphemisms; a vocabulary that somehow speaks more to the truth than the official 'diplo-speak' and that reveals the divide between what a diplomat says he or she does and what he or she actually is doing (see: FLETCHER, 2017):

- '*Back-channel diplomacy*': This is the technique of discussing the most important issues of a controversy in a backchannel of which not only the public at large but even the official delegations entrusted with the negotiation of that same issue are kept out and sometimes not even informed (Richard Holbrooke, the architect of the Dayton agreements, liked it).
- '*Cold call*': A surprise call from one leader to another, over the head of their counsellors and diplomats, perhaps to discuss an important and urgent matter, and sometimes tactically inspired to take the other leader aback (Reagan liked it).
- '*Concorde diplomacy*': The practice of leaders to directly meet *in person* thanks to speedy means of communication, thus diminishing the role of intermediary played by diplomats (Kissinger was one of its first practitioners).
- '*Vanilla communication*': The standard exchanges of platitudes in ministerial (and other) high-level meetings without any importance but sold to the outside world as of transformative significance.
- '*Behind the scenes*': The technique of negotiation based on secrecy; the role of secrecy in negotiation is not a relic from the past, it is crucial to its success as much as transparency can be deadly. 'Once your fall-back positions are known to your opponent, you have already fallen back to them' (EBAN, 1998, p. 81).

The **discrepancy between 'belief' and 'action'**, between 'pretence' and 'reality', sometimes reaches schizophrenic levels, as we can see in the 'secrecy versus publicity' debate, in diplomacy generally and in negotiation specifically:

- **Diplomacy generally**, first. As is well known, it was President Wilson who, in 1919, formulated the biblical text for public, open diplomacy in the first of his Fourteen Points: 'Open covenants of peace, openly arrived at, after which there shall be no private international understanding of any kind, but diplomacy shall proceed always frankly and in the public view'. Wilson was reacting against a 'conspirational' tradition in which a few major powers used to decide the future of smaller nations. But having thus *proclaimed* his attachment to 'open covenants openly arrived at', he *acted* quite differently when joining the leaders of Britain, France, and Italy in one of the most closed and indeed 'conspirational' conferences in history, the Versailles peace conference ending World War I. Another example showing the split between saying and doing concerns Jimmy Carter's human rights policy which, in the late 1970s of last century, appeared to be compatible with effusive support for the Shah of Iran and an attitude of commendation to the Nicaraguan dictator Somoza.

- **Negotiation specifically**, next. Building on Wilson's 'open covenants openly arrived at'-idea, a whole trade in 'transparency' has grown, based somehow on the assumption that secrecy is inherently sinful while transparency is inherently virtuous. And so, diplomats end up professing transparency, while knowing full well that negotiation cannot be effective when exposed to the public view. 'The best results of negotiation cannot be achieved in international life any more than in our private world, in the full glare of publicity'. This is what Dag Hammarskjöld, the former United Nations (UN) Secretary General from 1953 to 1961, who might have been expected by reason of his office to be the high priest of open diplomacy, had to say on it. Referring to the 'Behind the Scenes'-technique used in negotiation, Abba Eban comments: 'Hammarskjöld saw no reason for the existence of scenes except for the possibility of operating secretly behind them' (EBAN, 1998, p. 78).

I.4 Realist diplomacy

The diplomat-at-work does not speak the exalted language of textbooks. He or she pursues relatively modest goals, like prolonged political stability, rather than dreaming up 'new world orders'. He or she accepts the notion that rivalry is endemic to interstate relations and that the best that can be done is to keep conflict within tolerable limits. He understands that war prevented is a kind of peace, perhaps the only peace attainable. Such approach is sobering. It is what makes the professional diplomat to be a sober realist.

Realism is usually opposed to *Idealism*. But that opposition is both overblown and misdirected. Let us take both points in turn. **Overblown** first. The realist is not the hard-minded diabolic egoist, nor is the idealist the soft-minded angelic altruist. Most realists pay sincere attention to ethical values and most of the idealists acknowledge the overriding importance of national interest. **Misdirected** next. The real difference between the realist and the idealist lies elsewhere than in a difference in perspective. Realism is a *descriptive* category, it simply tells us how this world is, how it functions, what its imperfections are – whether we like it or not. Idealism, on the contrary, is a *normative* category, it tells us what we should aspire for, what we should aim at, what values we should pursue. Both realism and idealism operate at different levels. They concern two different realms, which are not incompatible with each other but in fact complementary to each other. That is why the realist is sensitive to ethical values, and the idealist knows about national interest. On closer analysis, therefore, the opposition between realism and idealism disappears. Except in one respect: that idealism dominates *the rhetoric of diplomacy* even when its actual practice is guided by realism. And so it happens that most of our governments *take* their decisions in terms of self-interested egoism but *explain* them in terms of self-sacrificial altruism. Which brings us back to the distinction we made between what a diplomat *says he or she does* and what a diplomat *actually is doing*, in his or her practice. And if it is the practice that we are primarily interested in investigating, then, of necessity, we will have to adopt the realist stance.

A realist is someone who believes that self-interest is what determines the behaviour of states, that insecurity and rivalry are inherent to the international system, and that power is the final arbiter in that rivalry. But not all realists are alike. Realists come in different shapes, not all of them attractive or illuminating. Owen Harries, former editor of *The National Interest*, distinguishes five types of realists; a distinction that we find illuminating (HARRIES, 1998, p. 7). First, there is the *scholastic and doctrinaire* realist, lost in his elaborate closed system of Hobbesian truths. Second, the *cynical and gleeful* realist delighted to find hypocrisy and gullibility all around him, without doing anything about it. Third, the ostentatiously *tough and assertive* realist, forever flexing his muscles. Fourth, the *attenuated* realist – an accountant's realism, who insists on reducing all human affairs to what is palpable and measurable and dismisses such things as ideas and ideals and passions from his calculations. And finally, there is what Harries considers the best sort of realist, the **reluctant realist**, the one who is sceptical rather than cynical, and pragmatic rather than dogmatic. The reluctant realist is characterised as much by reservation as by assertion. He is cautious about generalisations and has a keen eye for the particularities that mark international events. Realism is much healthier when it is characterised by the tension that such reluctance conveys, by an *ultimate uncertainty and modesty* concerning the world. This is the kind of sober realism to which we subscribe.

I.5 Interdisciplinary approach

Our sober realism follows from our methodological principle: if you want to understand something, observe it in action. If you want to understand diplomacy, look at diplomatic practice, at what diplomats do, not at what they say they are doing. We will be sceptical with regard to learned treatises approaching problems and issues from above, rather than bottom-up, be it on conflict resolution (prescribing neat scripts and scenarios for conflict resolution, for example, where in fact much of it is just muddling through) or on negotiation (overly theorising a skill that essentially is a matter of good sense). We will be sceptical as regards the 'professed' rationale or 'official' explanations and justifications given for diplomatic actions (think of the 2003 Iraq war) in the form of press releases, public statements in conferences, hearings before parliamentary committees, etc. We will be primarily interested in examining the *unmentioned* factors leading to decisions or actions that are presented as rational, certain, and definite. These factors may range from cognitive traps (such as the 'availability trap': seeing suffering children in Syria, but not in Yemen) over weakness of will and defects in reasoning (groupthink, for instance, or false causality: correlation is not causation) to cultural and ideological prejudices (in the field of Human Rights, for instance). When we thus substitute the diplomacy-in-books with the diplomacy-in-action, there should be no limits as to the resources we rely upon to get a proper take on what diplomacy is really about. Hence the interdisciplinary approach which will be ours. We will in particular rely on:

- *Decision Theory and Pragmatic Logic*: Deciding/acting under uncertainty (ignorance, risk), the practical syllogism, the logic of consequences rather than antecedents.

- *Game Theory*: Strategies (competition *versus* cooperation, zero-sum and win-win) and games (prisoner's dilemma – one-shot and iterated, stag hunt, dictator game...).
- *Behavioural Economics*: Cognitive traps, heuristics, biases, role of framing and nudging.
- *Social Psychology*: Role of stereotypes and clichés, groupthink.
- *Cultural Anthropology*: Role of 'culture' and 'identity', understanding the mind of another – 'rational empathy'.

I.6 Diplomacy as a craft

Diplomacy is a practice, a craft, an art if you wish. It is not a body of knowledge, a science, or a study. Which does not mean that it cannot be studied; indeed, this book is primarily a study of diplomacy as a practice. 'Art' is what the Ancient Greeks called '*technè*' and the recurrent example they gave was that of the '*kybernètes*', the steersman (captain) of a ship: his is not the 'knowledge' of a ship or of the seas (an '*epistemè*'), but of the way a ship is steered trough sometimes rough waters (a '*technè*'). *His is not a know-what, but a know-how*. The same goes for the diplomat. Not the field (domain, subject-matter) she is working *on* (say trade, energy, environment) is what makes her a diplomat, but the way she approaches and manages these different subjects, the 'techniques' she employs, the 'strategies and tactics' she deploys, her 'public speaking' and 'negotiation' styles. The centrality of these how-questions to a diplomat's job explains why the skills part of the job should not be neglected.

In the past few decades, we have witnessed the emergence of all kinds of so-called **'new diplomacies'**, which has confused the debate on what *diplomacy* is at its core. Economic diplomacy and cultural diplomacy had been around for some time already. More recently, they have been joined by environmental diplomacy (eco-diplomacy), energy diplomacy, health diplomacy, and population diplomacy. And then it went on: from public diplomacy and virtual diplomacy over citizen's diplomacy and celebrity diplomacy to panda diplomacy and most recently vaccine diplomacy. Whether all these new diplomacies should be taken at face value is questionable. In fact, one could construct a 'diplomacy' around any public good one can think of. People seem to be fascinated by labels. By just giving it a name, it looks as if one has created something new. We will try to put some order in this panoply of diplomacies.

The proliferation of diplomacies has been **misleading** as *it confuses the craft (the 'know how') with the subject matter* on which it bears *(the 'know what')*. The new diplomacies are *domain-specific,* which diplomacy seen as a practice is not. Diplomacy as a practice is *domain-independent*. A craft can come to bear on *any* domain imaginable (from environment and energy to vaccines). That is why there are **not multiple diplomacies**, there is just one. There are no more eco-diplomats than there are energy-diplomats. There are just plain diplomats who today will work on environmental matters and tomorrow on energy issues. Somewhat simplifying, diplomats are generalists, they know how to handle problems; experts are specialists, they know the whereabouts of the problems. Diplomats sit in all kinds of different meetings covering the most diverse, sometimes arcane issues, not because they are the specialists in the matter but because as generalist practitioners they know (or are supposed to know) how to navigate the ship of diplomacy. The domain-independent skills of the diplomat are brought to bear on the domain-specific knowledge of the expert. That is where the **complementarity** between the **diplomat** and the **expert** shows: the expert provides the hardware, the diplomat the software.

It is the craft that is the diplomat's distinguishing feature, not the domain on which he or she operates. That is why a diplomat's agenda can be extremely diverse: politics in the morning, economics in the afternoon, and culture in the evening. That is also why it is often a diplomat who will be entrusted with leading a conference delegation or presiding over a negotiation team, whatever the subject matter under discussion might be. Just watch a day in the life of an ambassador (Permanent Representative) to the UN. He or she starts their day with a working-breakfast with some NGOs on, say, children in armed conflict; then moves on to the Peace Building Commission (PBC) to continue the negotiation of an assistance program for the Central African Republic (CAR); at noon he or she lunches with the deputy to the Prosecutor of the ICC (International Criminal Court) to discuss the political fall out of some recent indictments... and that is how the day goes on.

I.7 Summing up

The reader will have noticed the adjectives used in this introduction to characterise the book's underlying pragmatic outlook: practical, instrumental, empirical, sceptical, realist. This outlook has grown *out of* experience. It is not an ideological postulation. This is perhaps the place then to briefly say what that experience has been, what I have learned from practising diplomacy over the years:

First, that in diplomacy one should not be misled by great *concepts* and lofty *principles* as if they had an immutable, sacrosanct value on their own; they are tools that should help us getting things done. If they do not work, just set them aside.

Second, that *ideas* in diplomacy should be tested on their real meaning and practical value. Ideas, to be fruitful, must make a difference in the facts, not just in our heads.

Third, that only clear ideas can be clearly *articulated*. And only through articulated language will a diplomat be able to persuade others. Ideas wrapped in obfuscated language mislead and confuse.

Fourth, that diplomacy is not about *grand schemes* or great *visionary constructions*. However intellectually entertaining architectural debates may be, they are most often a waste of time, an *ersatz* that distracts from the real work at hand.

Fifth, that diplomacy is not about *reforming the world,* but just about making it a slightly better place through patient *problem-solving* and that each new problem asks for a new solution.

Sixth, that *institutions* are not fixtures that once created must go on living a life on their own. They are instruments to be judged on their operational value. The question to be asked is: 'does it work?'

Seventh, that although diplomacy needs secrecy and confidentiality, to be effective diplomacy must *also* know when to *go public*. Diplomacy is about influencing the behaviour of others.

Eighth, that in diplomacy one must learn to live with the suboptimal (not the perfect), the partial (not the total), the provisional (not the final), the feasible (not the principled), the plausible (not the certain), the reasonable (not the rational).

Ninth and concluding, that diplomacy is *parsimony of thought* and *modesty of expectation* and that it is to be conducted with *patience* and *calm*.

I.8 What to expect

Now that we have sketched **how** we will approach diplomacy as a practice, let us give a brief overview of **what** will be covered in this book.

We obviously need to start with saying something on the *organisation of diplomacy*, which we will do in *Part I* of this book. In Chapter 1, we present the standard state-based model of doing diplomacy. We look at the Ministry of Foreign Affairs (MFA) and its main actors, from the Minister down to the desk officer and ask which are the main tasks of a Ministry. From headquarters we will move to the periphery: Embassies, Consulates, and Permanent Representations. We focus on a diplomat's daily work and life: what is expected from them and how do they go about it and what challenges does diplomatic life bring with it. From the standard model we move on in Chapter 2 to look at different ways and means of doing diplomacy: most of us are familiar with the distinction between 'bilateral and multilateral' diplomacy, and that between official 'Track I' and non-official 'Track II' diplomacy. 'Networked' diplomacy is less familiar. We will look at it and make a short inroad in 'virtual' diplomacy. 'Public' diplomacy too deserves a brief comment and will offer us the opportunity to say something about 'cultural', 'diaspora', and 'sports' diplomacy. Along the road, we will discover all kinds of 'new diplomacies'. We will try to put some order in them and will close with the critical question whether they challenge the more traditional concept of state-based diplomacy.

In *Part II* we get at the real work: building a diplomat's *conceptual toolbox*. We first look in Chapter 3 at some reasoning processes that are said to underlie diplomatic thinking, but we soon discover that reasoning in diplomacy is more about justifying decisions *ex post* than reaching them *ex ante*. Decision-making in diplomacy is an interactive process. You do not decide on your own. Effective action in diplomacy requires you to take into account what others are saying, thinking, and doing. That is what we take up in Chapter 4. We can learn from game theory, sometimes called the theory of *interdependent* decisions. We will review different 'diplomatic' games and illustrate their relevance for strategic thinking with examples drawn from diplomatic practice. In order to properly assess what others say and think we need a specific capacity: 'rational empathy'. It is the capacity that allows you to enter into another's mind so that you not just *understand what* he is saying but *comprehend why* he is saying it. In Chapter 5, we warn for all kinds of fallacies and delusions that threaten proper diplomatic thinking. They range from formal errors in logic to so-called cognitive traps; some of them are recurrent in diplomatic practice. We will illustrate them with examples. Concepts and principles play an important role in diplomatic thinking, they constitute a diplomat's basic vocabulary. In Chapter 6, we approach concepts as flexible tools for political analysis and principles as guides for action. We will list them according to their nature: political, legal, or diplomatic.

In *Part III* we address the pre-eminent topic of diplomacy: international peace and security. In Chapter 7, we discuss the 'conflict cycle': pre-conflict prevention and post-conflict management. Preventing conflicts is difficult; there are limits on what a diplomat can do. Managing post-conflict situations is no less a challenge; that of having former enemies make peace. We will study issues regarding peace settlement, state building, and transitional justice. When conflict cannot be prevented, parties may have recourse to the 'use of force'. That is the topic of Chapter 8. 'Armed conflict' – war – is not a free for all; there are questions of legality, legitimacy, and political prudence to be addressed when launching a war no less than in its actual conduct. These questions lay at the basis of the distinction between 'war of choice' and 'war of necessity'. When discussing the 'use of force' one cannot ignore the crucial role of the UN Security Council. So that too is something to be looked at.

A diplomat's life does not unfold in a normative vacuum. Values, standards, principles, and rules constrain states' behaviour in many ways. We will take up a diplomat's *normative framework* in *Part IV* of the book. We start in Chapter 9 with looking at international law. We are interested in uncovering its specific nature, its scope, and limits, not so much in reviewing its substantive provisions. We will see that lawyers and diplomats do not always see eye to eye, they approach international law from different perspectives. Next, in Chapter 10, we move to the place of 'human rights' and the 'Rule of Law' in the conduct of diplomacy. The central question we will address is how come that ministers and their diplomats have such a hard time in credibly defending human rights. We identify some vulnerabilities which are inherent to the concept of human rights: we question their universality, criticise their proliferation, and regret the growing banalisation of human rights discourse. We suggest that the concept of 'Rule of Law' may offer an alternative model to that of human rights. In passing, we will say something about attempts at building an 'ethical foreign policy' and try to understand why these often fail. With that we have reached the end of the book. In a short conclusion, we reflect on how a diplomat's life is intertwined with his or her job. Diplomacy is not just work to be executed, it is a habit, an attitude, ultimately perhaps a 'way of life'.

Bibliography

AMSTRONG, David, FARRELL, Theo & LAMBERT, Hélène (2012), *International Law and International Relations*, Cambridge University Press, Cambridge.

BURNS, William (2019), "The Lost Art of American Diplomacy", *Foreign Affairs*, May/June 2019.

COHEN, Felix S. (1937), "The Problems of a Functional Jurisprudence", *The Modern Law Review, 1*, pp. 5–26.

COOPER, Robert (2021), *The Ambassadors – Thinking about Diplomacy from Machiavelli to Modern Times*, Weidenfeld & Nicolson, London.

DER DERIAN, James (1987), *On Diplomacy*, Blackwell, Oxford/Cambridge.

EBAN, Abba (1998), *Diplomacy for the Next Century*, Yale University Press, New Haven, CT/London.

FERREIROS, José (2016), *Mathematical Knowledge and the Interplay of Practices*, Princeton University Press, Princeton, NJ.

FLETCHER, Tom (2017), *The Naked Diplomat*, William Collins, London.

HARRIES, Owen (1998), "A Reluctant Realist", *The New York Times*, March 29, 1998.

HOLTON, Gerald (1973), *Introduction to Concepts and Theories in Physical Science*, Princeton University Press, Princeton, NJ.

JÖRGENSEN, Knud Erik (2010), *International Relations Theory*, Palgrave, New York, NY.

KISSINGER, Henry (1994), *Diplomacy*, Simon & Schuster, New York, NY.

OLIVERI, Gianluigi (2010), "For a Philosophy of Mathematical Practice", in: VAN KERKHOVE, Bart, DE VUYST, Jonas & VAN BENDEGEM, Jean Paul (Eds.), *Philosophical Perspectives on Mathematical Practice*, King's College, London.

POSNER, Richard (1995), *Overcoming Law*, Harvard University Press, Cambridge.

POSNER, Richard (2001), *Frontiers of Legal Theory*, Harvard University Press, Cambridge.

SIRACUSA, Joseph M. (2010), *Diplomacy – A Very Short Introduction*, Oxford University Press, Oxford.

Part I

The organisation of diplomacy

1 The organisation of diplomacy

The standard model

1.1 A preliminary question: what is diplomacy *for*?

It does not make much sense to start discussing the organisation of diplomacy without first asking the question: 'What is diplomacy *for*?'. That question is different from the question what diplomacy is. As we said in the Introduction, diplomacy can best be understood when seen as a practice, a craft, a way of doing. And then the question obviously arises: 'for doing what?' Making the distinction between the practice and that for which it is a practice is important. Quite often that distinction is not made. Paul Sharp notes that the Chinese tend to simply equate diplomacy with foreign policy and that the Americans often take diplomacy to stand for international relations generally (SHARP, 2019, p. 13). But *diplomacy is not foreign policy* and even less international relations. Foreign policy is what diplomacy is *for*. Diplomacy is the *instrument* of foreign policy. A government's foreign policy is what diplomats are supposed to help shape, promote and defend, explain and clarify, execute and implement, thereby relying on their 'know how', that is the sum total of strategies, tactics, techniques, and skills for which they have been trained or that they have acquired over time. Diplomacy is in the service of foreign policy. Stronger still: diplomacy is the engine room of foreign policy.

But what then is a country's foreign policy? A country's foreign policy defines the kind of relations it wishes to entertain with other countries, the alliances it wishes to enter into, with a view of securing and defending its **national interests**. And among these interests, **security** comes first. That is why, in shorthand, diplomacy is often said to be about 'peace and security'. Security is *primary* in a fundamental sense, namely that without it a country may be unable to pursue its *secondary* goals: that of a strong economy, an efficient health and education system, an independent judiciary. In the wake of security comes **prosperity** (broadly understood as well-being). Once a foreign policy has thus been defined, it will be the task of the Minister of Foreign Affairs, the chief diplomat, to implement it and it is at that point that the diplomats enter into the picture. They are the day-to-day managers of the relations with other states; it is up to them to keep communication lines open, achieve understanding, and clear misunderstandings.

1.2 The Ministry of Foreign Affairs

The Ministry of Foreign Affairs (MFA) stands at the centre not only of the conception and execution of foreign policy but also of diplomacy's organisation. MFAs go by many names: they are called the *State Department* in Washington, the *MID* in Moscow, the *Quai d'Orsay* in Paris, the *Gaimusho* in Tokyo, and the *Farnesina* in

DOI: 10.4324/9781003298182-3

Rome. The Minister of Foreign Affairs (State Secretary in the US, Foreign Secretary in the UK) is the first diplomat, the *chef de la diplomatie*. He or she is a member of government who bears the political responsibility for a country's foreign policy and is accountable before parliament. Next to the Foreign Minister, who is the (temporary) *political* head of the Ministry, there is in most MFAs a (more permanent) senior official in charge of overseeing the *management* of the MFA. He or she is commonly called the *Secretary-General*. He or she is the top administrator of the MFA. Secretary-Generals increasingly adopt corporate approaches to their work. A Minister can either work directly with the senior officials of the Ministry, just relying on a small coordination cell headed by a *Chief of Staff* (as in the Netherlands, for example), or else have a full-fledged *cabinet* which acts as an intermediary (some would say buffer) between the Minister and his or her administration and is headed by a *Chef de Cabinet* (as in France, for example).

In many MFAs a distinction is made between the *internal* and *external careers* (sometimes called *foreign service* and *diplomatic service*, respectively), that is between officials who remain permanently based in the capital's MFA, often called international analysts, and those who can be assigned to Embassies, Consulates, or Permanent Representations abroad (diplomats). However, as happened in quite a few MFAs where the formerly distinct diplomatic and consular careers were merged, so too there is currently a tendency to integrate, at least partially, the internal career with the diplomatic service. These developments are part of an organisational evolution towards flexible horizontal organisational networks replacing former more rigid hierarchical vertical structures.

MFAs are differently organised in different countries, but there are some recurring patterns. A prominent one is the distinction between *geographical* departments which concentrate on individual countries, sub-regions (Central Africa, for instance) or regions (Latin America, for instance), and *functional* (or thematic) departments that typically deal with high-profile political issues such as security policy, arms control and disarmament, human rights, terrorism, climate change, refugees, and migration. The geographical department generally oversees bilateral diplomacy, whereas the functional department will be managing multilateral affairs. Both geographical and functional departments are primarily **political** in nature. Often there will be a separate department for the conduct of the **economic** relations, broadly understood, including questions regarding energy, transport, telecommunications, among others. Further, there will be a **consular** department in charge of the implementation of visa policy, of assisting the foreign diplomatic community living in the country and of overseeing the work of the consuls abroad. In the countries that are member states of the EU, and those that are associated with the EU, there will be a **Europe** department exclusively devoted to the formulation and implementation of European policy which increasingly affects domestic policies. Departments are generally led by a *Director-General* who oversees the work of directors, deputy-directors down the whole hierarchy, with the *desk officer* at the lowest level of the pyramid playing a pivotal role in the whole machinery, a role that is unfortunately not always recognised (see Box 1.1). The *desk officer* must master several requirements (see RANA, 2011, pp. 256–258):

- Read and absorb the many reports and dispatches received from the diplomatic missions in the country or region under charge.
- Gain insight into the country or region handled through an analysis of both its economics and politics and proceed to prudent policy recommendations.

- Do the routine business of drafting letters, messages, speeches, and answers to parliamentary questions.
- Write records of meetings.
- Keep in regular contact with the resident diplomatic missions of the country or region under charge.

Box 1.1 The Desk Officer

The desk officer is a key player in the geographical departments of the MFA. His or her job, however, has come under increasing pressure. Let me approvingly share with you what Rozental and Buenrostro have to say about him or her:

> The desk officer is generally responsible for a number of countries, which does not allow him to specialise. The speed with which global events unfold often only leaves time for *reactive diplomacy*. It is almost impossible for the desk officer to keep track of, let alone analyse developments in the countries he is responsible for. Nor is he in a position to prepare appropriate medium or long-term responses. This is often referred to as the *firefighting nature of foreign ministry work*. Urgent tasks tend to overshadow and displace the important ones. This leads ministries to spend much of their time in a defensive response-mode, rather than in thinking about what policy should be. Not surprisingly, many desk officers thus become mere paper pushers, overwhelmed by the numerous demands they face.
>
> (my italics, see ROZENTAL and BUENROSTRO, 2015, p. 239)

Without pretending to be exhaustive in this short outline of the organisation of MFAs, let us just further mention the **press** office (and the crucial role of the spokesperson of the Ministry), the **legal** department (also in charge of the formal aspects of treaty-making), the **protocol** office (assisting the foreign missions at home and organising incoming visits of foreign dignitaries: state, official, and working visits), the **archive** department (in charge of 'knowledge management' by keeping the MFA's institutional memory in good order), the **crisis centre** (which is the locus of emergency actions, also monitoring critical international developments and events on a continuous basis), and last but not least the **policy planning staff** (concerned with strategising: anticipating future challenges and opportunities and thinking through how they might be met and, in the process, challenging conventional wisdom).

Beyond all these substantive departments, there is the **administrative** department in charge not of the conduct of diplomacy but of its organisation both at home and abroad: recruiting and training incoming international analysts and diplomats, staffing and supporting the missions abroad, providing logistical support to the diplomats and their families, especially when they find themselves in hardship posts or in the midst of an emergency crisis, renting or acquiring suitable buildings (plus their equipment and furnishings), securing telecommunications, providing physical protection where necessary (guards, armoured cars), proceeding to periodic inspections of the posts abroad and evaluating personnel's performances (praising good work as well as drawing attention to failings), and last but not least … advising on cost-cutting measures.

The tasks of an MFA are diverse, but there are two outstanding tasks that need to be stressed: that of advising the Minister and that of coordinating foreign policy. Diplomats working at headquarters contribute *directly* to the shaping of foreign policy by **advising the Minister**. This advisory role is a continuing effort, but it starts on the very first day of the Minister's presence in the Ministry when he or she receives a *general briefing* about the way international relations work, the position and commitments of the country, and what are the big problems. This general briefing is for the new Minster an occasion to get to personally know those who will be his or her top advisers for the months or years to come. Once in office, the Minister will receive *daily briefings* about what is happening, how the country's policies are working, and what the advisers think should be done.

Although diplomats are often quite eager to be sent in postings abroad rather than staying at headquarters, it should be said that the most interesting and gratifying but also most demanding diplomatic work is carried out at home, in the MFA. That is where a diplomat can have a *direct* and effective impact on both the formulation and implementation of foreign policy; more than his or her colleagues posted abroad. The latter also contribute to the policy-shaping, but rather *indirectly* through their reports and dispatches. Your Minister is a busy person who inevitably must give priority to current events, which often reduce to the events of the day. Your Minister does not have the time to read, let alone digest the huge amount of information and analysis that the diplomatic missions abroad send home. That is your job as a senior adviser in the MFA. Advising your Minister is not an easy task, but when well done it can be quite rewarding. Here follows some advice for the Minister's chief adviser.

1.2.1 Some advice for the Minister's Chief Adviser

- The first thing to do is to put your overworked Minister *at ease* by telling him or her in a sober language what the problem (only) amounts to; many advisers do exactly the reverse: they inflate the issue, they exaggerate, as they feel this makes them more interesting and indispensable. The advice is no exaggerations, but, on the contrary, de-dramatisation.
- Second, have the courage to say things that you know your Minister does *not* like to hear (he or she will not say so on the spot but will tell you next day that he or she appreciated your 'inconvenient' advice); saying 'yes, Minister' is cheap; saying 'no Minister' requires courage; good advice is 'speaking truth to power'; of course you do not contradict your Minister when there are other people around; you do it discreetly, privately; your objective is not to score points with the bystanders, but to assist your boss.
- Third, offer solutions that are *simple* to grasp and easy to implement; your job is one of facilitation, not complication; complicated solutions are not solutions, they just show your own puzzlement and confusion.
- Fourth, let your Minister not be distracted by the babble of scary daily press headlines, put them in perspective; fifth, prick ideological bubbles, they don't serve any practical purpose; sixth, act as a filter for all those trying to bend your Minister's ear; seventh, beware of self-congratulatory groupthink.
- Finally, be strong enough to help drive policy forward through substantive advice and self-effacing enough not to put umbrage on your minister; the best advisers remain almost invisible.

Perhaps this short advice to the Minister's adviser should be complemented with a short *advice addressed to the Minister* himself or herself in *how to choose and use his or her advisers*. In his *The Ambassadors*, Robert Cooper remarks that 'Political leaders choose their advisers according to the policies they want to follow, not the other way round' (COOPER, 2021, p. 164). There is an implicit message here that may sound presumptuous. But think about it. Who wins and who loses in not following the advice?

1.2.2 Some advice for the Minister in choosing and working with his or her Chief Adviser

- First, choose men or women who will speak to you frankly (although privately); you learn nothing from people who are there to please you, the 'flatterers' against whom Machiavelli already warned and gave advice on how to shun them (see Chapter 13 of his *Il Principe*).
- Second, and closely related to the first point, do not seek confirmation of your views from your advisers, that is do not fall into the so-called *confirmation-trap* (on which more will be said in Part II of this book); on the contrary, look for disconfirmation and contradiction; ask your advisers to make the case *contra* your position or viewpoint.
- Third, choose men or women who have a different temperament from yours; they will complement you and act as a counterweight leading to the right balance.

The second important task of an MFA concerns the overall **transversal coordination of foreign policy**. Despite the MFA's continued central role in foreign policy formulation and implementation, it can no longer claim to have the monopoly power over foreign affairs. Increasingly other government departments – Economy, Finance, Defence, Interior, Environment, Energy, Transport – or other levels of government, particularly in federal states, have their own international relations agenda and may have their own international sections or agencies. There is no point in contesting these new developments or hankering for the old 'gatekeeper' role that the MFA once had. These developments cannot be wished away, and it is exactly because of them that the MFA had to reinvent itself as the 'grand coordinator' of all external activity. With a view to ensuring the overall *coherence* of foreign policy and its *consistency in time*, and to avoid that external partners would play off one ministry or government level against another, coordination of foreign activities is a necessity. An MFA can claim such coordination role because it is the only ministry to have the *'big picture' perspective* on international developments. Moreover, through its coordination role, the MFA contributes to *'whole of government' approaches* to policy-making by keeping different parts of government informed about each other's activities abroad. There are two important coordination mechanisms that should be mentioned. The first is **interdepartmental coordination** (the famous 'inter-agency' process in the US) where senior officials of the MFA meet with their counterparts of other ministries or government offices to *align* their positions within a coherent overall foreign policy framework. These coordination meetings are generally headed by a senior MFA representative. To facilitate this process, diplomatic personnel from the MFA are seconded to those other ministries or government offices. They act as liaison officers facilitating the communication. A specific form of coordination, and in fact the most important one for EU member states, is the **European coordination** covering the entire spectrum of EU questions which, by their very nature, more often than not involve competences that belong to other, perhaps more technical departments and only marginally to the MFA.

The task of coordination of foreign policy remains to this day largely entrusted to the MFAs although we lately witness a shift towards the chanceries of the Heads of State or Government in assuming (part of) this role (see Box 1.2).

Box 1.2 Coordination – MFA's Role under Threat?

Today, Heads of State or Government are more directly involved in external relations than ever before. Within their chanceries, diplomatic offices act as semi-autonomous entities 'usurping' some of the MFA terrain. Leaders travel abroad more often than before and engage in direct phone conversations with their colleagues, thus setting up their own communication channels. Presidents and Prime Ministers meet more often than ever in 'summits' (hence the new label 'summit diplomacy'). That is *what* we see around us. The more interesting question, however, is *why* leaders have become more directly involved in foreign affairs and *why* they increasingly become the arbiters of intra-government differences. Part of the answer, it seems, is that with globalisation, connectivity, and interdependence, the clean separation that in earlier times could be made between foreign and domestic politics has evaporated. New transversal topics have come to dominate the diplomatic agenda (climate change, migration, energy, pandemics, terrorism), involving core competences belonging to other departments than the MFA. In those circumstances, one can understand that aligning divergent interdepartmental interests, that is coordination, has become an 'all-of-government' affair that needs to be handled at the highest level of state authority, that of the President or Prime Minister. This evolution is even more pronounced as regards European Affairs for the simple reason that European questions bear essentially on matters of domestic concern. We have clearly seen that evolution happening in France (Elysée and Matignon) and Germany ('Bundeskanzleramt'), for instance.

Two recent cases where we have seen the coordination role of MFA's diminishing are Brexit and the Chinese 'Belt and Road Initiative'. After the June 2016 Brexit referendum, Prime Minister Cameron resigned and his replacement Theresa May faced the challenge of how to manage Brexit. She established two new government departments: the Department for Exiting the European Union (DEEU) and the Department for International Trade (DIT), both with their own minister (State Secretary) and some 300 staff members, leaving the role of the MFA (the Foreign and Commonwealth Office) in the whole process unclear, to say the least. Something similar happened with the October 2013 Chinese 'Belt and Road Initiative', a huge project involving massive investment worldwide in the most diverse sectors (mining, energy, infrastructure …). While this project involves extensive negotiations with multiple stakeholders, the MFA' role in the initiative has become rather marginal; essentially a public diplomacy role: explaining what the initiative is about and responding to criticism (see SHARP, 2019, pp. 7–8).

There are of course many other tasks that an MFA must perform; managing *economic/commercial diplomacy*, for instance, particularly in countries where MFA's have merged with foreign trade ministries. *Consular services* are offered to both nationals and foreigners in their more routine welfare needs. *Public diplomacy* engages in 'outreach' activities involving all actors interested in foreign policy, including NGOs and academia, offering them a platform for discussion and consultation as well as the possibility to engage with MFA officials, particularly at times when the country assumes specific responsibilities such as an EU Presidency or a non-permanent seat at the UN Security Council.

1.3 The Embassy, Consulate, and Permanent Representation

Embassy. We now move from headquarters to the periphery and start with the first kind of a country's representation of abroad: the embassy. Originally the term 'embassy' referred to a temporary assignment to an envoy (and his or her following) having full powers – *plena potentia* – to negotiate on behalf of his or her principal – the Prince or Sovereign – on a certain narrowly defined *ad hoc* issue. Such *temporary embassies* were expensive to dispatch, vulnerable on the road and often likely to cause trouble over precedence and ceremonial questions. As a result, when diplomatic activity intensified in the late 15th century, they were replaced by what came to be called *resident embassies*. Kishan Rana has given a crisp description of the resident embassy:

> It is at the heart of the diplomatic process; it represents the sovereign state, the principal actor in international affairs. The embassy is the field outpost of the foreign ministry, its eye-and-ears on foreign terrain, advising all government branches on developments important to the home country.
>
> (RANA, 2011, p. 131)

Although the term 'embassy' now refers to the building where the diplomatic activity takes place, the underlying idea remains one of continuous representation of a state by an ambassador and his or her entourage.

An *ambassador-designate* of a *sending state* cannot take up his or her job until after having been properly accredited by the *receiving state*. To obtain such **accreditation** a request for *'agrément'* must be introduced by the sending state to the receiving state ensuring that the latter does not object to the designation. Once obtained, the ambassador can travel to the receiving state informing the *Chief of Protocol* of its MFA of his or her arrival. It is the date of this official notification that determines the protocollary rank of the newly arrived ambassador within the *corps diplomatique* (see Box 1.3), the longest serving ambassador being accorded the highest seniority and hence acting as the *Dean* of the *Corps* (except in predominantly catholic countries where that honour is usually conferred to the papal envoy, the *nuntius*).

Box 1.3 *Corps Diplomatique*

Diplomacy is a 'profession'. Even more, it is a restricted profession, not unlike the medieval craft guilds. Entry to the profession is through the narrow portal of a demanding and highly selective 'diplomatic exam'. The successful candidate then goes through a one-to-two-year training period, an 'apprenticeship' often conducted in a 'diplomatic academy'. Once formally admitted to the 'diplomatic career' ('la carrière' as the French say), diplomats form a small, cosy, and homogeneous community. In the exercise of their profession, they benefit from 'privileges and immunities'. As an 'Ambassador extraordinary and plenipotentiary', the senior diplomat presents his or her 'letters of credence' to the Head of State of the country to which he or she has been duly 'accredited'. He or she then is addressed as 'Her Excellency'. All this contributes to a certain 'mystique' surrounding the 'high office' for which he or she has been chosen and a flattering self-conception of what it means to do, to be, to live in diplomacy. A warning may be appropriate here: as a diplomat, always be on your guards and don't let yourself be misled by honorific labels and glittering appearances, residences, and paraphernalia. If not, you risk being qualified as a 'self-important person of little use', an 'elegant, empty husk', or a 'striped pants cookie pusher' (SHARP, 2019, p. 124). The diplomatic career is treacherous.

One should note that an ambassador can only start having higher level, that is political contacts than after having presented his or her **letters of credence** (established to show that he or she is genuinely representing his or her state – see Box 1.4) to the Head of State of the receiving state such as the President of the US or the King of the Belgians. That is an example where protocol gets in the way of effective diplomacy.

Where there are normal diplomatic relations but there is no resident embassy, a sending state can appoint to it an ambassador based in a third country (most often a neighbouring country); this is called *concurrent appointment* as when, for instance, the ambassador of the Netherlands to the US is concurrently appointed and accredited as ambassador to the Bahamas.

Box 1.4 Letter of Credence – Example

PHILIP

KING OF THE BELGIANS

TO

HIS/HER EXCELLENCY MR/MRS

PRESIDENT OF THE REPUBLIC OF ...

Being desirous to maintain and strengthen the relations of friendship and good understanding which so happily exist between our two countries, I have chosen Ambassador ..., as Ambassador Extraordinary and Plenipotentiary of the Kingdom of Belgium to the Republic of .... The ability of Ambassador ... gives me full confidence that she is worthy of the high office for which she has been chosen and that she will discharge the duties of her mission in such a manner as to merit Your Excellency's approbation and esteem. It is in this conviction that I request Your Excellency to receive her favorably and give full credence to all that she shall communicate on My behalf and mere especially when she conveys My best wishes for Your Excellency's personal well-being.

(Source: Protocol Service, MFA Belgium)

Protocol rules have, not undeservedly, a reputation for stuffiness and excessive formality, but the fact is that the regulation of diplomatic precedence, for instance who comes first and who last – continues to prove useful in a world where vanity is never far away. Contests for precedence have been of all times. Cooper recalls the story of the Spanish ambassador in London who won the contest of precedence (and a better seat at the table) with his French colleague by detaching the horses from the latter's carriage and getting to the St James's dinner party ahead of him which caused such outrage in Paris that Louis XIV threatened war (COOPER, 2021, p. 21).

Diplomats enjoy special **privileges and immunities**. 'Privileges and immunities' is an unfortunate terminology as it gives the impression that diplomats are somehow *above the fray*. The irony, regrettably, is that some diplomats do indeed take themselves to be so, mistakenly considering the privileges they enjoy as reflecting their merits (something for which Machiavelli already warned us in the early 16th century – see BEECKMAN, 2020, p. 171). Nor are privileges and immunities granted on the basis of some old-fashioned theory of 'extra-territoriality' which mistakes a metaphor for a justification. Privileges and immunities are granted to diplomats on **functional grounds** and meant to facilitate the discharge of their *official* functions free from pressures or harassment coming from agents of the receiving state. And it is in terms of these functional grounds that states (and their courts and tribunals) have placed certain limits on the scope of these privileges and immunities.

Talk about 'privileges and immunities' may also misleadingly give the impression, again entertained by some, as if diplomats were *above the law*, which is not the case; diplomats must respect the laws and regulations of the receiving state no less than its own nationals. What they are **not subject to** is the **enforcement of the law**; diplomats may not be arrested or detained. If a diplomat is accused of committing a crime, he or she may well be obliged to leave the country. In such case, the receiving state may declare him or her *persona non grata*. Note that declaring a diplomat *persona non grata* need not any specific justification. Being declared *persona non grata* by the *receiving* state is one thing, being *recalled for consultations* by your own *sending* state quite another: usually the latter is a sign of a frost in relations rather than of any diplomatic misdemeanour. A recent example is when France recalled its ambassador from Canberra when in September 2021 Australia resigned on an earlier commitment regarding the purchase of French submarines in favour of American submarines. Declarations of *persona non grata* should not be confused with the *expulsion* of diplomats for political reasons. This happens regularly and sometimes spectacularly. In August 2017, Russia decided to expel 755 US diplomats and supporting staff. The Russians objected to economic sanctions that the US had placed on them for interfering in the 2016 presidential elections, and they retaliated saying that the US diplomats were interfering in Russian affairs and had to leave. A less spectacular case happened when in the space of one month (from mid-March to mid-April 2021) some 20 Russian diplomats were kicked out of the US, Bulgaria, the Chez Republic, and Poland for all kinds of transgressions (spying, involvement in plots, interference in elections). As could be expected (and is regular practice), tit-for-tat retaliatory expulsions by Russia followed.

Another immunity concerns the **inviolability of diplomatic premises**. Diplomatic premises (embassies and residences) may not be entered by agents of the receiving state, except with the consent of the head of mission. That is why London police were stationed for years *outside* the Embassy of Ecuador, where WikiLeaks founder Julian Assange took refuge in 2012 (he faced arrest and extradition to Sweden if he stepped outside the 'inviolable' premises of the Embassy). Diplomats are also exempt from local **taxation** (with sometimes tricky questions: does the London Congestion Charge constitute a tax or a permissible charge for services rendered?).

When speaking about diplomats one should not confuse administrative **rankings** (*titles*) with diplomatic **functions**, although both may and in fact often do overlap: a first secretary, for example, *normally* exercises the functions of a first secretary; but exceptions to the rule are plentiful. The administrative rankings are generally in descending order as follows: Ambassador, Minister-Counsellor (first, second, perhaps third), Counsellor (first, second, third), Secretary, Attaché. His or her Excellency *the* Ambassador (function), that is the head of mission, will most often be *an* ambassador (ranking). But many *a* minister-counsellor (ranking) in fact exercises the function of Ambassador, head of mission. The head of mission can be a mid-level diplomat (say a counsellor or even a first secretary), who will be called a *Chargé d'Affaires ad interim* if leading the Mission on a temporary basis (e.g. when the Ambassador has left the country for holidays) or a *Chargé d'Affaires en pied* if leading the mission on a permanent basis, as happens when the sending state refuses to be represented at ambassadorial level (*ranking*) in the receiving state, which was the case for quite a few countries in Chile during the Pinochet era. Finally, although a Defence Attaché bears the same title as the most junior diplomat of the Mission, the importance of his or her function, and indeed his or her military rank (which often is that of a General), exceeds by far that of the young diplomat.

The preceding remarks may give the impression that diplomacy is more a matter of *form* than of *substance*, of credentials and rules of precedence, titles, and privileges. Add to it the stereotypes regarding official ceremonies, diplomatic dinners, receptions, balls, and many other (superfluous) gallantries, and the picture is complete. Such presentation is, however, largely (although not entirely) unfair. First, because it ignores that there is an important symbolic dimension attached to diplomacy (think of the celebration of national days or the commemoration of tragic events such as the Holocaust). Second, and more importantly, because such presentation does not any longer fit with how contemporary diplomacy is practiced. Diplomacy today has increasingly become a pragmatic, no-nonsense, business-like profession. In this regard, it is gratifying to note that the stilted forms of credential ceremonies, the residual use of glitter in the diplomatic uniforms, as well as the obsession with precedence and titles have become gradually more obsolete. Gradually but not entirely.

Before moving on, let us briefly pause and address some issues that belong to **the micro-world of diplomacy**, issues that take a less prominent place in the overall organisation of diplomacy but are not without interest in the day-to-day world of the acting diplomat:

- **Poor Ambassador.** An ambassador is the boss of the embassy and will therefore generally be evaluated not only on his or her own personal performance but also that of his or her embassy as a whole. That leads to the question whether an ambassador has a say as to *who will be part of his or her team*. In the private sector, a leader of a team generally chooses its members making sure that all of them contribute to its cohesiveness and effectiveness. In most diplomatic systems, that is not the case. An ambassador may make suggestions and sometimes be consulted but the final decision is not his or her, but that of the headquarters, and he or she may very well end up with a dysfunctional team, the overall performance of which is sub-optimal. Should he or she be blamed for that? To remedy such situation, some countries have decided (or are considering) to introduce a system of *co-decision*. Capital and head of mission are jointly setting up a cohesive team, thus ensuring the overall optimal performance of the embassy. That should be the preferred option, but its practical implementation is far from simple.

- **Lucky Number Two.** Many people envy the position of the ambassador as head of mission. They should not, particularly not in bilateral posts. Sure enough, the ambassador is the boss and assumes the overall responsibility of running the embassy. But that does not mean that he or she does the most interesting work. A bilateral ambassador is very much a public figure. Much of his or her time and energy gets *diverted from genuine diplomatic work* to formal or ceremonial activities, public speaking, and social entertaining. It is his or her younger colleagues in the embassy, and in particular his or her 'number two' (formally called DCM, Deputy Chief of Mission) who end up doing the interesting, substantive diplomatic work: enquiring, analysing, and reporting to the capital.

- **Fighting your Way up.** We saw that diplomats have a dual career path. One concerns the advances in administrative rankings (from junior attaché to senior ambassador). The other concerns the kind of postings (from Bujumbura to Washington) and the functional positions within the mission (from attaché to head of mission) which diplomats succeed in obtaining. Interestingly, this dual career path and the rivalry that comes with it has resulted in making the diplomatic career one of the most *competitive* in the public sector. Such competition, *if fair*, no doubt contributes to the quality of the diplomatic apparatus. But is it always fair? (See below: politisation).

- **Career Planning: 'chi va piano, va sano, va lontano'.** A word on *career planning*. Many young diplomats aspire to start their career at once in prestigious posts: Paris, London, Tokyo, New York, the same capitals you find in advertisements for perfumes. Whether that is good strategy is questionable, for two reasons. First, once you have started in such first-class posts, your expectation may well be to remain in this category for your next assignment(s), and that is not likely going to happen. Then comes your first disappointment, something you will consider a demotion rather than a promotion. Second, as an incoming diplomat, you are young (and so is your family) and can easily cope with difficult postings (so-called exotic posts which in fact often are hardship posts), places where you learn diplomacy at its roots and in the field ('terrain-diplomacy' as some call it), a difficult but rewarding experience that your colleague in Paris has missed. People in headquarters will be grateful for your 'availability' and 'flexibility' and will value your experience. It is your turn now to go to Paris, or London ... .

- **Politisation of the Career.** This can mean two things. First, that the Head of State has the privilege to freely appoint the ambassadors of his or her choice, so they need not be career-diplomats. This is standard practice in the US and in quite a lot of Latin-American countries. The US President, for instance, regularly appoints people who have actively supported him in his election campaign (they can be businesspeople, bankers, lawyers, consultants, etc.). Such appointments need not be arbitrary; like all ambassadors-designate, they too will have to be confirmed by the Senate. Political appointees have an asset that career-diplomats may lack; they have a direct line to the Head of State; they can sometimes 'deliver' where a career-diplomat may not. But the system should not be over-used: first because political appointees are less familiar with the technical aspects of the job and may perform poorly, and second because it is demotivating for the career people. A second meaning of politization is what happens in countries which for their ambassadorial appointments rely on the existing pool of career-diplomats. Politisation then means that for major appointments, the Minister of Foreign Affairs (or the Head of State or Government) will favour diplomats known to have an affinity to or affiliation with his or her political party. This is a delicate issue. One cannot reasonably contest that a minister may have a margin of discretion in appointments of senior ambassadors (or, for that matter, senior officials in the ministry) as long as such appointments are *not only* motivated by political considerations but *also* take into account the objective qualifications of the appointee. If not, the Minister may end up not only with a less performing diplomatic service but also with a demotivated one. In some countries, unfortunately, the habit to appoint by the political affiliation only is deeply ingrained. Good diplomats then defect.

- **Sabbatical Year?** Some diplomatic services offer sabbatical leaves as a way for mid-career professionals not just to take a break in the career but also to expand their expertise, engage in specific projects that will enhance their knowledge of a country, region, or issue, or simply allow them to undertake an activity for which time is normally not available. The sabbatical can also take the form of a secondment to a research institute or think tank or to another non-governmental entity. Such pause in the career allows the diplomat to reflect on his or her career and reload the batteries while living through a new experience and acquiring new abilities. Such sabbatical year can be combined with mid-career examinations leading to a promotion or new post assignment.

- **The Woman-Diplomat.** Diplomacy, like any institution, has evolved as society itself evolved. Up to the 1950s of the last century, diplomacy was essentially an affair of male aristocrats, particularly in Western countries. Around that time, the 'career' was opened to all social classes and to both men and women. Sweden played a prominent role in what came to be called '*the gender turn*': it opened the diplomatic career to women in 1948 and attained gender parity in 1999. Prejudices against women in decision-making positions and stereotypes based on gender roles and men's and women's leadership abilities steadily disappeared in other countries as well. Today, the number of women joining the career is increasing every year as is the number of them that make it to the top. An interesting but difficult question is whether the woman-diplomat excels in certain diplomatic aptitudes and skills compared to her male colleague. Some approaches to the question are based on the *essentialist* assumption that women are inherently more peaceful than men which presumably explains their prominent role in conflict prevention and management, and their valued contribution to stabilisation efforts, peacekeeping, and post-conflict relief and recovery. It has been empirically established that peace tends to last longer when women have been involved in the peace talks (see THE

ECONOMIST, 2021). *Non-essentialist* approaches stress functional skills which women-diplomats display with more ease than their male colleagues: they are said to be better listeners showing a keener sense of respect for the other; being less arrogant and less self-assured, they demonstrate a keener sense of 'empathy', that is the capacity to enter into the mind of the other; being less self-centred than their male colleagues, they care less for their subjective 'persona' and more for the object at stake in the dispute under consideration which would explain their greater readiness to compromise. These and other features make them presumably more apt to be, for instance, good negotiators.

- **A Diplomat's family.** A 15th-century Italian regulation ordered the ambassador to take his cook with him (to avoid being poisoned) but to leave his wife behind (lest she be suborned). No longer. Today, a diplomat's job is a family business. Each of the family members somehow gets tangled up with the job. You arrive in that unknown country, far away from home, it looks strange; your partner looks sad, the children uncertain. You know you will have to make it with just the 'three' of you: partner, children, and you. Many diplomats *discover* their family for the first time when sent abroad, particularly when it is far abroad: far geographically, culturally, and linguistically. Expatriate life offers fantastic experiences but parts of it can be challenging: to find a job for your partner, to have your children like their new school … There is stress around and it permeates the whole family. How this works out differs from one family to another. In most cases, the bonds of family get strengthened, increasing its cohesiveness, everybody is winning; in others, however, the bonds risk to weaken, leading to estrangement among partners or between parents and children. That is why care for the family should be no less a priority than dedication to the job.

Consulates. An embassy is one kind of bilateral diplomatic mission and there can be only one of them in any single country, in its capital, or better its administrative capital (as, for instance, in The Hague, not Amsterdam). An Embassy's *jurisdiction* covers the entire country. Consulates are of a different kind and come in different shapes. A ***Consulate-General*** is usually located in a big commercial city, perhaps a port city (New York, Bangalore, Antwerp). Its jurisdiction may cover (one or more of) the following: a (Canadian) province, a (French) *département*, or (as in federal states) a (Belgian) region, a (German) *Land* or (American) state, or any well-defined geographic area. ***Consulates*** have a more restricted jurisdiction and are supervised by the Consul-General who himself or herself acts under the (administrative) authority of the Ambassador. Although embassies and consulates are different kinds of diplomatic missions, note that most embassies have *consular sections*, staffed by career consular officers, who together with their colleagues from the economic-commercial section of the embassy carry out the same responsibilities of a regular consulate (see below).

Although the distinction between the diplomatic and consular careers is slowly fading away, both being gradually fused in one single foreign service, there remains a great deal of difference between the typical consular work and typical diplomatic work. The former deals chiefly with the problems of individuals and companies; the latter is concerned mainly with issues of general policy regarding inter-state relations, especially those of a political nature. Consuls will be occupied with facilitating exports from their countries to the receiving state, facilitating outward and promoting inward investment, and – depending on their location – supervising and assisting national flag shipping and aircraft. In addition to this commercial work, they are expected to assist nationals administratively (renewal of passport, registration of birth and death, issuing of certificates of life) or provide help to those in need (loss of passport, accident, victim of crime, natural disaster) and more generally keep in touch with the expatriate community (businesspeople, university students, artists ...). They are also responsible for issuing visas to the numerous applicants for travelling to their countries, when required. Consulates increasingly outsource the initial examination and processing of visa applications, thus avoiding long queues for all to see outside the office. Career consular officers enjoy more limited privileges and immunities than diplomats in accordance with the separate Vienna Convention on Consular Relations of 1963 (to be distinguished from the Convention on Diplomatic Relations, also signed in Vienna, but in 1961).

Career consuls must be distinguished from **Honorary Consuls**; the former are officials belonging to the diplomatic service, whereas the latter are often nationals from the receiving state with close connections to the sending state; preferably though they are nationals of the sending state permanently residing in the receiving state; in either case, they know their way around, including with the local political establishment and are generally persons who have control over their own time. Honorary consuls are frequently self-employed businessmen or professionals (often lawyers). They undertake their role on a voluntary part-time basis; they may receive (at most) a small salary (usually none) as well as fees for certain special services and reimbursement for incurred expenses. But one may assume that most of them undertake the responsibilities chiefly for the social and perhaps economic advantages generated by the mere prestige of the office; they are quick to have their business cards printed.

Finally, one word on the recent trend consisting in the creation of so-called **virtual consulates**. These are websites that are locally branded and customised and are often supplemented by periodic visits to the capital city of the region in question by professional consular staff from the nearest 'real' consular post or from the consular section of the Embassy (we call them *flying consuls*).

Permanent representation. A third category of diplomatic mission along the embassies and consulates is the permanent representation of a state, not to another state but to an international organisation (IO) of which it is a member state. We now leave the world of bilateral diplomacy (two states) and enter the world of *multilateral diplomacy* (three or more states). IOs, such as the United Nations or the European Union, can be viewed as *standing diplomatic conferences*. It is this permanency that gives the IO its added value compared to the alternative of the periodic calling of temporary *ad hoc* conferences. In fact some IOs have grown out of conferences: the OSCE (Organisation for Security and Cooperation in Europe) out of the like-named Conference, the CSCE; the WTO (World Trade Organisation) out of the GATT (General Agreement on Tariffs and Trade) (see Box 1.5).

Box 1.5 Conferences and Organisations

There are three significant differences between international conferences (ICs) and international organisations (IOs): (1) IOs have an *open-ended time-frame*; they operate, in principle, on a permanent and continuous basis, whereas ICs most often have a temporary character; they last no longer than needed for agreeing on the issue for which they were convened. (2) IOs have an *open-ended agenda*: everything that can be subsumed under the broad-framed purposes, aims, and objectives of the organisation can, in principle, be discussed, whereas ICs generally are directed to a specific *ad hoc* issue to be resolved; (3) IOs benefit from an *institutional backing*; institutions give solidity to an organisation and ensure its longevity; ICs, being both time-limited (temporary) and agenda-specific (*ad hoc*), are not embedded in an institutional framework but most often rely on a light secretariat.

The member states of IOs need not all necessarily entertain diplomatic relations with each other. This does not constitute a liability for an IO; quite on the contrary, one of the assets of IOs is that they allow for a dialogue among those who need it most, countries that do *not* entertain diplomatic relations with each other (the United States and Iran or North Korea in the UN setting, for example). As far as the UN is concerned, this allows for a genuine *global conversation* through what has come to be called '*the New York channel*'.

A Permanent representation is headed by a senior diplomat, almost always of the rank of ambassador and is therefore designated as *Ambassador, Permanent Representative* (*to the African Union*, for instance), in short 'the PR' as diplomats refer to him or her. Since the ownership of an IO rests with its member states, a PR need not formally to be accredited to the organisation of which his or her country is co-owner (so no request for *agrément*, no *letters of credence*). In practice, a formal notification is made to the head of the international secretariat housed in the permanent headquarters of the organisation, such as the Secretary-General of the UN in New York. The broader the agenda of the organisation, the larger will be the staff supporting the PR; it will consist of career-diplomats and experts coming from different technical ministries. Its internal organisation is like that of an embassy with minister-counsellors overseeing the work of their colleagues down to the attachés under the overall direction of the PR. The privileges and immunities granted to embassies and consulates pursuant to the Vienna Conventions do not apply to permanent representations; these matters are usually regulated by specific agreements between the *host State* and the organisation concerned.

Before leaving the world of ambassadors, consuls, and permanent representatives, one final remark on a phenomenon called **going native**. Going native or succumbing to *localitis* as it is also sometimes called, is an occupational hazard experienced by professional diplomats who have been posted for too long in the same place, caring more about the country in which they are posted than their own. A related danger is **tunnel vision** resulting from too long an exclusive and tight focus on the target country, losing sight of the broader context including one's home country's objectives. A well-known story is that of former US Secretary of State Schultz asking his ambassadors to point to 'your country' on a globe. They would invariably indicate the country to which they were posted, allowing Schultz to spin the globe back to the US and remind them that *this* was in fact 'their country'. That is why diplomats generally are rotated between postings, typically after three to four years, and why after two consecutive postings abroad, they are being called back to the capital to serve for a couple of years at headquarters in the MFA. These changes in location between posts abroad, or post and capital, are commonly referred to as the *diplomatic movement* (the 'movement of the bodies' as an American diplomat once put it to me less respectfully).

1.4 What are diplomatic missions for?

What are the functions of a diplomatic mission? Before answering that specific question, let us ask the more general question: what is the **establishment of diplomatic relations** in the first place about? Diplomatic relations should not be confused with amiability or cordiality. Neither of these two concepts really belong to the diplomatic context. There is more sound sense in the observation of Winston Churchill who, in his inimitable style, puts it as follows: 'The reason for having diplomatic relations is not to confer a compliment, but to secure a convenience'.

Diplomatic relations are not a grace to be conferred but a convenience to be used. That is apparently the rationale behind the decision taken in 2020 by both the United Arab Emirates (UAE) and Bahrein to establish formal diplomatic relations with Israel, thus abandoning the old Arab orthodoxy of offering Israel full relations only if it withdraws from Palestinian lands. In their telling, they will now have more leverage to push for a two-state solution, not exactly Israel's preferred option. They came to realise, in the words of Anwar Gargash, the UAE's Minister of Foreign Affairs, 'that the policy of the empty chair has not served the Palestinians well' (or so he says).

This same rationale also tells us that nothing is more absurd than the **breaking off of diplomatic relations** in moments of crises. It is precisely when there is tension or conflict that there is most need of such relations, and yet it is in such conditions that they have often been sundered. That is how, between 1917 and 1934, the US denied itself relations of any kind with the Soviet Union. The US, interpreting diplomatic relations as a reward for good conduct (and their breaking off as a penalty for misdemeanour), thus made impossible any prospect of balancing the policies of these two great nations one against the other for a period lasting some 17 years.

Later, seven years had to pass between 1965 (when the US had decided in principle to recognise the People's Republic of China) and 1972 (when it actually did), thus denying itself the opportunity of conducting a dialogue the PRC during these critical seven years. Recognition of states is of course not the same as establishing diplomatic relations, but in practice the latter follows the first. The US had created a dilemma, called the **'circular dilemma'** (not unlike the one Cameron created in the UK in early 2000 with the Brexit-referendum); first it (he) persuaded its (his) own public opinion to hate China (leave the EU), and then it (he) overestimated its (his) own capacity to implement the wished-for-change, that is to recognise China (to remain in the EU). This behaviour reflected the erroneous belief that diplomatic relations, including their establishment and breaking off, have a moral, rather than utilitarian significance (see EBAN, 1998, p. 101).

Something similar happened when the Iranian leaders started qualifying the US as the *Great Satan*. Would the American people then accept that their President talks to the Iranian leadership and, conversely, would the Iranian people understand that their government wants to talk to the Great Satan? What is gained by identifying countries and their leaders in such a way when precisely because of the sour relationship they need to be worked with?

With these preliminary caveats in mind, let us now take up the more specific question regarding the functions of diplomatic missions. The simplest way to do this is to take the Vienna Convention on Diplomatic Relations of 1961 as a guide. In its article 3, it mentions five functions of diplomatic missions which we will present in a slightly *updated* language:

- **Representing your Country.** Representing the sending state in the receiving state can mean everything ranging from attendance at state ceremonial occasions over paying courtesy visits to local authorities and giving public lectures at universities, to appearing on television. Although that is also part of it, representation is more than organising nice dinner parties and glamorous receptions at the residence, as the *cliché* of the smooth diplomat sipping cocktails may make us believe. It is for fulfilling this representation function that the diplomat is given a monthly 'representation allowance'.
- **Promoting Friendly Relations.** What of the duty to promote friendly relations between sending and receiving states? Again, make no mistake. As Chris Patten once remarked, one should not 'confuse foreign policy with being nice to foreigners' (cited in FLETCHER, 2017, p. 100). The first duty of a diplomat is to advance and defend his country's interests, and this may occasionally require him to behave in an unfriendly (but always tactful) manner. What counts is efficacy, not sentimentality. The natural authority that a diplomat has acquired through his impeccable professional behaviour is what will impress on his interlocutor, not his smile or the colour of his tie. Marking important local events and making extensive social contact are a means to an end, and that end is gaining influence, which, of course, on itself, does not constrain one to be *un*friendly.
- **Gathering Information, Analysing and Reporting.** Gathering, and more importantly analysing information on political, military, economic, and other developments in the receiving state, and then reporting the analysis to the capital, has long been recognised as one of the most important functions of a diplomatic mission. *Gathering information* is not just blindly shopping around but must be done selectively, and with trusted sources only. Before you go out fishing for information, make sure you studied the file and ask the pertinent questions. Your interlocutor will judge *you* no less than you will judge him or her. In diplomacy, there is no time for small talk. As Joseph Nye puts it: 'In today's world, information is not scarce, but attention is, and attention depends on credibility' (NYE, 2015, p. 61). Also, go after the information your capital needs, not after what you somehow find interesting (see Box 1.6). You know that 24/7 global, real-time news gathering has rendered reporting of brute facts useless. That is why the crucial question you should address is not 'what is it?', but 'what does it all mean?'. That is where *analysis* comes in. Understanding is not the same as knowing. Understanding requires contextualising what one knows, placing it in a broader narrative, identifying the relevant variables of a problem, unearthing underlying motives, explaining. And then finally comes the *reporting* to the capital. Again, you do not report everything you know and understand, only what your colleagues at headquarters need to know and understand. And perhaps you may wish to share some prudent policy advice with them. Embassies do not *make* policy, headquarters do that, but they *contribute* to the *shaping* of policy.

Box 1.6 Requests and Instructions

The interaction forth and back between headquarters and periphery occurs through a flow of requests and instructions from the MFA to the missions abroad and reports coming back from the diplomatic missions to the capital.

Requests are general and can bear on anything in which your authorities are interested, not out of sheer curiosity but of necessity for the conduct of foreign policy. They can ask for an analysis of a particular issue or for an assessment of a general situation. The smart diplomat is the one that can **anticipate** what his or her capital needs. His or her report is in the capital before the request is sent out.

Instructions are more specific than requests. They often involve an *action* to be undertaken: a *démarche* to be performed at the MFA of your host country, an inquiry to be conducted, a public statement to be issued … . More specifically, instructions are what you ask for and get on a continuous basis in a *negotiation situation*. But instructions in such cases should leave you the necessary leeway allowing you to navigate intelligently the meanders of an evolving negotiation situation. That is why instructions coming from the capital and bearing on a negotiation should be *'framework-instructions'* outlining the direction to go and defining the upper and lower bounds of your negotiation space. Instructions, in particular when they bear on sensitive issues, should be clear and coherent and give you the necessary guidance on what lies *behind* them. Without such guidance, you would need to be clairvoyant to work with them. Also recall that the smart diplomat should never want to get an instruction from his capital that he has not shaped himself. And that shaping is what he will do, explicitly or implicitly, in his reporting on the status of the negotiation to his capital.

- **Explaining Policy.** It is important that the receiving state has a proper understanding of your country's policies. The receiving state needs explanation, sometimes reassurance, at other times warning. What you say in public may need clarification in a private *'one-to-one'* (*'tête-à-tête'*, *'face-to-face'*) encounter or *'in the margins'* of some other meeting. Explanation and clarification often mean making the underlying considerations and motivations of your county's policy, that is its *rationale*, more explicit. In fact, an embassy will often be asked by its capital to make representations to the authorities of the receiving state directly through a physical contact, a *'démarche'*, regarding issues that are of particular interest or concern (see Box 1.7) or more indirectly through written *'notes verbales'* (see Box 1.8).

Box 1.7 *Démarche* and *Aide-Mémoire*

These are yet again French diplomatic terms which have become part of the practising diplomat's daily vocabulary. A *démarche* refers to the act of taking up an issue with another government. Usually the *démarche* is made to the MFA of the receiving state, but it may also be made to another ministry or to the office of the Head of State or Government. A démarche is almost always made on specific instruction from the home MFA. Often the ambassador making the démarche will leave behind with the official of the receiving state an *aide-mémoire* which summarises the *démarche* that is usually made verbally.

- **Negotiating.** Although a diplomat posted abroad will almost never be called to take the lead in a bilateral negotiation (home-based senior officials or, more rarely, ministers will do that), embassies still may be associated to a negotiation and play an important although less visible role in it. The embassy may be entrusted with the preparation of the negotiations: agreeing on the agenda (the 'what' of negotiations), agreeing on the procedure (the 'how' of negotiations: format, venue, delegations, timing). Sometimes ambassadors are brought back home to reinforce a negotiating team that wishes to rely on their unique in-country knowledge and expertise. More often, the embassy will be asked to negotiate updates or amendments to existing agreements. It may negotiate 'understandings' of a more technical nature. Embassies are easily used as vehicles for secret negotiations. Negotiations with kidnappers, for example, under intense pressure from family and friends of the kidnapped person and which for good reasons governments regularly deny conducting, are often entrusted to local embassies familiar with the micro-political context of the case.

Box 1.8 *Note Verbale*

Notes Verbales are the most widely used form of diplomatic correspondence, both in bilateral and multilateral diplomacy. As English has become the *lingua franca* of diplomacy, *Notes Verbales* are increasingly referred to as *Diplomatic Notes*. They have a wide range of application: to inform, to request, to protest … . They are used in correspondence between the host country authorities and embassies, between embassies, and in international organisations. They generally open with a customary courtesy ('The Embassy of (country) presents its compliments to') and conclude in a similar manner ('avails itself of the opportunity to renew to the Embassy of (country) the assurances of its highest consideration'). The note is initialled but never signed.

Example: *Note verbale* from the UN Secretary-General to the President of the Security Council (source: BARSTON, 2019, p. 350).

> The Secretary-General presents his compliments to the President of the Security Council and, in accordance with paragraph 8 of Security Council resolution 816 (1993) of 31 March 1993, has the honour to bring to his attention further information received by the United Nations Protection Force (UNPROFOR) regarding apparent violations of the ban on flights in the airspace of Bosnia and Herzegovina.
>
> Between 29 November and 1 December 1994 there appear to have been 18 flights of fixed or rotary-wing aircraft in the airspace of Bosnia and Herzegovina other than those exempted in accordance with paragraph 1 of resolution 816 (1993) or approved by UNPROFOR in accordance with paragraph 2 of that resolution. Details as to the itinerary of flights in the reporting period are attached as an annex to the present *note verbale*.
>
> The total number of flights assessed as apparent violations is now 3,317. Etc.

Example: *Diplomatic Note* from the British Embassy in Washington, DC (source: Embassy of Belgium in Washington).

'Diplomatic Note N°030'

> The British Embassy in Washington, D.C. presents its compliments to the US Department of State and all Diplomatic Missions in Washington, D.C. and regrets to inform them of the death of the former British Prime Minister, Baroness Thatcher, on April 8 2013.
>
> Lady Thatcher was Prime Minister of the United Kingdom of Great Britain & Northern Ireland from 1979–1990.
>
> A book of Condolence will be opened at the British Embassy, 3100 Massachusetts Avenue NW, Washington, D.C. 20008, on Tuesday 9 April and Wednesday 10 April between 10 am and 4 pm.
>
> The British Embassy avails itself of this opportunity to renew to the US Department of State and all Diplomatic Missions in Washington, D.C. the assurance of its highest consideration.
>
> British Embassy
> Washington, D.C.
> 9 April 2013

In this chapter, we have reviewed the standard model of the organisation of diplomacy. In that model, the state remains the prime actor. That is why it is called state-based diplomacy. It is states that define foreign policy and it is for states to determine the nature of relations they wish to entertain with other states. Ministries of foreign affairs advise the Minister on the multiple contingencies of international life. Through coordination with other ministerial departments, they ensure the overall coherence of foreign policy. Diplomats are state officials assisting the Minister in the day-to-day conduct of foreign relations. They are sent abroad to work in Embassies and Consulates. Living and working abroad makes them privileged observers of the national scene. They contribute to the shaping of foreign policy and are entrusted with its execution. Diplomats represent their state abroad, promote and explain its foreign policy, and defend its national interests. They ensure that communication channels stay open. State-based diplomacy remains the dominant model for doing diplomacy. In the last few decades, however, new approaches to diplomacy have emerged. They complement and support state-based diplomacy, but do not replace it. This will be the topic of the next chapter.

Bibliography

AGGESTAM, Karin & TOWNS, Ann (2019), "The Gender Turn in Diplomacy: A New Research Agenda", *International Feminist Journal of Politics*, 21, 2019, nr.1.

BARSTON, Ronald. Peter. (2019), *Modern Diplomacy*, Routledge, Abingdon/New York, NY.

BEECKMAN, Tinneke (2020), *Machiavelli's Lef*, Boom, Amsterdam.

BERRIDGE, G. R. (2010), *Diplomacy. Theory and Practice*, Palgrave, New York, NY.

COOPER, Andrew E., HEINE, Jorge & THAKUR, Ramesh (eds.) (2015), *The Oxford Handbook of Modern Diplomacy*, Oxford University Press, Oxford.

COOPER, Robert (2021), *The Ambassadors – Thinking about Diplomacy from Machiavelli to Modern Times*, Weidenfeld & Nicolson, London.

EBAN, Abba (1998), *Diplomacy for the Next Century*, Yale University Press, New Haven, CT/ London.

FLETCHER, Tom (2017), *The Naked Diplomat. Understanding Power and Politics in the Digital Age*, William Collins, London.

NYE, Joseph (2015), *Is the American Century over?*, Polity, Cambridge.

RANA (2011), *21st Century Diplomacy – A Practitioner's Guide*, Continuum, London/ New York, NY.

ROZENTAL, Andrés & BUENROSTRO, Alicia (2015), "Bilateral Diplomacy", in: COOPER (2015), p. 239.

SHARP, Paul (2019), *Diplomacy in the 21st Century – A Brief Introduction*, Routledge, Abingdon/ New York, NY.

THE ECONOMIST (2021), *Sex and Geopolitics – Why Nations That Fail Women, Fail*, 11 September 2021.

WOUTERS, Jan, DUQUET, Sanderijn & MEUWISSEN, Katrien (2015), "The Vienna Conventions on Diplomatic and Consular Relations", in: COOPER (2015), pp. 510–543.

2   Ways and means of doing diplomacy

2.1 The one old and the many new diplomacies – a preliminary exploration

In Chapter 1, we looked at the *standard model* of diplomacy: how diplomacy is structured through ministries and embassies, what their functions are and how they operate. This *classic* model is state-centred; diplomacy is about managing relations among states, it is the state that has the *monopoly* of dictating foreign policy and diplomats, which are official agents of the state, are its instrument. This model is called **state-based diplomacy**. The slightly outmoded Vienna Convention on Diplomatic Relations of 1961 reflects this Westphalian model pretty well.

Although the state remains very much at the centre of diplomacy, there is no denying that *new non-state actors* have joined the international scene lately doing 'their' own diplomacy (from civic organisations over big corporations to celebrities) and that *new issues* have been added to the diplomatic agenda as globalisation has engendered an increasingly interconnected world (climate change, migration, pandemics). It is no surprise then that next to the 'old' state-based diplomacy, **'new diplomacies'** have emerged. What we have been witnessing, however, is not just the emergence of *some* new diplomacies but a *numerical* explosion of *all kinds* of them, all thrown in the same 'diplomacy' bag: climate diplomacy, summit diplomacy, virtual diplomacy (also called e-diplomacy or digital diplomacy), people-to-people diplomacy, citizen's diplomacy, diaspora diplomacy, face-to-face diplomacy, refugee diplomacy, back-channel diplomacy, health diplomacy … and one could go on for another ten lines. This proliferation of diplomacies has led to much confusion and to misunderstandings as regards the nature of diplomacy, as we will see in the last section of this chapter. What one notes when looking at this list is not just that there are *many* of them (quantity), but also that they seem to be quite *different as regards their nature* (quality).

In what follows we will attempt to *de-confuse* the matter by making a few *basic distinctions* among these numerous and diverse 'diplomacies' in terms of *four categories: forms, kinds, ways and means*. Our endeavour is not just one of **clarification** but also of **demystification**. Some of the 'new' diplomacies seem to be just gadgets or empty labels: 'ping-pong diplomacy', 'panda-diplomacy', 'vaccine-diplomacy'; and what about 'citizen's diplomacy', 'celebrity diplomacy', 'conference diplomacy', 'disaster diplomacy' (none are my invention). Do we really need these concepts, do they somehow advance our understanding of what diplomacy is? Some fear that they obscure rather than illuminate matters. Take 'disaster diplomacy'. What does this concept add to our common understanding that in cases of emergencies and disasters people of the Ministries of Foreign Affairs' (MFAs') Crisis Centre will be set to work and actively

DOI: 10.4324/9781003298182-4

engaged in trying to address the matter. Perhaps they will prepare an evacuation operation or send out a rescue team. Does that make them 'disaster diplomats' engaged in 'disaster diplomacy'?

Distinguishing among those **four categories of diplomacies** may help bringing some order where currently disorder reigns. The reader should not be concerned too much about understanding the examples given for each category. For now, the objective is simply to give an initial feel as to what these categories amount to. Most of the examples will be examined further down this chapter.

- *Forms* of diplomacy. *Forms are **models** in which diplomacy can be conceptualised, they speak about different **approaches** to diplomacy.* The *state-based* diplomacy that we studied in the preceding chapter clearly is a model, indeed it is the standard model of diplomacy; it says that it is states and their official agents, diplomats, that take centre stage in diplomacy. Other approaches to diplomacy are *non-state-based.* A good example is 'Track II diplomacy', often also called *non-official* diplomacy, as distinct from state-based 'Track I diplomacy'. Another example of a non-state-based diplomacy is 'networked diplomacy', an interesting model that we will study in detail below. Most people would *not* consider non-state-based forms of diplomacy as *alternative diplomacies*, displacing state-based diplomacy, but rather as complements to it. Most often they support state-based diplomacy.
- *Kinds* of diplomacy. *Kinds simply refer to the **subject-matter**, the **domain** covered by specific diplomacies, they tell us what these diplomacies are **about**.* A kind of diplomacy that has been with us for quite some time is 'economic diplomacy'. Newcomers are 'energy diplomacy', 'environmental diplomacy', 'health diplomacy', and perhaps 'population diplomacy' (should we add 'refugee diplomacy' and 'disaster diplomacy' as well?).
- *Ways* of doing diplomacy. *Ways are the **methods** that are being used in the actual conduct of diplomacy, the **manners in which** diplomacy is executed.* As could be expected *forms* and *ways* are closely linked and the distinction between both is therefore not always easy to make (most diplomats, for instance, will consider 'Track II diplomacy' not as a *form* of diplomacy, but as a *way* of doing it). Examples of ways of doing diplomacy are 'bi- and multilateral diplomacy', 'public diplomacy', 'virtual diplomacy', and 'summit diplomacy' (should we add 'back-channel diplomacy' and 'conference diplomacy'?).
- *Means* for doing diplomacy. *Means are **tools, instruments, vehicles** on which one relies, or to which one appeals for doing diplomacy.* Examples are 'cultural diplomacy', 'sports diplomacy', and 'diaspora diplomacy' where culture, sports, and a country's diaspora abroad are used as vehicles for doing diplomacy (should we add 'celebrity diplomacy' to it?).

Equipped with these categories allowing us to generally distinguish among different diplomacies, we can now briefly look at how these play out in the diplomacies that we will be reviewing in this chapter. **'*Bi- and multilateral diplomacy*'** clearly are two different *ways* of doing diplomacy (methods), but as we will see they also point to two very different *approaches* to diplomacy which are captured by the concepts of '*bilateralism*' and '*multilateralism*' (somewhat akin to the distinction commonly made between 'globalisation' and 'globalism'). And these may be considered *forms* of diplomacy rather than just *methods*. **'*Track II diplomacy*'** is also an interesting case. As a *non-official* diplomacy, Track II diplomacy looks like a genuine alternative *form* (*model*) to *official* Track I diplomacy; some, however, consider Track II to be just another *way* (*method*) of doing diplomacy. Diplomats will tend towards the second view, but non-diplomats may be sympathetic with the first. *'Networked diplomacy'* is an interesting non-standard *model* of diplomacy that has become quite prominent lately. It is a *form* of diplomacy that is *not* meant to be a *substitute* to classic state-based diplomacy, but rather a complement to it. Networked diplomacy leads rather naturally to *'virtual diplomacy'*, a novel and somewhat trendy concept to be handled with some caution. It is *not* a *form* of diplomacy but simply a new *way* of doing diplomacy. *'Public diplomacy'* has been around for some time and is a rather well-established practice, at odds with the traditional concept of closed diplomacy where confidentiality and secrecy prevail. Is it a way of doing diplomacy or a form? Most diplomats would probably just consider it as a *way* of doing diplomacy. But others may disagree. Woodrow Wilson, well known for his attachment to 'open covenants openly arrived at', would consider public diplomacy as a *form* of diplomacy. So here we meet the same ambiguity that we met when comparing bi/multilateral diplomacy (means) with bi/multilateralism (forms). Public diplomacy is closely linked to *'cultural diplomacy'*, which refers to a *means* for doing diplomacy, and is not a *kind* of diplomacy (cultural diplomacy is not *about* culture but uses culture as a vehicle for doing diplomacy). Finally, there are the *'new vintage diplomacies'*, some of them trendier than others, each with their own label. Some of those labels refer to *forms* of diplomacy: 'sub-state diplomacy', for instance; others refer to *kinds* of diplomacy as they are subject-related: 'energy diplomacy', 'health diplomacy', and 'eco-diplomacy'. Still others refer to *ways* of doing diplomacy: 'summit diplomacy' and 'conference diplomacy', for instance. And finally there are those that refer to *means* for doing diplomacy: 'sports diplomacy' and 'diaspora diplomacy', for example.

2.2 Bilateral and multilateral diplomacy

Diplomacy is about the conduct and management of foreign *relations*. Foreign relations are what link one country to another. That is why the concept of *unilateral diplomacy* looks awkward. In fact, it does not exist: a country can *act* unilaterally, but it cannot *conduct* a unilateral diplomacy. A relation is minimally entertained with one other party. *Bilateral* diplomacy is about the conduct of such *one-to-one*, country-to-country relationship. There can be many of them, but then in parallel. Relations can also simultaneously and jointly be entertained with more than just one other country, with a group of countries (minimally three), informally (as with the G20) or within a pre-established framework: a conference (on climate change or disarmament, for instance) or an international organisation (the UN, ASEAN, African Union …). *Multilateral diplomacy* is about the conduct of such *many-to-many* relationships.

Bilateral diplomacy is the standard operational procedure for the conduct of foreign relations. It is the *default procedure* through which relations between states are being managed. *Bilaterality* reflects a core principle of diplomacy: *reciprocity,* which is itself based on the principle of *equality.* Bilateral diplomacy has one big advantage. The relationship among any two countries can be tailor-made. It can directly address the specific interests of the two countries involved in the relationship. The two countries are in full control; no other country looks over their shoulders. Full control does not mean total freedom, however; bilateral diplomacy will have to take into consideration the regional and global context in which it operates. Still, it is easier to align interests and preferences of two countries than it is when more are involved. A bilateral relationship is also more direct, more intimate and generally more gratifying for the countries involved than relations in a multilateral setting which are more distant, more anonymous. But bilateral diplomacy is no panacea. The transaction costs involved in establishing as many bilateral relationships as there are outside parties may be prohibitive. That is what post-Brexit UK has been experiencing. It also explains why small states with limited resources cannot afford to do it the bilateral way. Cost-effectiveness is an asset of multilateralism.

Bilateralism is something different and should not be confused with bilateral diplomacy as such. The latter refers to a *method*, a way of conducting foreign relations. Bilateralism is more than the mere choice of a certain *method*; it involves a political choice as to how to *approach* international relations generally. There is an ideological element at play in bilateralism. To call yourself a 'bilateralist' is to make a *political statement*. Bilateralism has gained new traction lately. In a world marked by rivalry and competition, particularly among the Great Powers, we witness the re-emergence of the strong sovereign and independent state, the self-assertive state. Bilateralism then questions the 'Rules-based World Order' which emerged after the World War II and came alive again in the early 1990s with the end of the Cold War. When in May 2010 William Hague became the new UK Foreign Secretary, he packed out with his *'New Bilateralism'* predicated on the premise that what one does on its own (or just with two), one does better. Managing relations on a bilateral basis, Hague said, is not just easier but much more effective. You do not have to carry the multilateral ballast behind you. In a bilateralist approach there is no such thing as a 'lowest common denominator'. As is well known, a similar move happened in the US when Donald Trump took over from Barack Obama (who wasn't a convinced multilateralist either). On his first day in office in February 2017, Trump signed an executive order unpacking the 12-country trade deal known as the Trans Pacific Partnership (TPP). Other withdrawals from multilateral arrangements or organisations followed suit: the 2015 Paris Climate Change accord, the 2015 Iran nuclear deal known as the JCPOA (Joint Comprehensive Plan of Action), the UN Human Rights Council, UNESCO, and UNRWA (the UN refugee agency for Palestine).

The distinction between bilateral diplomacy as a *method* and bilateralism as a political stance, a doctrine, a *form* of state-based diplomacy can be replicated in the multilateral dimension.

Multilateral diplomacy then simply refers to a *way* of conducting foreign policy, in this case through coordinated diplomatic interaction between three or more states. It rests on the premise that cooperation is a winning strategy. Multilateral diplomacy is less transactional than bilateral diplomacy: in the latter you bargain and make a 'deal' ('what's in it for me?'), in the former you negotiate and make an 'agreement' ('what's in it for us?'). Such understanding of multilateral diplomacy is essentially *procedural*; it is about the 'how to' conduct diplomacy (the way, the method), not the 'what of' diplomacy (the form, the model). Globalisation and the growing interdependence between states have made multilateral diplomacy a growth industry. International organisations (the UN, the Bretton Woods twins IMF and World Bank), specialised agencies (WTO, ILO, WHO, IAEA), regional organisations (EU, AU, ECOWAS, ASEAN), global conferences (on the Law of the Sea, on Climate Change), and *ad hoc* summits (G7, G20), all are multilateral *ways* of doing diplomacy.

Multilateralism, however, is something else. Now we are no longer talking about a mere method or procedure for the management of foreign relations. Like bilateralism, multilateralism is a political statement. It involves a *substantive* commitment to a certain world order. It rests on values and normative principles, not just interests. Dialogue and cooperation lead to collective action. Examples of such multilateralist commitments are George Bush's 'New World Order' of the early 1990s or today's 'Rules-Based World Order' defended by most liberal democracies. Multilateralism in this sense is no longer primarily *a way* of acting together with others (method), but is rather about sharing and securing objectives and interests that together constitute a political worldview, an ideology. That is what the first ever EU High Representative Javier Solana had in mind when launching the concept of '*effective multilateralism*' in his 2003 security strategy. It is also the sense in which the '*Alliance for Multilateralism*' launched by Germany and France in September 2019, should be understood. Multilateralism in this substantive sense is axiomatic for the foreign policies of many European countries as it is of the European Union's external policy itself. Confusing multilateral diplomacy with multilateralism, the procedural with the ideological, is what allows Vladimir Putin and Xi Jing Pin to claim to be no less multilateral-minded than Angela Merkel or Emmanuel Macron. The first, however, are 'methodological' multilateralists only and do not share the latter's 'substantive' multilateralism.

With these distinctions and caveats in mind, let us now look at the **strengths and weaknesses** of multilateral diplomacy as a way of conducting foreign policy.

Some of the **strengths** are:

- *Cost-effectiveness.* Multilateral diplomacy lowers the high transaction costs involved in 'do-it-alone' bilateral diplomacy. Economies of scale benefit all participants. International organisations provide for low-cost cooperation.
- *Predictability.* Working within a pre-set multilateral framework, such as an international organisation, where principles and norms as well as procedures and working methods have been agreed beforehand, reduces uncertainty and enhances predictability.
- *Rulemaking.* Multilateral diplomacy facilitates cooperation based on trust. Its long-term norm-setting addresses issues that states on their own cannot resolve (climate change and migration, for instance). International conferences and organisations are like an open market where participants trade proposals and concessions in an ongoing negotiation process.
- *Compliance.* This ongoing negotiation process affects participants' calculations of self-interest and induces compliance with the multilateral discipline (see Box 2.1).
- *Communication.* Multilateral fora have a unique 'convening power' that single states rarely have; they facilitate informal contact and communication among officials of the most diverse countries.

We will look at what diplomacy can learn from *game theory* in a later chapter. But it is worth noting already at this stage that multilateral diplomacy, with its multi-party conferences and international organisations, creates situations that are like that of the *iterated, open-ended Prisoners' Dilemma* in which cooperation is a rational and beneficial strategy for all, resulting in a collective win-win.

> ### Box 2.1 Multilateral Discipline
>
> Pursuit of one's farsighted long-term self-interests leads states to eschew their myopic short-term self-interests. Social pressure, exercised through *linkages* among issues, provides the most compelling reason for states to comply with their commitments. That is, egoistic states, pursuing their myopic short-term interests, may still end up complying with the rules of the multilateral game because they know that if they fail to do so, other states will observe their behaviour, evaluate it negatively, and perhaps take retaliatory action against the egoistic states thus undoing whatever short-term benefit they may have gained. Even in the absence of retaliation, states may still have incentives to comply with the multilateral discipline if they are concerned about precedent or believe that their reputation is at stake (see KEOHANA, 2013, p. 98).

What are some of the **weaknesses** of multilateral diplomacy?

- *Low content effectiveness.* While multilateral diplomacy may result in weighty agreements obtained through protracted and broad-based negotiations (high legitimacy), it may not be very effective on content because agreements in the multilateral context are often the result of contorted compromises reflecting the *lowest common denominator*. The inverse relationship between legitimacy and effectiveness is a recurring theme in diplomacy that we will meet regularly in this book.
- *Poor real-time problem-solving capacity.* Multilateral diplomacy may be good in long-term norm-setting on fundamental issues of international governance (think of the Sustainable Development Goals (SDGs) or Climate Change) but is *poor in addressing urgent problems* requiring rapid and decisive action, in particular military action. That is why international security organisations (such as the UN or the OSCE) are no substitute for a foreign policy based on the realities of power.
- *Inertia.* Once multilateral mechanisms are set in place, they tend to endure and start having a life on their own. This is particularly true of international organisations. They embody '*sunk costs*': giving up on the organisation is felt as a loss, even though its persistence does not any longer serve any useful purpose. The high costs of institution-building helps explaining why existing organisations with poor performance tend to persist in time (UNCTAD is the classic example).
- *False impressions.* Multilateral diplomacy is sometimes said to be *misleading*: artificial pomposity and fake nervousness create the false impression (perhaps the illusion) that important things are being decided while no significant results are produced (the Conference on Disarmament in Geneva is an example of a multilateral forum that has been unable to achieve any significant outcome over the last few decades).

Multilateral diplomacy is generally a win-win strategy. As Robert Cooper says:

> The multilateral order changes everything. One state on its own is isolated. Two states, and relations will be transactional – 'the art of the deal'. Three is the magic number. When three or more states are gathered together, there is transparency and very likely rules, written or unwritten.
>
> (COOPER, 2021, p. 488)

Everybody comes out better than when they came in. Which is true. What Cooper does however not mention is that some come out better than others, or to put it differently, that the distribution of the 'wins' is uneven.

In relative terms, small and medium-sized states tend to get more out of multilateral cooperation than larger states. The latter obviously need it less than the former. They benefit from 'strategic autonomy'. For them, multilateral disciplines can occasionally even be more of a burden than an asset. The strongest anti-multilateralist statement ever made was when John Bolton (later to become Trump's National Security Adviser) expressed a desire to lop off the top 10 floors of the UN Headquarters in New York.

Small and medium-sized states' commitment to multilateralism is not due to some natural inclination for its noble causes, an inclination that the Great Powers would lack. Small and medium-sized states' commitment to multilateralism is no less the result of a self-interested rational calculus than the one explaining Great Powers' relative disinterest for multilateralism. Great Powers manage a global agenda and are therefore more actively engaged in the world at large (think of the American military deployments worldwide). As a result, they risk being more affected by multilateral disciplines decided in multilateral fora than small and medium-sized countries (think of their greater exposure to possible International Criminal Court (ICC) prosecution for military misconduct). If the balance of relative 'wins' between the big players and the small fish gets too uneven, the first may *not* even be interested in *joining* the multilateral undertaking in the first place (that is why, to stay with our example, the US refused to join the 1998 Rome Statue instituting the ICC or, in another context, to sign the 1997 Ottawa Convention on Landmines). Or they may *quit* an organisation when they deem their interests no longer served (or perhaps disserved) by it. That is why, as already noted, the US left UNCTAD and UNWRA, as well as the UN Human Rights Council (temporarily), and why it is wary of many Geneva-based UN Agencies, in particular the WTO and WHO.

It is to address such possible imbalances that certain mechanisms have been devised to make multilateralism attractive for greater powers too. Obviously, the 'one state – one vote' rule contradicts the reality of how power is distributed in the world. No wonder then that one of the mechanisms to redress imbalances is to revisit that rule, for instance through the system of weighted voting rules. The European Economic Community (1958) and its successor European Union would never have come into existence if *qualified majority voting rules* had not been adopted. The same holds for *the veto right* of the UN Security Council permanent members; take their veto away, and they would be gone as well (at least the three bigger ones). Another mechanism that helps setting imbalances in multilateral diplomacy somewhat straight again is by way of *de facto* leadership groups (variously called 'contact groups', 'core groups', *'directoires'*, 'troikas', 'quartets', 'quints', etc.) which give a privileged position to some more powerful members that steer and thus to some extent dominate the multilateral process. Classic examples are the *Balkan 'Contact Group'* during the 1990s (France, Germany, Italy, Russia, UK, and US) and the *Franco-German tandem* in the history and development of European integration. Contesting such leadership groups is tantamount to ignoring that the voice of power cannot be ignored, even in multilateral diplomacy.

2.3 Track II diplomacy

Track I diplomacy is *state-based diplomacy*, carried out by government representatives, officials, and diplomats whose duty it is to defend their state's '*interests*'. *Track II diplomacy*, on the contrary, generally involves a '***third-party***' engagement by **impartial non-officials**. Track II diplomacy therefore is often referred to as *non-official diplomacy*, sometimes also as *quiet diplomacy* or as a form of *citizen-based diplomacy*.

Track II diplomacy is particularly relevant in conflict-related situations which can only be defused by an impartial outsider not bound to serve the interests of a particular state or institution. Such outsider can more easily offer his or her good offices or act as a facilitator, mediator, onciliator or arbitrator. Good offices, facilitation, mediation, conciliation, and arbitration are indeed the primary forms of Track II involvement. An acting minister or a diplomat in active service will rarely be called upon to take up a mediation role, for instance, whereas former politicians or retired diplomats or diplomats that left official Track I life, certainly can. That was the case with Harold Saunders, a former Assistant Secretary of State who left the State Department to assist President Carter in negotiating the *Camp David agreement* between President Sadat and Prime Minister Begin in 1978. The mediation carried out by former UN Secretary General (UNSG) Kofi Annan in the *post-electoral crisis in Kenya* in 2007 is another example. What has been called 'Track one-and-a-half' diplomacy is what Marti Ahtisaari, the former President of Finland, was involved in as of November 2005 when dealing with the *Kosovo question* (this involvement has been called 'one-and-a-half', because although nominally independent, Ahtisaari still acted as a Special Envoy of UNSG Kofi Annan – see AHTISAARI, 2015, p. 344).

The **strengths** of Track II diplomacy thus lie in the relative advantages that nonofficial actors possess over official actors. Many contemporary conflicts are not inter-state but intra-state and preclude official intervention because they involve non-state actors, such as insurgents, ethnic groups or militias. Diplomatic practice, geared to managing disputes among states, often denies non-state actors any recognised role. That is what prevented direct Israeli-PLO talks for many years, as the PLO was considered a terrorist organisation. For non-officials such *questions of recognition and status* do not arise. They do not face the so-called '***entry-problem***' of getting talks going in the first place. Their independence can facilitate the building of trust. They can more easily be dismissed without causing embarrassment. They are free from the constraints of diplomatic protocol. They can move about more freely without the kind of publicity that diplomats often attract.

The characteristic features of third-party engagement are:

- **Disinterest**. The third-party acts with no interest other than the parties' interest, particularly *not a state or private interest.*
- **Independence**. Within its mandate the third-party has a degree of freedom of action and *independent* decision-making, apart *from any government.*
- **Neutrality**. The third-party has no *a priori* position on *the issue* at stake, is not prejudiced in one way or another as regards the substance of the dispute.
- **Impartiality**. The third-party has no preference as among *the parties* to the dispute (impartiality does not imply 'equidistance', which is a very misleading concept; in fact, equidistance would more often than not result in partiality).

Nonofficial Track II diplomacy is **quiet diplomacy**. Quiet diplomacy is not 'public' diplomacy, much less 'megaphone' diplomacy. It is defined by confidentiality and discretion. This is another reason why a politician will but rarely be called upon to mediate: he or she is too eager to run to the press, aspiring for political advantage, which is understandable – there is always a next election coming up. Track II diplomacy and active politics are difficult to reconcile.

The **aim** of quiet diplomacy is to create conditions in which parties feel *comfortable*, allowing them calmly to evaluate positions and interests, to weigh options and consider independent and impartial advice. It does so by allowing dialogue to take place without the public scrutiny that risks parties losing face or hardening their positions. In short, the primary function of quiet Track II diplomacy is to create a *space for dialogue* and to establish and maintain *confidence* among the parties by putting them at ease.

Track II diplomacy is **not**, however, a **substitute for official Track I** diplomacy although that is often the way it is presented. Track II is not an alternative to Track I state-based diplomacy, it is a *complement* to it. A diplomat would rather consider Track II diplomacy as a *way* of doing diplomacy, indeed as the un-official way. Track II is designed to *support* traditional diplomacy by exploring possible solutions out of the public view and without the requirements of formal diplomacy. Once Track II diplomacy has succeeded in assisting the opposing parties overcoming their differences, Track I diplomacy can and indeed must *take over*. Because only governments can guarantee the ultimate delivery and enforcement of whatever deal has been reached in Track II. This is what we have witnessed in the *India-Pakistan* Track II diplomacy on nuclear non-proliferation, in the use of Track II methods to advance the dialogue among the parties in the *Northern Ireland* conflict, and in the more than four decades long investment in Track II diplomacy in the *Israeli-Palestinian* dispute.

Track II diplomacy has its strengths, but that is not to say that everything is perfect with it. Track II diplomacy is **no miracle diplomacy**. Often it does not work. Millions of Euros have been spent on dialogues for Syria and Yemen in the 2011–today period that have had practically no impact on ending the violence. Occasionally this leads to cynicism towards Track II 'diplomats' which some consider to be 'either free-booting amateurs, or para-diplomats with valuable but limited usefulness' (BERRIDGE, 2010). Moreover, there are two dangers that potentially haunt Track II diplomacy more structurally. The first is that it risks becoming a business on its own. People start speaking about the 'peacebuilding industry' with its 'peace-making firms' that range from 'big-budget operations' over 'for-profit consultancy' to so-called 'boutique firms'. The Middle East is said to be a 'healthy market' for 'conflict resolution shops'. Government contracts can be highly 'lucrative'; millions of Euros and dollars have been spent on dialogues and forums for conflict-hit countries. A second danger that looms over Track II diplomacy is that it is not taken seriously as it is suspected to be manipulated by Track I diplomacy. Track II offers a nice pretext for Track I to appear to be doing something through the non-official channel for causes which they consider lost anyway, while relieving them of active engagement and responsibility; as Martti Ahtisaari says: 'Sometimes the goal of mediation is merely to create political cover; a state may send an envoy to a conflict zone so as to be seen doing something, but the conflict may actually receive little attention' (see AHTISAARI, 2015, p. 342).

2.4 Networked diplomacy

In the early 1990s of last century, after the fall of the Berlin wall and the implosion of the Soviet Union, it was quite fashionable to proclaim 'the end of the nation-state' and the advent of a 'post-territorial' era. Hoping to capitalize on the so-called 'peace-dividend', some believed in a 'New World Order' where state rivalry would be replaced by cooperation and understanding. But that dream was short-lived. As of the beginning of this new century, power politics has come back, and so has the strong state, alive and well. In terms of geopolitics, the billiard-ball model is still with us, a system of self-contained states colliding with one another, answering to the Hobbesian laws of power. The results of these collisions are essentially determined by military and economic power.

Still, something has happened in the meantime. The world has become networked. As William Hague, a former UK foreign secretary, stated it: 'Today, influence increasingly depends on fluid and dynamic networks, alliances and often informal links that require new forms of commitment' (cited in RANA, 2011, p. 4). In the networked world, power is distributed horizontally. It is a world that exists above the state, below the state, and through the state, a world where the new measure of power is **connectivity** (or connectedness), a world driven by globalisation, powered by the information and communication revolution, the so-called digital revolution. It is a world of global networks among businesses, civic organisations, individuals (including criminals), all of them non-state actors, but also among state actors: governments, their leaders, and officials. Anne-Marie Slaughter, a former Harvard Law School professor and currently the president of New America, a think-tank, has been active in researching the concept of a networked world and we will rely on that research for those aspects that are relevant for diplomatic practice.

For the sake of clarity, we will work with contrasting pairs of concepts, one referring to the classical geopolitical approach, the other to the more recent connectivity approach, so that what makes the one approach differ from the other becomes more apparent:

- A state operates through *government*, a network trough ***governance***; but while no world government has emerged, global governance has. If government denotes the formal exercise of power by established institutions, governance denotes cooperative problem-solving by a changing and often uncertain cast.
- In networks we see a shift from the *vertical* world of (state) hierarchy to the ***horizontal*** world of (network) 'heterarchy', where power is laterally distributed among peers, the participants in the network.
- In networks the centralised constraining power of states is replaced by ***voluntary association***. The power that flows from networks is not a power that imposes outcomes. Networks are not directed and controlled as much as they are managed and orchestrated. Multiple players are integrated into a whole that is greater than the sum of its parts.
- Network power flows from the ability to make the maximum number of valuable connections. In the networked world it is ***connectivity***, not wealth or status, that determines individual power.
- In a networked world ***human security***, broadly understood, takes centre place, rather than *state security*.

Networks can be as malign and deadly (think of drug cartels, human traffickers, traffickers in organs, terrorists) as they can be productive and beneficial. Also note that the gap between those who are connected to global networks and those who are not, sharply multiplies existing injustices. Existing (income) *inequalities* between the 'have' and 'have not' may well become exacerbated by the *inequities* resulting from the divide between the 'connected' and 'not-connected', between those who 'know' and those who 'know not', the 'know' and the 'know not'.

The vocabulary of networks can be heavy to swallow:

- **De-territorialisation.** A network has no 'place', it is nowhere and everywhere, perhaps somewhere in open (cyber) space.
- **De-institutionalisation.** The decision-making process is taking place outside (and sometimes against) institutional frameworks.
- **Proliferation of actors.** The more players there are in the network, the more newcomers will join (exponential growth) and the stronger the network will become, to the benefit of each of the participants.
- **Interdependence.** All players in the network are linked to each other and constitute a collective mind.

Networks should not be misunderstood. **First**, *network power is **no substitute** for state power*, network power *supplements* state power but does *not replace* it. Consumer boycotts of multinationals exploiting child labour, for instance, may have more than just marginal impact, but most human rights activists will still prefer government intervention, for example through effective legislation (think of the *Magnitsky Act* in the US). Swedish teenager Greta Thunberg's passionate campaign on climate change is laudable but cannot do much without the COP states' decisive involvement (COP stand for *Conference of Parties*: the latest one was the COP21 in Glasgow in December 2021). It is true that, historically, NGO's and governments have often seen each other as rivals, not partners – and in some cases rightly so. But with the emergence of networked diplomacy a relationship of trust between state and civil society is gradually being developed. **Second**, the power shift from state to non-state actors is ***not a zero-sum game***; a gain in power by non-state actors does not necessarily translate into a loss of power by the state.

Examples of networked diplomacy where states and civic society joined hands are the *Ottawa Convention on Anti-personnel Landmines* of 1997 and the *Rome Statute* of 1998 creating the *International Criminal Court* (ICC). The momentum for the Ottawa Treaty arose in the aftermath of the Cold War, increased during the early 1990s as NGOs united around the notion of a ban on anti-personnel mines, and sped to its conclusion when major governments embraced the movement. The Nobel Peace Prize committee awarded the 1997 prize to the International Campaign to Ban Landmines (ICBL) and to Jody Williams, an American activist, for their effective contribution. As already noted, NGOs and governments have not always seen each other eye to eye. At first, many in the NGO mine-ban community worried that governments were going to 'hijack' the issue in order to undermine the ban. But a relationship of trust among a relatively small 'core group' of governments (notably Belgium, Canada, and Norway) and the ICBL leadership quickly developed. Eventually this relationship became known as '*citizen diplomacy*' (see below). It was Jody Williams who acknowledged at an early stage that governments were essential to the success of the initiative (see John English, 'The Ottawa Convention on Anti-Personnel Landmines', in: COOPER, HEINE & THAKUR, 2015, pp. 797–801). The ICC too came into being as the result of a combination of traditional diplomacy with networked diplomacy, of efforts made by civil society and interstate diplomacy. As of the early 1980s, NGOs have played an important role in generating ideas, and political and operational support for the concept of an ICC. And it is largely motivated by NGOs that, in 1989, the UN General Assembly (UNGA) requested the International Law Commission to develop a draft statute for such court.

What does all this mean for **state-based diplomacy**? Not that states and their diplomatic services have become obsolete, but that they may have to shed some of their old-fashioned manners and must learn to see themselves and the world differently. If power is derived from connectivity, then the diplomatic focus should be on making connections to solve shared problems. The problems will remain the same (global issues such as terrorism, climate change, and pandemics and local issues such as linguistic, ethnic, and religious tensions), but the ways (the methods) to address them will have to be different. Diplomatic problem-solving will need to be *less institutionally constrained, less procedural, and more pragmatic, informal, and ad hoc.* The range and complexity of foreign policy challenges and the speed with which crises can escalate mean that knowing the right people and organisations to call and the right levers to pull in any corner of the world must be a key element of a country's diplomacy.

In this century, global power will increasingly de defined by connections – who is connected to whom and for what purposes. In the networked world the states with the most connections will be central players, and these need not necessarily be great powers (think of small states such as Singapore or Switzerland). The network approach also leads to a different concept of **diplomatic leadership**, a concept in which a single leader cannot any longer be in charge of everything. Different countries or groups can mobilize diverse coalitions for specific purposes: the French-led Takuba operation to tackle insecurity in the Sahel, the Normandy format for the stalemate in Ukraine (Germany, France, Russia, and Ukraine), the 2+2 Group for the North Korean nuclear impasse (US, China, North and South Korea), the Quad (US, Japan, India and Australia) for Australasian security. Regional powers can address crises in particular parts of the world better than global organisations such as the UN (the EU, for example, in stabilising the Sahel region, the US-led coalition in fighting Daesh/ISIS terrorism in the Middle East).

2.5 Virtual diplomacy

From networked to virtual diplomacy. The Covid-19 pandemic has given a boost to the concept of networked diplomacy by adding a virtual dimension to it. Videoconferences have become the new forums for human interaction and dialogue. There is no doubt a sense of loss. Lost is the physical presence, the personal rapport, the body language, the sense of action…even the sense of political momentum. But there are gains too. Thanks to improved technology, meetings among government leaders and diplomats can now be held rapidly online and in response to rapidly evolving crises. Meetings with civil society and a wide variety of diplomatic actors have become less cumbersome. And work has become paperless. The increased use of new media has made it easier to get closer to the ground. Paradoxically, with travel restricted, contact with those living through conflicts and crises has become faster and more direct. Directly addressing the parties to a conflict, including non-state actors, used to be difficult. Now this has become routine. Transparency too has been enhanced by these new working methods. Informal meetings are now being regularly broadcasted; documentation is made more broadly available and posted online. The UNSG Antonio Guterres has been quite excited about these new Covid-induced developments and has spoken of three main elements for 'the future of multilateral diplomacy': the need for it to be networked, inclusive, and transparent. 'The pandemic, he said, offers a glimpse into what this future could look like' (see UN PS Forum, 2021). Really? Is virtual diplomacy going to be the new panacea for conducting diplomacy?

Virtual diplomacy: *E-diplomacy, digital diplomacy.* The mere multiplication of names standing for the same thing should warn us that we may be dealing with a buzzword, a trendy concept that needs careful analysis. It is no doubt a merit of the Covid pandemic to have brought the concept of virtual diplomacy to prominence and increased our awareness of its potential. But from there to state, as UNSG Antonio Guterres suggested that it may tell us what the future of diplomacy will look like, may be a bridge too far. Before speculating about that future, some proper analysis of the concept may be in order. What is virtual diplomacy, what are its strengths and weaknesses, its scope and limits?

Scope. Virtual means of communication such as videoconferences are certainly not an innovation brought about by the outbreak of the pandemic. They have been around for decades. What is new is their *generalised use* as a tool for communication. The UNGA meets every year in New York on the second Tuesday of September with large delegations flying into New York from all over the world. In 2020, the GA for the first time met virtually in cyberspace with leaders joining via screens. The experience made diplomats speculate that in future similar big multilateral meetings could also be scaled back given that much of their routine business can be done perfectly well online. Such big multilateral meeting is what happened on Earth Day in April 2021 when the White House convened world leaders to make on-screen statements about tackling climate change. It is also via videoconference that in February 2021 President Biden joined his fellow G7 leaders in London without leaving the White House. Clearly, virtual meetings are becoming a much more generalised practice in diplomacy, they have enlarged a diplomat's toolkit. Let us look at some benefits that are said to accrue to the way of doing diplomacy through virtual communication.

- ***Efficiency***. Interaction with people around the world is much *simpler* through virtual means than in person; no *time* is lost in travelling and in airports and less travel also means less harm to the *environment*. Virtual meetings are *easier to organise*, they can be organised rapidly online in response to rapidly evolving developments, and they are *cost-effective* – they cost only a fraction of what physical meetings cost. Virtual meetings cut out a lot of the formalities and pomposity of traditional diplomacy, they are *less cumbersome* and almost 'paperless'.
- ***Effectiveness***. Virtual meetings allow to reach out to more people simultaneously and to connect with new players in international society outside the traditional diplomatic in-crowd – to NGO's, businesses, think tanks, universities, journalists, etc. It is a strong instrument for *public diplomacy* (see COPELAND, 2015, pp. 453–456). Virtual diplomacy makes things happen that otherwise would not happen; thanks to Zoom, Teams, and other platforms, it has become possible for diplomats and political leaders to show up for speeches and meetings that they would not have attended had their physical presence be required. Also, virtual meetings make it easier to get closer to the ground with those living through conflicts and crises and bring in people who are not normally consulted or involved on political or peace processes. Such '*digital dialogues*' have already successfully been held in Yemen and Libya (see THE ECONOMIST, 2021, pp. 49–50).

These benefits accruing to the tools of virtual communication are no doubt real. But that it is Covid-19 which made diplomats discover them is not true. It is fair to say that these tools would most probably have been put to use in diplomacy sooner or later anyway, with or without Covid-19. Covid-19 has not so much innovated on them than *hastened and generalised* their adoption, given the circumstances, that is, out of necessity, not of choice.

Limits. The efficiency and effectiveness gains outlined above essentially bear on *the public face* of diplomacy: addressing large audiences (public speaking), making broad policy statements (as in the UNGA), reaching out to targeted publics (public diplomacy), and consulting with grassroots communities (conflict resolution). *The essence of diplomacy, however, lies elsewhere.* Trust is the currency of diplomacy and trust is not something you build on the marketplace. You build it behind closed doors. It is quite interesting to note that, contrary to the UNGA-experiment, the UN Security Council did not go virtual. Personal rapport is something you can only establish through direct physical contact. What you are missing in virtual contact are the subtle signs you pick up about an interlocutor in a face-to-face encounter: their body language and facial expression which can be more eloquent than words. In negotiation, for instance, the difficult part must be done in person. If things are not going well, a chat at the bar or a stroll on the grounds may help create a breakthrough. The plus side of virtual meetings, their efficiency gains, are also their minus side: you lose the opportunity to work on the margins of the meeting; you miss the space for informal conversation that is key to establish trust. Difficult messages, the stuff of diplomacy, can be delivered with more nuance in a face-to-face contact than when struggling with a poor connection. At a distance it is easier for your interlocutor (as it is for you) to camp on 'red lines' than when you sit in the same room. At a distance it is easier for your interlocutor (and again for you) to turn around questions asked. Confidentiality is another concern; delicate issues are not amenable to be divulged through cyberspace.

So, virtual meetings have their limits. Physical meetings will not disappear. Particularly not when they touch the core of diplomacy, dialogue ('talking it over'), and negotiation ('talking it through'). And what is true for multilateral diplomacy is even more true for bilateral diplomacy. Despite the ease of direct digital communication between Ministers and high officials, the role of the resident ambassador does not seem under threat. There is no substitute for the man or woman sitting in the foreign capital, soaking the politics, the media, the arguments, and the culture, and being the trusted interpreter and reporter of all that, back to his or her own capital.

2.6 Public diplomacy

Public diplomacy is a rather recent invention. The term was coined by Edmund Gullion, Dean of the Fletcher School of Law and Diplomacy, in the 1960s during the Cold War (see SHARP, 2019, p. 108). Until a few decades ago, diplomats thought that diplomacy had to be conducted in closed circles. They quietly enjoyed the conspiratorial atmosphere of their job. **Confidentiality and secrecy** were their trademark. And nobody will contest that diplomatic work, to be successful, does indeed often need to be done discreetly, far from the public *agora*. But the love for secrecy among diplomats was not only motivated by the necessities of the job. There was also a psychological factor at play; secrecy gave the diplomat that pleasing feeling that what he or she was dealing with was important and that as the bearer of secret and confidential information he or she belonged to a privileged elite group.

This tendency for confidentiality and secrecy was always more prominent in continental Europe than in the Anglo-Saxon world. No surprise then that it was there that things really started changing. It was particularly in the US, sometime in the early 1980s of last century, that diplomats realised that for diplomacy to be effective, they had to go public. The underlying rationale of this insight is rather straightforward: diplomacy is about influencing the attitudes and beliefs, and ultimately the behaviour of others; so, if you want the others to be on your side, you'd better tell them what your side stands for, what your policies are. Marc Rutte, the long-time Prime Minister of the Netherlands, stated it succinctly: 'If you don't speak, you can't be heard' (he made his statement in German: 'Wer nicht redet, wird nicht gehört'). And with that **public diplomacy** as a pervasive practice was born. Public diplomacy is not primarily meant to inform but to influence; it is one of the instruments a state appeals to for achieving its strategic purposes and defending its core interests. But make no mistake, public diplomacy is one tool among others for doing effective diplomacy. **Backroom diplomacy**, far away from the public eye, remains no less alive and well. Both practices, public and backroom diplomacy, are not so much contradictory to each other as complementary; they operate in different contexts and for different purposes.

Public diplomacy is about promoting a country's foreign policy, and more generally its standing in the international community. And this can be done towards two distinct audiences: the domestic and the foreign audience. When the target group of public diplomacy is **a state's own population**, one generally speaks of a *narrative*, a compelling, mobilising 'story' that people can easily assimilate and identify with, and which makes them not only consenting to, but also supporting a state's foreign policy. Such narrative needs of course to be developed and adjusted as the situation evolves and that is an important job of the foreign ministry spokesperson. In fact, domestic publics have increasingly become important as home reactions to foreign affairs may directly affect domestic politics and politicians alike. Even on overseas visits, leaders may be much more interested in what the home media (will) say than on reaching out to foreign publics via the media in the countries visited (see Box 2.2).

Box 2.2 The 'Domestification' of Foreign Policy

The definition and execution of a country's foreign policy is no less part of domestic politics than any other government policy of the country. To put it succinctly: domestic politics dictate foreign policy. And it has done so increasingly as domestic publics have become more and more well informed and critical as regards international politics. Leaders are accountable before their *national* parliament and their *domestic* public opinion. No wonder then that they will see to it that their domestic political position *not be hurt* by their foreign policy actions; perhaps they will even try to shape foreign policy in terms of *how it helps* strengthen their domestic political position.

Whatever the importance of the domestic audience may be for promoting and consolidating a country's foreign policy, most would still consider public diplomacy as targeting **foreign audiences** first. The effort then consists in trying to influence another country's government and possibly also its public and elite opinion, for the purpose of turning the foreign policy of the target country to advantage. Note that there are *two* possible *sub-audiences* involved here. Traditionally, it was *foreign governments* and their leaders that were the prime target of public diplomacy. This fitted in well with the concept that governments were supposed to interact with other governments, not with their people, as this could be seen as an unwelcome interference with another country's domestic affairs. But things evolved and increasingly states have been trying to influence other country's *people*, hoping perhaps that in so doing they would *also* influence their governments. An example is the extensive programmes of the US during the Cold War directed at shaping the attitudes of Soviet citizens and those of Soviet-dominated Europe. Such 'hearts and minds' efforts directed by governments at whole groups of people have now become common practice applied by not only the US but also Russia, the EU, and China.

Public diplomacy has always had its 'low road' and 'high road' approaches (SHARP, 2019, p. 108). The *'low road'* speaks the language of 'brands' and 'images' and aims at showing one's country at its best thus hoping to advance its external interests: 'Fiji me' is the catchy slogan that this Pacific Island state has chosen for itself, as did Malaysia with its euphonic 'Malaysia, truly Asia' (see RANA, 2011, p. 76). Many countries have adopted the idea of national branding, providing their states with simple but strong identities: German 'grundlichkeit', British 'cool', Japanese reliability. Such approaches adopt marketing techniques used by private companies and come close to advertising and propaganda. It is often linked to promoting culture and tourism, rather than promoting and explaining a country's foreign policy. The latter is what the *'high road'* is about. Promoting and explaining foreign policy is very much a diplomat's job in which his or her skills at meeting and connecting with people are at a premium. Public speaking in different fora, lecturing at universities, and interacting with the media take centre stage in this effort. Convening people at the residence is also part of that effort. Expensive residences are not there for the glory of the ambassador. They are attributes of a country's image that enable the envoy to play the public functions that go with the job. People love to be invited to events at the residence and it gives the ambassador a unique opportunity to pass on messages to an often select audience (see Box 2.3).

Box 2.3 Some Golden Rules for Effective Public Speaking

- Open strong. Together with your close, your opening is what your audience will remember from your speech.
- Think carefully about what your core message will be. State it clearly and put it up front of your speech. Having more than one core message is self-contradictory.
- Inspire. Engage with your audience. Speak with courage and character. Slack language will not sway your audience. Avoid platitudes.
- Use the language of your audience. A speech is not about what you say, it is about what your audience will hear. Avoid jargon.
- Structure your speech well. Use the 'rule of three': first, say what you are going to say; then, say it; and finally, say what you said.
- Be aware that the attention span of your audience is limited, both in time and in scope. So, make your speech no longer than necessary. And make it as focused as possible.

- A speech is not a lecture. 'Speeching' is about performing, convincing, persuading, not about transmitting knowledge, let alone information.
- Avoid preaching and moralising. People do not like to be told what to do or not to do. They get your point without you needing to force it on them.
- End strong. Wrap everything up in one single memorable line.

Public diplomacy has a direct link with diplomacies that can be considered means to an end rather than ends in itself: diaspora diplomacy, cultural diplomacy, and sports diplomacy.

Diaspora diplomacy. A diaspora community is constituted of people (and their descendants) who originally were citizens of home country A but have settled in foreign country B where they may have acquired the citizenship of that new country (perhaps in the second generation), sometimes without losing their original citizenship, thus obtaining dual citizenship. Most countries have such overseas diasporas whose members are 'living links' (relatives, friends, former business partners, etc.) between their country of origin and their newfound host country. For some relatively small states (Lebanon, Armenia, Ireland, Israel) the diaspora may be much larger (and wealthier) than the home population. Embassies have been quick in discovering the *untapped potential* that these communities represent for the promotion and defence of the interests of their country of origin. For the embassies concerned it can be important to keep in constant contact with the leaders of the diaspora communities and to sensitise them on issues of concern to the country of origin. Such outreach can be a delicate task given that members of the diaspora often have a dual allegiance, both to their country of origin and their new host country. The golden rule for the diplomat is to act with transparency and responsibility in view of *the interests of both states*. When well handled, diasporas become a valuable part of a country's public diplomacy (see RANA, 2011, pp. 94–110). Public diplomacy is also closely related to cultural and sports diplomacy.

Cultural diplomacy has been called by the US State Department 'the lynchpin of public diplomacy', for it is in cultural products and activities that a nation's idea of itself is best represented (see GOFF, 2015, p. 421). Cultural diplomacy can be helpful in bridging differences and in opening new avenues of communication. Even when relations are at their worst, a cultural exchange can take place. Cultural diplomacy fosters mutual understanding and respect among states and their people. It provides a positive agenda for cooperation. It creates a neutral platform for people-to-people contact. Cultural diplomacy can be directed from the foreign ministry which then provides an official framework for action and funding. That is how cultural centres and education facilities (in particular for language learning) are being set up and how student exchange and scholarship programmes are being provided for. But often, cultural diplomacy efforts are undertaken more directly by the ambassador and his or her staff. An engaged diplomat is always looking for ways to connect with the people of his or her host country, and culture provides an easy inroad for doing so. Again, it will be their residence that will be the venue for welcoming visiting artists and cultural personalities, scholars and academics and organise events where the local population is invited to meet and interact with those visitors. That is how a diplomat can also create the necessary goodwill for carrying out his or her mission effectively.

Sports diplomacy too is public diplomacy. It capitalises upon the role that international sport can fulfil in improving international understanding as well as improving the status of both the hosting and the competing states (see SHARP, 2019, p. 133). The emergence in the early 2000s of a 'Sport for Development and Peace' movement as well as the appointment by UNSG Kofi Annan of a 'Special Advisor' on 'Sport for Peace and Development' are emblematic of this interest in sport from a diplomatic perspective. Given the great visibility and popularity of sport, joined to intense manifestations of national identities, it is hardly surprising that sport teams, events, and venues have been viewed as vehicles for political and diplomatic ambitions. Sports diplomacy is, like public diplomacy more generally, a 'two-level game', targeting international and domestic audiences simultaneously. Today, the Olympic Games – both summer and winter – the football, cricket, and rugby World Cups, and various international tennis and golfing competitions provide opportunities not only for national glory but also for *bringing states and nations all together*. Let us also remind that international sports organisations, such as the International Olympic Committee, pay increasing attention to environmental and human rights considerations in their hosting decisions. And that too is a positive development to the benefit of the world community (Box 2.4).

Box 2.4 Public Diplomacy and Soft Power

As most of us know, Joseph Nye is the intellectual father of the distinction between 'hard' and 'soft' power. Hard power is the power to coerce, to force the other to do what you want. It coincides with the traditional definition of power: A has power over B to the extent that that he or she can get B to do something that B would not otherwise do. The power base of hard power is tangible, material assets: territorial size, number of population, economic strength, military capabilities, and technological development. Soft power is also the ability to get what you want, but this time not through coercion or force, but through attraction, persuasion, and co-optation as opposed to coercion. Hard power is the power of the sword, soft power that of the word. The soft power base is constituted mainly by intangible, immaterial assets such as: national image, reputation, credibility, tolerance and respect, social capital, language, and culture. Soft power is what is being applied in public diplomacy. Public diplomacy encompasses building a strong national image but goes beyond propaganda. Simple propaganda can even be counterproductive. Nor does public diplomacy reduce to merely public relations campaigns. Its ultimate target is mutual understanding and dialogue among nations, building long-term relationships that create an enabling environment for a country's foreign policy.

Before closing this section, a brief warning is in place. In public diplomacy there is a treacherous **trap**, that of *'over-selling'* **one's policy**. Doing so backfires for sure. When you oversell your foreign policy, or certain aspects of it, you raise the level of expectations of your audience (local, national, or global), and when these do not come out, you end up in a situation worse than the one you started with. This is what has happened for too long with the EU in its outreach and public diplomacy activities: claiming or promising a lot and not delivering that much. A similar danger exists when one overestimates the reach of his/her message. When in 2006, Condoleezza Rice, George W. Bush's Secretary of State, was advocating the concept of a 'transformational diplomacy' (making democracy, human rights, and good governance global standards) she simply assumed her (American) values to be a universal good; placed before Asian audiences she became aware of her ethnocentric bias and lack of intercultural understanding (RANA, 2011, p. 86).

2.7 The 'new diplomacies'

Diplomacy has traditionally been the preserve of the state. Diplomats are, by definition, representatives of their state, and their work is intended to advance the interests of that state. Historically, the term *diplomacy* came into being to describe relations between sovereign, territorial states, and a certain way of conducting those relations, while the term *diplomat* came into being to identify the officials who did diplomacy on behalf of those states. The idea thus was that *only sovereign states* could engage in diplomacy. States had the **monopoly** for dictating and conducting foreign policy. A practical institutional consequence of this conception was the creation of MFAs staffed with professionals called diplomats. As already mentioned, this view of diplomacy is called **state-based diplomacy**.

As of the end of the 20th century and even more so in this 21st century, this monopoly authority of the state as regards both conception and execution of foreign policy has been questioned. Some observers have spoken about a paradigm shift in the concept itself of diplomacy, others went as far as to announce *The End of Diplomacy* (see SHARP, 2019, p. 88). Since Francis Fukuyama's *The End of History*, we have learned to be cautious with announcements starting with 'the end of...'. Each age tends to believe its own time to be unique. So, what's happening? We will look at **two interrelated developments** that are said to have changed the diplomatic landscape: **new topics for** diplomacy, **new actors in** diplomacy (see generally SHARP, 2019).

2.7.1 New topics for diplomacy

Until about two generations ago, in the Cold War era, *politics* was in command and was the prime focus of foreign ministry work, both at headquarters and in the periphery. *Security* was each state's greatest concern. In most ministries the Political Director General was the *primus inter pares* and the Directorate for Politico-Military Affairs the most respected among the directorates. Similarly, in embassies abroad, it was the trio of ambassador, political counsellor, and military attaché who were in charge of the serious stuff. These were the times of *'high diplomacy'* involving issues of 'war and peace', arms control and disarmament, nuclear questions, Great Power relations, and post-World War II European integration. Then, commencing around the 1970s, economic diplomacy began to emerge as a component of external relations with export promotion and foreign direct investment (FDI) mobilisation taking center stage. Ministries were rebaptised as Ministries of Foreign Affairs *and* Foreign Trade. *Prosperity* became a prime national interest next to security. Diplomats started spending much of their time on economic issues, particularly as regards countries that offered sizable economic opportunities (US, Japan, China, South Korea). Next to *economic, trade, and agricultural attachés* we saw *science and technology attachés* emerging, soon joined by the *cultural and media attachés* as attention was also increasingly given to expressions of soft power: culture, education, and the media. With that the politically incorrect concept of *'low diplomacy'* was born. And then, after the fall of the Berlin Wall, in the early 1990s came globalisation powered by the ICT revolution: the world became one single arena on which both states and non-state actors spread a dense web of interactions going well beyond the contacts that states used to entertain. As Andrew Cooper put it: 'with accentuated forms of globalization the scope of diplomacy has moved beyond the traditional core concerns to encompass a myriad set of issue areas' (COOPER, 2015, p. 36). The current buzz word 'connectivity' captures it well. With connectivity come new opportunities but also challenges: vulnerabilities within and dependencies among states which demand to be managed. Today we see migration pressures on America's and Europe's borders, Europe's energy dependency from Russia, the global vulnerability induced by the Covid-19 pandemic, industry's dependency on scarce raw materials, and last but not least the latent threat of terrorist attacks. These new challenges have claimed diplomacy's attention and have given birth to **new *kinds* of diplomacy**, each with their own **domain** of action (subject matter):

- *Economic-financial diplomacy.* In its beginnings economic diplomacy had better been called *commercial diplomacy* given its almost exclusive focus on export promotion and FDI mobilisation; later its field broadened to encompass questions regarding trade and investment regimes, generally, and the stability of the international financial system, particularly after the 2007–2008 financial crisis; today, much attention goes to governance questions related to globalisation and to the strategic impact of major geo-economic projects such as the China's 'Belt and Road Initiative'.

- *Environmental diplomacy* (eco-diplomacy, climate diplomacy) focussing, among others, on biodiversity and even more on climate change (an 'urgency' that has been with us for some 30 years) which directly impacts on human security and raises difficult questions regarding national mitigation and global responsibility.

- *Health diplomacy,* for long concerned with diseases such as tuberculosis and malaria, and more recently with epidemics (HIV/AIDS) and pandemics and their destabilising and sometimes devastating effects on fragile and even less fragile states (Ebola in Liberia and Sierra Leone (2004), and in the DRC (Democratic Republic of Congo) up to this day; SARS in China some 10 years ago; Covid-19 and its multiple mutants worldwide today).

- *Population diplomacy*, concerned with demographic pressures resulting from population explosions (Egypt's population is expected to double in the next 30 years) which are often causes of tension and conflict (as was the case in the 1994 genocide in Rwanda).

- *Migration diplomacy*, addressing the challenges caused by mass movements of people, whether seeking fresh opportunities in new lands given the unsustainable global economic inequalities or escaping cycles of violence, famine, persecution, bad governance, and corruption.

- *Energy diplomacy* which is concerned with energy autonomy and dependency (think of the contested Nord Stream project), and related questions such as renewable energies, interconnections among states, energy corridors.

- *Terrorism* has re-emerged as a new item (but, remarkably, not as a new *diplomacy*) on the international security agenda, particularly since 11 September 2001, and has led to intensified cooperation among states exchanging information and coordinating action, either multilaterally in the UN framework or on an *ad hoc* basis as happened with the anti-ISIS coalition set up in 2014 under US leadership.

Increased *interdependence* among states thus naturally leads to *new issues* becoming part of the diplomatic agenda. These 'new' diplomacies have now joined the older ones (trade, investment, agriculture, culture...) and with them new experts with in-depth knowledge in specific areas have joined the dance. This then is a first new development which has led to the ***diversification of the diplomat's portfolio***.

2.7.2 New actors in diplomacy

A second, parllel development concerns the emergence of new actors on the inter-national scene, eroding perhaps the monopoly of states to dictate and conduct for-eign policy. Most of them are ***non-state actors***. With them we enter the field called ***'people-to-people diplomacy'*** which covers many different types of activity. **First,** there is ***'citizen diplomacy'***, diplomacy carried out by people like you and me, groups and individuals who travel to other (sometimes unfriendly) states to meet with people there and develop relationships with them; or they are students going to study abroad either just on their own or in the framework of established programmes (such as the EU Erasmus Programme). The new slogan of 'citizen's diplomacy' is, predictably: '*We are all diplomats*'. **Second,** there is what we commonly call the (international) ***civil society***, a broad assembly of groups interested in international affairs and operating some-where between government and society, within one state and among states. These can be social movements (Gaia), charities (Bill and Melinda Gates Foundation), academic institutions (the UN universities) and 'think tanks' (Brookings Institute in Washington, Chatham House in London), humanitarian organisations, or civic groups (often international NGO's) that seek to promote and defend their values and beliefs in such fields as human rights and the environment (Human Rights Watch, Transparency International). **Third,** there are the ***transnational corporations***, those with a global reach (which we used to call 'multinationals') such as Amazon, Ali Baba, or Microsoft that seek to advance their own economic interests but also altruistic interests such as respect for human rights or labour and environmental standards (Nikè in apartheid South Africa was a pioneer). They interact with counterparts and government author-ities across borders to negotiate agreements on production and supply chains and tech-nology exchanges, for instance. Often, they have their own international departments and so-called government relations people. Linked to these are consultancy firms, lobbying groups, and professional associations (lawyers, accountants) that entertain relations with their counterparts abroad. **Finally,** there are ***prominent individuals***, per-sonalities ranging from celebrities (George Clooney, Angelina Jolie), for whom the term ***celebrity diplomacy*** was coined, over former presidents (Nelson Mandela, Jimmy Carter) to UN 'Goodwill Ambassadors' (Queen Mathilde of Belgium) and 'Messengers for Peace' (film star Michael Douglas).

Next to these non-state actors we should also briefly mention ***sub-state actors*** which have emerged from what historically used to be the single, unitary, and strongly centralised state. The idea here is that the monopoly power of the classic state has been shared with other levels of governance ultimately reaching that of municipalities. Sub-state entities are as varied as the autonomous regions in Spain (Catalonia and the Basque region), the Québec Province in Canada, the 'states' in the United States of America, the 'Länder' in the Deutsche Bundesrepublik, the 'Regions and Communities' in Belgium, the devolved entities (Scotland and Wales) in the United Kingdom of Great-Britain and Northern Ireland, etc. The claim that these sub-national entities have gained some margin for action in the field of international relations, de facto or de jure, has given rise to yet another diplomatic denomination: ***sub-state diplomacy***. To be complete we should also mention ***supra-state actors***. There do not seem to be many of them, but the European Union certainly is one given that sovereign state powers have explicitly been transferred by treaty from the member state level to the EU supra-national level, even though as far as foreign and defence policy is concerned (CFSP and CSDP), these transfers remain limited in scope. This then would be an example of ***supra-state diplomacy*** which together with its sub-state alter ego would be subsumed under yet another new concept, that of '*para-diplomacy*' (which stands for *parallel diplomacy*).

2.7.3 The changing nature of diplomacy

What do we have to make of both these new developments? First, the diversification of the diplomat's portfolio to which new topics have been added lately; second, the arrival of new actors on the diplomatic scene, all with their own activities. The question is: to what extent have these developments changed diplomacy as we commonly understand it, that is, **what it means *to do* diplomacy** and **what it means *to be* a diplomat**? Diplomats should dare to approach this question with calm and not be on the defensive. There's nothing to be frightened of. Interpreting these questions as threatening is misdirected. There is no denying that the emergence of new domain-specific diplomacies together with an increasing number of new non-state, sub-state, and supra-state actors has changed the diplomatic scene. International society evolves and so does diplomacy. But from that to conclude that state-based diplomacy has had its time and that we near '*the end of diplomacy*', is preposterous. Perhaps a few simple observations may help clarifying the issue:

*   As a start, let us not take all 'new diplomacies' at face value. Their mere numerical proliferation has proven to be self-defeating; the more there are, the less one takes them seriously. There is no denying that the enthusiastic **search for diplomatic 'newness'**, particularly during the last two decades, has given rise to some extravagancies. Examples are 'panda-' or 'vaccine diplomacy'. In the introduction to this chapter we already mentioned '*disaster diplomacy*' and said that there is nothing intrinsically wrong with talking about it, as there is nothing wrong with talking about '*celebrity diplomacy*', but whether that helps us in better understanding the workings of diplomacy, is doubtful. To call oneself a diplomat, as in the case of '*citizen diplomacy*', by the mere fact of having spent a year studying abroad is questionable and arguably even flimsy (see Box 2.5).

Box 2.5 Hyphenated Diplomacies

In addition to the domain-specific diplomacies (environmental, health, population, etc.) that we have reviewed earlier, all kinds of other new 'diplomacies' have proliferated: *sports-diplomacy* (with its derivatives: ping-pong, cricket, golfing, tennis, and football diplomacy), *diaspora diplomacy* (as part of public diplomacy, as we saw), *celebrity diplomacy* and *citizen's diplomacy* (both part of *people-to-people diplomacy*). These new diplomacies have one thing in common, ironically designated by still another new label '*hyphenated diplomacies*', a term that refers to the simple practice of putting an adjective before the noun 'diplomacy'. By just giving it a name, it looks like one has magically created something new (see SHARP, 2019, p. 102).

- The proliferation of all **kinds** of new **domain-specific** diplomacies, each with their own subject-matter (environmental, energy, population, health…) can be misleading. It may give the impression that next to state-based diplomacy there is now also, let's say, environmental diplomacy – **on the same plane** as it were. But doing so is making a **category mistake**, it is *confusing* two distinct categories, that of a *form* of diplomacy (state-based) with that of a *kind* of diplomacy (environmental). State-based diplomacy, as a **form** of diplomacy, is *not domain-specific*. Such form of diplomacy can come to bear on *any* domain imaginable (including, if one would insist, on disasters). The reason for this **domain-independence** is that classic diplomacy is not about policies as such (energy, climate change) but about the **international politics of policies**, particularly their **security-related aspects**. To illustrate: take energy, what a diplomat is interested in is not energy corridors as such, but their geo-political consequences such as the *political* dependencies they can create; and the same goes for climate change, not desertification as such is a diplomat's prime concern, but the destabilising effects on the countries concerned and the migratory pressures on third countries that it can generate (think of the link between the drying up of Lake Chad, the rise of the terrorist organisation Boko Haram, and the destabilisation of the entire four-country region around the lake; such examples can of course be multiplied and generalised: 'climate change threatens our national security' is what one can read in a Pentagon report of end 2014).
- Another way of stating this point is that a domain-specific diplomacy (what we called a *kind* of diplomacy) can never replace a domain-independent diplomacy (a *form* of diplomacy). A form of diplomacy can only be 'threatened' by another form of diplomacy. We have seen that next to *state-based* diplomacy only two other **forms** of diplomacy had to be considered (all the others were kinds, ways, or means of doing diplomacy): **networked** diplomacy and **Trak II** diplomacy, and we have noted that neither pretended to be a substitute (or replacement or alternative) for state-based diplomacy, but that on the contrary they should be seen as complementary to and in support of state-based diplomacy. Ultimately, therefore, state-based diplomacy remains intact. We come back to the old orthodoxy that diplomacy is a state affair: only states engage in diplomacy, and it is states that dictate and conduct foreign policy. That is not to say that non-state actors do not actively *participate* in the diplomatic process or cannot influence foreign policy (Ahtisaari in his Track II Kosovo mediation certainly did so, but still remained accountable to the member states of both the UN Security Council and the Balkan Contact Group; also recall the examples we gave of how we got at the Ottawa Convention on landmines and the Rome Statute instituting the ICC, where civic organisations were quite active via networked diplomacy, but it is states that ultimately signed the Ottawa Convention and the Rome Statute).

- The proliferation of 'new diplomacies' has made people think that we have now a **multiplicity of diplomacies**, which again can be misleading. From what was said in the two preceding paragraphs it follows that ultimately there cannot be but one (*form* of) diplomacy: 'state-based political diplomacy' (an awkward tautology, but one that has been forced upon us given the proliferation of new labels for new diplomacies from which it needed to be distinguished). That there cannot be but one diplomacy, properly understood, does not mean that there cannot be multiple *kinds* of diplomacy, as we saw in the preceding paragraphs, or multiple *ways* of conducting diplomacy (virtual diplomacy or summit diplomacy, for instance), and multiple *means* on which to rely in doing diplomacy (cultural diplomacy or sports diplomacy, for instance). The reason why we made the distinction between different categories of diplomacies aimed exactly at de-confusing matters, as we said earlier.
- As a profession, diplomacy is **not domain-specific**. There are no more eco-diplomats than there are energy-diplomats. There are just plain diplomats. That is why the diversification of a diplomat's agenda following the introduction of new *kinds* of diplomacy (or for that matter new ways and means of doing diplomacy) does not affect the profession. What is it then that the diplomat brings to the table? A diplomat brings **domain-independent practices** to the table. Not the *field or domain* he or she is working in (say energy or the environment) is what makes the diplomat, but the *way* he or she approaches and manages these different subjects, the 'techniques' he or she employs and the 'strategies and tactics' he or she deploys, his or her problem-solving capacity, and his or her ability as a negotiator, debater, drafter, among others. Diplomacy is a practice, a craft, an art, a *way of doing*.
- A diplomat's 'knowledge' is indeed not a *'know what'* regarding a certain subject matter (the French *connaitre*) but a *'know how'* to handle problems (the French *savoir*). And that is where the **complementarity** between the **diplomat and the expert** comes in. The diplomat is a *generalist,* the expert is a *specialist*. The domain-independent skills of the diplomat are brought to bear on the domain-specific knowledge of the expert. Both need each other, they are partners in a common endeavour. The software of the diplomat needs the hardware of the expert, and *vice versa*. The distinction between diplomat and expert is a functional one. Line ministries have valuable domain-specific knowledge that an MFA lacks; experts bring that knowledge to the table, diplomats act on it. The centrality of *how-questions* to a diplomat's job explains why the skills part of his or her job is important: communication, negotiation, writing and drafting, knowledge of foreign languages.
- A final but important asset that the generalist diplomat brings to the table is his or her panoramic, holistic, **'big picture'- perspective** on a particular issue which allows to see things in context, to see the forest through the trees thanks to what has been called a diplomat's *'broad bandwidth'* quality (see RANA, 2011, p. 252). What he or she must bring to the table is the wider *relationship management* expertise, including knowledge of interconnections between different issues that are at play in interactions with other states, allowing to see points of leverage and trade-offs.
- Does that mean that the new non-state actors that have emerged on the international scene are not diplomats? Or that, conversely, the 'old' diplomats, those in the employ of the state, have been overtaken (at least in part) by the 'new' diplomats? This, we think, are largely *definitional questions*. The classic definition of diplomats as 'agents' of the state would appear to exclude non-state actors. Still, few diplomats would contest that civic organisations, transnational corporations, and

prominent individuals have become *part of the diplomatic process* and **recognised** as such with the **status** of *'relevant others'*, as Andrew Cooper calls them – *'actors with whom a diplomat engages in the conduct of diplomacy'* (COOPER, 2015, p. 42). Such engagement is what we already noted when studying *networked* and *Track II diplomacy*. Neither pretends to be a *substitute* for state-based diplomacy. These are not rival diplomacies. And the same holds for the activities deployed by non-state actors generally. As regards the question of *status recognition* for non-state actors it is interesting to look at what *in fact* has happened with intergovernmental organisations; their *'civil servants'*, as they used to be called and officially still are, have been largely accepted in terms of possession of a **diplomatic standing** and are indeed sometimes referred to as the *'new diplomats'*. Similar developments may happen elsewhere. But note that we are talking here about organisations that are *state*-owned (hence the denomination 'inter-*governmental*') which again seems to suggest that the link with the state (states) is difficult to be ignored. What is true of the diplomat in the national context, is true of the civil servant in the international context: both are accountable to states.

In this chapter, we have explored different approaches to diplomacy. Some of them have been with us for some time already, others are quite new. Most of us are familiar with the distinction between *bilateral* and *multilateral* diplomacy, both being *ways* for conducting state-based diplomacy. *Track II* diplomacy is different. In it non-official third parties get involved. Still Track II diplomacy needs official Track I diplomacy because only governments can ensure the actual implementation of whatever deal has been reached at Track II level. A similar remark is true for *networked* diplomacy. Here too, we see the involvement of non-state actors such as civic organisations building networks in which power is distributed horizontally rather than vertically as in state-based diplomacy. But that private power is not meant to replace state power, but rather to complement it. *Public* diplomacy is a *way* of doing diplomacy. It complements *backroom* diplomacy which diplomats need when negotiating, for instance. Public diplomacy has grown out of the rather straightforward premise that if diplomacy is about influencing the behaviour of others, then diplomats had better go public. Next to these rather well-established ways of doing diplomacy we have recently witnessed the emergence of all kinds of so-called *new diplomacies* such as environmental diplomacy, summit diplomacy, celebrity diplomacy, or even vaccine diplomacy. We deem their proliferation to be potentially misleading. Distinguishing between different categories under which these new 'diplomacies' could be brought has clarified the landscape, or so we hope. It has enabled us to note that what is 'new' in these 'diplomacies' is not the concept of diplomacy as a practice as such, but merely the *subject matters* on which diplomacy bears (environmental diplomacy, for instance), or the *ways* in which it can be conducted (summit diplomacy), or the *means* on which it relies in doing diplomacy (celebrity diplomacy). Further, we have concluded that diplomacy as a domain-independent practice is compatible with any of these new diplomacies.

Bibliography

AHTISAARI, Marti (2015), "Mediation", in: COOPER (2015), pp. 338–348.
BERRIDGE, G. R. (2010), *Diplomacy: Theory and Practice*, Palgrave, New York, NY.

COOPER, Andrew F. (2015), "The Changing Nature of Diplomacy", in: COOPER (2015) pp. 35–53.

COOPER, Andrew, HEINE, Jorge & THAKUR, Ramesh (Eds.) (2015), *The Oxford Handbook of Modern Diplomacy*, Oxford University Press, Oxford.

COOPER, Robert (2021), *The Ambassadors – Thinking about Diplomacy from Machiavelli to Modern Times*, Weidenfeld & Nicolson, London.

COPELAND, Daryl (2015), "Digital Technology", in: COOPER (2015), pp. 453–472.

CSIS (2007), *The Embassy of the Future*.

GOFF, Patricia (2015), "Cultural Diplomacy", in: COOPER (2015), pp. 419–435.

HANDLER, Scott P. (Ed.) (2013), *International Politics – Classic and Contemporary Readings*, CQ Press, Los Angeles, CA.

KEOHAN, Robert O. (2013), "Harmony, Cooperation, and Discord", in: HANDLER (2013), pp. 92–99.

MAHBUBANI, Kishore (2015), "Multilateral Diplomacy", in: COOPER (2015), pp. 248–262.

MAULL, Hans W. (2020), "Multilateralism", *SWP Comment*, No. 9, March 2020.

RANA, Kishan S. (2011), *21st Century Diplomacy – A Practitioner's Guide*, Continuum, London/ New York, NY.

ROZENTAL, Andrès & BUENROSTRO, Alicia (2015), "Bilateral Diplomacy", in: COOPER (2015), pp. 229–247.

SHARP, Paul (2019), *Diplomacy in the 21st Century – A Brief Introduction*, Routledge, London/ New York, NY.

SLAUGHTER, Anne-Marie (1997), "The Real New World Order", *Foreign Affairs*, 76, 5.

THE ECONOMIST (2021), *Hybrid Diplomacy – The Virtue of Virtual*, 1 May 2021.

UNITED NATIONS (2021), PS Forum: "Is COVID-19 Forcing a Rethink of UN Diplomacy", retrieved from: https://dppa-ps.atavist.com/is-covid19-forcong-a-rethink-of-un-diplomacy.

Part II
A diplomat's conceptual toolbox

3 Reasoning in diplomacy

An exploration

Practical thinking is thinking about how to act, thinking that results in *action*. Diplomacy, as any action-oriented practice (as in law, medicine, engineering), is primarily concerned with practical thinking. That is not to say that reasoning about beliefs has no place in diplomacy. To get an action going one needs to decide. And *decisions* are beliefs that often, but not always, come from reasoning, a discursive activity that links distinct pieces of information (variously called propositions, beliefs, opinions) with each other. In reasoning, we establish links called *inferences* from established beliefs, the *premises,* to new beliefs, the *conclusion*. In an action-oriented practice such as diplomacy, the conclusion of reasoning is a *performative* statement, a statement with which you do (perform) something, a decision to act: 'invade Iraq'.

Reasoning in diplomacy has a lot of similarities with reasoning in law. When a judge decides a case, he or she does not end up with a mere statement of belief that is either true or false, they end up with a decision (for instance an injunction: 'two years jail') which is considered right or wrong. Similarly, when a diplomat faces a controversial situation, she acts as a problem-solver and aims at a solution that settles the matter. A solution is not true or false, it works, or it doesn't. There is a sense of kinship between diplomacy and the legal profession as far as the reasoning process involved is concerned. Diplomacy can learn lessons from legal reasoning.

3.1 The practical syllogism

'The life of the law has not been logic: it has been experience'. This well-known statement made by Justice Holmes, the father of the so-called *realist school* in legal thinking, would certainly also apply to diplomacy (just replace 'the law' by 'diplomacy'). What Justice Homes and his fellow American 'realists' of the 1930s did is to open men's eyes to *what actually goes on* when judges decide cases by drawing the contrast between the actual facts of judicial decision-making and the traditional terminology for describing it as if it were a wholly logical operation. To further paraphrase Justice Holmes, replacing 'diplomats' for 'judges' and 'diplomatic' for 'legal', one could say

> that the felt necessities of the international situation, the prevalent political mood, all kind of intuitions and prejudices that diplomats share with their fellowmen, have a good deal more to do in the search for a diplomatic solution than the formal rules of reasoning prescribed by pure logic.
>
> ('The Common Law', *Harvard Law Review* 593, 1958)

DOI: 10.4324/9781003298182-6

Take George Bush's decision to launch 'Operation Desert Storm' against Iraq in 1991. This decision to act was not the outcome of the mechanical application of the standard syllogism:

> *Major* (a general principle): article 51 of the UN Charter recognises 'the inherent right of individual or collective self-defence if an armed attack occurs against a member of the UN'.

> *Minor* (a factual situation falling under the general principle): in August 1990 Iraq invaded and then occupied Kuwait.

> *Conclusion* (a decision to act): use military force to push Iraq out of Kuwait (US-led coalition of 30 countries, 600,000 troops).

George Bush's decision was primarily the result of a serious preoccupation with the political stability of the Arab peninsula and its strategic role in providing the required energy resources. Had a similar Article 51-type aggression occurred in sub-Saharan Africa at the time, American action would have been unlikely. Also, America's status at that time as the only remaining superpower made such action in the UN Security Council an easy ride; in fact, it reinforced that superpower status. Moreover, action by the US gave credibility to Bush's proclaimed but not yet substantiated 'New World Order'. Finally, the dollar-cost of the operation for the US government was next to nothing thanks to the significant contributions of the coalition states. All these considerations entered into a global cost-benefit assessment in which the syllogism providing for the legitimacy of the operation by invoking the general principle enshrined in Article 51 of the UN Charter may well have been rather marginal. *Marginal* in the *build-up* of the decision but *crucial* in its *justification*, as we will see.

In diplomatic thinking we do not start out with neat premises, majors, and minors, smoothly leading up to an unquestionable conclusion. What we start out with is some messy, complicated, and confused situation that seems to admit of alternative modes of treatment and solution. Premises only gradually emerge from the analysis of the situation. The problem is not that it is difficult to draw a conclusion from given premises; our laptop can do that. The problem is the premises. As a matter of fact, we generally begin with some vague anticipation of a conclusion, that is, the decision to act, the one that seems most plausible to us or that suits our interests best, and then we look around for premises, principles that may act as the major and factual data that may act as the minor, which together will substantiate the conclusion.

No diplomat ever thought of solving a problem in terms of a syllogism. He or she begins with the conclusion, the decision they want to reach, and then they analyse the facts of the situation *selecting* those data that allow them to construct a favourable statement of the facts (the *minor*). Simultaneously, they identify some rules and general principles (the *major*) which they *interpret* so that they fit the facts, hoping that both major and minor will substantiate the pre-set conclusion. And as over time their acquaintance with the rules and principles grows, so will their perspective in the selection of the facts change. And conversely, as they learn more of the facts, they may change their interpretation of applicable rules and principles.

As we see, this procedure is strongly *pre-committed* to the establishment of a particular and possibly partisan pre-set conclusion and has therefore for a long time been held 'un-scientific', 'non-rational' (until such time, that is, that scientists themselves in the mid-20th century started realising and then admitting that their own scientific *modus operandi* is not that different from the one just sketched). It does illustrate that in practical thinking the formation of both major and minor premises proceeds tentatively and correlatively in the course of the decision-making process to suit the preferred outcome. In strict logic, the conclusion does not *follow* from the premises; it is rather the premises that follow from the conclusion. Conclusions and premises end up being two ways of stating the same thing. But then, *the whole point of distinguishing premises and conclusion, and hence of speaking about a syllogism, becomes moot.*

To illustrate this way of proceeding, let us have a look at the decision-making process (a questionable label) that led to the 2003 so-called second Iraq war. George W. Bush's decision to go to war was pre-set: Saddam had to go or, in diplo-speak, 'regime change'. The whole discussion turned (1) around the *framing of the facts* in such a way as allowing some generally agreed diplomatic or legal principle regarding the proper use of force to apply and conversely (2) around the *interpretation of the principles* in such a way that they could cover the facts. Either approach separately or both simultaneously could work, as long as the objective of 'regime change' could be attained. One will recall the contorted arguments constructed by the US and the UK in a desperate attempt to justify the armed invasion of Iraq: first, there was the openly contested question regarding the 'weapons of mass destruction program' that Saddam was presumably conducting ('principle of non-proliferation'), then came the implausible claim of Saddam's involvement with international terrorism (post 9/11 'fight against terrorism'), followed by recalling the atrocities committed (use of chemical weapons) and suffering inflicted by the regime on its own people, in particular the Kurds, in the wake of the first Gulf-war ('respect of fundamental human rights' if not 'crimes against humanity'). The mere consecutive shifting of reasons and grounds invoked to justify the invasion – an exercise in 'trial and error' – totally undermined the credibility of the whole operation.

3.2 Finding and justifying decisions

The preceding discussion points to an important distinction that we need to make when discussing diplomatic reasoning, the distinction between the *motives* that as a *matter of fact* lead to a decision to act (*ex ante*), and the *reasons* that as a *matter of principle* are invoked for the rational justification of the decision (*ex post*). Remember what Justice Holmes said about judges, and what we said in the introduction about diplomats: what a judge/diplomat says he or she does may differ from what he or she actually does. Most often, in diplomacy as in most action-oriented practices, the actual decision will rest not only on one's worldview, on the dominant political narrative of the day, but also on motives of a questionable nature, personal hunches and inarticulate feelings, intuitions and impressions linked to considerations of political necessity, or convenience dictated by the concrete situation. Its rational justification, on the other hand, will set forth lofty grounds for the decision reached, so as to make it not appear as an arbitrary dictum; it will therefore be presented in terms of presumably undisputed general principles, standards, and rules.

Let us recall the 1991 Iraq case which we discussed in the preceding paragraph and where we showed that the *nominal* justification of the operation in terms of general principles (that of legitimate self-defence, but also the principles of territorial integrity and inviolability of borders) did not tell us much of the *real* thinking which led to the decision (regional stability, energy security, superpower status, costs of the operation).

In practice, it will not always be easy to find out what the real motives for an action were, given that the decision-maker will try to cloud, at the earliest stage possible, his real motives under the cover of more worthy or noble reasons. Whether he does so successfully is another matter, as we have seen with the contorted arguments invoked for the justification of the 2003 Iraq invasion.

To wrap up. Earlier we asked: what is the point of distinguishing premises and conclusion, antecedent, and consequent, if both end up stating the same thing? Why, in those circumstances, insist on having diplomatic reasoning fit the paradigm of a syllogism? Better just drop it; it is pure fiction, illusion, and artificiality. But the perspective changes fundamentally when we move from the consideration of our ***actual thinking ex ante*** to the ***justification ex post*** of our decisions (see Box 3.1). Then the appeal to some kind of logic is no longer fiction, illusion, and artificiality but becomes vital and eminently political. Decisions must be expounded, and the exposition must set forth grounds for the decision, state its justifying reasons, and show how these grounds and reasons logically support the decision. Being able to give reasons for our decisions and actions is a political requirement called *accountability*. The difficult debates in the UN Security Council in the spring of 2003 did not turn around the question of how President Bush junior had *in fact (de facto)* come to the conclusion to go to war with Iraq, but on how *in law (de jure)* he could justify that decision.

Box 3.1 Non-logic of Discovery versus Logic of Justification

The American philosopher-scientist *Hans Reichenbach* is the intellectual father of the distinction between what he called the *context of discovery* and *the context of justification*:

> The act of discovery escapes logical analysis; there are no logical rules in terms of which a 'discovery machine' could be constructed that would take over the creative function of the genius; it is not the logician's task to account for scientific discoveries. Logic is concerned only with the context of justification.
> (The Rise of Scientific Philosophy, Berkeley, 1951, p. 231)

The moral philosopher *John Ladd* has this to say on the question:

> Discovery, that is the resolution of practical problem-situations, is not even the principal way in which (practical reasoning) is used. More often it is used to defend one's acts (...) in the sense that the aim of the person presenting reasons is to procure acceptance of some sort on the part of others (...). I think it is also obvious that a person is able to explain (that is, justify) a past action by using a practical syllogism, even though the premises of the syllogism were not consciously present in his mind when he performed the act.
> (LADD, 1964, p. 134)

The pragmatist philosopher *John Dewey* goes so far as to state that there probably never would have been any question of logic in decision-making, were it not for the need of justification: 'It is highly probable that the need of justifying to others conclusions reached and decisions made, has been the chief cause of the origin of logical operations (...)', and further: 'It is quite conceivable that if no one had ever to account to others for his decisions, logical operations would never have developed, but men would use exclusively methods of inarticulate intuition and impression, feeling' (DEWEY, 1924, p. 24).

Having thus disentangled the confusion between the *non-logic of discovery* and the *logic of justification*, two questions remain: first, the question how in fact we reach our decisions to act; and second, what kind of reasoning patterns can do the job of justification of decisions. Let us start with the first question.

3.3 A non-logic of discovery?

If there is no proper **logic** of discovery, at least we may try to see whether there is something like a non-logic of discovery, a **mere practice** that would describe, and perhaps to some extent explain, how, *as a matter of fact*, decisions are reached in action-oriented thinking. Different models have been advanced. We will just look at one of them. This model is known as reasoning by consequences. Let us have a look at it and then make a critical assessment.

3.3.1 Reasoning by consequences

We have seen that the empirical claim that decisions flow with logical necessity as conclusions from antecedent premises is absurd. The converse is true: conclusions *precede* their premises. If that is the case, it is conclusions that should be the starting point of the analysis. Things must be turned upside down. Practical reasoning is ***means-end reasoning***. A rational action is an action that is performed because it is believed to be a means to a predetermined end. The kind of rationality involved here is called *instrumental rationality*. Such approach is (somewhat misleadingly) called a **'logic' of consequences** rather than antecedents, a 'logic' of prediction of *probabilities* rather than one of deduction of certainties. A pragmatic approach to problem-solving is one where the diplomat asks which of the possible solutions has the best consequences. Diplomats use consequences to guide their decisions (POSNER, 1995, p. 400).

The means-end schema can be developed in three steps:

- In a *first* step the desired **end state** (objective) is clearly spelled out.
- In a *second* step we identify and evaluate the **means** that can contribute to the realisation of the end: (1) exhaustive *identification* of all alternative action patterns (not necessarily mutually exclusive) that can possibly contribute to the realisation of the end state; (2) critical *evaluation* of each of these alternative action possibilities *in terms of the consequences* they entail, for good or for bad.
- In the *third* and last step a *choice* is made among the alternative action patterns, the **decision** to act.

This sequence can be illustrated again with the 1991 Iraq war example:

Step 1 (spelling out *the end* state): ensuring the stability in the Arab peninsula and restoring the *status-ante-quem* after the invasion of Kuwait by Iraq in 1990; that end state may be formulated in terms of general principles (peace and security, self-defence, territorial integrity, inviolability of borders).

Step 2 (identifying and evaluating *the means* to get to that end):

- First, *identification* of alternative action possibilities which could be (1) negotiating Iraq out of Kuwait, (2) imposing a sanctions regime on Iraq, (3) launching a limited war aimed only at restoring Kuwait's territorial integrity, (4) launching an all-out punitive war so as to durably disable Iraq's military apparatus, and (5) *idem* but also targeting the regime (regime change); some of these courses of action can be realised simultaneously (for example, limited war and sanctions imposition).
- Second, *evaluation* of these alternatives in terms of their consequences: (1) negotiation is out of order as a response to armed aggression, (2) sanctions may be envisaged only in conjunction with more forceful intervention, (3) limited war may not durably avoid future Iraqi misbehaviour but can be conducted with minimal losses of lives and at reasonable cost, (4) and (5) would lead to uncertain outcomes with risks of entanglement, would be costly both financially and in terms of human lives, and could be seen as disproportionate and unlikely to be endorsed by the UN Security Council in an authorisation resolution.

Step 3 (choice – *decision*): alternative (3), limited war, is withheld.

Step 1 may seem easy: you just state your objective. But in real life, we all simultaneously pursue different objectives which are not necessarily compatible. An example: the objective of non-intervention in the domestic affairs of another state (Art. 2, para 7 of the UN Charter) is difficult to reconcile with the objective to ensure the respect fundamental human rights or with the Responsibility to Protect (R2P) peoples subjected to atrocities (such as genocide and ethnic cleansing). Such conflicting ends must be weighed against each other. Pursuing one end does not mean reneging the legitimacy of rival ends.

Step 2 is the crucial step in this means-end decision-making scheme. It is the deliberative stage in which common sense and practical wisdom join to properly evaluate what your possible action means in terms of *probable consequences*, not of certain outcomes, and how one action compares to another taking into account these probabilities.

Step 3 is the final step: you decide, that is, make a final *choice* among the possible actions on the basis of the cost-benefit analysis of the probable consequences of the alternative action patterns made in the second step.

Whether this model adequately reflects practical thinking as it *actually* unfolds in decision-making remains questionable. No doubt this model comes already closer to the actual practice of decision-makers compared to the implausible deductive model – the practical syllogism – sketched earlier, but we doubt that this is what really happens when a decision is in the making. For that, the model is still too neat, a 'model' indeed, something that idealises, simplifies, and rationalises what is intrinsically more confused and complex. Here is what John Kay has to say on this and to which we are tempted to subscribe:

> There is an appearance of describing objectives, evaluating options, reviewing evidence. But it is a sham. The objectives (our ends) are dictated by the conclusions,

the options (our means) presented so as to make the forward course look attractive, the data (our facts) selected to favour the required result. Real alternatives are not assessed rigorously: *policy-based evidence supplants evidence-based policy*

(KAY, 2010, p. 165, my italics)

3.3.2 Muddling through?

What are we to make of this and similar attempts to get to grips on reasoning in diplomacy? Some think such attempts are misguided, even futile. *They look for something that is not there.* Practical reasoning is not as linear as one should wish, it is oblique. An oblique approach involves no sharp distinction between means and ends and often proceeds through problem-simplification and ignoring many potentially available options.

We see that various people involved in the decision-making process find themselves directly agreeing on a policy. The idea is that decision-making in politics and diplomacy, in law and business, and indeed in everyday life is often based on a common, implicit, unarticulated view of what to do, which does not require an explicit, conscious awareness of the reasons for doing it.

Decision-making is a process of experiment and discovery, of successes and failures which allow us to reassess our ends and means in a process of constant adaptation. We improvise, we combine means with ends, and rather than proceeding to a comprehensive evaluation of all available options we just look at a relevant subset of them. All this is what Cass Sunstein called an 'incompletely theorised agreement' (SUNSTEIN, 1996, p. 27). Yet, this approach also goes by a less mundane and more straightforward name: 'Muddling Through'.

The intellectual father of this concept is Charles Lindblom who launched it in his 1959 book 'The Science of Muddling Through'. He contrasted two modes of reasoning. The root, rational, comprehensive method is open and direct, and involves a single overall evaluation of all options in light of the defined objectives. He thought such mode of reasoning to be utopian. The oblique approach is characterised, not by a single comprehensive assessment of the problem situation but by what he called successive, limited, incremental comparisons. 'Muddling through' is a process of 'initially building out from the current situation, step-by-step and by small degrees' (KAY, 2010, pp. 59–67).

In diplomacy, we often meet areas of discourse where a lack of common ends, conflicting interests, or incompatible values precludes a rational resolution. The pragmatic counsel to the practitioner of diplomacy then is to muddle through, preserve avenues of change, and not roil the political waters unnecessarily. What a pragmatic approach to diplomacy connotes is – to paraphrase Posner – a rejection of the idea that diplomacy is something grounded in permanent immutable principles and realised through logical manipulation of those principles, and a determination to look at principles as instruments for *finding solutions here and now* (POSNER, 1995, pp. 404–405).

3.3.3 A way out: distinguishing fast and slow thinking

The preceding considerations may still leave many of us perplexed. Is there a way to get out of the puzzle? We think a key to unlock it is given by Daniel Kahneman in his *Thinking, Fast and Slow* (KAHNEMAN, 2011). In this seminal work, the author distinguishes between two ways of thinking: fast thinking, which is the kind of spontaneous, intuitive thinking that is involved in *leading* us to certain decisions to act, and slow thinking, which is the kind of articulate, discursive thinking that is involved in *explaining and justifying* our decisions.

Thinking Fast is automatic, quick, and associative. It is effortless and spontaneous. Information processing is unconscious. Thinking fast jumps to conclusions on the basis of what is readily available or accessible. It looks for coherence and uncritically relies on stereotypes and prototypical situations (such as 'diplomats are often lawyers'). It easily sees connections where there are none (temporal and causal connections, for instance, as wrapped up in the dictum: 'post hoc, ergo propter hoc'; 'the Queen died – The King died from sadness'). Fast thinking is also sensitive to emotions and prone to all kinds of misleading heuristics (on which more in a later chapter). It is uncritical and systematically looks for *confirming* evidence, ignoring what is at odds with its dominant thinking. Thinking fast is efficient but it can be misleading.

Thinking Slow is conscious, articulate, and explicit. It is what we call *discursive* thinking, directed and purposeful. It consumes a lot of cognitive energy and demands effort. Whereas thinking fast has been evolutionary selected because it allows making quick and efficient decisions in familiar and recurring routine situations, thinking slow is helpful and indeed necessary whenever we meet new situations for which no readymade solutions are available or when we have to critically evaluate what intuitively looks plausible but is not. Also, it is generally agreed that automatic fast thinking's intuitive processes operate via multiple *parallel* systems that generate quick decisions at low cost, whereas the slow thinking system's analytical processes unfold *sequentially* and demand concentration and attention.

*Thinking slow acts as a **corrective** on the decisions made by thinking fast*. According to Jonathan Haidt, in an article titled 'The Emotional Dog and its Rational Tail' (*American Psychologist*, 108 (2001), pp. 814–834) most political decisions (and presumably also diplomatic decisions) are taken on the basis of *thinking fast* and only later get scrutinised by the *thinking slow* system, in particular with a view to constructing *ex post* justifications for the decisions.

3.4 The logic of justification

The distinction between fast and slow thinking allows us to understand the distinction we made between the non-logic prevalent in finding decisions (the context of discovery) and the logic prevalent in justifying them (the context of justification). In addressing the issue of the justification of decisions we now move from the descriptive question of 'how *do* people *actually* make their decisions' (which requires an empirical, *in casu* psychological investigation) to the normative question of 'how *should* people *ideally have made* their decisions', decisions that would pass the test of accountability, which brings us into the realm of logic.

We already noted that the real, final reckoning in politics, diplomacy, and law is not about how *in fact* we get at our decisions but about how well we can justify and explain them, and for that we need some solid grounding. In what follows we will explore three ways of reasoning which are considered standard in logic: inductive, abductive, and deductive reasoning. The respective strengths of the conclusions to which they lead (reliability, plausibility, and validity) will determine whether and if so, to what extent, the justifications of decisions relying on these logics are convincing.

3.4.1 *Inductive reasoning*

Inductive reasoning starts out with *specific* (particular) observation statements that act as premises (such as 'democratic regime A [Austria] eschews aggressive behaviour', and so does regime B [Belgium], C [Canada], D [Dominican Republic], E, etc.). It then *generalises* over them by way of a *general* (universal) statement covering not only the observed cases (of democratic regimes) but also those that have not yet been observed (in particular future cases, as happens in 'early warning', 'foresight', and 'strategizing' fields that have become increasingly important in diplomacy). Note that the conclusion in inductive reasoning (in our example the general statement: 'democratic regimes eschew aggressive behaviour', known as the *Democratic Peace Theory*) does not necessarily or conclusively follow from the premises (we may come across a democratic regime that does not eschew aggressive behaviour). The conclusion is therefore said to be only **reliable**. That is why in inductive reasoning, one generally assigns *probabilities* to the conclusion, a conclusion which holds, *given* the premises (called 'conditional probability'). Much reasoning in diplomacy is inductive. We observe all kinds of regularities, on which we build our policies and decisions ('identity politics leads to polarization and violence, fuelling intra-state conflicts'; 'climate change increasingly affects human security, particularly in fragile states'). But inductive reasoning is fallible. Reliability is not certainty. Counterexamples falsify an inductively reached conclusion or decrease its probability (thus diminishing its reliability). That is why we should be on our guards for fallacies in inductive reasoning: the most obvious one is unjustified and hasty *over-generalisation* (concluding too much and too fast on the basis of too small a sample); another frequently occurring fallacy is *stereotypical or exemplary thinking* (basing your generalisation on one single or just a few 'typical' observations or on merely anecdotal but somehow 'significant' evidence).

3.4.2 *Abductive reasoning*

Abductive reasoning starts out with a fact or situation that is unexpected or surprising and that needs explaining. Abductive reasoning is called '*inference to the best explanation*': it links the fact or situation to be explained (the *explanandum*) to one or more hypotheses which would *explain* them (the *explanans*). What such reasoning does is to put the facts in a *broader context* which sheds light on them, makes sense of them, and as a result makes them comprehensible (in this process one often relies on some implicit general principle that acts as intermediary between *explanandum* and *explanans*). To illustrate, let us look at an example of abductive reasoning. The context is the civil war in Libya. As you may remember, in the last months of 2020 the balance of war between the renegade general Khalifa Haftar (supported by i.a. Russia) and the UN-endorsed government in Tripoli (supported by i.a. Turkey) suddenly shifted to the latter's advantage. The surprising fact to be explained was this sudden shift. The explanatory hypothesis that has been advanced referred to a deal signed in November 2020 between Turkey and Tripoli pursuant to which Ankara would provide military support to the Tripoli government. Note that this 'inference to the best explanation' rests upon an unspoken, implicit premise intermediating between the facts and the explanation, namely that when one party in a conflict is provided game-changing military support, the balance of war is likely to shift to its advantage, a premise that could be kept hidden because unproblematic. Also note that alternative explanations could have been given (for example: internal strife within the Haftar camp weakening its resolve, or diminished support by the Russians to Haftar) but that the one offered seems the best, that is, the one with the greatest explanatory power. While conclusions from an inductive reasoning are said to be (more or less) reliable, conclusions from abductive reasoning are said to be (more or less) **plausible**.

Inferring to the best explanation generally means going for the explanation that is:

- *Conservative:* Adopting the explanation does not constrain you to *revisit* other beliefs in your belief system (in our example: the explanation offered (increased military support to the Tripoli government) does not constrain you to revisit your belief about the well-known cohesiveness of the Tripoli government).
- *Simple:* The explanation stands on its own and does not need additional, perhaps less credible *ad hoc* hypotheses that may themselves require an explanation (in our example: suppose my explanation would have been that Russia had diminished its support to Haftar, then I would need to explain that fact in turn, for instance by postulating a shift in Russia's policy regarding Libya).
- *Fits well* with much that we more generally already know about the world at large, going beyond the specific case at hand (in our example: military support to one party in a two-party conflictual situation upsets the balance among them; relations between Ankara and Moscow have been volatile lately; Ankara's diplomatic ambitions in the region have been steadily increasing in the last decade). This requirement is the (tautological) converse of the first one on conservativeness: not having to revisit your belief system means compatibility with that system.

3.4.3 *Deductive reasoning*

Deductive reasoning also establishes an inferential link between premises and conclusion but is much more stringent than inductive or abductive reasoning. In deductive reasoning, whenever your premises are taken to be true, your conclusion must, *of necessity*, be true. That is why a deductive reasoning is said to be truth-preserving. This is a *first* important difference between deductive reasoning on the one hand and inductive or abductive reasoning on the other hand. In the two latter ways of reasoning your premises also support your conclusion, but the link between both is not one of necessity but one of *probability* or *explanation*. A *second* important difference between deductive reasoning as compared to inductive and abductive reasoning is that in the latter it is the *content* of the premises (what they say) that will determine the reliability and plausibility, respectively, whereas in deductive reasoning the *validity* of the reasoning is a *question of form only*.

In sum, valid deductive reasoning means *truth-preservation on the basis of form only*; *if* all premises are taken to be true, *then* the conclusion *must* be true (whatever the content of premises or conclusion may be), or conversely, *if* the conclusion is untrue, *then* at least one of the premises must also be untrue. It is because deductive reasoning is **content-independent** that its study is part of what is called *formal* logic (of which inductive and abductive reasoning are not part).

'If p implies q', and moreover 'p', then of necessity 'q'. This is a purely formal statement that remains valid for whatever 'p' and 'q' stand for:

- 'If a country has been invaded by another country, then it is entitled to defend itself using force' (Art. 51 of the UN-Charter).

- 'Kuwait has been invaded by Iraq in the summer of 1990'.
- Hence: 'Kuwait can defend itself using force against Iraq'.

Now consider the following:

- 'If a country has been elected as a non-permanent member of the UN Security Council, then it can exercise its veto-right'.
- 'Estonia has been elected as a non-permanent member of the UN Security Council'.
- Hence: 'Estonia can exercise its veto-right'.

Both preceding reasonings are deductively valid. The only difference is that in the first reasoning the premises are true and so is the conclusion, while in the second reasoning the first premise is untrue and so is its conclusion. But that does not affect the formal **validity** of the reasoning. Validity only requires that *if* the premises are taken to be true, *then* necessarily its conclusion must be considered true; or in other words that a conclusion is *conditionally* true, true *only if* all premises are true.

To bridge the gap between these two cases, we need an additional concept beyond validity, that of **soundness**: a deductive reasoning is sound when it is *both formally valid and all its premises are true*. Importantly, *whether premises are true or untrue is not a matter of logic*. It is a matter of the knowledge you have, for instance as a diplomat; in the first example, you knew what Article 51 of the UN Charter states, but in the second example you apparently did not know what Article 27, paragraph 3 (on the veto right) is saying. That knowledge of the UN Charter is clearly not a matter of logic.

3.4.4 Conditional reasoning

Reasoning with conditional statements is pervasive in diplomatic thinking. Conditional reasoning is an important aspect of deductive reasoning. It is what we did in both the Kuwait and Estonia examples cited above. A **conditional statement** has the 'if...then'-form, it links an antecedent to a consequent. Conditional statements have a significant intrinsic structure linked to the concepts of sufficient reason and necessary condition. In a conditional statement, the truth of the antecedent is a **sufficient reason** for the truth of the consequent: given the antecedent, the consequent follows (which is a straightforward reading of 'if p then q'). Moreover, in such statement, the consequent is a **necessary condition** for the antecedent: the antecedent cannot be true unless the consequent is true, which is *not* to say that given the consequent the antecedent follows; what it *does* say is that if the consequent is not true then the antecedent cannot be true ('if not-q then not-p').

Let us illustrate this with the following example drawn from one of the darkest pages of the Yugoslav war in the 1990s: the Srebrenica massacre (SM) over which the International Criminal Tribunal for the former Yugoslavia (ICTY)) has claimed jurisdiction. As a result, Radoslaw Karadzic (RK) was brought before the Tribunal. The following conditional statement could then have been made by the prosecutor: 'If RK ordered the SM, then he will be condemned by the ICTY'. This conditional statement says two things: first, that it suffices for RK to have ordered the massacre for him to be condemned by the ICTY; second, that should RK not be condemned by the ICTY, it could not have been the case that he ordered the SM. So far, so good.

We now move from a mere conditional statement to **conditional reasoning**. From the conditional statement on its own nothing can be concluded. It is simply expressing a conditional relation between two other statements. For conditional reasoning we need more. We need an inferential relation between one or more premises and a conclusion. For the sake of clarity, we will simplify (and indeed formalise) the preceding conditional statement regarding RK into: 'if p then q'. What can we do with it?

First, we can add to it the statement 'p'. We thus have the following scheme:

- If p then q (here we do not say that p and q are true, we only say that if p is true then q is true).
- p (here we say that p is true).
- Therefore: q (here we conclude that q must be true).

As a matter of fact, in the Karadzic-case p proved to be true (RK had ordered the SM) and so was q (the ICTY sentenced RK to 35 years' imprisonment for the Srebrenica massacre which it qualified as genocide).

This mode of deductively valid reasoning is called *modus ponens* (you posit the antecedent p).

Second, we can add to the conditional statement 'if p then q' the negation of q: 'not-q'. As we saw in the preceding paragraph the conditional statement 'if p then q' (sufficient reason) is equivalent to the conditional statement 'if not-q then not-p' (necessary condition). So, the two following schemes can be freely interchanged:

- If not-q then not-p; not-q; therefore not-p (which simply is an application of the modus ponens), or equivalently.
- If p then q; not-q; therefore: not-p.

In our example, this would have meant that if RK, while being prosecuted, would not have been condemned by the Tribunal then we must conclude that he cannot have ordered the massacre.

This new way of reasoning is called *modus tollens* (you negate the consequent q).

What else could we do with our conditional statement 'if p then q'?

First, we could be tempted to *deny the antecedent* 'p' (that is: affirm not-p) and then conclude to 'not-q', or schematically:

- If p then q.
- Not-p (here we say that p is untrue).
- Therefore: not-q (here we conclude that q is untrue).

This is *not a valid reasoning*. The conclusion does not follow from the premises.

In our example such reasoning would mean: if RK would not have ordered the massacre, he would not have been condemned by the Tribunal. But how do you know this? He could very well have been condemned for a crime against humanity other than the Srebrenica massacre. This logical fallacy is known as *denying the antecedent*.

Second, we could be tempted to *affirm the consequent* 'q' and then conclude to 'p', or schematically:

- If p then q.
- q (here we say that q is true).
- Therefore: p (we conclude that p is true).

This is again *not a valid reasoning*. In our example it would mean that if the Tribunal has condemned RK it must have been the case that he had ordered the Srebrenica massacre. How do you know this? Yes, he must have been condemned for a crime against humanity, but not necessarily for ordering the Srebrenica massacre. This logical fallacy goes by the name of *confirming the consequent*.

This fallacy and other forms of invalid reasoning are particularly misleading when the conclusion happens to be true. Take the following example:

- If Commission President Mrs. von der Leyen is German, she is also European.
- Mrs. von der Leyen is a European.
- Therefore Mrs. von der Leyen is German.

All the statements (both premises and conclusion) are true, and this is what tempts us to consider the reasoning as valid (which it clearly is not, it is a case of *confirming of the consequent*). But things can get even more insidious. A true conclusion may not just make you think that the reasoning is valid (where it is not); it may even misleadingly make you think the premises are true (where they are not). Take the following example:

- 'All headquarters of international organisations or agencies are located in the capital of their host country'.
- 'The World Bank and IMF have their headquarters in Washington, DC'.
- Therefore: 'Washington, DC is the capital of the USA'.

For the sake of completeness, let us just mention another mode of valid deductive reasoning that also appeals to conditional statements, called **hypothetical syllogism**. The mechanics of this extremely simple reasoning relies on the transitivity of conditional statements. Example: 'if p then q' and 'if q then r', then 'if p then r'.

3.4.5 *Reasoning by analogy*

We close this chapter with a short comment on what is called reasoning by analogy. Reasoning by analogy is a pervasive feature of diplomatic thinking. But it does not have the analytical strength of any of the reasoning patterns that we studied earlier. Rather than reasoning about a certain situation, it is a technique of *interpreting new and unfamiliar situations by comparing them to known situations*, then noting similarities among them to finally conclude to treat the unknown situation in the same way as the known situation is treated.

Relying on **past experience** (the known) in addressing **current problems** (the unknown) is something diplomats do all the time. Often, as we will see, all too often, and all too easy.

Reasoning by analogy has two great advantages. First, it is *economical*. Once the analogy is established one can rely on past solutions for solving similar current problems; it spares us time and effort. Second, it ensures coherence, continuity, and stability in thought and action; thinking and acting today as we did in the past provides us and others with a *sense of certainty*, and therefore predictability. But mental economy and psychological certainty will not by themselves make reasoning by analogy a suitable model of reasoning.

Indeed, reasoning by analogy is conceptually very *fragile*. Reasoning by analogy tells us that *similar cases should be treated similarly*. Note that this is not a rule of logic but one of simple prudence or perhaps convenience. Thus stated, the rule seems fair enough. But the critical question in reasoning by analogy is how to judge the similarities. Similar cases are not identical cases: they resemble each other in certain aspects but differ in others. Hence, such cases could *a priori* give rise to *both* reasoning by *analogy* and reasoning by *disanalogy*. The critical intervening factor is relevance. It is said that reasoning by analogy holds when the **similarities** between the cases are **relevant** *and* the **differences** between them are **irrelevant**. But this *simply pushes the question one step further*. The crucial question now becomes whether a similarity or difference is or is not relevant. Relevance is far from being an objective datum but involves subjective appreciation. That is why caution should prevail in reasoning by analogy.

Analogy tells us that *if* two situations, past and present for instance, may be *considered* as similar in *some* respects (the relevant ones), they *then* may be *treated* as similar in *all* respects, that is, identically. And if they cannot so be considered because they are dissimilar in *some* relevant respects, then they must be treated differently. The critical point is the transition from 'some' to 'all' or 'none'.

There are thus three sides to this issue. First, *the no-paradigm case*, that is, the case where we judge the similarities between both situations, past and present, between the potential paradigm situation and the instant one, to be too weak to allow reasoning by analogy. Second, *the single paradigm case*, the one where there is a unique paradigm fitting the situation under consideration. And third, *the multiple paradigm case* where multiple plausible similarities between past and current situations can be established leading to competing past paradigms among which we will have to make a reasoned choice (based on considerations other than similarity because if so there would not have been multiple paradigms in the first place).

In a chapter titled 'The Perils of Analogy' of his book *Diplomacy for the Next Century*, Abba Eban (EBAN, 1998, p. 50) recalls the following (rather simplistic but nevertheless helpful) anecdote from a lecture he gave at Cambridge University:

> I brought into the Senate House a red rubber ball and a shiny red apple, and then described the analogy in the following terms: 'This apple is round, red, shiny, and good to eat. This rubber ball is round, red, and shiny. Therefore, there is at least a strong probability that it will be good to eat'.
>
> (EBAN, 1998, p. 50)

In diplomacy, we do not compare rubber balls with red apples, but most often one past crisis with a current one. Therefore, the underlying preliminary question regarding the legitimacy of analogical reasoning is **whether history repeats itself or not**. There are two opposing views on this:

* The first one is that history does indeed repeat itself, that lessons can be learned from past experience and that the professional diplomat therefore needs to be familiar with diplomatic history, the history of international relations. In its strongest form, this view, known as *historicism*, says that there are 'laws of history', regularities which are similar to those we find in the physical world where they are known as 'laws of nature'. This view is shared by many International Relations scholars and, obviously, most historians.

- This view has been strongly criticised by the philosopher Karl Popper in his well-known short essay *The Poverty of Historicism*. Diplomats too (George Kennan is one of them) are generally critical of the 'history repeats itself'-thesis. They would rather agree with Paul Valéry's one-liner: 'History is the science of things which do *not* repeat themselves' or with what Will and Ariel Durant had to say on this: 'History smiles at all attempts to force its flow into theoretical patterns and logical groves: it plays havoc with our generalisations, breaks all our rules. History is baroque' (both quoted in EBAN, 1998, p. 59).

To illustrate the frivolity of analogical reasoning let us look at two particular cases, one mistakenly *seeing analogies* between the *Korea war* of the early 1950s and the *Vietnam war* of the 1960s, and the other mistakenly *not seeing analogies* between the *Korea war* and the first *Iraq war* of 1991:

- **Seeing analogies where there are none (or ignoring the differences).** The advocates of the US *intervention in Vietnam* from the 1960s onward sought support for their position by comparing it with the *Korean war*, which had been acceptable to American public opinion. George Ball, the then Under Secretary of State, who opposed the war, felt bound to make a patient analysis of the *differences* which violated the analogy. He pointed out that the Korean intervention had been sustained by the United Nations; that the US, as a result, had the active support of a large group of other countries, including 53 that contributed troops, whereas in Vietnam the US had gone in alone. He further pointed out that South Korea, unlike South Vietnam, had a stable government. The South Koreans were ready to fight for their independence, whereas the South Vietnamese, who had been at war for 20 years, had no such energy or commitment. Most observers would agree that George Ball got it right. The lesson to be learned from this case study is not that reasoning by analogy is wrong but that such reasoning is wrong when badly performed, which in this example clearly was the case: the *dis-analogies* that Ball identified were simply ignored.
- **Ignoring analogies where there are (or seeing differences were there are none).** In its early stages, the first Iraq war proved not uncontroversial. Opponents to the war recalled that Vietnam had been an attempt to solve a problem by military means. Vietnam was a failure. Therefore, so said opponents to the Iraq war, the attempt to solve the Kuwait problem by military means should be avoided. But this was just lazy thinking, reducing to the simplistic argument that since *a* war (in Vietnam) was a failure, *all* wars (including the Iraq war) will be. There was not even an attempt to see similarities or dissimilarities between both situations. Establishing analogies requires careful analysis. The analogy to be made as regards the 1991 *Iraq war* is not with the Vietnam war but with the *Korean war*. The Korean war was a response to a classic aggressive land invasion by thousands of troops across a recognised border. And so was the aggression and invasion by Iraq of Kuwait in 1990. In both cases, the US and its coalition partners had a strong case to make before the UN Security Council thus having an unassailable political and legal base for war.

We close with a controversy closer to our current concerns, Trump's **cold war metaphor**, which he used to describe the *Sino-American confrontation* and which was intended intended to rally US allies to the cause. It is a good example of how we are inclined to make sense of the present by reaching out onto the past. Not so long ago the fashionable commentary on the US-China rivalry summoned up the Athenian historian Thucydides who predicted inevitable conflict between an established hegemon (then Athens, now the US) and a rising power (then Sparta and now China). The mechanism is known as the Thucydides-trap. Now, the **favoured analogy** is the **cold war**, the west's fight against the Soviet Union. Neat as it may seem, the analogy is more confusing than illuminating. (1) The cold war between the West and the Soviet Union was a struggle between competing systems, whereas the current rivalry between the US and China is a contest between states. (2) The cold war focused on ideology and nuclear weapons; the new battlefield is information technology (data, 5G mobile networks, artificial intelligence [AI]). (3) And finally, the US and the Soviet Union lived in separate bubbles, whereas the protagonists today are interconnected. China knows fully well that its claims must be managed in the context of economic interdependence with the West. The Soviets thought they could crush capitalism. China depends on it. Remember that a reasoning by analogy requires not only that there be relevant similarities between both cases *but also that there be no relevant differences between them.*

What should we make out of all this? Not more than what we already said: analogy should be handled with care and requires that unique diplomatic capacity for judgment called 'prudence'. Reasoning by analogy has two major weaknesses. *First*, at the *conceptual* level. Everything hinges on the dual test whether the similarities are relevant *and* the differences irrelevant. If so, you construct an argument by analogy; if not, an argument by disanalogy. Who will decide? Relevance is an extremely subjective category: relevant for whom, for what purpose, in what context. The *second* weakness involves a principled question, perhaps one of worldview. Reasoning by analogy in politics and diplomacy rests upon a questionable premise as regards the existence of regularities in social life generally and politics specifically. *Social life is not persistent in time*; history does not repeat itself and the past may not be a good guide for the present and future. The situation is quite different from the one we encounter in physics. Natural phenomena are persistent in time. They recur and show regularities that are captured by the stable laws of nature. On the law of gravity, there are no exceptions and water will still be H_2O over 50 years' time.

In this chapter, we have explored different reasoning processes that are said to underlie diplomatic thinking. We have elegantly dismissed the so-called practical syllogism as clearly misrepresenting actual thinking in diplomacy. We then explored a less stringent mode of reasoning, reasoning by consequences, but again questioned whether it properly reflected practical thinking as it actually unfolds in decision-making. Instead of concluding that thinking in diplomacy is just some way of 'muddling through', we came to understand that our search was perhaps misdirected. We discovered that thinking in diplomacy is more about justifying decisions *ex post* than about reaching them *ex ante*. And this fits rather well with political reality: leaders are not expected to explain how they reach their decisions; rather they are expected to give a solid justification for them. This is what the concept of political accountability is all about; and solid justifications should rely on solid thinking. That is why we made a short detour in standard logic which also allowed us to shed some light on two ways of reasoning that are pervasive in diplomacy: conditional reasoning and reasoning by analogy. Throughout this chapter we have illustrated the rather abstract concepts with concrete examples drawn from actual diplomatic practice.

Bibliography

BUEKENS, Filip & DEMEY, Lorenz (2017), *Redeneren en Argumenteren*, Acco, Leuven/ Den Haag.

COHEN, Felix (1937), "The Problem of Functional Jurisprudence", *Modern Law Review,* Vol. 1, pp. 5–26.

DEWEY, John (1924), "Logical Method and Law", *Cornell Law Review* Vol. 10 (pp. 17–27). 1924–1925.

EBAN, Abba (1998), *Diplomacy for the 21st Century*, Yale University Press, New Haven, CT/ London.

ELSTER, Jon (2007), *Explaining Social Behavior*, Cambridge University Press, Cambridge.

FRIEDMAN, Lawrence M. (1975), *The Legal System – A Social Science Perspective*, Russell Sage Foundation, New York, NY.

GENSLER, Harry J. (2002), *Introduction to Logic*, Routledge, Abingdon/New York, NY.

KAHNEMAN, Daniel (2011), *Thinking, Fast and Slow,* Allen Lane, New York, NY.

KAY, John (2010), *Obliquity*, Profile Books, London.

LADD, John (1964), "The Place of Practical Reason in Judicial Decision", in: FRIEDRICH, Carl J. (Ed.), *Rational Decision*, Atherton Press, New York, NY, , pp. 126–144.

LEVI, Edward (1949), *An Introduction to Legal Reasoning*, University of Chicago Press, Chicago.

PETERSEN, Martin (2009), *An Introduction to Decision Theory*, Cambridge University Press, Cambridge.

POSNER, Richard (1995), *Overcoming Law*, Harvard University Press, Cambridge, MA.

SUNSTEIN, Cass R. (1996), *Legal Reasoning and Political Conflict*, Oxford University Press, Oxford.

WASSERSTROM, Richard A. (1961), *The Judicial Decision. Toward a Theory of Legal Justification*, Stanford University Press, Stanford, CA.

4 Interactive diplomacy
Game theory and rational empathy

Game theory provides useful insights for diplomatic practice. Until now we looked at decision-making mainly from the perspective of a *single decision-maker*, one who does not take into account what other decision-makers are doing. Many decisions, however, are not like that, and certainly not in diplomacy. Diplomacy is an essentially interactive activity. Effective action in diplomacy requires *taking into account what others are saying, thinking, and doing*. A diplomat is not there just for making decisions on their own. Not taking into account what others say, think, and do would spell disaster. And that is true even for a country that is keen on acting unilaterally, as America was under President Trump.

The central point in game theory, which has been called the 'theory of **interdependent decisions**' (ELSTER, 2007, p. 312), is that the outcome of your decision will depend on what others are doing. Many decisions that a diplomat needs to take, from intervening in a negotiation situation to having recourse or not to the use of force, have this basic strategic interactive structure: if your opponent is clever enough to foresee what you are likely to do he or she will adjust their strategy accordingly and you, no less rational and self-interested than your adversary, will of course also adjust your strategy based on what you believe about your opponent (and this mirroring process can be stretched further down the line).

The value of game theory is both explanatory and conceptual. Explanatory, because it allows you to understand behaviour that previously appeared as puzzling. Conceptual, because it illuminates the structure of social interaction generally and interaction in international politics specifically. Often, the underlying structure of how and why countries interact with each other the way they do is not immediately visible. Through the **modelling** of real-world situations, past and present, game theory forces us to be explicit about the structure of such interactions and can reveal unsuspected subtleties and perversities. *Models are guides to policy-making*. The diplomat can learn from them.

In what follows we will briefly review a few strategic games that have direct relevance for diplomatic practice.

4.1 The one-shot Prisoner's Dilemma

We start with the mother of all games, the so-called *Prisoner's Dilemma* (PD). In this section, we consider the game as a *one-shot* event: two players play the game; they never met before and know they never will meet again. In the second section, we will consider the *iterated* version of the game; the players know they will meet again, and they know

DOI: 10.4324/9781003298182-7

they will play the game all over again. According to the scenario envisaged the strategies deployed by the players will differ fundamentally.

PD is so called because the following slightly adapted story was used to illustrate it in an early discussion. Two drug dealers, John and Marc, have presumably been involved in the same deal. They are now in separate cells and cannot communicate with each other. They are told by the prosecutor that they can either *confess* their crime or *deny* the charges. The prosecutor informs them that there is not enough evidence for convicting them for all their offences unless at least one of them decides to confess. He tells them that:

- If both confess, they will get ten years in prison each.
- If one confesses and the other does not then the prisoner who confesses will be rewarded and get away with just one year in prison, whereas the other will get 20 years.
- If both deny the charges, they will nevertheless be sentenced to two years for a series of well-established traffic offences.

The following matrix (Table 4.1) summarises the situation with the two strategies (Confess or Deny) and the four possible joint outcomes. The minus sign indicates years lost in prison.

Marc must decide which strategy (row) to play, whereas John must decide his strategy by choosing which column to play. The row and column chosen by them together uniquely determine the outcome for both players. For each outcome, the first entry refers to what will happen to Marc and the second entry to what will happen to John. If we look at the first entries of the first *column*, we see that Marc would be better off confessing than denying: 10 years in prison is better than 20 years in case of denying. And the same holds for the entries in the second column: one year in prison after confessing is to be preferred to two years after denying. So, as far as *Marc* is concerned, he *should confess, no matter what John may decide*. Let us look now at John's situation. If we look at the second entries of the first *row*, clearly 10 years in prison after confessing is better than 20 years after denying. And the same holds for John's entries in the second row: confessing means one year in prison, while denying would cost him two years. So, as with Marc, *John too should confess, no matter what Marc decides* to do.

Hence, both players, on undisputable rational grounds, will confess and therefore end up with ten years in prison each. Under such circumstances, confessing is said to be the *dominant strategy*. This holds true, despite the fact that both prisoners would get just two years had they both decided to deny. The PD shows that **what is optimal**

Table 4.1 One-Shot Prisoner's Dilemma

		John	
		Confess	*Deny*
Marc	Confess	−10, −10	−1, −20
	Deny	−20, −1	−2, −2

for each individual need not coincide with what is optimal for them as a group. Individual rationality sometimes comes into conflict with group rationality.

It is a common misunderstanding that the dilemma is a problem of communication. Note that the (misleading) initial assumption that the players were not able to communicate was in fact superfluous. Rational players, who are not necessarily moral players, will confess even if they get the opportunity to coordinate their strategies. Suppose both would promise to deny the charges, which would bring them to the optimal collective outcome: two years prison for each. If *Marc* thinks that John will *honour* his promise, he has an incentive to defect, that is: not to honour his own promise, as this would half his prison term from two years to just one year. Furthermore, Marc has a very strong incentive to confess if he suspects that John will *cheat* on him and confess, in which case he would end up with 20 years in prison instead of 2 years. So, Marc will confess, no matter what. However, given the symmetry in the structure of the PD, *John* will make exactly the same reasoning: he too will confess. Hence again, both will confess and end up in prison for ten years. As Elster remarks, this outcome is generated by a combination of the 'free rider temptation' (getting only one year) and the 'fear of being suckered' (getting 20 years) (ELSTER, 2007, p. 319).

The PD is much more than just an odd and somewhat artificial example of how people interact. PDs, and similar non-cooperative games, occur everywhere in society, including in the 'society of nations'.

A classic example is **OPEC**, the *Organisation of Petroleum Exporting Countries*. For each member state of the cartel, it is better to break out and produce a high volume of petroleum to exploit the high prices resulting from the output restrictions respected by the other member states ('free riding'). But if all do so, prices fall back to competitive levels and the whole point of the cartel disappears. Profit maximisation by each member undermines joint profit (group) maximisation.

Another example concerns the '*nuclear arms race*' between the US and the (former) Soviet Union which was essentially a race to get to parity, if not superiority, over the numbers and types of nuclear weapons possessed by the other (in the mid-1980s of last century there was enough nuclear firepower to destroy humankind several times over). So, what was at stake was *relative* military capability, not absolute. It is this basic insight that led to nuclear disarmament talks: bringing down the absolute levels of armament while respecting the relative position of quasi-parity among the contending parties. That is what happened with the New START treaty of 2010 (Strategic Arms Reduction Treaty) which reduced the number of deployed warheads for both parties to 1.550 over seven years. New START has been extended for five years on 26 January 2021.

Closer home we have of course the challenges posed by *pandemics* and *climate change*. Here too the issue is how to escape from the self-defeating competitive logic of PD and to embrace a cooperative logic instead. International cooperation is crucial in controlling the spread of *infectious diseases*. Somewhat simplifying, in the interdependent world which is ours, if one or a few countries fail to take the appropriate measures, others will not be able to protect themselves. An example in the context of *global warming* is the ongoing negotiation over emissions cuts. The European Union (EU) has regularly stated that it is prepared to reduce its emissions significantly, but only if the *others* too agree to do so. Here again, the worry is that others may unfairly gain benefits by free riding on the EU's actions. That was a serious concern with the US until President Biden decided to rejoin the 2015 Paris agreement.

As a final example, consider ***counterterrorism*** measures. If only one of two countries invests in such measures, it benefits the other as well as itself. If the costs exceed the benefits to itself, it will not invest unilaterally. Yet if both invest, their cooperation (the ability, for instance, to pool information) may lead to a greater security level for each than it could achieve by exploiting the investment of the other.

4.2 The iterated Prisoner's Dilemma – tit for tat

The preceding examples show that to escape from the competitive logic of the PD and get at a cooperative logic instead one needs to transition from the one-shot version of the game to its iterated version. In the standard version of the PD as presented above, the players had no reason to believe that they would ever meet again and face the same decision. However, in many cases, this restriction to *one-shot* games makes little sense. Many games are played many times. In iterated games, the strategies chosen by the players may very well be different from those chosen in one-shot games. To explain why this is so, we must distinguish between finitely and infinitely iterated games. In a finitely iterated game, the players know that at some stage they will be playing the last round. In infinitely iterated games, even though the game may actually end at some point, there is no point in time such that the players *know* that they are about to play the last round of the game. The distinction plays a huge difference to the analysis of iterated games.

Finitely iterated game. Suppose Marc and John play the iterated PD a *finite* number of times. Now, as they are about to play the last round, they both know that it is the last round and they both know that the other knows this as well. Hence, in the last round, both players will confess (for the reasons we gave in the one-shot scenario discussed earlier). Now, as the players are about to play the penultimate round, they both know that each of them will confess in the last round. Hence, a player who decides to cooperate (deny the charges) knows that he or she will not be rewarded for this in the next round. The other player will confess no matter what happens. Knowing all this, it is clearly better for each to confess also in the penultimate round. And that is what both players will also do in the pre-penultimate round of the game, and so on and forth. This pattern of interaction is called '***backward induction***'. The conclusion of this analysis is simple: in a finitely reiterated game, rational players will behave in exactly the same way as in the one-shot version of the game.

Infinitely iterated game. Now consider the *infinitely* iterated PD. Every time the players make their moves, they believe the game will be played again, against the same opponent. This stops the backward induction getting off the ground. In such infinitely iterated game, each player will adjust their next move to what the opponent did in the previous round. If she was cooperative (deny charges), so will I. If she defected (confessed), so will I. Both of us will soon see that playing the mutually beneficial strategy pays. In fact, by behaving in this way, players have adopted the clever strategy that goes by the name of 'tit for that': always cooperate in the first round, and thereafter adjust your behaviour to whatever your opponent did in the previous round.

An important point to stress in this regard is that transiting from playing 'one-shot' games to playing infinitely 'iterated' games actually means replacing **short-term tactical calculation** with **long-term strategic thinking**, which is key to effective diplomacy. Two points can be made in this regard.

One of the key features of a healthy **democracy** are its electoral cycles. This means, however, that a politician is virtually always in an electoral mood, wishing to ensure that next time again she will be elected. Democratic governance thus rewards politicians for placing the acceptability of short-term political action above the effectiveness of long-term, reasoned policy. Tactical moves then dominate strategic thinking. And it is not just elections that are to blame. More generally, the 'push and pull' of democratic politics (elections, partisan wrangling, legislative-executive discord, public opinion) is very much a mixed blessing when it comes to policy formulation, including foreign policy formulation. Already in the 1940s of last century, George Kennan lamented the inefficiencies of democratic foreign policy as did, one generation later, Nixon and Kissinger (BRANDS, 2014, p. 201). This is not to say that authoritarian regimes are necessarily better in formulating long-term foreign policy, but they seem to have an easier ride (think of 'the long view'-approach in foreign policy by China).

A second point to be made in this short-/long-term debate concerns the role of multilateral diplomacy generally and international organisations (IOs) particularly. **Multilateral diplomacy** can be seen as an *ongoing* process of negotiation characterised by its *serial* form of interaction – as opposed to the one-shot *ad hoc* form of interaction. In a continuous negotiation you never know whose help you may need tomorrow. You can never break with anyone, no matter how bad the quarrel. That is why multilateral diplomacy can be called a *regime of compulsory friendship* (COOPER, 2021, p. 483). A similar remark can be made as regards the nature and role of **international organisations**. An IO is an arrangement aimed at *facilitating cooperation*, in the game-theoretic sense of this word. An IO can best be conceived as a *standing* diplomatic conference, replacing its alternative – the periodic calling of distinct *ad hoc* conferences (BERRIDGE, 2010, p. 145). An example of such transition from conference to organisation is the Organisation for Security and Co-operation in Europe (OSCE) which, in 1984, replaced its predecessor, the Conference on Security and Cooperation in Europe (CSCE). The *permanent* nature of IOs, that is the fact that the interactions among its member states (*via* their *Permanent* Representations) take the form of an infinitely iterated game, is what allows a culture of cooperation and trust to prosper where group rationality trumps individual rationality, and everybody ends up better off.

Both these points are linked, of course. It is because multilateral diplomacy takes 'the long view' that IOs can be long-term norm-setters. And that is what we see happening; think of the 2000 UN Summit agreeing the *Millennium Development Goals* (updated in 2015 as *Sustainable Development Goals*) or the current debate on *climate change*. In fact, as we discussed in Chapter 2, that is what IOs are strong in: *norm-setting*. Compared to national governments, they are not (or at least less) hostage to the vicissitudes of the democratic process and can therefore do things that a state has difficulties doing. One should point to an irony in this regard. Decisions that are difficult to take at the national level are sometimes willingly relegated to the international level and then presented as 'imposed' by the relevant IO, without however being formally contested. Such contorted ways of acting (which are recurring in the EU, for instance) may not look very elegant but have the merit that they are far from useless. Being unfairly blamed (as often happens with the EU Commission, for instance) for doing what a national Government wishes to, but cannot do, is, all well considered, a rather small price to pay.

4.3 Other 'diplomatic' games

Other games that deserve attention from the point of view of diplomatic practice are the Game of Stag Hunt, the Battle of the Sexes, the Chicken Game, and finally the Ultimatum Game. We will treat them in that order.

Let us start with the **Game of Stag Hunt**, originally discussed by Jean-Jacques Rousseau. Two members of a pre-historical society must choose to either cooperate to hunt for stag together or go and hunt for hares each on their own. If the hunters cooperate and hunt for stag, each of them will get 25 kilos of meat; this is the best outcome for both hunters. Indeed, a hunter who hunts for stag when the other hunts for hare gets nothing. This is the worst outcome. A hunter hunting for hare on his own can expect to get a hare of five kilos.

In this game, there are *two equilibrium points*, not just one as was the case in the PD (these equilibrium points are 25, 25 and 5, 5). And this gives rise to two interesting concepts we often encounter in diplomatic practice: that of *risk aversion* and *trust*. To explain why, let us see how both hunters can reason. If hunter 1 is confident that hunter 2 is going to hunt for stag, then hunter 1 would have no reason to switch from 'hunting stag' to 'hunting hare'; nor would hunter 2 have any reason to switch from 'hunting stag' to 'hunting hare' if he knew that hunter 1 was going to hunt stag. Hence, hunting stag by both is in equilibrium, which means that each player's strategy is optimal against that of the other. However, note that this also holds for the opposite strategy: both hunting hare. If hunter 1 knew that hunter 2 was going for 'hunting hare', then hunter 1 would not be better off were he to switch from 'hunting hare' to 'hunting stag', and the same holds true of hunter 2 *mutatis mutandis*. Hence, hunting hare by both is again in equilibrium. The matrix for the Game of Stag Hunt looks as follows (see Table 4.2).

Note, however, that in the preceding analysis we used words like 'is confident' and 'thinks'; a player who is not that confident in what the other player will do, that is a player that is '**risk averse**', may always prefer to hunt for hare, since that will give him 5 kilos of meat for sure, that is, he runs no risk of ending up with nothing. Therefore, each player may stop worrying (that is: being confident, thinking) about what the other player will do, since it is better to be safe than sorry. This leads to a conclusion that is familiar from the study of PD: what is best for each (risk-averse) individual may not be the best for the group as a whole. To reach the outcome that is best for the group, we have to ensure that the players are prepared to take at least a moderate risk. Stag Hunt can therefore also be seen as illustrating the importance of **mutual trust** in human interactions. And that is no less true for international relations, including in a diplomat's dealings with colleagues (for example in a negotiation situation). We all benefit from optimal cooperation (as citizens, as nations), but to get there we need to trust each other. As we have seen, the benefits of trust can be undone by risk-averse players lacking confidence in the other players, in which case all end up with sub-optimal decisions.

The **Battle of the Sexes** is a game that illustrates the importance of **coordination** among players for them to reach a decision. The matrix for this game looks as follows (see Table 4.3).

Table 4.2 Stag Hunt Game

		Hunter 2	
		Stag	*Hare*
Hunter 1	Stag	25, 25	0, 5
	Hare	5, 0	5, 5

Table 4.3 Battle of the Sexes

		Marc	
		Opera	Football
Mary	Opera	2, 1	0, 0
	Football	0, 0	1, 2

Unlike Stag Hunt, this game cannot be dealt with by 'merely' establishing a certain degree of trust among the players. Consider the following story. Marc and Mary are lovers and wish to spend the night together and think about either going to the opera or attending a football match. They definitely prefer to do something together than going alone. Mary prefers to go to the opera, while Marc prefers to go to the football stadium. But again, both activities are worth undertaking just in case the other comes along. As in the Stag Hunt game, there are *two points of equilibrium* (2, 1 and 1, 2), but the payoffs for each partner are different. If you are Mary you will opt for the Opera-row since that will give you a payoff of 2 rather than the payoff of 1 if you were to choose the Football-row. For exactly the same reason Marc will opt for the Football-column, which gives him a payoff of 2 while the Opera column gives him a payoff of only 1. However, the problem is that these options, *taken jointly*, result in both Mary and Marc getting a payoff of 0. Fearing this, and definitely wishing to do something *together*, Mary may consider giving in and opt for the Football-row; after all, although 1 is less than 2 it is still more than 0. But if that is what Mary may be inclined to do, there is no reason why Marc would not also feel inclined to give in; he thus opts for the Opera-column. As in a Greek tragedy, these choices again end up with Mary and Marc getting a payoff of 0. Note that the *only assumption* made here is that *both players are very likely to reason in the same way*. What this game teaches us is that under the reasonable assumption just mentioned it seems almost certain that players will fail to reach an equilibrium point. The structure of the game is such that rational agents will not know how to meet on a common point. The situation is said to be **indeterminate**. The only way not to remain hostage of the 'internal' structure of the game, is to escape from the game and make an explicit 'external' agreement, that is, **coordinate** on meeting either on the opera or the football match.

In diplomacy, we often meet such coordination problems. They arise when *different* alternative solutions to a problem or controversy exist, *all of which* are better for all agents than no solution at all, but *each of which* is preferred by some agents to the others. In game-theoretic language: there are multiple equilibrium points and agreeing on one of them is better than not agreeing on any of them. Unless the agents involved step out of the scheme to see the global benefit of having a solution over having no solution at all, all loose.

As an example, consider **post-conflict peace-building**: *all* parties are convinced that having a political constitution (within a certain range of possible regimes) is necessary for long-term stability and is therefore much to be preferred to not having a constitution at all, but they fail to agree on a specific constitution within the range of possible regimes (parliamentary *versus* presidential regime, federal *versus* centralised state, proportional *versus* winner-takes-all electoral system). The common preference of all to have a constitution rather than no constitution trumps the different preferences of some

Table 4.4 Chicken Game

		John	
		Straight	*Swerve*
Marc	Straight	−100, −100	+1, −1
	Swerve	−1, +1	0, 0

for specific constitutions. Cooperation through coordination will allow them to escape from the dilemma.

The **Chicken Game** shows how players can rationally *win* a game only by not opting for the best outcome. Its matrix is as follows (see Table 4.4).

Two drivers, Marc and John, are driving at high speed in a straight line against each other. If neither of them swerves, they will both crash and die (−100). For both players, the best outcome (+1) is achieved if the other swerves (the other then gets −1 and is the 'chicken'). If both swerve no one gets anything (0). As in the Battle of the Sexes, there are *two equilibria points* (+1, −1 and −1, +1), but we cannot predict which of the two (if any) will be chosen. Again, from the point of view of rational choice, the situation is *indeterminate*.

The **Cuban Missile Crisis** is the most told and retold of all diplomatic stories and often cited as a case in which the two superpowers, the US and the Soviet Union, were locked in a Chicken-Game-like confrontation. In this situation, the Soviet Union 'blinked first', that is, in the example's terminology, swerved. If it had not and the US would also have persisted in its strategy of not-swerving, a nuclear confrontation between both great powers could have resulted in the 'crash and die' outcome of the game.

Some fear that a similar Chicken-Game-like confrontation, but this time between the US and China, may be in the making over **Taiwan**. For 71 years Taiwan's existence as a self-ruled island has relied on deterrence of Chinese aggression by the US. Observers of the Taiwan-scene note: first, that China is *losing patience* with Taiwan, as appears from recent military, economic, and diplomatic attempts at intimidation; second, that talk about 'peaceful reunification' is being replaced by *cold calculation*; to the hard men who rule China, history is not written by the squeamish; third, that China's single-minded pursuit of *militarisation* (advanced weapons and skills) may well be such as to keep US forces at bay in case of an invasion; and finally, that it is uncertain whether America's regional allies would be keen to join the US in defending Taiwan against China as they do not consider Taiwan's survival as a vital interest over which it is worth angering China, often their largest trading partner. In such context, the *potential for accidents and miscalculation leading to the 'crash and die' scenario* is never far off. In its very early days (January 2021) and in response to these fears, the Biden administration has declared its commitment to the island to be 'rock solid'. But some doubt that such verbal declaration is credible and think more should be done. One suggestion is to end the US policy of 'strategic ambiguity', which avoids making explicit pledges to respond to aggression against Taiwan (this policy is meant to discourage rash moves by Taiwan itself but also to avoid enraging China). Others want the US to shore up its military deterrence with credible 'geo-economic deterrence' (such as making clear that China will be expelled from the dollar-based financial and trading system if it attacks Taiwan) (see Chaguan, 'How to kill a democracy', The Economist, 20 February 2021).

Up to this point, we have been looking at games where the players were assumed to be rational and self-interested. But in diplomacy (as in real life) that is not always the case. Often factors such as *honour and pride* play an important part in the decision-making process; non-strategic considerations might be as important as strategic ones. Just to give the reader a taste of what is at play in these kinds of situations we now briefly present the *Ultimatum Game* which is of particular relevance in the context of negotiation.

The Ultimatum Game. You are given 100 Euro and must share it with another person, unknown to you. You can decide how it is divided up between you and the other. However, if he or she turns down the offer, you must return the entire 100 Euro; then, no one gets anything (that's 'the ultimatum'). How do you split the sum? It would make sense to offer the stranger very little (5 Euro, say). After all, from a *purely* rational point of view, something is better than nothing. But experiments show that this is not the way things work out. The other too has leverage. He knows that you will end up with nothing if he refuses your offer. So, you may not wish to press the lemon too much and therefore make a more *honourable* offer. This situation has been studied experimentally. The results obtained were that on average the offers fluctuated between 30 and 50 per cent. In many situations, particularly in a negotiation situation, you may find yourself in an 'ultimatum' scenario having the upper hand on your rival. But what the Ultimatum Game teaches us is that you had better not exploit your advantage to its full extent. If you do, you may end up with nothing rather than something.

Let us see how non-strategic considerations play out in politics generally and diplomacy specifically:

- At the **Federal Convention in Philadelphia in 1787,** there was a heated debate over the terms of accession to the Union of future western states. Some Convention members argued that while these states should be welcomed in the federation, they should be admitted only as second-rate states, so that they would never be able to outvote the original 13 states. Against this view, George Mason argued strongly saying that the new states would be unlikely to accept such *degrading* proposal. These were his words: 'They will have the same *pride* and other *passions* which we have, and will either not unite or will speedily revolt from the Union, if they are not in all respects placed on an equal footing with their brethren' (quoted in ELSTER, 2007, p. 332).

- Mason said that if the western states would not be treated honourably, and instead be offered unequal terms of accession, they 'will speedily revolt from the Union'. Something like that is what happened with the unfair deal that was the **Versailles Peace Treaty** of 1919. This treaty, closing World War I, but containing the seeds of World War II, has been decried as a *punitive treaty*, not a peace treaty. One may have crushed the enemy, won the war and be the undisputed victor, that is not enough to ensure lasting peace. The incapacity of the allies, or at least some of them, to make a balanced peace deal is what brought us from World War I to World War II. In his well-known stinging critique 'The Economic Consequences of the Peace' (published in 1919), John Maynard Keynes, a representative at the Paris Peace Conference who resigned in protest at the treaty's terms, denounced the treaty and its creators. He was kindest with Lloyd George, much more critical of Woodrow Wilson, but openly scornful of Georges Clemenceau, the man who viewed the affairs of Europe as 'a perpetual prize fight, of which France has won this round, but of which', Keynes adds, 'this round is certainly not the last'. Keynes unfortunately was proven right in his prediction (see SIRACUSA, 2010, pp. 48–51).

4.4 Rational empathy – entering into another's mind

In this section, we change track. From a strategic point of view, interactive diplomacy obliges us to take into account (or perhaps even anticipate on) what others are (or will be) saying, thinking, and doing so that we can adjust our responses adequately to it. That is what we looked at in the preceding sections. However, taking into account what others are saying (thinking, doing) *presupposes* that we got a proper understanding of what they were saying (thinking, doing). Understanding the mind of the other comes first. That is what 'rational empathy' is about. And that is no less a part of interactive diplomacy.

'Diplomacy must look at the situation from the point of view of other nations'. This is one of the six principles that Hans Morgenthau has spelled out in his so-called realist program. It is a crucial rule in diplomatic thinking. A diplomat will never be successful in their work if he or she does not come to terms with *why* other nations act as they do, with *what reasons* other people have in saying what they say. As one of the great characters in American fiction, Atticus Finch, once said: 'You never really understand a person until you consider things from his point of view…until you climb into his skin' (or rather – we would say – into his mind) 'and walk around in it' (see Box 4.1).

Box 4.1 McNamara on Vietnam

Here is what Robert McNamara, then Secretary of Defence, had to say about his greatest failure, Vietnam:

> 'We *misjudged* then – as we have since – the geopolitical intentions of our adversaries (…), we viewed the people and leaders of South Vietnam *in terms of our own experience*'. (…) 'our *misjudgement* of friend and foe alike reflected our profound ignorance of history, culture, and politics of the people of the area, and the personalities and habits of their leaders' (my italics)
> (McNAMARA and VAN DE MARK, 1996, pp. 321 and 339)

Entering into the mind of another is not just understanding what she says as a matter of communication (surface understanding) but grasping the very reasons or motives that make her say what she is saying (deep understanding, comprehending). In the context of diplomacy, this is not an easy task. Understanding may already be difficult when interacting with your neighbour next door, it becomes particularly challenging when discussing, debating, and negotiating with your colleague from the other hemisphere. Understanding the mind of another, deep understanding – *comprehending* – goes by the name of rational empathy. And empathy is not to be confused with sympathy.

Sympathy is also a way of putting yourself in another's place, but it differs from empathy in two respects. (1) Sympathy starts from the *assumption that the way you think and feel about the world is also the way others think and feel about the world*. Only then does it work. It is because of that *assumed* commonality in worldview and value-system that sympathy is not, as empathy is, a question of *understanding* the other's mind but rather of *identifying* with it, in particular with its owner's *feelings*. With sympathy, you take *your* feelings and simply project them onto others as a way of grasping how they presumably *also* feel about a particular situation. (2) As a consequence, with sympathy, you *side with* the other, you signal that you are with her, that she can count on you. That is not necessarily the case with empathy, which involves a cool, emotionless understanding of another's mind, including the mind of somebody for whom you may happen to have antipathy.

As a strategy, sympathy is only effective when people share a common worldview and common values. Sympathy ignores human cultural differences. In seeking to communicate with people from other cultures, however, it is simply not enough to imagine how *one's self* as a European, or American, or Asian might feel in a given situation. That is where empathy comes in.

Empathy is almost the reverse of sympathy. Empathy is what you need when you deal with people with a worldview and value-system that differs from yours. With empathy, you do *not assume* the other's worldview and value system to be yours. Empathy relies on one's ability to temporarily set aside one's own worldview and value-system. It invites us to recognise that the way we look at the world is not universal. But not only that. Getting out of your mindset is the first stage. Next comes getting into the other's mindset, being able to assume an alternative perspective. And that is the most difficult part. Getting into another's mind is *not just 'imagining how things would look to us' from the other's point of view, but to 'understand how they look to him' from his point of view* (BAGGINI, 2018 , p. xix). In a negotiation situation, for instance, when you, being a Canadian, are confronted with a statement made by your Chinese colleague that does not make much sense to you, the challenge is to get to see how it makes sense to him. In this, you will need to be 'charitable', that is: making a genuine effort to reconstruct the other's thought as good as you can (see Box 4.2).

Box 4.2 The Rule of Charity

The rule of charity plays an important role in negotiation. But it can easily be misunderstood as it touches upon an intrinsic ambivalence in negotiation, which is *a cooperative undertaking among competitors*. The rule of charity, its name notwithstanding, does not prescribe that you must be 'understanding' of your opponent's position, give in to him or somehow sympathise with his point of view (you are in competition); what it says is that, given the shared objective of reaching an agreement (cooperation), it is in both his *and* your interest to genuinely understand the point your opponent is making. For this, you will try to mentally enter into his mind so as to not just understand *what* he is saying (language) but comprehend *why* he is saying it (thought). And your opponent should do the same with you.

Once you come to see how your opponent sees things *from their point of view*, you can crawl back to your ways of seeing and adjust to the situation; you may, for instance in a negotiation situation, find out that the controversy rests on a misunderstanding, or you may come to understand that your argument was misdirected. It should be stressed again that empathy is not to be confused with sympathy. Empathy is not about feelings;

it is not a sentimental affair; it is about intellectually understanding in the coolest way possible another's thoughts. Empathy does not aim at being nice to others or being sympathetic towards them. More often, in diplomacy, the other will be your opponent in negotiation or your adversary in a tense or conflictual situation. Your basic attitude towards him will probably be one of scepticism and perhaps even antipathy. When George Kennan wrote his *Long Telegram*, it was essentially meant as a warning for a certain *naiveté* in Washington; his message was: do not think these people are like us. Empathy is about understanding the mind of another, particularly when the other happens to be your enemy.

Let us illustrate the preceding remarks and make matters more tangible by considering the Western mindset (Europeans, Americans, and Australasians) and compare it with the Eastern mindset (particularly, the Far Eastern mindset of China, Korea, and Japan). For the sake of clarity, our approach will be schematic and as a result simplifying. The core question that needs to be addressed is whether, notwithstanding our different ways of looking at the world (Western and Eastern), we still are in a position to bridge the divide; or whether, conversely, the Western and Eastern *worldviews* (the fundamental beliefs we entertain about the world), *value-systems* (the values that subtend it), and *cognitive* apparatuses (the characteristic thought processes) are that far apart from each other that it becomes virtually impossible to get to understand each other; in such extreme situation, they are said to be '*incommensurable*', which means – literally – that there is no common measure that allows us to talk to and understand each other; our mental languages are then simply too far apart.

To see what we mean, let us point to some of the differences between the Western and the Eastern mind as far as their **belief systems and cognitive processes** are concerned (NISBETT, 2003, passim):

- The Western mind thinks in terms of discrete *objects* (atomistic, modular), whereas the Eastern mind attends to continuous *events*, that is relations between objects in their broad situational context (holistic, relational).
- The Western mind organises the world in substantive *categories* (space, time, quantity, quality, etc.) and explains events in terms of straightforward rules such as the laws of physics (*simplicity*), whereas the Eastern mind sees *part-whole* relationships which can only be understood by taking into account a host of factors that operate in relation to each other in no simple way (*complexity*).
- The Western mind sees the world as closed, *static*, linear, and governed by strict causality between discrete objects, and hence as *deterministic* and predictable, whereas for the Eastern mind the world is open, *dynamic*, cyclic, and in constant flux and reflux with continuous events being *context driven*. Where Westerners see stability, Easterners see change.
- As a result, for the Western mind, the world, because of its simplicity, is *controllable*, whereas for the Eastern mind the world is *complex and diffuse*.
- The Western mind relies on rigid *logic* in problem-solving, whereas the Eastern mind relies on a less articulate but also more versatile *dialectical* approach to problem-solving.

With this last point regarding **logic** *versus* **dialectic**, we get rather deep down in the minds of Westerners and Easterners. That is reason enough to briefly elaborate on the point as it sheds a clear light on rather fundamental issues (at least for a Western mind, less for an Eastern mind who would consider the western obsession with logic as a token of immaturity).

Let us have a look at the *three most basic laws of formal logic* as we in the West know them. First, there is the *law of identity*, which holds that a thing is itself and nothing else: 'A=A'. Second, there is the *law of non-contradiction*, which holds that a statement cannot be both true and false: 'not (A and not-A)'. And third, there is the law known as the *law of the excluded middle*, which holds that a statement is either true or false, so 'A or not-A'; there is no middle, third alternative. Note that the second principle states that *at most* one of the two alternatives A and not-A must be true while the third principle states that *at least* one must be true. These three laws of logic have baffled many a potential student of logic, while attracting those of a more mathematical bent.

The Western insistence on this triple of logical principles and the Eastern spirit of dialecticism are, on the surface at least, in direct opposition to each other. The *law of identity* insists on cross-situational consistency: 'A=A' regardless of the context. The Eastern *principle of holism*, on the contrary, tells that a thing differs from one context to another, so: 'A=not-A'; a man is a different person in the family than in his role as a businessman; Zen: 'The Bodhi tree is not a tree, and the bright mirror is not a mirror'. The *law of non-contradiction* says that a statement and its negation cannot both be true. The *principle of change* indicates that the world is in a continuous flux from one state to another, so that what is, is also not, and vice versa, so: 'A and not-A'; wealth means poverty is around the corner; wealthy now, poor tomorrow; Daoism: 'Sometimes diminishing a thing adds to it; sometimes adding to a thing diminishes it'. The *law of the excluded middle* says that for any statement, at least one of the two truth-values must apply: true or false, and nothing in between. Not so for the Easterners, however, for them: 'not (A or not-A)': Brahman is 'not this, not that'; given the limitations of human language, the nature of Brahman cannot be captured by it (NISBETT, 2003, pp. 177–185).

We, Westerners, will of course easily point to the fact that the family father and businessman are indeed the same man, but not in the same way, and that the wealthy and poor man too are the same man, but not at the same time. What have we to make of all this?

- For the either-or logic to work it is essential that there is no ambiguity (when the meaning is unclear) or equivocation (when more than one meaning is possible). And the Easterners would probably agree with that. For them, however, the real controversy between West and East as regards the laws of logic is how useful they are, given that the world itself *is* often 'unclear and ambiguous', that is, indeterminate, and that, as a consequence, we must learn to live with a measure of uncertainty, something that the Western mind, at unease in a world lacking certainty, would resist.
- The Easterner would also contend that language falls short in capturing ultimate reality because even if it were clear and unambiguous, reality defies the neat categorisations of our limited words and concepts; and he would therefore add that attempts to get to ultimate reality are futile and misdirected anyway.

The difference, then, between the dominant ways of thinking in the West and the East is not that the former embraces the three basic laws of logic, which the latter rejects. Rather, the difference is the extent to which these laws are foregrounded and taken to be practically important. And this has important implications going beyond questions of logic and thinking proper. Western binary and dichotomous thinking ('either-or' rather than 'both-and') has permeated political and diplomatic culture. An antagonistic spirit of enquiry is antithetical to cooperation, compromise, and seeking common ground. Also, a dichotomous and adversarial mindset leads to polarisation, it allows only for true or false, winner and loser. A logic of either-or easily turns into the logic of the zero-sum game in which only one side can win. And when there are several plausible views, a binary mindset finds it hard to manage the complexity that this creates (BAGGINI, 2018, pp. 56–59). One can understand that such differences easily translate into different *'styles' of diplomacy*, that is *ways* of approaching diplomacy and of doing it. That would merit a study on its own.

Having thus looked at the dominant belief systems and cognitive processes of Westerners and Easterners we can come to a better understanding of **the social structures** and the **sense of self** that are characteristic of both groups. Not surprisingly these fit hand in glove with their belief and cognitive systems. The communitarian nature of Asian society (interdependency), where the *community prevails on the individual*, and its stress on harmony, is consistent with Asian's contextual, holistic view of the world and their belief that events are highly complex and simultaneously related to many intervening factors. The individual is not defined as a self-standing entity but as part of a network. The individualistic nature of Western society (independency), where *the individual trumps the community*, is consistent with the Western atomistic focus on objects in isolation from their context and with the Westerner's belief that they can know the rules (laws) governing the behaviour of objects and therefore control them. From there we can again move one level up. If people really do differ profoundly in their systems of thought – their worldviews and cognitive processes – and in their social structures then differences in people's **attitudes** and **values and preferences**, might not be a matter merely of different inputs and teachings (nurture), but rather an inevitable consequence of using different tools to understand the world (nature). And if that is true, then efforts by us, poor diplomats, to improve international understanding may be less likely to succeed than we might have hoped.

When we looked at reasoning in diplomacy in the preceding chapter, we were approaching decision-making essentially from the perspective of a single decision-maker. But much of what we decide in diplomacy will depend on what others are saying, thinking, planning, and doing. And we had better take this into account when making our own decisions. That is where interactive diplomacy comes into play. There are two aspects to it. The first concerns strategic thinking, that is working out a winning strategy. The merit of game theory is that it explicitly uncovers the structure of interactions that may not be immediately visible, particularly not in the context of international politics. That is why the study of game theory can be useful for diplomacy. Just recall how the strategies deployed by the players differ according to whether they operate in the context of the one-shot or the iterated PD. Uncovering the structure of the game allowed us to get a grip on the underlying logic of such concepts as short-term tactical calculation *versus* long-term strategic thinking, or the difference between a one-shot *ad hoc* bilateral arrangements *versus* iterated interactions occurring in multilateral diplomacy. The other aspect of interactive diplomacy concerns 'rational empathy'. You cannot effectively interact with another without making sure that you properly understand him. Misunderstandings easily lead to miscalculations. The central point here is that understanding is not just a matter of *what* but of *why* things are being said or done. To stress that distinction we introduced the concept of 'comprehending', that is deep understanding. For that, one needs to enter into the mind of another. Getting out of your own mind (habits, preconceptions, prejudices...) is already difficult enough. Entering into that of another adds to the challenge as we saw when comparing the Western with the Eastern mind.

Bibliography

BAGGINI, Julian (2018), *How the World Thinks: A Global History of Philosophy*, Granta, London.

BAIRD, Douglas G., GERTNER, Robert H. & PICKER, Randal C. (1994), *Game Theory and the Law*, Harvard University Press, Cambridge, MA.

BASANEZ, Miguel E. (2016), *A World of Three Cultures*, Oxford University Press, Oxford.

BINMORE, Ken (2007), *Game Theory – A Very Short Introduction*, Oxford University Press, Oxford.

BRANDS, Hal (2014), *What Good Is Grand Strategy?*, Cornell University Press. Ithaca, NY.

ELSTER, Jon (2007), *Explaining Social Behavior*, Cambridge University Press, Cambridge.

GLADWELL, Malcolm (2019), *Talking to Strangers: What We Should Know about the People We Don't Know*, Penguin, New York, NY.

HARGREAVES HEAP, Shaun, HOLLIS, Martin, LYONS, Bruce, SUGDEN, Robert & WEALE, Albert (1992), *The Theory of Choice – A Critical Guide*, Blackwell, London.

HAZAREESINGH, Sudhir (2015), *How the French Think*, Basic Books, New York, NY.

MERNISSI, Fatema (2001), *Sheherazade Goes West – Different Cultures, Different Harems*, Washington Square Press, New York, NY.

McNAMARA, R. S. & VAN DE MARK, B. (1996), *In Retrospect – The Tragedy and Lessons of Vietnam*, New York, NY.

NISBETT, Richard E. (2003), *The Geography of Thought. How Asians and Westerners Think Differently... and Why*, Free Press, New York, NY.

PETERSEN, Martin (2009), *An Introduction to Decision Theory*, Cambridge University Press, Cambridge.

SIRACUSA, Joseph M. (2010), *Diplomacy – A Very Short Introduction*, Oxford University Press, Oxford.

STEWART, Edward C. & BENNETT, Milton J. (1991), *American Cultural Patterns. A Cross-Cultural Perspective*, Intercultural Press, Boston, MA/London.

VAN IJZERDOORN, Patrick (2008), *London Denkt*, Boom.

5 Logical fallacies and cognitive traps

When reasoning in diplomacy, as in our daily lives, we are prone to make errors. The difference is, however, that for reasons of magnitude and importance, making errors in diplomacy will generally be more consequential than errors made in our daily lives; directing states' behaviour differs from conducting one's life as an individual. There are two kinds of errors in reasoning that need to be distinguished: formal fallacies and cognitive traps. There is a third kind of 'error', not in reasoning, however, but in argumentation where it can be used as a deceptive tactic; we will just mention it for the sake of completeness but not study it.

(1) Errors in logic are called **formal fallacies**. When somebody tells you that whenever A occurs, B must occur (if A, then B) you will be tempted to conclude that since B occurred, A must have occurred (B, hence A), which is not correct. You are making the *logical fallacy* called *affirming of the consequent*. When somebody asks you about 'the taste of the moon', he is making the *quasi-logical fallacy* that goes by the name of *category mistake*: taste is not a predicate (attribute) that fits the moon.

(2) Logical and quasi-logical fallacies are not the only threats to clear thinking. **Cognitive traps** are no less menacing. These are systematic errors we commit in reasoning and are called traps because of their insidious character. They are linked to Kahneman's intuitive, spontaneous 'Thinking Fast' mode of reasoning that we discussed earlier and against which we had to erect the 'Thinking Slow' mode of reasoning as a corrective. The latter is the conscious, articulate, and discursive way of reasoning that we find in logic. Among the cognitive traps, a distinction is often made between heuristics and biases. *Heuristics* are shortcuts in reasoning that we readily (most often unconsciously) use to solve routine problems in a simple and efficient manner, but which become unreliable when tackling more sophisticated questions. The *availability heuristic* is a well-known example (see below). *Biases* are deep-seated tendencies or hidden presuppositions or presumptions rooted in our psychology and often related to the preservation of our self-image. The *confirmation bias* that we discuss below together with the availability heuristic is a prominent example.

(3) There is a third kind of 'errors', one that we meet in persuasive *argumentation*, and which are closely linked to diplomatic practices such as debate and negotiation. These, however, are 'errors' which we may make on purpose (examples are the 'ad personam' argument or the 'straw man' fallacy). They then function as a deceptive tactic in argumentation. Their specific characteristic is that they break or tamper with one or more of the often-implicit rules governing the proper conduct

DOI: 10.4324/9781003298182-8

of a debate or a negotiation. Traditionally, they were called *sophisms* but today are known as **informal fallacies**. As these fallacies concern argumentation, rather than reasoning, we will not consider them here.

To see how cognitive traps and logical fallacies interact, and more broadly how Fast Thinking relates to Slow Thinking, let us have a look at a pleasant and intriguing puzzle known as the '**Wason selection task**'. It is a perfect illustration of how cognitive traps (in particular the *confirmation bias*) can get us *astray* of proper thinking into logical fallacies (in particular the *affirming the consequent fallacy*) and how, conversely, proper logic must come to the rescue to *correct* improper thinking and get us *back again on the right track*. The Wason selection task runs as follows: you receive four cards of a game of cards. One side of each card shows a letter which will be either a vowel or a consonant. The other side of each card shows a number, either even or uneven. The four cards are:

A D 4 7

You are given the following rule:

If on one side a card shows a vowel,
then on the other side it shows an even number.

You no doubt recognise the form of this rule. It is that of a conditional statement, the kind of statement we met when studying conditional reasoning. It is now up to you *to verify the truth of that statement.* Your task is: which card (or cards) must I turn to know for sure that this conditional statement is true, that is that the rule has been properly followed? Take your time to reflect on this puzzle. It is worth it. Let us see what the right answer is:

- If you turn ***card A***, then you can verify whether the 'if' – part (vowel) is indeed followed by the 'then' – part (even number). Suppose an uneven number shows up, then you know for sure that the statement is untrue (you have falsified it), that the rule has not been followed. So, *you must turn card A.*
- If you properly understand the 'if...then' – sentence, you will also understand that *you must turn **card 7***. Suppose you see a vowel on its other side. Then this is a card with a vowel on one side (the 'if' – side) and an uneven number on the other side (the 'then' – side). You have again falsified the conditional statement.
- You *need not turn **card D***. The statement tells you what you should see on the other side of a card showing a vowel, not what you should see on the other side of a card showing a consonant. Whether on the other side of card D you see an even or uneven number is if no significance. Card D is irrelevant.
- Card 4 is irrelevant as well. You *need not turn **card 4*** either. Suppose you find a consonant on its other side. Is that a problem, is the rule falsified? No, it is not, because the rule is simply not applicable. We are back to the preceding case (card D). And if on the other side a vowel shows up, does that help you in verifying the statement? No, whether a vowel or consonant shows up on the other side is of no help to you to decide on the truth of the statement.

On average, only half of the participants succeed in solving the Wason selection task properly. The culprit is the so-called **confirmation bias**, a very pervasive cognitive trap that makes us systematically look for (positive) facts that confirm, not (negative) facts that disconfirm a rule that we must evaluate. Almost everybody reads an 'if…then' – sentence as an instruction to look for confirmation of the 'if' – side. And that is why most of them turn card A, rightly so. But then they continue searching for confirmation of the 'if' – side by turning card 4, hoping to see a vowel appear there as if this were of any help, *quod non* (as we have shown above). Few people see that the other critical card to be turned is card 7, because this can lead to the falsification of the rule. In short, most people focus on cards that can confirm the rule, but they do not search cards that could disconfirm it (see Box 5.1).

Box 5.1 An Old Joke

This is the story of a policeman who sees an inebriated man searching for his keys under a lamp post and offers to help find them. After a few fruitless minutes, the officer asks the man whether he is certain he dropped his keys at that particular location. No, says the man, he lost them in the park. Then, why search here, asks the officer. The man answers: 'Because that's where the light is' (see The Economist, 'Free exchange. A question of illumination', 12 December 2020).

5.1 Logical and quasi-logical fallacies

We will distinguish logical from quasi-logical fallacies. The first, the logical fallacies, contradict logic proper, they are **invalid** reasonings. The second comes in two categories: those that do not contradict logic and hence are valid reasonings, but happen to be inert, unhelpful, or misleading; and those that fall outside the scope of logic proper.

5.1.1 Logical fallacies

We start with recalling without further comment the fallacies we already met when discussing **conditional reasoning** earlier and which we illustrated with the Karadzic-Srebrenica example. We will simplify that example and present its underlying logic in terms of 'raining' and 'wet streets'. Remember, a conditional statement has the form of 'if…then…'; it is the kind of statement we met in the Wason selection test. Recall that there are two valid ways to reason with such conditional statement:

• Either you *affirm the antecedent*, and the consequent follows necessarily: 'if p, then q', and: 'p', therefore: 'q' (for example: 'if it rains, then the street is wet', and: 'it rains', therefore: 'the street is wet').
• Or you *deny the consequent* and then the denial of the antecedent follows necessarily: 'if p, then q', and: 'not-q', therefore: 'not-p' (for example: 'if it rains, then the street is wet', and: 'the street is not wet', therefore: 'it does not rain').

In conditional reasoning, *two fallacies* lurk around the corner:
Denying the antecedent (rather than *affirming* it).

'If p, then q'
But: 'not p'
Hence: 'not q'

For example: 'if it rains, then the street is wet', but: 'it does not rain', therefore: 'the street is not wet'. The conclusion does not follow from the premises. The conclusion would have followed from the premises if the conditional statement read as follows: 'if not p, then not q'. But that is not what we started with.

Affirming the consequent (rather than *denying* it).

'If p, then q'
And: 'q'
Hence: 'p'

For example: 'if it rains, the street is wet', and: 'the street is wet', therefore: 'it rains'. Again, this is no valid reasoning. The conditional statement flows from p to q, not the other way round. The conclusion would have followed from the premises if the conditional statement read as follows: 'if q, then p'.

A *third fallacy* that is recurrent in politics and diplomacy is the **False Dilemma**. To properly understand this fallacy, one needs to clarify the distinction between contradictory and contrary statements. Two statements p and q are **contradictory** when it is *impossible that both are true*, and it is *impossible that both are untrue*. So, out of a pair of contradictory statements, one of them must necessarily be true. Take the following two statements: 'All Europeans (defined as nationals of any of the 27 member states) are European citizens' (which is true by virtue of the Treaty on European Union [TEU], the so-called Lisbon Treaty) and 'Some Europeans are not European citizens'. These statements are contradictory: if the first of these is true the second cannot be true (it is impossible that both are true), and if the first one is untrue as was the case before the adoption of the TEU, then the second must be true (it is impossible that both are untrue). The situation is different in the case of statements that are **contrary**. Two statements p and q are contrary when it is *impossible that both are true*, while it is *possible that both are untrue*. 'Bolsonaro is an American citizen' and 'Bolsonaro is a European citizen'. If one of these statements is true, then the other must be untrue, but the untruth of one statement does not imply the truth of the other; it is perfectly possible (and in fact the case) that Bolsonaro is neither an American nor a European citizen. With contrary statements you are not locked up with an *either-or dilemma* as you are with contradictory statements: there is a way out, a *third possibility*. And that is where the false dilemma shows up. A false dilemma emerges when contrary statements are presented as contradictory statements. The classic example is Dostoyevsky's famous statement 'If God does not exist, then everything is permitted' (which is equivalent to stating 'Either God exists, or everything is permitted'). An example of such logical fallacy in politics is the well-known statement made by George W. Bush in the context of the 9/11 events and his declaration of war on terror with fundamentalist Islam as the new enemy: '*You are either with us, or against us!*'. Both statements ('either with us' and 'against us') are presented as if they were contradictory, that is as if there were no third possibility, while, in fact, they are contrary statements leaving a third possibility open: one can be neither with nor against the US in its war on terror (see Box 5.2). Let us close with one more example. In Europe, a fruitless debate has been going on for decades as regards the 'nature' of the EU: is it an 'international organisation' or is it a 'state'. Partisans of either option have been trapped in a false either-or dilemma. The answer may well be that it is neither: no longer a classic intergovernmental organisation but not yet a federal state.

Box 5.2 Us and Them

Identifying threatening enemies is often central to crystallising a sense of purpose and identity. An example is the concept of 'Cold War' that provided a clear sense of purpose and direction around the notions of **'East' and 'West'**. Indeed, with the end of the cold war and the enemy gone, the question arose as to what *the West's purpose, role, and identity* were in the new context. More specifically the question arose of what NATO could still be about. A question that was openly asked by the then Deputy Secretary of State Strobe Talbott in 1994. The short answer could have been that NATO had no role to play anymore and could be disbanded, as the Warsaw Pact had been. But the answer went in the opposite direction. Instead of disbanded, NATO was set on a new course: first, through its enlargement program and second, with the so-called new out of area missions assigned to it.

In diplomacy, avoiding being trapped in a false dilemma is what the principles of *neutrality and impartiality* aim at safeguarding, principles that we met when studying mediation as a form of Track II-diplomacy in chapter 2 of this book. Avoiding to become hostage of the false dilemma between capitalism and communism was also what the *Non-Aligned Movement* (NAM) during the cold war was about; not surprisingly the movement 'moved' into a diplomatic dead-end after having lost much of its meaning, and therefore of its clout and appeal, with the disappearance of the bipolar world.

5.1.2 *Quasi-logical fallacies*

Quasi-logical fallacies come in two groups. The first group encompasses reasonings which, although logically valid, somehow show features that make them suspect or unsuitable for effective reasoning. The second group encompasses reasonings that are not logically valid, not because they infringe the rules of deductive logic, but simply because they do not belong to the realm of deductive logic proper.

Let us start looking at the sparsely populated *first group*, that of the logically valid reasonings that are, however, for reasons that we will spell out, inert, unhelpful or misleading. Take **circularity**. In circular reasoning, the conclusion is somehow presupposed in the premise(s), implicitly or explicitly. That is why such reasoning is known as '*begging the question*' (in more learned language: '*principio principii*'). From a purely logical point of view, there is nothing wrong in deducing A from A; 'A, therefore A' is valid reasoning, but it is trivial reasoning, not in any way helpful, because the premise *does not support* the conclusion. An example of circular reasoning would be: 'The principle of sovereign equality among states is unassailable, since any infringement of the principle is considered to be an open breach of public international law'. With this, you have said nothing; your conclusion ('being unassailable') is a mere paraphrase of your premise ('an infringement being a breach'). Still, such misleading although logically correct reasoning is not always easy to detect, particularly not when one or more premises are hidden or tacitly assumed to be true. An example: 'No uncertainty exists as regards the legality of the principle of territorial integrity, because as all states adhere to this principle of public international law, its legality is uncontested'. Here the circularity is between 'no uncertainty' (conclusion) and 'uncontested' (premise), which virtually mean the same thing, while the premise that 'all states adhere to this principle' is tacitly assumed to be true. A good trick to detect a circular argument is to see whether you can easily inverse the reasoning 'A, because B' ('no uncertainty' because 'uncontested') into 'B, because A' ('uncontested', because 'no uncertainty').

The **Slippery Slope Fallacy** also belongs to the category of valid but misleading deductive reasonings. How did you go bankrupt, asks a character in the Hemingway novel *The Sun also Rises*. 'Two ways', comes the reply, 'gradually, and then suddenly'. This fallacy occurs when a sequence of closely linked similar steps ultimately leads to an unacceptable result. It starts with acknowledging that a given difference between A and B is not significant, and since A is acceptable so is B. Then, since there is a similar relationship between B and C, as there was between A and B, it *must be* conceded that C is acceptable as well. This step-by-step reasoning continues until, eventually, one arrives at some absurd or disastrous result (see Box 5.3).

Box 5.3 The Sorites Paradox

The Slippery Slope Fallacy is a direct descendant of a paradox with an ancient pedigree, known as the Sorites paradox or the *paradox of the heap*. The reasoning is disarmingly simple:

- One grain of sand does not constitute a heap. If one grain of sand does not constitute a heap, then two grains of sand do not constitute a heap. Therefore: two grains of sand do not constitute a heap.
- Two grains of sand do not constitute a heap. If two grains of sand do not constitute a heap, then three grains of sand do not constitute a heap. Therefore: three grains of sand do not constitute a heap.
- …
- 999,999 grains of sand do not constitute a heap. If 999,999 grains of sand do not constitute a heap, then 1,000,000 grains of sand do not constitute a heap. Therefore: 1,000,000 grains of sand do not constitute a heap.

This is a valid deductive reasoning. The two premises are: *(1) one grain of sand is not a heap; and (2) if n grains of sand do not constitute a heap, then neither do n+1 grains of sand.* The conclusion is: *any number of grains of sand do not constitute a heap.* Both premises are indisputably true, and the conclusion is indisputably untrue. Hence the label 'paradox'. To solve the paradox, more than two values (true or untrue) need to be attributed to statements. In between true (1) and untrue (0), there are infinitely many values one can postulate: 0.01, 0.553, 0.89, and so on. The statement 'one grain of sand does not constitute a heap' gets the value 1 (manifestly true) and the statement '1,000,000 grains of sand do not constitute a heap' gets value 0 (manifestly untrue). And the statements in between these two (for example: '4867 grains of sand do not constitute a heap' will get some value in between 1 and 0, for example: 0.234 [neither manifestly true nor manifestly untrue]) (see Louis Demey, 'Waarheid', Leuven, 2019, pp. 156–158).

Escalation and spiralling are well-known concepts in international security studies. As fear grows in a state due to perceived hostile actions by another state, this will cause an escalation in hostile behaviour and fear among the states, adding to the tense situation and perhaps leading to pre-emptive war. The development and proliferation of nuclear weapons during the Cold War provides a good example of how the *security dilemma* can produce spirals of insecurity and arms races (see Box 5.4).

Box 5.4 The Security Dilemma

The security dilemma is a central concept in international security studies and is directly linked to the concepts of *anarchy* and *self-help*. Kenneth Waltz, the father of the neo-realist school in international politics, explains why states do what they do by focusing on the *structure* of the international system rather than the strategies and motivations of national leaders. Here is what he has to say on this:

> 'With many sovereign states, with no system of law enforceable among them (*anarchy*), with each state judging its grievances and ambitions according to the dictates of its own reason or desire (*self-help*) – conflict, sometimes leading to war, is bound to occur'. (…) 'Because each state is the final judge of its own cause, any state may at any time use force to implement its policies. Because any state may at any time use force, all states must constantly be ready either to counter force with force or to pay the cost of weakness'.
> (quoted from his 'Man, the State and War: A Theoretical Analysis', New York, NY, 1959, reprinted in HANDLER, 2013, p. 31)

An example closer to diplomacy concerns the *constitution of ad hoc groups* of countries called upon to manage certain crisis situations. One generally starts out with a restricted group, but then comes diplomatic pressure to admit another country to the group. This admission in turn raises a legitimate claim for yet another country to be admitted and so on. In EU foreign policy, it often happened that once you started opening a core group (say, Germany, France, and pre-Brexit UK) to others, say Italy, then you had to go further and include Spain, in which case you could not avoid taking up Poland as well, at which point The Netherlands made its claims known too, and so on. A good case of such slippery-slope group expansion was the so-called Balkan Working Group (BWG) that in the mid-1990s supervised EU's policy regarding the former Yugoslavia. Almost any member of the then 15-member EU claimed to have some good reason to be part of it; with expansion came dilution and with dilution substitution of the BWG by a smaller core group where the real business was carried out. A similar development has been noted in the G20, established in 2008 mainly as a response to the 2007–2008 financial crisis, which started as a closed club of 20 countries but where soon several countries have been invited (generally by the host country) to join the permanent members on an *ad hoc* basis first and a *semi-permanent* basis later (invited countries include The Netherlands, invited by Canada, Ethiopia [Chair NEPAD], Malawi [Chair AU], and Singapore [invited by Korea] [see BARSTON, 2019, p. 138]). It is worth pondering what President Obama, not without some irony, said when arguing for a limited size of the G20: 'Everyone wants the smallest possible group that includes them'.

There are a few other logically valid reasonings that deserve the label quasi-logical fallacy. As they are of marginal utility for our purposes, however, we will skip them, except one: the simple rule that *from inconsistent (that is contradictory) premises, any (arbitrary) conclusion follows*. In such situation **everything goes**, an idea captured in the Latin sentence with which logicians refer to it: '*ex falso sequitur quodlibet*'. Such reasonings cannot prove anything since the premises, being contradictory, can never be jointly true, and hence everything can be concluded from them. So, although valid, such reasonings can never be sound. Their interest for the diplomat is that it suffices for him to point to a contradiction among the premises of his opponent's reasoning to reject the conclusion outright.

We can now move to the much more populated **second group** of quasi-logical fallacies, those that fall outside the realm of deductive reasoning. We can be brief in our review as these fallacies do not require elaborate comments.

We start with **over-generalisation,** a fallacy we briefly touched upon when discussing inductive reasoning; it is also known by its Latin name of *secundum quid*. Over-generalisation is unjustified or hasty generalisation: *concluding too much and too fast on the basis of too small a sample*, as in the statement that 'all failing states are badly governed'. Some states may fail for reasons other than bad governance such as demographic pressure, climate change (desertification), pandemics (Ebola, SARS, and Covid-19), and endemic instability. Think of Afghanistan after President Ashraf Ghani took over from Hamid Karzai. An integer and former high-level World Bank official, Ghani made very serious efforts in good governance but still did not succeed in redressing his country out of the 'failing states' – category.

Variants on this fallacy are stereotypical or exemplary thinking. *Stereotypical reasoning* is what happens when you generalise on one single or just a few '*typical*' observations. The Chernobyl and later Fukushima nuclear fallouts were generalised over all nuclear installations as being intrinsically vulnerable and made many governments turn away from nuclear energy, thus creating new energy dependencies not without geo-economic implications (think of the Nord Stream 2 controversy). *Exemplary reasoning* generalises on merely anecdotal but somehow '*significant*' evidence (as when you generalise from Vladimir Putin as a 'model' for defining what a strong leader looks like). The culprit in this kin of generalisation is the so-called *availability heuristic* which we will study in the next section.

An important and recurrent fallacy is the result of confusing correlation with causation. It is known as the *post hoc, ergo propter hoc* fallacy, but we will simply refer to it as the **correlation-causation fallacy**. The confusion is facilitated by a mistaken reading of the conditional 'if…then…' statement as establishing a causal relation rather than a mere logical one; compare 'if we are the 4th of July today, then it is America's Independence Day' (correlation) with 'if an atomic bomb is dropped over Hiroshima, then many of its citizens die' (causation). Three points should be stressed: (1) Causes *precede* their effects. Causes have a temporal direction (from cause to effect). Therefore, only correlations which are temporally asymmetric can give rise to the fallacy. (2) Causes are not just followed by their effects, they *produce* them; lift the cause, and the effect is lifted too. (3) Correlated facts which are not causally related often can be explained in terms of a third intervening variable which is their *common cause*.

An example of a *clear causal relation* is the civil-disobedience movement in Myanmar in early 2021 in the wake of the military *coup d'état* ousting President Aung San Suu Kyi. A *questionable causal relation* is the one suggested by European populists who state that immigration is the main cause of the continent's socio-economic malaise. An example of a *correlation* in Covid-19 times is the one between doubting the safety of vaccines and voting for populist parties (a correlation established by Jonathan Kennedy of Queen Mary University of London). As regards this last correlation, it has been suggested that a common cause lies at the heart of both: a distrust of experts, officials, and institutions (see The Economist, Charlemagne, 'Republic of cranks', 12 December 2020).

The **is/ought fallacy**, also known as the *naturalistic fallacy*, consists in deriving *norms*, telling us what *ought* (not) to be the case, from *facts*, that *is* what is (or was) the case. Facts do not dictate anything; they have no normative power. Take gender. Men and women obviously differ from each other, but that does not imply anything in terms of differential treatment, nor for that matter, of equal treatment. The Srebrenica massacre was a fact, a horrible fact, but only after its normative (legal) qualification as 'ethnic cleansing' (or indeed 'genocide') did it become a crime to be prosecuted by national tribunals and courts and ultimately by the International Criminal Tribunal for former Yugoslavia (ICTY).

The **category mistake** occurs when there is a misfit between subject and predicate, as when we ask for the smell of music or the taste of the moon. Closer to our diplomatic concerns: you can dispute the legitimacy of a regime, but not of a state; you can ask about the legality of a military action but not of a negotiation.

Next comes the fallacy of **composition and division** also known as the *part-whole fallacy*. Composition is when you attribute a feature of a part to the whole of which it is part *(pars pro toto)*. Division is the reverse, attributing features of the whole to its parts *(totum pro parte)*. All members of the European Union (EU) are states, but that does not make the EU a state (composition). A government may be notoriously corrupt, but that does not mean that any single member of government is corrupt (division). The fallacy also easily shows up with the use of the terms 'all' and 'some' as in the following: 'all A are B' and 'some B are C', therefore: 'some A are C', which is invalid. For example: 'all members of the EU are members of the UN' (true); 'some members of the UN are microstates' (true). Therefore: 'some EU members are microstates' (which is untrue; Luxembourg is a small state, not a microstate). Replace 'microstates' with 'island states' and the conclusion becomes true (Cyprus and Malta are island states), although the reasoning remains invalid.

Some more fallacies are:

- **Unreflective Extrapolation.** This fallacy occurs when there exists a positive (negative) relationship (correlation) between A and B, and one then infers that more (less) of A will result in even more (less) of B. In thus extrapolating, however, one neglects that a positive (negative) relationship between two variables A and B often only exists within a certain range, and not beyond (below) that range. Not all relations are linear. Take *'transparency'*. Until the 1970s of last century, much of diplomacy was couched in a veil of confidentiality and secrecy. Only gradually did the world of diplomacy open up to wider audiences, in particular civil society (sharing of documents, debriefings, joint initiatives…). But soon one realized that too much transparency would clash with effective diplomacy, particularly in negotiation which, as is well known, is key to diplomacy. As the Danish permanent representative to the EU once stated it in a COREPER meeting in 1993: transparency is not striptease. Transparency works only within a certain range. Too much of it is bad. The Oslo peace negotiations of 1992, for example, which revolutionised the strategic balance in the Middle East could not have proceeded very far without a good amount of secrecy.

- **Cause-Effect Reversal.** This fallacy consists in taking the effect for the cause (and vice versa). It is generally agreed that the main cause of uncooperative behaviour among states is a lack of trust, but some argue that it is uncooperative behaviour that causes trust to be lacking. Both statements cannot simultaneously be true regarding the same event. They can, however, be both true sequentially in regard to different, perhaps successive events (as happens in escalation and spiralling situations – see above). An example is what we have seen in the Prisoner's Dilemma: in the *one-shot scenario* of the game, it is lack of trust that causes uncooperative behaviour, but in the *iterated scenario* it is the reverse: uncooperative behaviour generates mistrust, while cooperative behaviour causes trust.

5.2 Cognitive traps

Cognitive errors are systematic deviations from optimal, rational, or reasonable thought leading to wrong decisions. By 'systematic' we mean that these are not just occasional errors in judgment but rather routine mistakes we stumble over again and again. The study of cognitive errors is not new (see Box 5.5) but was only recently revisited in a new branch of economics called 'behavioural economics' which integrates psychology into economics. The lessons taught by behavioural economics go well beyond the field of economics proper and should interest the diplomatic practitioner no less. A careful study of these traps must guard us against falling in them. Machiavelli already warned for them when he said that 'one must be a fox to recognise traps' ('Bisogna essere volpe a conoscere i lacci', Il Principe, Capitolo XVIII).

Box 5.5 Francis Bacon's 'Idols'

Francis Bacon (1561–1626), a sharp-minded English philosopher who revolutionised scientific method, insisted that the first thing anybody should do before starting any enquiry is *to purge himself of prejudices and predispositions*. He called them 'idols' which beset men's minds. He distinguished four of them:

Idols of the Tribe have their foundation in human nature itself. Bacon noted, for example, that human understanding is prone to generalise hastily and to overemphasise the value of confirming evidence (we already met the 'overgeneralisation fallacy' and the 'confirmation bias' earlier).

Idols of the Cave, by contrast, are directly linked to the situated individual ('for every one has a cave or den of his own') and concern his idiosyncratic attitudes arising from his specific upbringing and education.

Idols of the Marketplace 'are formed by the intercourse and association of men with each other', in particular their discourses which lead to distortions as regards the meaning of words, concepts, and ideas.

Idols of the Theatre 'have immigrated into men's minds' from all sorts of received dogmas and principles through credulity, negligence, and mere tradition. Bacon calls them idols of the Theatre because he deems 'all the received systems (to be) but so many stage-plays, representing worlds of their own creation after an unreal and scenic fashion'.

(Source: Francis Bacon, Novum Organum, 1620, Paragraphs 39–68.)

Although all cognitive errors contain valuable lessons for any human being, and certainly no less for diplomats than for others, we will concentrate on those errors which we think have special relevance for diplomatic practice and gloss over the more common delusions and traps such as:

Groupthink, where a group of smart people makes bad decisions because everybody aligns his position to that of the others in what results to be (taken for) a genuine consensus; often, however, the consensus is the effect of dissonance-reduction, caused by the discomfort of finding oneself disagreeing with the majority.

Belief Echoes is what occurs when, knowing that a piece of information is untrue – 'Barack Obama is a Muslim', it still has the power to resonate and affect how we think.

The **Halo Effect** implies the unjustified transfer of a particular positive (negative) quality of a person or entity to the whole of that person or entity; 'Obama is a great politician; he speaks so well' (this effect is linked to the 'fallacy of composition and division' that we met earlier).

Loss Aversion Trap. Losing something hurts much more than failing to get something worth as much; it has been experimentally established that losses hurt about twice as much as gains make us feel happy (see THALER, 2015, p. 58).

The **Amnesia Bias** is the tendency to focus on recent experience and forget about experience further back in the past.

The **Objectivity Delusion** consists in people thinking that the way they see the world is how the world truly is. If that were true for all, we could never meet someone whose views conflict with our own because we all should see the world as it truly is. But we do meet with people whose views conflict with ours, and then we at once believe that *they* must be deluded, rather than realising that perhaps *we* are the ones who are mistaken and could learn something from them.

The **Overconfidence Delusion** says that people systematically overestimate their *own* knowledge, abilities, and virtuousness.

The **Optimism Bias,** closely linked to the former, says that we are often too optimistic, at least about our *own* situation, even amid generalised pessimism. Both the Overconfidence Delusion and Optimism Bias are closely linked to the Wishful Thinking Delusion discussed below (see Box 5.6).

Box 5.6 America's Retreat from Kabul – Overconfidence, Optimism, and Wishful Thinking

President Biden's decision in spring 2021 to pull America's remaining troops out of Afghanistan has been criticised as a '*withdrawal of choice*', not of '*political necessity*'. Being on the defensive, Biden tried to explain his decision in terms of delusions and traps that America had fallen into. He characterised America's record in Afghanistan

> as a triumph of *wishfulness* over political prudence. The campaign's spiralling cost was long fuelled by an *assumption* that well-resourced American soldiers and diplomats could deliver a stable, democratic Afghanistan. This was a *delusion* based much less on Afghan reality than American politics, an *overestimation* of American military force and a *desire* to maintain the brief moment of post-9/11 national unity.
>
> (the quote is drawn from: The Economist, Lexington, 'Retreat from Kabul', 17 April 2021)

The **Over-Interpretation Trap** says that we try to make sense of the world even when there is no sense to be made, for instance in reconstructing history. We have already met this cognitive trap when questioning the principle that history repeats itself which *reasoning by analogy* presupposes.

Cognitive errors that are more directly relevant for diplomatic practice are:

- **The Sunk Cost Fallacy.** The more significant the effort, time, energy, or (mental) investment spent on a project, the more you will stick to it, even when you have come to realise that the whole project is a lost cause. That is why the fallacy has also been called '*escalation of commitment*' (by Barry Staw, a professor of organisational behaviour, see THALER, 2015, p. 65). The greater the investment, the greater the sunk costs, and the greater the urge to continue. The 'sunk cost fallacy' helps explaining why the Americans extended their involvement in the *Vietnam War* even though most thought that it had become a totally futile enterprise into which the US should never have entered in the first place. The thinking was: 'We've already sacrificed so much in this war, including thousands of human lives and billions of dollars, that it would be a mistake to give up now', whereas the right response should have been to declare defeat and move on, in accordance with the saying: 'let bygones be bygones'.

- **The Availability Heuristic.** We tend to pay too much attention and attach too much importance to what is readily available to our mind, either because it is dramatic and spectacular (a plane crash) or because we can conceive of it more easily (it is still fresh in our memory). Shortly after the *Fukushima* nuclear accident in 2011, Chancellor Merkel decided (perhaps too quickly) to change Germany's decades-old policy on nuclear energy, a decision that many observers thought unfounded. In a 2007 experiment by psychologist Paul Slovic, people were asked to give a donation. One group was shown a *photo* of *Rokia from Malawi*, an emaciated child with pleading eyes. People donated eagerly. The second group was shown *statistics* about the *famine in Malawi*, including the fact that more than three million malnourished children were affected. The average donation dropped by 50 per cent (DOBELLI, 2013, p. 261). Until recently, this bias went by the name of the CNN-effect: the pictures of starving children in Syria made the conflict world news while an identical but unnoticed drama in Yemen remained unnoticed for years. As a result, humanitarian relief does not necessarily end up where it is most needed.

- **Hyperbolic Discounting.** We tend to place huge value on the short term and low value on the long term, discounting the future in favour of the present. If you are offered 1,000 Euro today or 1,100 Euro in a month, you will go for the 1,000 Euro today. If you are offered 1,000 Euro in a year or 1,100 Euro in a year and a month, you will go for the 1,100 Euro in a year and a month. The closer the reward (pleasure, gratification), the higher our (subjective) interest rate rises, and the more we are willing to give up in exchange for it. This explains the prevalence of *short-term thinking* over long-term thinking and the difficulties we encounter in tackling global problems such as climate change and migration and trans-generational issues such as pension reform. We have already noted that democracies are more vulnerable to such hyperbolic discounting than (semi-)authoritarian regimes. We will see that hyperbolic discounting helps explain why *preventive diplomacy*, an honourable notion on paper, often remains a dead letter in practice. The capacity to avoid the trap of narrow, short-term reasoning is an asset: in diplomacy, it goes by the name of *'Strategic Patience'*; substituting a short-term tactical advantage for a long-term strategic one is an endemic feature of thinking which in diplomacy more than elsewhere need to be overcome.

- **The Confirmation Bias.** We already met this bias when discussing the *'Wason selection task'*. Confirmation bias is the tendency to *interpret* incoming information so that it confirms or at least is consistent with your existing beliefs and convictions (see Box 5.7). You filter out any new information that contradicts or sits uneasily with your existing views ('dissonant information', 'disconfirming evidence'). This is the mechanism which is at work in 'Covid denialism', for instance, as professed for too long by Presidents Trump, Bolsonaro, and most tragically by John Magufuli, who after denying the existence of an illness that has ravaged his country Tanzania, himself succumbed to Covid-19 on 17 March 2021. This obviously is a self-deluding strategy. The right strategy is exactly the reverse: look for contradictions, for contrary opinions, not in the masochistic hope of weakening your beliefs and convictions, but on the contrary to make them rock solid.

Box 5.7 Surprises and Lenient Interpretations

'Why is there so much surprise rather than foresight in the international history of the twentieth century', asks Abba Eban. The Soviet Union was surprised when invaded by Germany. So did the US when its fleet was destroyed at Pearl Harbor. The US was again surprised when North Korea invaded South Korea… And it goes on: the US surprise by the Soviet introduction of missiles in Cuba in 1962, Western surprise by the landing of Turkish troops in Cyprus in 1974. 'The explanation of this extraordinary record of surprises does not lie in inaccurate information', says Eban, 'In every case the physical facts about troop concentrations and political hostility were known and often documented in the media. Yet those who were threatened by them lent themselves to *lenient interpretations*' (EBAN, 1998, pp. 41–42, our italics).

Cognitive traps are often at work in a *negotiation situation*. The negotiator who is keenly aware of them, both in his own and in his opponent's behaviour, has a competitive advantage.

- **The Endowment Effect.** People generally overvalue what is theirs. When you succeeded in buying a car for 40,000 Euro from a seller that was pushing for 50,000 Euro, and the next day somebody offers you 53,000 Euro for the car, you probably will not sell it. Rationally, you should, given that you considered it worth 40,000 Euro. In other words, when selling what we own we charge more than what we are willing to pay for it when we do not own it. In a negotiation situation, we often do the same: when working towards a compromise we tend to *overvalue our offer* (concession) and *undervalue our opponent's counter-offer*. We consider our concession to be *a sacrifice*, the other party's concession just a *trifle*.
- **The Wishful Thinking Delusion.** People find it hard to distinguish between *what is* true or fair, and *what they wish were* true or fair. In a negotiation situation, you are often biased by your own self-interest and misperceive what would be a fair deal. Wishful thinking about the outcome (perhaps in conjunction with the Overconfidence and Optimism Bias) leads you to *overestimate your chances* of winning and *underestimate* the chances of *your opponent* winning. No wonder negotiation's give-and-take mechanism does not work in these circumstances, and you fail to reach an agreement. In the meantime, and were it not for your bias, you may have let go an 'advantageous' deal.
- **The Opportunity Cost Neglect Trap.** Opportunity cost is a standard concept in economics: it is the idea that *the value of what you have or get is to be judged by what you have to give up to keep it or get it.* If you have a ticket to a game that you could sell for 1,000 Euro, the opportunity cost of going to the game is what you could do with those 1,000 Euro. You should only go to the game if that is the best possible way you could use that money. Is it better than 100 movies at 10 Euro each? In a negotiation situation, when you are about to make (or agree to) a compromise proposal first think about what you will have to give up in making (or agreeing to) it. You may soon realise that the proposed deal is much too 'expensive' considering its opportunity costs, or conversely that this is the very deal you need to make. What reasoning in terms of opportunity costs does is to allow you *to let the possible trade-offs of a compromise explicitly cross your mind.* You may of course also try to find out what the opportunity costs of your offer are *for your opponent* (through empathetic thinking: putting yourself in his place) and come to understand why it is unbalanced from his perspective and then see that a slightly different concession may work out. Situations of underestimating opportunity costs for your opponent easily arise when highly symbolic issues are at stake for which you may be less sensitive than the other; think of border issues (the decades-old standoff between Ethiopia and Eritrea) or questions related to sacred cities such as Jerusalem (with its holy sites the Temple Mount and Al Quds) (see Box 5.8).

Box 5.8 Neglecting Opportunity Costs – The Case of Jerusalem

In diplomatic negotiations it happens that opportunity costs linked to highly symbolic, often religious issues risk being underestimated. Such issues constitute diplomatic no-go areas. The status of Jerusalem, which for decades has been disputed in international law and diplomatic practice is a case in point. The establishment of Jerusalem as a *separate international entity* ('*corpus separatum*') under the auspices of the UN goes back to a resolution of the UN General Assembly of 29 November 1947. That special status, while aimed at protecting the specificity of the city, has made it very difficult to find any accommodation. Jerusalem is claimed by both Israeli and Palestinians as their 'exclusive' capital. Given the intractability of the Jerusalem-question, it is generally agreed that its resolution should only be addressed in the final stage of Israeli-Palestinian peace talks, if ever such *final* talks will take place.

In Chapter 3, we explored reasoning in diplomacy. And we found that it was far from perfect, particularly in the ascending phase of *reaching* decisions, as distinct from the descending phase concerned with their justification for which some ways of reliable, plausible, and sound thinking were available. Following Kahneman's distinction between fast and slow thinking, we noted that much of the thinking that is involved in *reaching* decisions is fast thinking, the kind of spontaneous, intuitive thinking that easily leads us astray, both in terms of making logical errors and falling in cognitive traps. Errors and traps obviously need to be avoided. Explicitly stating what these are was the object of the present chapter. We started with pointing out recurrent errors in logic, called formal fallacies, such as the False Dilemma ('you are either with us or against us'), the Slippery Slope Fallacy (leading to escalation and spiralling in conflicts up to a point of non-return) and the Over-Generalisation Fallacy (leading to stereotypical reasoning). Cognitive traps are even more insidious. They are deep-seated habits of thinking which often mislead us. They are commonly called 'Biases' and 'Heuristics'. Some of them are quite familiar such as the Availability Heuristic (we are more impressed by a picture of one starving child in Syria than by statistics reporting the death of hundreds of children in Yemen), the Endowment Effect (in a negotiation: my concession is a sacrifice, your counter-offer is a trifle), the Confirmation Bias (eagerly looking for evidence that confirms your views and filtering out disconfirming evidence as in 'Covid denialism'). Being thus equipped against errors in logic and cognitive traps, in the next chapter, we can look at the tools we need for sound decision-making.

Bibliography

AJDUKIEWICZ, Kazimierz (1965), *Pragmatic Logic*, Reidel Publishing Company, Boston, MA/Warsaw.

ARIELY, Dan (2008), *Predictably Irrational – The Hidden Forces that Shape Our Decisions*, Harper, New York, NY.

BUEKENS, Filip & DEMEY, Lorenz (2017), *Redeneren en Argumenteren*, Acco, Leuven/Den Haag.

DOBELLI, Rolf (2013), *The Art of Thinking Clearly*, Harper, New York, NY.

HARFORD, Tim (2007), *The Undercover Economist*, Oxford University Press, Oxford.

KAHNEMAN, Daniel (2011), *Thinking, Fast and Slow*, Allen Lane, New York, NY.

SHAROT, Tali (2011), *The Optimism Bias – A Tour of the Irrationally Positive Brain*, Epub,London. .

TALEB, Nassim Nicholas (2007), *The Black Swann – The Impact of the Highly Improbable*, Random House, New York, NY.

THALER, Richard (2015), *Misbehaving. The Making of Behavioural Economics*, Norton, New York, NY.

VAN BENDEGEM, Jean Paul (2005), *Inleiding tot de Moderne Logica en Wetenschapsfilosofie*, VUB Press, Brussels.

ZIEMBINSKY, Zygmunt (1976), *Practical Logic*, Reidel Publishing Company, Boston, MA/ Warszawa.

6 Concepts and principles in diplomatic thinking

We have seen that diplomacy, as an action-oriented practice, is concerned with *practical reasoning*, reasoning which results in action rather than belief. Diplomats are not in search of new truths derived from old truths, as scientists are. Diplomats are problem-solvers, they start out with a problematic situation and look for solutions that could settle the matter. We have seen that in practical reasoning two interlocked steps are involved: one regarding the (messy) *facts* of the case which require a political analysis by means of *concepts;* the question here is, simply put: **what** *is going on, what is the problem*?; the other step concerns the solution to be adopted to solve the problem, to act upon it, and that requires the appeal to *principles* allowing you to decide **how** *to act*; the question here is, simply put: *what should be done* about this situation, what is the *solution*? As we discussed earlier, there is a subtle (some would say perverse) dialectic going on between problem-identification and solution-elaboration: the *principles* may be so interpreted as to fit the facts of the case, or the *facts* may be so construed as to favour a certain rule (or both). Facts and principles are no independent variables. The only independent variable often is the preferred solution to which we are pre-committed.

6.1 The nature of concepts and principles

Concepts and general principles are **ready-made tools** that we use, respectively, in the *descriptive political analysis* of a problematic situation first and then in the *prescriptive build-up of a decision* to act (*ex ante*) or, as is more often the case, in its justification (*ex post*). Concepts and principles are no doubt useful in our work, but we should avoid relying on them unreflectively. Carl von Clausewitz pointed out that a primary concern in any endeavour should be 'to clarify concepts and ideas that have become, as it were, confused and entangled' adding that 'not until terms and concepts have been defined can one hope to make any progress in examining a question clearly and simply' (cited in Hal Brands, 'What Good is Grand Strategy?', Cornell University Press, Ithaca, 2014, p. 1).

Concepts are **cognitive instruments**; they are the main *tools* we use in *political analysis*. They have a **descriptive** character.

Once developed, concepts tend to have a kind of *intrinsic inertia*; the 'law of habit' applies to them. It is in the nature of any concept, as it is of any habit, to change more slowly than do the circumstances with reference to which it is employed. It is practical and economical to use ready-made concepts, rather than to take time, trouble, and effort to change them or to devise new ones. Moreover, the use of familiar concepts with their relative fixity gives us a specious sense of assurance against the troublesome flux of events. It flatters that deep-seated longing for *certainty and stability* which is in every

DOI: 10.4324/9781003298182-9

human mind. But we should be on our guards. That sense of stability and certainty is often an illusion. The meaning of concepts is rarely as fixed as it may seem (see Box 6.1).

Box 6.1 An Operationalist and Pragmatist on the Meaning of Concepts

For the influential American physicist-philosopher Paul Bridgman, the father of operationalism, 'the true meaning of a concept is to be found by observing what *a man does with it, not what he says about it*' ('Logic of Modern Physics', New York, 1927, p. 47, my italics). And for the influential American lawyer-philosopher Richard Posner the question to be asked as regards a concept is: 'Does it work?'. For him, the antidote to an abstract conceptualism is pragmatism, the theory (or anti-theory) that debunks all pretences to having constructed a 'pipeline to the truth' (POSNER, 1995, pp. 2 and 399).

Concepts are not there to live a life on their own. They are instruments meant to assist us in thinking through the problems we face in diplomatic practice. We should work with them, manipulate them, perhaps change them. Concepts in diplomacy, as elsewhere, are not absolute, they have meaning only in terms of what diplomats can do with them. Creativity in diplomacy is closely related to what has been called 'the juggling with concepts'. Instead of forcing diplomatic practice into the mould of existing concepts viewed as immutable, the smart diplomat will make concepts subservient to their practice (finding the right solution for the problem at hand) and will therefore be open to adjust or revisit concepts to fit that practice.

Principles, as distinct from concepts, are **guides for action**. They have a **prescriptive** character. What has been said of concepts is, however, largely true also of general principles. They too have a kind of inertia and instil a (false) sense of certainty and stability. General principles are often presented as intrinsically *absolute and intangible*. It is the *sanctification* of ready-made universal principles as tools for thinking that is, however, often the chief obstacle to finding the right response to the problems we face.

General principles often *contradict* each other. They have a habit of running in pairs. As in the domain of popular proverbs one appeals with equanimity to the caution, 'Look before you leap', or to its opposite, 'He who hesitates is lost', so too in the domain of diplomacy (as we saw in discussing 'reasoning by analogy'), there is the appeal to 'Lessons learned from history' against the warning that 'History never repeats itself'. Legal principles too are often difficult to reconcile, as we will see further down in this chapter. In such circumstances one would be tempted to agree with Napoleon's remark to Talleyrand: 'I like principles, they don't commit to anything' (cited in COOPER, 2021, p. 486).

To overcome these drawbacks, it is best to consider general principles, both diplomatic principles and principles of international law, as **working hypotheses**, which need to be constantly tested by the way in which they work out in applications to concrete situations. This was an insight that the 'realist' Niccolo Machiavelli has been stressing time and again in his *Il Principe* when asking us to pay attention to '*la qualità dei tempi*', which I would simply render as 'the circumstances'. It is what in modern diplomatic parlance is called **situational awareness**: taking duly account of situational factors when devising diplomatic solutions. Great principles should not be taken at face value, *in abstracto*. Their real value consists in what you can and cannot do with them, given 'the circumstances'.

As a problem-solver, a diplomat's job is to find suitable solutions to complex problems. That requires flexibility. Most of a diplomat's solutions will not be judged as optimal when seen in the light of so-called universal and eternally valid principles. But that is not the ultimate test to which diplomatic solutions should be submitted; their ultimate test is: *'does it work'*. Abstract formula or rigid axioms will seldom allow you to catch the complex, the moving, the living, the human, and hence the passionate in international relations. Principles are there to assist you, not to block you. They should be guides for action, not obstacles.

What we learn from these preliminary caveats is not that concepts and general principles should be rejected altogether as tools for analysis and decision-making in diplomacy, but that they should be handled with care. The lesson to be drawn from these caveats is that concepts and principles do not decide on their own what course to take; they may help us in finding our way, but it is ultimately for us to decide. It is for us to recognise that there is an *element of choice* when we appeal to concepts or principles, and that underlying these choices it is *conflicting interests* that are at stake. And it is interests, not concepts and principles, that are the ultimate stuff of diplomacy.

6.2 A diplomat's vocabulary

Having made these caveats, let us now proceed with the risky job of establishing a list of concepts and principles that we think are relevant for diplomatic practice; a risky job indeed given what we said on the need to avoid looking at them as static and determinate. We will not cover concepts that are closely related to International Relations Theory (anarchy, self-help, the security dilemma, balance of power, free riders...) although we recognise that International Relations Theory influences and shapes foreign policy and diplomatic practice; we would certainly recommend the alert diplomat to be familiar with its main tenets. The list that follows does not claim to be exhaustive, nor should its ordering be seen as 'fixed'. For each of the concepts and principles mentioned we give a short description and, occasionally, a short comment. This section is meant to be informative and help the reader to find their way in the labyrinth of diplomat's vocabulary.

6.3 Concepts

Concepts, we said, are the tools we use in the *political analysis* of a factual situation. Political analysis is the starting point in diplomatic reasoning. A diplomat does not just gather information (that is the easy part), he or she must figure out what it all means. Knowing some facts does not amount to understanding. Understanding is putting the facts in context. Understanding a situation is conceptualising it. Only then can we start thinking what to do about it. And for that we will need principles (on which more below). For the ease of reference, we have subdivided the concepts listed below in political, security, and diplomatic.

6.3.1 *Political concepts*

- **Power**: is the capacity to effectively *influence* or affect other country's behaviour to get outcomes one wants ('power to'), with at its extreme the capacity to *impose* one's will on others ('power over') (see Box 6.2).
- **Power Base**: is the whole of material and immaterial resources and capabilities on which the exercise of effective power rests.
- **Power Distance**: measures the degree of asymmetry in power between countries, or between leader (great power) and follower (allies).
- **Hard Power**: is the power of *coercion*, not only military power first but also economic power.
- **Soft Power**: is the power of attraction or *persuasion*, or by example, based on the capital of 'goodwill' of which a country benefits (reputation, trustworthiness, predictability).
- **Connectivity Power**: is a newcomer in the diplomat's vocabulary and refers to the control overflows of people, goods, money, and data via connections (and the ensuing dependencies) they establish. The geo-economic Chinese 'Belt and Road Initiative' is a prime example.
- **Power Conversion Capability**: is the capacity (and willingness) to convert economic into military power. A country (or region) may have major power resources but have a poor power conversion capability. The US in the 1930s had the largest economy in the world but did not engage with the world preferring to follow an isolationist policy. The European Union (EU) today offers another example. Nobody would contest Europe's strong economic power base, but this power base is only hesitantly being converted in 'hard' military power.

Box 6.2 The Impulse to Power

The first line of *Bertrand Russell*'s 'Introduction' to his little book on *Power* reads as follow:

> Between man and other animals there are various differences, some intellectual, some emotional. One of the chief emotional differences is that some human desires, unlike those of animals, are essentially boundless and incapable of complete satisfaction. Power is one of these insatiable human desires. The more power one has, the more power one wants.

In his book *The Power Paradox*, Dacher Keltner tells us that Machiavelli was wrong in thinking that being feared was better than being loved. Leaders get power, Keltner thinks, not by force, but by winning the approval of others, and this they obtain not by frightening them, but by acting in accordance with the greater good. But then comes *Keltner's paradox*: we get power by being good but once we have power it makes us bad. The knowledge that power corrupts is not new. Montesquieu already warned for it: 'power corrupts, and absolute power corrupts absolutely' (« le pouvoir corrompt, et le pouvoir absolu corrompt absolument »). Power is **cumulative**, there is no saturation point in power accumulation, nor is there negative marginal utility: the more power, the better. Power is also **monopolistic**; power is what you seek for yourself, not for others, rather to the detriment of others; one does not share power with others. Power is a **comparative** notion: it is less than, equal to, or more than another's power; it is measured in relative, not in absolute terms. Power is always relative power.

- **Great Powers versus Global Players**: the critical factor for distinguishing between 'Great Powers' and 'Global Players' is power conversion capability. The US today is a Great Power, as are China and Russia; not so the EU, which is a Global Player.
- **Middle Powers**: also called *Pivotal States* are states that without having the power to dictate the course of world events, still can make a significant difference in world developments. Countries that are considered pivotal are, among others, India, Egypt, Pakistan, Turkey, Israel, and perhaps Brazil and South Africa.
- **World Order**: refers to the structure of power distribution among the Great Powers. *Uni-, Bi-, and Multi-polar world orders* reflect different structures of power distribution. The Cold War era was characterised by a bi-polar world order with the US and the Soviet Union in the driver's seat. After the implosion of the Soviet Union, we got a short-lived uni-polar world order when power was concentrated in Washington (known as the 'unipolar moment'). Today we live through a period of flux with power *shifting* among the Great Powers (most significantly from the US to China) in a multi-polar world order (or rather disorder) still in search of a new equilibrium.
- **Alliances**: are most commonly viewed as a response to threats. When entering an alliance, states may either *balance*, that is ally with the power that opposes the threatening country, or else *bandwagon*, that is ally with the threatening power. When balancing is the dominant strategy, threatening countries face combined opposition. But if bandwagoning is the dominant tendency, threatening is rewarded (Box 6.3).

Box 6.3 No Eternal Allies, Only Perpetual Interests

The American alliance system has come under increasing criticism lately. In a 2016 Brookings paper authored by Jeremy Shapiro and Richard Sokolsky 'How America enables its allies' bad behaviour', focussing on the deteriorating relations with such perennial malcontents as Saudi Arabia, Egypt, and Turkey, the authors claim that the Cold War legacy – either 'with us' or 'against us' – has created pathologies that have become deeply embedded in America's foreign policymaking machinery. Their analysis in terms of 'reverse leverage', 'moral hazard', and 'endless reassurance' reminds one that alliances are not there to make allies happy but to make them behave like allies should – responsibly. There may be a lesson here for NATO allies as well. It was Lord Palmerston who, in 1848, coined the unforgettable phrase: 'We have no eternal allies, and we have no eternal friends. Our interests are eternal and perpetual, and those interests it is our duty to follow'.

6.3.2 Security concepts

- **Force**: the use of force is the effective exercise of military (coercive) power ultimately resulting in physical violence. A *threat of the use of force* is the non-coercive use of power signalling the possible consecutive use of coercive power to the opposing party.
- **Threat versus Risk**: a threat is a patent, clear, and imminent danger; a risk is the probability of a latent danger becoming a threat.
- **War:** is an all-encompassing military event, using force and intended to attain a *political outcome*, involving crucially but *not exclusively* the armed forces. Diplomacy plays an important role in war, as we will see in the chapter on 'The Use of Force'. One of the distinguishing features of modern diplomacy is the blurring of the line between diplomatic activity and use of force. War, for instance, is viewed by some as a means of pressure aimed at the continuation of negotiation.
- **Battle**: is part of war, it is a fight, relying *solely* on armed force and aimed only at a *military outcome*, not a political one. Diplomacy has no role to play in battles.
- **Escalation and De-escalation**: refer, respectively, to increasing or decreasing the intensity of a conflictual situation, or extending or limiting its scope.
- **Retaliation**: is a military response meant as *punishment* for a hostile action by an opposing party. An example is the repeated attacks by the US against Iran-sponsored militias in Iraq in the spring of 2020 in response to the killing of US soldiers.
- **State Security versus Human Security**: 'State Security' traditionally focuses on questions of national interest, territorial sovereignty, and nuclear deterrence. But such questions may seem far removed from the security concerns faced by most ordinary people: hunger, disease, education, housing, and employment. Placing humans at the heart of debates about international security is what 'Human Security' is about. The concept was for the first time developed by the United Nations Development Program (UNDP) in its 1994 report 'Redefining Security: The Human Dimension'.

Note that in the forthcoming chapters on 'The Conflict Cycle' and 'The Use of Force' many other security-related concepts will be analysed (such as 'peace-enforcement', 'pre-emptive' and 'preventive war', 'war of necessity', and 'war of choice').

6.3.3 Diplomatic concepts

- **Power versus Authority**: power is the capacity to influence or affect the behaviour of other countries and, *in extremis*, to impose your will on others; power works from the outside. Authority works from the inside; it is the capacity to have others internalise your will and voluntarily accept and recognise it as their own. It is what President Obama once called 'real' power: 'the ability to get what you want without having to exert violence'.
- **Legality versus Legitimacy**: legality is a legal concept and presupposes the existence of a legal order; legality then is conformity with the law. Legitimacy is a political concept linked to a political order; it is more fundamental than 'legality'; lawfulness may be an element of legitimacy, but legitimacy does not reduce to lawfulness. Hitler's regime was lawful but not legitimate. International legitimacy is

increasingly linked to what is broadly called 'good governance', the set of norms embracing democracy, the rule of law, openness and transparency, and respect for human rights.

- **Legitimacy versus Efficacy**: efficacy is the capacity for getting things done, efficiently and timely. Efficacy and legitimacy have an inverse and therefore tense relationship: the more legitimacy, the less efficacy, and *vice versa*. A legitimate (democratic) regime has transaction costs for getting things done (elections, freedom of speech, political accountability, independent judiciary …) that an illegitimate (authoritarian) regime has not. *Principled Pragmatism* is an attempt to find the right balance between both.

- **Unilateralism**: is the policy of a country acting on its own in the conduct of its foreign policy, without much consultation or regard to others (not to be confused with isolationism). *Bilateralism*: the policy of a country privileging the bilateral channel in its conduct of diplomacy. *Multilateralism*: the coordinated diplomatic interaction among three or more states, perhaps within the framework of an international organisation.

- **Isolationism**: is the policy of a country not to get involved with (the fate of) other countries, regions, or perhaps the world at large. In the 19th century, following George Washington's advice to avoid 'entangling alliances' and in line with the Monroe Doctrine, the US played only a minor role in the global balance of power. After a brief engagement at the end of World War I when in 1917 Woodrow Wilson for the first time in US history sent American troops to fight in Europe, the US in the 1930s returned to its isolationist policy.

- **Spheres of Influence**: are established either as the result of intimidation and force, in which case they are considered illegitimate (on the basis of the right of Freedom of Alliance), or else result from the willing consent of the countries involved, based on the idea that all nations can do it 'their own way' (pleasantly known as the 'Sinatra-doctrine'). Both China and Russia somehow claim that they should have veto rights about what goes on in their immediate neighbourhoods. Russia argues that it is unacceptable that Georgia and Ukraine – a country ruled from Moscow for centuries – should join the western alliance. Similarly, China lays territorial claims on the South and East China Sea as belonging to its sphere of influence.

- **Transactional foreign policy**: involves a *calculated* approach based on self-interest and often relying on rewards and punishments.

- **Interest-based versus Value-based foreign policy**: two approaches to foreign policy prioritising interests above values, and *vice versa*. Both approaches need not be incompatible; indeed, most often interests and values will converge since the definition of a country's interests is normally based on and includes the values it cares for.

- **Short-termism versus Long-termism**: concerns the time-horizon envisaged by a foreign policy. States tend to focus on the short-term (electoral deadlines oblige); international organisations can afford having the longer view and are therefore generally better than states in long-term norm-setting (Sustainable Development Goals, Climate Change, Migration…).

- **Grand Strategy**: is not foreign policy, it is the overall architecture that lends structure to foreign policy; it aims at defining a coherent, purposeful approach to international politics and involves a long-term vision defining key objectives, identifying means, and the way to proceed; what makes a strategy 'Grand' is not the strategy itself, but the questions on which it bears. Grand strategy is essentially a matter for the Great Powers.

- **Cooperation versus Competition**: are two strategies to engage with a rival; these strategies seem to contradict each other, but they need not: we often cooperate because we are competitors, for example in negotiation where we have a *common* desire to overcome our *differences.* Sometimes being cooperative even increases one's competitive position, a paradoxical idea that is encapsulated in the notion of *competitive altruism* (see Box 6.4).

Box 6.4 Frenemies

In the past few years, China has variously been regarded both as a partner and a systemic competitor or rival or even enemy. Martin Wolf of the Financial Times, alarmed by a possible breakdown of relations between the US (the West) and China thinks that 'the right path is to manage relations that will be both competitive and cooperative and so to recognise that China can be both foe and friend'. 'In other words', concludes Wolf, 'we must embrace complexity. That is the path to maturity'. Being both friend and enemy, China may have become our 'frenemy'.

- **Containment versus Engagement**: containment involves the imposition of limits on your rival's freedom of action through appeal to hard power; engagement, on the contrary, involves showing willingness and openness to work with your rival by appealing to the soft power of persuasion. 'Containment' was George Kennan's 'invention' that became US policy as of 1947 to counter increasing Soviet influence and hinder Soviet territorial expansion.
- **Deterrence versus Compellence**: both involve threatening a potential aggressor either *not to act* so as not to upset the *status quo* (deterrence), or in case the *status quo* has been upset, *to act* in such way as to revert to the prior situation (for instance, to withdraw behind the 'Line of Control' [LOC] in a disputed boundary area after the line has been trespassed). Deterrence and Compellence will only work when the other party is convinced that the threats can and will be executed in case of non-compliance. They thus constitute a serious credibility-test for the threatening party (as we have witnessed with Obama's 'red lines' on the use of chemical weapons in the Syria conflict).
- **Confidence Building Measures (CBMs)**: are understandings (often related to arms control regimes) aimed at avoiding or at least reducing misunderstandings and at maintaining or restoring trust among opposing parties.
- **Contingency Planning**: is part of early crisis management and encompasses a set of measures, procedures, or scenarios to control or stabilise a tense situation *awaiting* a more durable solution.
- **Retorsion**: is the imposition of unfriendly measures (or the removal of friendly concessions) that does not involve the breach of any legal obligation (for example, the withholding of foreign aid, the imposition of visa requirements, the withholding of overflight rights, or of awards of government contracts, the imposition of restrictions on imports or exports, the imposition of travel bans).
- **Countermeasures** (also called *reprisals*): are justified (and therefore lawful) breaches of international legal obligations when a state is injured by an unlawful act of another state. An asset freeze, for example, is tantamount to the seizure of foreign

property, and as such forbidden; it becomes lawful, however, if it can be justified as a countermeasure. This was the case, for instance, with the 12 billion dollar freeze on Iranian assets imposed after the 1979 hostage-taking in the US Embassy in Tehran. A recurrent example of countermeasure is when a state no longer fulfils *its* treaty obligations after they have been disregarded by another state. This was the underlying logic of Iran's behaviour after President Trump unilaterally withdrew from the ACPJ Treaty; Iran then claimed to be relieved from its own treaty obligations (from a legal point of view things were a bit more complicated).

- **Blockade**: is a means of exercising diplomatic pressure and involves a military action aimed at cutting off a country (or part of it) from outside interaction (for example, Berlin by the Soviet Union in 1948 and Cuba by the US in 1962 – the latter operation was called a 'quarantine').
- **Embargo**: is also a means of diplomatic pressure; it institutes a prohibition on *exports* of products and services *to* a country; an embargo can be total or partial (for example, of weapons only); when instituted by the UN Security Council it is called 'a mandatory embargo' as it binds all UN members. A total UN trade embargo has been instituted against Iraq after the Kuwait invasion in August 1990; a partial (weapons only) UN embargo was instituted against Yugoslavia at the start of the Balkan wars in September 1991.
- **Boycott**: is also a means of diplomatic pressure; it is a decision to restrain commercial relations, particularly targeting imports. A boycott is a perfectly legal action.

6.4 Principles

Only after the political analysis of a situation has led to its proper understanding can we meaningfully address the question what to do about it. We then move from the *descriptive* level of analysis of a situation ('what is the problem') to the *prescriptive* level of acting upon it ('what should be done about the problem'). A diplomat's job does not end with offering a keen political analysis of a particular situation ('here is the problem, Minister, for you to solve it'). A diplomat must offer suggestions as to how to act upon that situation. He or she then contributes to the *shaping of policy* through advice and recommendations. For that he or she needs to rely on principles which are guidelines for action. We will distinguish two different kinds of principles: legal principles and diplomatic principles.

6.4.1 *Legal principles*

The 'official language' of the diplomat is very much couched in the language of international law. So, it is no surprise that legal principles will play a prominent role in diplomatic thinking. The general principles of international law define the basic framework of the international legal order and act as guidelines for diplomatic action. They would not be called 'principles' if they were not considered as carrying prescriptive force. We just mention a few of these principles without much comment. Comment will be provided when we proceed to their in-depth analysis in the chapter on 'International Law'.

- **Sovereignty**: is, at its most basic level, the right of each state to determine its own fate.

- **Freedom of Alliance**: this principle is a derivative of the Principle of Sovereignty; since sovereign states have the right to determine their own fate, they are entitled to freely choose their own allies.
- **Independence**: this principle is a corollary of the Sovereignty Principle; if sovereignty amounts to the right of each state to determine its own fate, then it follows that no state is subject to the authority of any other state.
- **Equality**: this principle is again a corollary of the Principle of Sovereignty; if sovereignty is the right of each state to determine its own fate, then each of them has an equal standing in relation to the others.
- **Reciprocity**: this principle is a derivative from the Principle of Equality; reciprocity means that each state can expect to be treated by other states in the same way as it treats them.
- **Territorial Integrity**: territory is a crucial attribute of a state; the Principle of Territorial Integrity protects a state's territory against intrusion, invasion, or annexation.
- **Inviolability of borders**: this principle is a derivative of the Principle of Territorial Integrity; borders, as we have seen, are the most sensitive part of a state's territory.
- **Self-Determination**: is the right of all *peoples* to freely determine their own destiny; the essence of this principle is that no people should be subject to alien domination, particularly of the colonial variety.
- **Non-Intervention**: this principle is a corollary of the Principle of Sovereignty and is generally understood as prohibiting interference in the domestic affairs of another state.
- **Responsibility to Protect** (R2P): this principle, adopted at the UN Summit of 2005, constitutes an exception to the Principle of Non-intervention and has therefore a clearly defined and limited scope.
- **Necessity:** is when in an exceptional situation a state may for its own survival be constrained to act contrary to its international legal obligations; necessity is not to be confused with '*force majeure*' when a state finds itself in a situation where it is simply impossible for it to conform to its legal obligations.
- '***Pacta sunt servanda***' ('agreements must be executed'): this is the principle according to which states are legally bound by their agreements, as recalled in the Preamble of the UN Charter ('respect for the obligations arising from treaties and other sources of international law').
- '***Exceptio non adimpleti contractus***' ('exception of non-fulfilment of obligation'): if state A does not respect its treaty obligations vis-à-vis state B, then state B is relieved of its own treaty obligations vis-à-vis state A. State's B action can then be seen as a legitimate *reprisal*. This principle is flows from the Principle of Reciprocity.
- '***Rebus sic stantibus***' ('provided things stay as they are'): this principle states that an agreement may lose its binding character if important conditions for its applicability have materially changed.
- '***Suum cuique tribuere***' ('to each his due'): this dictum is often said to express the *principle of justice* in its barest form: that similar matters must be treated similarly and dissimilar matters dissimilarly to the extent of their dissimilarity.

At first sight, these revered legal principles look neat and clean, but as we had occasion to say in the introduction to this chapter, principles should never be taken to be absolute and intangible. Under a sceptical gaze, a good many of the legal principles turn out to be pious frauds ('Equality of States'), systematically infringed (what remains of the 'Principle of Territorial Integrity' when we see Russia brazenly grabbing pieces of Ukraine or China occupying disputed territories in the South China Sea), contradictory (how do we reconcile the 'Principle of Non-intervention' in domestic affairs of with the demand to promote and ensure the 'Respect of Human Rights'), others turn out to be so ambiguous that they have no predictive value ('Principle of Self-Determination'), and still others turn out to be disguised tautologies (such as the 'Sovereign Equality of States', or the pair 'Inviolability of Borders' and 'Territorial Integrity').

Beyond these *substantive* general principles of international law, there is a family of *formal* rules which are valid not only in national legal systems but also in the international legal order. In diplomatic thinking one often, perhaps implicitly, relies on them. By way of example, let us mention the following ones (for the lawyers among the readers, their pedant Latin pedigree is added when they have one):

- Only serious matters deserve due consideration ('De minimis non curat praetor').
- Always hear both sides to a controversy ('Et audiatur altera pars').
- When in doubt, go for the least exacting option ('In dubio pro libertate').
- No one can take advantage from their own wrongdoing ('Ex iniuria ius non oritur').
- What is factually impossible cannot be obligatory ('ad impossibile nemo tenetur') and what is factually necessary cannot be prohibited.
- A legal provision that is more recent in time (or more specific in scope) prevails over an older (or more general) one with which it is incompatible ('Lex posterior derogat legi priori' and 'Lex specialis derogat legi generali').
- Exceptions to rules must be interpreted restrictively.

6.4.2 Diplomatic principles

Beyond legal principles, there are diplomatic principles. Diplomatic principles do not have a strong doctrinal basis compared to the principles of international law and lack their venerable standing but are certainly not less normatively relevant. Diplomatic principles have emerged from diplomatic practice, and that is their strength.

- **Respect and Recognition**: one of the most fundamental features of the international order is the desire of states to be recognised, respected, and accepted by other states. This *battle for recognition* is not about material advantages but about symbolic goods such as honour and pride or its inverse, humiliation. This battle is going on everywhere in diplomacy and has too often been neglected. Many observers would agree, for instance, that Putin's 'revanchist' foreign policy is linked to the humiliation inflicted by the West on the Russian nation during the Yeltsin years of the early 1990s shortly after the Soviet Union implosion.
- **Fairness**: states, like people, wish to be treated fairly. Fairness does not reduce to formal justice ('equality before the law') and is closer to such concepts as *'equity'* and *'fair play'*. This principle should work as a check against arbitrariness. Selective indignation (so-called *double standards*) in the field of Human Rights, for example, is said to infringe this principle; it is a complaint that African countries have often made as regards Western criticism of their human rights record.

- **Trust:** is the cement for international understanding and cooperation. Trust is a scarce resource that deserves to be protected. Trust should pay, deceit should make the other pay.
- **Promises**: even though promises are not legally binding (that is what distinguishes them from formal agreements), they must be honoured no less. From a diplomat's non legalistic perspective, not honouring one's promises is no less condemnable as not complying with a formal agreement (see above: 'Pacta sunt Servanda').
- **Predictability**: involves the coherence of a country's statements and acts and their persistence through time within the overall framework of a consistent foreign policy.
- **Reliability**: being trustworthy, predictable, and honouring promises altogether amount to reliability. When President Trump abandoned the US's Kurdish allies in Syria in an overnight decision in 2019, he forfeited any amount of reliability he might still have had at the time.
- **Credibility**: is about being taken seriously; truthfulness plays an important role in this regard; when people do not (or no longer) believe what you say you get nowhere. When threatening an opposing party (by stating 'red lines', for instance) that party should believe you for the threat to be effective. Credibility is also critical when making a peace deal such as the one President Trump made with the Talban in early 2020, which seemed to be more about the withdrawal of the US troops in Afghanistan than about anything resembling a genuine peace, something which the Taliban had quickly understood.
- **Proportionality**: any diplomatic action should be proportionate to the objective sought by the action. This is a core principle in judging the legitimacy of the use of force (as we will see in the chapter on the 'Use of Force'). But it goes well beyond that single application and is recurring in diplomatic practice. The EU Schengen rules, for instance, give member states the discretion to reintroduce border controls in response to a 'serious threat to public policy or internal security' provided such tightening is last resort, time-limited, and restricted to the *minimum needed* to deal with the problem.
- **Prudence**: is not about caution or wariness but about judgement and measure; perhaps it is more like a virtue than a principle, but then the less virtuous may need the principle. Prudence makes one ask simple questions. I mention three of them. **Feasibility**: this is a pragmatic principle prescribing to proceed to a reality check on the practical 'implementability' of any prospective action; bright projects too often grind and come to a halt when getting at the implementation stage. **Precaution**: the precautionary principle prescribes not to act unless and until all possible negative consequences of a prospective action have been properly assessed. **Means-End Adequacy**: this principle prescribes you to check your means against the ends; never pursue ends for which you lack the adequate means.

Such list can be extended in many directions but then risks becoming a 'pot-pouri' that is useless as a guide for action. So, we will keep it at that except for Hans Morgenthau's six principles of effective diplomacy (see Box 6.5).

Box 6.5 Six Principles of Effective Diplomacy

Six principles of effective diplomacy as formulated by Hans Morgenthau in his
Politics among Nations (1948):

* Diplomacy must be divested of its crusading spirit.
* The objectives of foreign policy must be defined in terms of national interests
  and must be supported with adequate power.
* Diplomacy must look at the situation from the point of view of other nations.
* Nations must be willing to compromise on all issues that are not vital to them.
* The armed forces are the instrument of foreign policy, not its master.
* The government is the leader of public opinion, not its slave.

In this chapter, we have reviewed a diplomat's working vocabulary distinguishing
between concepts and principles. We conceived of them not as abstract entities but as
ready-made tools to be used in descriptive political analysis and in the prescriptive build-
up of a decision to act, respectively. We have stressed that concepts and principles do
not decide on their own what course to take. They are instruments meant to assist us
in thinking through the problems we face in diplomatic practice. We work with them,
manipulate them, perhaps change them. Whereas concepts are tools we use in political
analysis, principles are guides for action. Concepts help us to answer the question: what is
going on here, what is the problem? Principles help us to answer the question: what should
be done about it, how should we act on it? Establishing a list of concepts and principles
is a risky business. The lists we have established are meant to be exemplary, certainly not
exhaustive. We have distinguished between political, security, and diplomatic concepts.
Such distinction is not watertight, but it may help putting some order in what otherwise
may seem confusing. A similar remark applies to the distinction we made between legal
and diplomatic principles. The first largely derive from international law, while the second
have emerged from diplomatic practice. There is nothing doctrinaire about these lists, they
are just meant as practical instruments to be put in a diplomat's toolbox.

Bibliography

AMSTRONG, David, FARRELL, Theo & LAMBERT, Hélène (2012), *International Law and
    International Relations*, Cambridge University Press, Cambridge.
COOPER, Robert (2021), *The Ambassadors*, Weidenfeld & Nicolson, London.
DE DIJN, Herman (2003), *Erkenning, gelijkheid en verschil*, Acco, Leuven.
LOWE, Vaughan (2015), *International Law: A Very Short Introduction*, Oxford University Press,
    Oxford.
NYE, Joseph S. (2015), *Is the American Century over?*, Polity, Cambridge.
PERELMAN, Chaïm (1976), *Logique Juridique: Nouvelle Rhétorique*, Dalloz, Paris.
POSNER, Richard (1995), *Overcoming Law*, Harvard University Press, Cambridge, MA.
RUSSELL, Bertrand (1995), *Power*, Routledge, New York.
STRUCK, Gerhard (1971), *Topische Jurisprudenz*, Athenäum, Frankfurt.
WILKINSON, Paul (2007), *International Relations: A Very Short Introduction*, Oxford University
    Press, Oxford.
WOUTERS, Jan (2006), *Internationaal Recht in Kort Bestek*, Intersentia, Antwerpen/London.

Part III

Diplomacy's first call

International peace and security

7 The conflict cycle

International peace and security is the prime concern of diplomacy. To get a grasp on this preeminent concern, we will start in this chapter with a discussion of the 'Conflict Cycle' which has proved to be a useful instrument for conflict analysis. This instrument allows us to do two distinct things: first, to clearly identify each of the different stages in the build-up of a conflict (pre-conflict) and its consequent management and resolution (post-conflict), and to define the role of the diplomat, if any, at each of these stages; and second, to study the conflict dynamics, both in the escalation (build-up) and de-escalation (resolution) phases of the cycle, by paying attention to the sequence of events and actions required as we move through it.

A note of caution is in place here. When we speak of 'different stages' and the 'sequence of events' within the conflict-cycle, this should not be taken too literally; things are less 'linear' in this 'cycle' than this language may suggest. In our analysis of the conflict cycle, we will not be concerned with what constitutes its high point, the 'armed conflict', but only with its 'before' and 'after' (we leave the 'armed conflict' for the next chapter on the 'Use of Force').

Before embarking on our study of the 'Conflict Circle', let us make a few preliminary points.

7.1 Security first

Not everybody would agree that international security is or should be a diplomat's preeminent concern. Many would argue that questions regarding migration, climate change, and energy, for instance, are no less important. And they are right. But from a diplomat's perspective, such questions are important mainly *because and to the extent* that they actually or potentially affect security as he or she understands it. And security as he or she understands it is *primary* in a fundamental sense, namely that *without it we may be unable to pursue the secondary goals* of the 'good life'. This needs some clarification.

7.1.1 Hard and soft security

As the reader probably already guessed, underlying this controversy there is a confusion between *two concepts of security*, a narrow, hard and a broad, soft one. The narrow, traditional (critics would say old-fashioned) concept of security is about threats of violence, repression, military force, war and peace, physical integrity, and survival. Until recently, these matters were labelled 'politico-military affairs'. The broad, new (some would say fashionable) concept of security is not about existence and survival but about

DOI: 10.4324/9781003298182-11

conditions of existence such as provision of minimum levels of welfare (basic human needs) or the preservation of minimum values (human rights). This new, broad concept of security is a rather recent invention that has been strongly promulgated by the United Nations (UN) in the 1990s of last century.

Once the distinction between both concepts is established, one is surprised that they are considered as rival rather than simply different and indeed complementary approaches to security, each important in its own right: the first one focuses on *'freedom from fear'* and the second on *'freedom from want'* (see BROWNING, 2013, p. 6). Put this way, it seems rather obvious that a diplomat's concern is primarily, although not exclusively, about the first of these: the narrow, traditional, hard concept of security. Which is not to say that a diplomat does not recognise the relevance of the broader concept of security. It is simply that this is not what their job description tells them that they should do first. Which brings us to a second, similar point that needs clarification.

7.1.2 State security versus human security

Traditionally, questions of international security have been *state-centred*. This needs to be understood in two different ways; first, that it is the security *of* the state that takes centre stage when discussing security matters, and two, that it is the state who is the prime provider of security. It is the first aspect that interests us now. 'State security' traditionally focuses on questions of national interests, sovereignty, territorial integrity, intangibility of borders, defence, and deterrence. But such questions may seem far removed from the security concerns faced by most ordinary people in their daily life: hunger, disease, education, housing, and employment.

It has therefore been suggested that security should be deepened beyond the state and focus on people who, without being the victim of direct 'physical violence' may very well be the victim of indirect 'structural violence'. Placing humans at the heart of debates about international security is what *'human security'* is about. The concept was for the first time developed by the UN Development Program (UNDP) in its 1994 report 'Redefining Security: The Human Dimension'. Human security is about such things like having a secure and stable income, the ability to access educational and health systems, and living in an unpolluted environment.

As we did in distinguishing between hard and soft security, here too we need to understand that state-centred and human security are not, as is sometimes suggested, two contradictory concepts of security, but rather two different but complementary ways to approach security. And when talking about diplomacy and diplomats, it is the state-centred approach that will be privileged. Not because the human security approach is mistaken or worthless, but simply because diplomacy is, by its very nature, a state-centred business.

7.1.3 Integrated approach to security

Although hard security differs from soft security, and although state-centred security is not the same as human security, a diplomat's role cannot be seen in isolation from the role played by other actors involved in preventing and managing conflict. Indeed, the complementarities between hard and soft, state-centred and human security require an integrated approach to conflict, which involves the broadest simultaneous application of all elements of power: not only diplomacy but also defence and development, among others. The diplomat will therefore have to interact and cooperate with the military and the aid and development workers as well as with commanders of UN operations, Special Representatives and Envoys of states or international organisations, the NGO community, and perhaps even private security contractors. It is the interaction between diplomacy and the military in particular that has come under critical scrutiny lately.

Rupert Smith is one such critical observer. In his *The Utility of Force*, he insists that while a *military* operation does indeed aim at creating the *conditions* in which *political* objectives set by politicians and diplomats can be achieved, *military operation and political stabilisation should not be confused*. Military force may restore military security, but it cannot restore political security let alone resolve the underlying social, economic, and cultural sources of the conflict. This is an important point: while military force can restore short-term security, absence of violence, that is *negative peace*, it is for diplomacy and other actors to build long-term stability through institutional structures based on trust and understanding, that is *positive peace*. We will revert to this issue in the chapter on the 'Use of Force'.

7.2 Pre-conflict – Conflict Prevention

7.2.1 Conflict analysis

Confronted with a simmering dispute or a messy situation of rivalry and hostility among opposing parties, potentially spilling over in an open conflict, the first thing to be done is to proceed to a **cool analysis of the risks and causes** of the tense situation, particularly in so-called fragile states. In this regard, one should distinguish between structural (underlying) causes, proximate causes, and actual triggers of conflict. Such situational/ contextual conflict analysis is a diplomat's job. A diplomat is *in situ*, lives and works in the country, the fragilities of which (ethnic tensions, structural poverty, historic legacies…) he or she is familiar with and is best placed to put into context. Cool analysis also means not to be misled by false signals, such as exaggerations and dramatisations, which are intrinsic features of *tense* situations.

7.2.2 Negotiation and mediation

Talking with and among the opposing parties should help calm down spirits. Such **anticipatory talking** can be done through official channels, government officials mediating and perhaps bringing the parties to the negotiation table. Sometimes though such formal governmental arrangements are resented by the opposing parties, who may dislike the publicity it generates and be suspicious about the intervening country's intentions. Discreet diplomacy led by 'insider mediators', specialised NGOs or other third-party actors may then be the best way to handle the looming tension. This is what happened in Kenya, for example, where former UN Secretary General Kofi Annan rescued the country from a descent in large-scale conflict after hotly disputed elections in 2007.

Mediation, official and nonofficial, can be useful in both conflict-prevention and conflict-resolution. The record is mixed, however. Mediation efforts were successful after a coup in Guinea following the death of its long-term President Lansana Conté (23 December 2008) but less so, just one month later, after a coup in Madagascar (31 January 2009) where the three mediators (the UN, the African Union – AU, and the South African Development Community – SADC) got embroiled in institutional competition about the leadership of the mediation. Building on these successes *and* learning from failures, UN Secretary General Antonio Guterres some years ago set up a 'High Level Advisory Board on Mediation' (see below: Track II diplomacy).

7.2.3 Early warning

Once a simmering dispute seems to have reached the threshold of potential conflict, early warning should **alert stakeholders that time for action may have come**. Early-warning systems (such as those of the UN and EU) monitor the threats to peace and systematise the unstructured flow of reports coming from observers, both private and public (including reports coming from in-country diplomats), who happen to be on the ground in places that are ripe for conflict. Early-warning systems allow stakeholders (1) to design a strategy and plan of action in case the conflict could not be contained; (2) to build political support for action (for instance through coalition building); and (3) to plan for possible assistance and rescue operations for nationals living in the conflict area.

7.2.4 Preventive diplomacy

The concept of preventive diplomacy is ambiguous and is used with three different meanings. (1) Sometimes it refers to a *specific set* of individual or collective *actions* aimed at preventing a potential but *pre-identified* conflict. This rather narrow definition lays stress on preventive *actions* that address the *immediate and proximate* causes that can lead to the outbreak of a conflict. This is the concept most people would consider as being part of a diplomat's job. We will critically review this narrow concept further down. (2) At other times, preventive diplomacy is said to include *all kind of measures and policies* aimed at *removing* the underlying *structural conditions*, the so-called *root causes* of a potential conflict (such as poverty, demographic pressures, corrupt governance). This approach to conflict prevention goes beyond trying to avoid well-defined situations of potential physical harm and involves the engagement of the entire development community as well as that of diplomats. (3) Finally, preventive diplomacy is sometimes understood as referring to *a whole set of initiatives* (including the short-term actions and medium-term measures and policies mentioned above) that can or need to be taken in the *pre-conflict phase* (essentially the list of actions we are currently reviewing) and which aim at the 'prevention and removal of *threats* to international peace and security' generally, as stipulated in Article 1 of the UN Charter (and as further elaborated in the 'Declaration' of the UN General Assembly of 5 December 1988 'on the Prevention and Removal of Disputes and Situations which may threaten international Peace and Security and the Role of the UN in this field'). Below we will briefly review some approaches to peace as presented by former UN Secretary General Boutros Boutros-Ghali in his *Agenda for Peace* of 1992 and which can also be seen as instruments of preventive diplomacy thus broadly understood.

7.2.5 Incentives and disincentives

Incentives and disincentives, means of cajoling and coercing, constitute strategies available for directly engaging in tense situations as they escalate, and include:

- **Persuasive measures** (*'carrots'*) such as payments for assistance programs or confidence building measures (CBMs) designed to lower the uncertainty, reduce the anxiety, and eliminate the misperceptions inherent in any unstable situation.
- **(Non-coercive) dissuasive measures** such as 'naming and shaming' and threats of international legal action should atrocities occur.
- **Coercive measures** (*'sticks'*) such as the institution of selective embargoes or restrictions on weapons transfers, for instance; the imposition of 'no-fly zones' or the establishment of 'safe havens'; or the imposition of more specific sanctions targeting individuals or entities (companies, agencies…) such as travel bans and the freezing of assets. Sanctions regimes turn out to be rather complex instruments of foreign policy generally and conflict-prevention specifically (see Part IV). To be effective, sanctions need international backing and must be buttressed by military force. Even in ideal circumstances, sanctions tend to be limited in what they can accomplish. They may affect the population more than the targeted leadership. They can influence behaviour but are unlikely to produce fundamental changes in actions and capacities of the targeted party. Sanctions could not force Saddam Hussein, for instance, to leave Kuwait.

7.2.6 Deterrence

Deterrence is coercive diplomacy *based on* the **power to hurt**. Deterrence is not hurting, it is threatening to hurt. Diplomacy, you will recall, is about influencing another's behaviour. The power to hurt is bargaining power. To exploit it is diplomacy – vicious diplomacy, but diplomacy nevertheless. As Thomas Shelling remarks in his *The Diplomacy of Violence*, 'Violence is most purposive and most successful when it is threatened and not used. Successful threats are those that do not have to be carried out' (in HANDLER, 2013, p. 221). Deterrence is about *intimidation and threats* and may encompass limited military actions that are calibrated in such a way that while sending a **strong message** to the enemy they would not be so strong as to necessarily spark serious retaliation. As examples of deterrence, one may refer to the ongoing nuclear and ballistic stand-off with North Korea where military people have been thinking about striking an air base or naval facility *not* associated with the ICBM program itself (Inter-Continental Ballistic Missiles), or destroying one of Kim Jong-Un's residencies, or targeting a missile during a test.

7.2.7 Last effort diplomacy

When conflict seems unavoidable, making a last effort serves a double objective: first, genuinely trying to **give peace a last chance**, and second, signalling that, in case of failure, there is **no other option than resorting to military action** (last resort). This was the meaning of the January 1991 meeting between the US Secretary of State James Baker and his Iranian colleague Tarek Aziz at the eve of the first Gulf War, as it was of the

February 1999 Rambouillet meeting with Slobodan Milosevic at the eve of the NATO-led Kosovo intervention. At that meeting US Secretary of State Madeleine Albright, who had been counselled by her advisers to leave the meeting as the discussion turned in rounds, decided to stay on, knowing that such last diplomatic effort would (1) show the **commitment to avoid war**, (2) shore up **support** at home and in the international community for a possible military intervention, and (3) give **legitimacy** to the only remaining alternative of war in case of failure.

7.2.8 Pre-conflict diplomacy

Once armed conflict is inevitable, responsibilities obviously shift from the diplomat to the military. The **diplomat's role** now becomes one of **supporting the military commanders** in getting what they need to make the conflict as short as possible, with the fewest casualties possible. In preparing for the post-9/11 invasion of Afghanistan in October 2001, for instance, US diplomats secured transit and overflight rights with Central Asian states, while in preparing for the Second Gulf War in March 2003 they negotiated access to facilities for US forces in Europe. In preparing the fight against ISIS/Daesh in 2014 diplomats of all countries participating in the broad-based Coalition were involved in ensuring sufficient support for the operation, including through public diplomacy, as well as coordinating actions, both military and civilian, in the field.

7.3 From Pre-conflict Prevention to Post-conflict Management

At this stage in the conflict-cycle, we are faced with the inevitability of armed conflict, which closes the pre-conflict phase. Armed conflict is what we will study in the next chapter on the 'use of force'. When the armed conflict is over, and some fragile cease-fire has been secured, comes the real thing: **winning the peace**. We then enter the post-conflict phase of the conflict-cycle.

Once war is over, that does not mean peace is there. What you normally get is an extremely messy situation. It is an illusion to think that you will at once be able to apply neat, ready-made recipes telling you what to do. As a diplomat you must be willing to accept that your 'solutions' too will be messy to some extent. It is a frequent mistake to be willing to get at once at the optimal solution to the problem, the one you read about in textbooks. *Humility and patience* are what you will need most. Be content to make some progress. Work step by step. Go for the feasible and the workable even when that will often not amount to much in the early stages of the post-conflict phase.

Crucial in the early stages of the post-conflict phase is that you must be prepared to **build the peace with the very people who made the war**. Some diplomats, the purists, find this abhorring. And yet, quite often there is no alternative. Of course, the legitimacy of former fighters and warlords may be very questionable, but then consider (1) that they often continue to benefit from the support of large swaths of the population that backed them during the armed conflict, and (2) that even when this may not be the case, they often retain a considerable amount of *power of nuisance*. The outer limit of tolerance in dealing with them should turn on the question whether they were involved in war crimes or crimes against humanity. And even then, considerations of *transitional* justice for the sake of peace may have to prevail, as we will see below. The former rebel leader in what was then Zaire and is today the Democratic Republic of Congo (DRC), Jean-Pierre

Bemba, put many of us in the mid-2000s facing this delicate balance between peace and justice.

Based on these preliminary remarks, let me state a few **rules of thumb for sober yet effective conflict-management**:

- Do **not** primarily think of **solving** a conflict, **but** rather about **how to cope** with it, and that will consist in some 'muddling through'. Your first call is conflict-management, not conflict-resolution.
- Think of conflict management not so much in terms of static, substantive solutions, but rather in terms of a dynamic but time-consuming **process**.
- Do not ask 'what is the solution', but rather 'how do I get out of this mess', **slowly progressing** towards some perspective on a solution.
- And even then, do **not** look for the **perfect** solution. Perfection is not of this world, particularly not in a context of conflict and war. Just ask how you can get things moving, how to get from here to there, which direction to go.

7.4 Post-conflict – Conflict Management and Resolution

7.4.1 No relapse

Throughout the conflict management phase, particularly in its early stages, it is imperative to ensure there will not be any reigniting of the armed conflict. Relapsing simply means having to go through the pre-conflict phase all over again. Relapsing is what happened in South Sudan where after a peace deal in 2015 the country spiralled back into civil war the following year. A more recent example of relapse is Myanmar, where the army took complete control of the country again in a coup on 1 February 2021, leading to an economic collapse and widespread social unrest. Some predict that Myanmar will be 'Asia's next failed state' (THE ECONOMIST, 2021). Oxford development economist Paul Collier has established that a country that has just ended a civil war has a 40 per cent chance of **falling back into conflict** within a decade (the risk falls by about a percentage point for each year of peace).

7.4.2 Stability

That is why the first thing to do once the armed conflict is over and the military are gone, and some precarious peace is in place, is to consolidate that peace through the establishment of a **sustainable secure environment**. Providing urgent humanitarian relief and protecting the civilian population might well be the first thing to be done. Separating the warring factions is not enough. Active disarmament is a must. Since the late 1980s there have been more than 60 '*Disarmament, Demobilisation and Reintegration*' (**DDR**) programmes in countries as diverse as Liberia (2003, UNMIL) where it was a success and Haiti (2004, MINUSTAH) where it was not. The idea behind DDR is simple: part fighters from their weapons, discharge them from their militias, and help them reintegrate civilian life with money or training – or, in the case of children, with schools.

Once DDR has been implemented time has come to set up effective security structures, perhaps with the support of partner-countries or regional/international organisations, who may dispatch integrated *Security Sector Reform* (**SSR**) missions, as the EU has done in the Central African Republic (CAR), Mali and Somalia during the past 15 years.

The deployment of a UN multi-agency mission or a UN peacekeeping force can very well help (see below).

7.4.3 State building

Next to establishing a secure environment comes 'state building', *not* 'reconstruction and rehabilitation', as many are tempted to think. 'State building' involves the setting up of a new political infrastructure, which should reflect the **new political order** transcending the rivalries of the formerly warring parties. In the very short term, some kind of transitional political arrangements may need to be negotiated. But central to 'state building' at an early stage is agreement on a **constitutional framework** that should resolve upfront the issues that were at the core of the conflict and allow new political institutions to emerge. *Elections* have a role but closer towards the end of the state building process than at the start. Special attention should obviously go to the question which type of state needs to be built (centralised, federal, confederal). This will very much depend on the internal configuration of the different groupings (ethnic, religious, linguistic) that will have to learn to live together under one single political roof. When working out a new constitution, make sure you are guaranteed the lasting adherence of the different parties around the negotiation table. As Carl Bildt once put it: 'a lasting solution is one that meets the minimum demands of all, while most probably not meeting the maximum demands of anyone'.

State building is notoriously difficult. It delivered unconvincing results in Iraq and Afghanistan at a huge human and fiscal cost. The difficulties of state building most recently showed in the **Afghan peace negotiations**. After six months of intransigence and delay, the Taliban and Afghan government leaders at last agreed to sit down together on 12 September 2020 in Doha to seek agreement on how to run their country. The talks focused on the shape of the country once the Americans would have gone as they had promised they would. The talks were difficult. At some point the thorniest issues would have to be tackled (how should the country be governed? how to allocate power? what rights will be enshrined in a constitution?). But they never were. With the precipitate withdrawal of the US (and NATO) troops in 2021 the whole question of Afghan state building has been kept on hold.

7.4.4 Reconciliation and transitional justice

Reconciliation is a key for stability. A healthy society is one that has come to terms with itself, overcoming the demons of past hatred and resentment. Justice is the key here. But justice will somehow have to be **accommodated** (see Box 7.1). As we said, the fact is that you need to build the peace with those who made the war. You cannot have the latter simply locked up in jail, as classical justice might require. That is where transitional justice comes in. *Transitional justice aims at restoring the maximum of justice while preserving a workable perspective for peace.* Delicate questions are involved here, including questions of amnesties or pardons. Many ordinary citizens resent seeing former warlords and fighters transformed into political leaders. But evidence suggests that, when they are, the peace is more likely to hold. The importance of transitional justice has been *a contrario* demonstrated in the case of Uganda where the publicity given to the International Criminal Court's arrest warrants for the leaders of the Lord Resistance Army (LRA) disrupted the peace negotiations, generated a new round of violence and exposed potential witnesses to unacceptable risks.

Box 7.1 Transitional Justice – Conceptual Challenges

Should peace (in terms of the end of violence) be prioritised over justice when the pursuit of justice might destabilise the peace process? Or are justice and peace mutually reinforcing, and if so, how much justice is necessary to ensure peace? Pursuing justice may endanger the peace process such as when political bargains must be made with powerful and armed groups complicit in terrible human rights abuses. Political bargaining for the sake of peace is what happened in Sierra Leone (with the RUF) and Cambodia (with the Khmer Rouge): peace was traded for justice in the early post-conflict stages in order to prevent a return to full-scale civil war. It was only years later when that danger had largely passed, that prosecutions against the most notorious war criminals were initiated.

Sometimes past arrangements for transitional justice can come back with a vengeance. When democracy came to Spain in the late 1970s, it arrived through agreements between moderate Franco supporters and a realist democratic opposition. At their heart were an amnesty law and an understanding not to use the past as a political weapon. The seamless transition that followed risks however being upset by a draft law of 'democratic memory' proposed by the Sanchez government in 2020. The law would set up a special prosecutor to investigate human rights abuses from 1936 to 1978. Not only would this be futile (most perpetrators are dead), but it comes close to overturning the amnesty law based on the conviction *that justice and truth should retroactively outweigh peace and reconciliation.* Retroactive justice may not just be unwise, it may be dangerous. Reopening the past may aggravate political conflict (as in El Salvador where the amnesty law of 1993 was declared unconstitutional by the Supreme Court in 2016) or may make achieving peace or democracy in other countries more difficult (as in Venezuela where generals do not believe the amnesties offered by the opposition in return for their turning against the authoritarian rule of Nicolas Maduro).

7.4.5 Reconstruction and rehabilitation

Only after a durable secure environment has been established and a blueprint of a constitutional framework has been agreed, should one address the issue of *reconstructing* the **material infrastructure** of the country (housing, schools, hospitals, roads, and industrial base) and *rehabilitating* its **immaterial infrastructure**, such as its economy, finances, banking system, education system. This is essentially the job of aid and development workers. Essentially, but not exclusively. As said earlier, an integrated approach to peacekeeping, state-building, reconstruction, and rehabilitation requires a joint long-term effort of military, diplomats, and development workers. The minimalist approach we witnessed in Afghanistan where some thought that by overthrowing the Taliban and setting up the Karzai government, the job was done, has not worked. And similar lessons have been learned in Iraq after the second Gulf War.

7.5 Four approaches to peace – the UN vocabulary

In 1992, former UN Secretary General Boutros Boutros-Ghali presented his *Agenda for Peace* which provided analysis and recommendations on different approaches to strengthen the UN's capacity to maintain world peace. Some of those approaches to peace are outlined below.

When it comes to UN action in conflict situations, we need to recall the distinction between Chapter VI and Chapter VII operations. **Chapter VI** of the UN Charter is concerned with the *pacific settlement of disputes*, while **Chapter VII** allows the Security Council to authorise *coercive action, including military action*, when it deems this necessary to maintain or restore international peace and security.

- **Peace-making** is the general term to refer to any peaceful attempt at bringing the parties to a dispute to agreement by appealing to *traditional diplomatic tools* such as negotiation, mediation, and arbitration. We will come back to this when looking into Track II diplomacy (see below).
- **Peace-enforcement** involves the **imposition** of peace **by force**; peace-enforcement is a Chapter VII **coercion-based** action which requires the prior authorisation by the Security Council. Unlike peacekeeping, which is premised on the consent of the parties, peace-enforcement is more divisive as it entails taking sides among the parties. The imposition of peace is often carried out through an *ad hoc* multi-national 'coalition of the willing' (as in the 1991 US-led Iraq operation) or, less frequently, through a regional organisation such as the Economic Community of West African States (ECOWAS) or NATO (as in the 2011 NATO-led Libya intervention). The first UN-authorised peace-enforcement operation ever was decided in June 1950, sanctioning action against North Korea following the invasion of South Korea (ironically, that action was only possible because the Soviet Union was at that time boycotting the Security Council in protest at the continued occupation of the Chinese seat by the nationalist government based in Taiwan). The last UN-authorised enforcement operation was in Libya in 2011 authorising the international community to take 'all necessary means' in protecting civilians under threat of attack.
- **Peacekeeping** aims at the **preservation of peace** either in a pre-conflict scenario (avoiding deterioration and thus preventing armed conflict) or in a post-conflict situation (avoiding relapse after a precarious peace-deal has been found). Peacekeeping operations are known by the larger public as **PKO's**. Peacekeeping is a Chapter VI **consent-based** enterprise decided by the Security Council; consent-based means that the country where the PKO is to be deployed must assent to it. As a Chapter VI operation, a PKO should normally **not** have recourse to the **use of force**, except for self-defence, i.e. the protection of the UN mission itself. However, as a benign situation can turn sour, and to allow the mission then to respond with force, if necessary, usual practice is now for a Chapter VII mandate to be given for peacekeeping operations as well. Such hybrid operations are therefore sometimes called 'Chapter VI and a half' missions.
- Peacekeeping is normally carried out by so-called **Blue Helmets**, military operating under direct UN command and made available by troop-contributing countries (so-called TCCs). Bangladesh, India, and Pakistan have traditionally been the largest troop contributors. The developed states have a poor record in this regard, which is

to be regretted. Their involvement would add to the operational strength of PKO missions and, on a more symbolic plane, to their credibility. It is unfortunate that in contributing troops, some TCCs seem to be primarily motivated by cashing in the 'per diems' to which the military, not the government, should be entitled (as was the case with Burundi when it contributed troops to the UN operation in Somalia). Peacekeeping was until recently an almost exclusively male enterprise, but things have been changing in the last decades (see Box 7.2).

Box 7.2 The Woman-Soldier in UN Peacekeeping

Between 1957 and 1989, only 20 women ever served as UN Peacekeepers. But as the number of female soldiers in the army has been growing (in the US Army, for example, they currently make up one fifth of all officers) and as they have been allowed to serve in combat roles once reserved for men, so have their number and role in UN peacekeeping increased significantly during the last 20 years. The UN has in fact played a leading role in championing female soldiers. It has pledged to increase the share of women in military forces from 1 per cent in 1993 to 15 per cent by 2028 and 20 per cent in police units (in 2020, these percentages stood at 5 and 17, respectively). Among the pioneers were 103 Indian women sent to Liberia in 2007 as the first all-female police unit. This increased role of women in peacekeeping is not just a question of numbers but is directly related to what female soldiers can bring to soldiering. In modern wars, soldiers do more than just inflicting violence on enemies. The woman-soldier is better at building trust and therefore at gathering intelligence. Not surprisingly, she is also better able than her male colleague to engage with women and children without being seen as a threat. Also, it has been found that male fellow soldiers behaved with more restraint in joint male-female police and army patrols than in male-only patrols.

The PKOs in East Timor (1999, UNTAET) and Ivory Coast (2004, UNOCI) were a success. Less so the PKO established in the Democratic Republic of Congo (DRC) in 1999 (MONUC), one of the world's most expensive and largest peace-keeping mission (20,000 blue helmets) in the history of the UN. Less successful too, to say the least, were the missions in Rwanda in 1993 (UNAMIR) and Darfur in 2007 (UNMIS). The longest lasting PKO is UNFICYP, a mission dating back to 1964 meant to supervise the ceasefire lines and maintain a buffer zone between the Turkish and Greek Cypriot communities; the mission has in fact been freezing rather than resolving the conflict.

The **weak spots** of quite a few PKOs are twofold: mandates are often poorly defined and resources are often insufficient; in addition, and crucially, PKOs are dependent on the goodwill and cooperation of the host-government. Preserving the consent of the host country may oblige peacekeepers to abstain from directly intervening in conflicts as this could be construed as breaching impartiality. That is why UN peacekeepers may at times be helpless to protect civilians and prevent atrocities as happened with the massacre of 8,000 Bosniaks (Bosnian Muslims) in Srebrenica in 1995. More recently, the futility of UN missions was painfully demonstrated when the observers of the

UN Supervision Mission in Syria (UNSMS, deployed in April 2012 to monitor the cessation of violence) could not even reach the sites of conflict they were supposed to 'supervise'.

- **Peace-building.** *Keeping* peace may well have been what the first peace operations aimed to do, but the far more arduous task is the *building* of peace. Peace-building is essentially targeted towards states under stress (failing or failed States) and aims at avoiding pre-conflict 'state collapse' and even more often post-conflict 'relapse'. Peace-building is, like peacekeeping, consent-based and aims at addressing the root causes of (potential) conflicts and creating structures to bring or restore security, stability, and confidence. To be successful, peace-building should work bottom-up: more time should be spend working with communities, understanding their grievances, and earning their trust, rather than hobnobbing with government officials; more responsibility should be given to locals (see AUTESSERRE, 2020). In addition to their traditional military functions, peacekeepers also play an important role as peace-builders in assuming various police and civilian functions. At the September 2005 Summit in New York, a new institution, the UN Peacebuilding Commission (PBC), was created. It is an advisory body that works by consensus and that reports both to the Security Council and the General Assembly. When the PBC started working in 2006, Burundi became the first country on its agenda. The PBC's record so far has unfortunately not been quite convincing.

7.6 Preventive Diplomacy – Some Critical Remarks

As already said, the concept of 'Preventive Diplomacy' gained prominence and became quite 'trendy' in the wake of the former UN Secretary General Boutros Boutros-Ghali's 1992 *Agenda for Peace*. It is, however, a concept that has been criticised for its vagueness and ambiguity. For the sake of clarity, let us first briefly recall the three possible meanings of the concept:

- In its most general sense, preventive diplomacy is understood as referring to the whole set of *initiatives* (short-term *actions* and medium-term *measures and policies*) that can or need to be taken in the *pre-conflict* phase. This definition is much too broad to be of any practical use for diplomatic practice.
- Sometimes preventive diplomacy is said to refer to *policies and measures* aimed at removing the underlying *structural conditions* (the so-called *root causes*) of a potential conflict. This approach is still too broad as it does not target well-defined situations of potential physical harm. Removing negative structural conditions is an all-encompassing job for development workers and diplomats alike.
- The concept of preventive diplomacy that diplomats would consider part of their remit is the one that refers to a *specific* set of *actions* aimed at preventing a potential but *pre-identified* conflict. This rather narrow definition lays stress on preventive actions that address the *immediate or proximate* causes that can lead to the outbreak of a conflict. It is this concept that we will critically review below: specific actions aimed at preventing specific events. How come we did not prevent the invasion of Kuwait by Saddam Hussein in 1990? How come we did not prevent the Rwandan genocide in 1994?

Preventive diplomacy is a noble concept. Learned books have been written on it. Whenever you invoke it, you get applause. But for this concept to merit applause, one should be able to explain its mechanics, to tell how it exactly operates as a tool for diplomats to work with. As we will see, preventive diplomacy rests on two assumptions which are quite questionable. The first one is that *to prevent a future event you must have foreseen it*. The second assumption is that even when some reasonable prevision has been made, you will *act on it*. The first assumption is the no-surprises assumption. The second one is the action-assumption. Before looking at each of these, let us give some examples where preventive diplomacy failed and one single example where it presumably succeeded. We start with the latter.

Examples. Examples of so-called successful preventive actions are scarce (see Box 7.3); the most cited one is the *Ohrid Framework Agreement* of 2001 which presumably rescued Northern-Macedonia (formerly called FYROM – Former Yugoslav Republic of Macedonia), then on the brink of civil war, from disaster. But this was an exception. And even then, it is not clear what action prevented what non-event.

It is much easier to give examples of cases where preventive diplomacy failed. In many cases, governments seem to have been taken by surprise, as was the case with the Arab uprisings starting in 2011 (Tunisia, Egypt, Libya, and Syria) or they were slow to act as in the crises in Rwanda (1994), Darfur (2004), South Sudan (2013), and the CAR (2004 and 2013). One could go further back in the past and cite as 'historic' surprises the North Korean invasion of South Korea in 1950, the Soviet introduction of missiles into Cuba in 1962, the Egyptian (and Syrian) attack against Israel on 6 October 1973, the landing of Turkish troops in Cyprus in 1974.

Box 7.3 A Logical Quandary

For amateurs only. There is a logical problem at the core of the concept of prevention: since what has pretendedly been prevented does not happen (it is a 'negative fact' – 'the dog that did not bark at night'), you cannot know for sure whether you prevented it. That is why, ironically, the concept of 'preventive diplomacy' only seems to apply in the context of events ('positive facts') that, as they happen, have not been prevented.

This paradox explains why it is difficult to give examples of successful preventive diplomacy. Conversely, the paradox explains why talk about preventive diplomacy is most often linked to events that (could) have been foreseen but were *not* prevented. And then the question is: how come?

There seems to be something built into the international consciousness that prevents it from foreseeing future problems or, if foreseen, acting on that knowledge.

On not foreseeing what in retrospect seemed inevitable. As we said, the first assumption for preventive diplomacy to work is that you must have been able to foresee the event in order to prevent it. This assumption is far from obvious. 'Personne ne prévoit jamais rien' (Nobody ever foresees anything). With its four consecutive 'negatives', this statement leaves no doubt as to its categoricity. The statement is from Gérard Errera, former Political Director and Secretary General of the Quai d'Orsay (French MFA). As examples of not-foreseeing, he cites the Iranian revolution in 1979 and the implosion of the Soviet Union some ten years later, events that appear **inevitable *a posteriori* and impossible *a priori*** ('inéluctable *a posteriori* et impossible *a priori*') but that no intelligence service of no country had anticipated (Le Monde, 15 February 2011). The fallacy that is at work here is known as the ***hindsight fallacy***. It consists in judging a situation based on knowledge that is available *only after* the facts have occurred. Such *ex post factum* knowledge creates the illusion of inevitability to which Errera was pointing. Many so-called failures in preventive diplomacy are based on this hindsight fallacy. Take the Rwanda genocide in 1994. It was only after the atrocities took place that people highlighted reports of an impending disaster that had been circulating well before the events. Then everybody seemed to recall the reports that they had gently ignored before the events. Or take the *coup d'état* in Burundi in the spring of 1987 when President Bagaza was set aside by Colonel Buyoya. After the *coup*, everybody had his theory over the predictability and inevitability of the event, but they forgot that news of an impending *coup* had been around for over a year and that many *coups* had been announced with the regularity of a Swiss clock, which all turned out to be fake. Many events become self-evident only in retrospect. Could anybody have foreseen the proximate cause of the Rwandan genocide, the downing of the airplane carrying President Habyarimana? Could anybody have foreseen that President Bagaza would have been out of the country, which *ex post factum* may help explain the timing of the coup, if not the coup itself.

On foreseeing but getting it wrong. In diplomacy, *strategic foresight and anticipatory governance* have become trendy concepts. Outside the field of diplomacy, foresight, and anticipation is at the core of the flourishing business of *forecasting and risk management*. And although it is generally recognised that developing a 'culture of preparedness' has become more difficult and testing in a complex world that is changing at an unprecedented pace, many people still underestimate the intrinsic vulnerability of foresight and forecasting. Foresight easily falls prey to the so-called ***extrapolation fallacy***, a fallacy we already met when studying reasoning in diplomacy. Foresight is based on the idea that the future can be neatly extrapolated from the past as if time were linear, which it is not. History does not run in straight lines. And reasoning by analogy is, as we saw, perilous. In the context of conflict prevention, linear thinking shows in the tendency to believe that habits of an adversary in the past are bound to arise in the future. Take the Egyptian (and Syrian) attack in October 1973. Israeli intelligence *knew* about Egyptian troop concentrations but did not believe they were a signal of an impending war, because similar troop concentrations a few months earlier, in May 1973, had not led to war. Israeli intelligence knew but got it wrong.

On foreseeing but not acting on it. Often the explanation of 'surprises' is not, as in the last case, due to a miscalculation based on faulty extrapolation. Most cases of predictable surprises are cases where, not lacking accurate information, analysis or early warning and *full well knowing* the risks that lay ahead, we still *fail to act* simply for reasons of *mental comfort*. The German invasion of Denmark in April 1940 is a case in point, an event that everyone 'had predicted but which was still a shock when it happened' (COOPER, 2021, p. 119). Darfur is another example: the first alerts of an upcoming crisis were already clearly present in 2002, but the crisis only got on our agenda in 2004. No miscalculation was involved. We simply felt more comfortable ignoring the alerts and forgetting about Darfur altogether. As Henry Kissinger says in his *A World Restored* (LONDON, 1999, p. 329): 'Nations learn only by experience. They 'know' only when it is too late'.

How come? The problem lies in what Abba Eban has called 'the *psychological structure* of governments and statesmen', more specifically the easiness with which politicians and diplomats lend themselves to *lenient interpretations* (EBAN, 1998, p. 42). What is at play here is the habit to formulate assessments and appraisals of problematic situations that suit us well, and then to reject as inconvenient truths any information that contradicts them.

Humans are prey to 'cognitive traps' as we have seen in Chapter 6. In the context of our discussion on preventive diplomacy, the following traps merit special mention:

- First comes the all-pervasive **Confirmation Bias**. Confirmation bias is the tendency to *interpret* incoming information so that it confirms or at least does not disturb our existing beliefs and convictions. We filter out any new information that contradicts or sits uneasily with our existing views ('dissonant information', 'disconfirming evidence'). Closely linked to the confirmation bias is our seemingly limitless capacity for **Wishful Thinking**. In a complex world, we are surrounded by contradictory clues and differing opinions. And we eagerly do seize upon whatever clues and opinions happen to support the conclusions we wish to reach.
- Second, there is the **Hyperbolic Discounting of the Future Bias**: the future is worth less than the present (that is why we are ready to make a sacrifice – go to the dentist, quit smoking – over a month, but not tomorrow); or conversely: we value the present well above the future (that is why we prefer a more limited benefit today over a larger one tomorrow). So, preventing foreseeable future events is less rewarding than acting on current events, even though the former may intrinsically be much more important than the latter. This bias is reinforced by **the logic of politics**. Politics is short term. Politics is about survival here and now. What counts for the politician is winning the next election. So, the next electoral deadline is what defines the politician's time horizon. The politician must act *now* on questions which are relevant *now*. Being busy with questions about the future is a luxury he or she cannot afford.
- Third, there is the **Optimism Bias**: when something bad might happen, but also might not happen, we will favour the last contingency. An extended version of the same bias is that while bad things happen, they just do not happen to us, but to others.

All these biases are obviously *self-deluding strategies*. They have been wrapped up under what Robert Meyer and Howard Kunreuther have called the '**Ostrich Paradox**': for individuals and governments alike, it is common to make poor decisions in the face of clearly foreseeable but unpleasant events; rather ignore them than face them. While the world is an unpredictable place, unpredictability often is not the problem. The problem is that faced with clear risk, we still fail to act.

7.7 Conflict and Track II diplomacy

When studying the pre-conflict phase of the Conflict-Cycle we met 'mediation' as a useful instrument to defuse emerging conflict situations. Mediation, when done by *non-officials*, belongs to what is called Track II diplomacy, a way of doing diplomacy that we introduced in Chapter 2. But mediation is only one of the multiple ways Track II diplomacy can be carried out in the context of conflict-prevention and -resolution. In this section, we will review the different **forms** of conflict-related **Track II diplomacy**.

Facilitation: Facilitation is a minimal form of third-party engagement in a parties' dispute. The facilitator's role is limited to providing an appropriate forum, space, and environment conducive to the settlement of the dispute. The facilitator creates the conditions for parties to initiate and maintain their own dialogue process, but he or she does not enter into the substance of the dispute unless, as is often the case, their facilitation is linked to mediation (then called facilitated mediation).

Good offices: Through good offices, a third-party intermediary tries to bring about or initiate negotiations between the parties or bring parties back to the negotiation table after negotiations broke off. The good officer is a mere 'go-between'. Contrary to what happens in mediation, in good offices there is no direct active engagement in the discussion on the substance of the dispute. What the good office provider does, however, is indirectly support the negotiation, e.g. by providing information and expertise. He or she may be doing fact-finding or assist in the determination of legal rights and duties of the parties. An important role may consist in setting up enquiries, perhaps through an international enquiry commission (so-called *fact finding commission*) whose aim is to present a detached, objective insight in the real whereabouts of the dispute. Such enquiry normally results in a factual report, without advice or recommendations. An outstanding example of good offices is the role played by Pakistan in the Sino-American rapprochement in the early 1970s. When Pakistan found the two parties ready to talk directly it withdrew from the process.

Mediation: Contrary to the other forms of third-party engagement, mediation implies the *active participation* of the mediator in the negotiation. He or she actively seeks to solve matters by bridging positions, advancing alternative proposals to those on the table and making proposals on their own. Mediation involves the non-coercive and often non-binding intervention of the mediator, whose objective is to support the negotiation by influencing the perception of the parties of what is at stake and by motivating them to reach an agreed outcome, perhaps by using subtle pressure. The mediator is there to affect, change, resolve, or otherwise influence the course of the negotiation. As a third party, he or she may be better able to identify and then draw attention to the enlightened self-interest of the parties, devising genuine and workable solutions to real problems, advancing arguments, and perhaps using experience and prestige to influence the process and change the parties' perceptions or behaviour. The parties may commit themselves to respect the determinations and decisions of the mediator.

Conciliation: This is a method of conflict-resolution whereby the parties jointly create a commission (most often on an *ad hoc*-basis) entrusted with an impartial and independent enquiry on the dispute. As a rule, each party will designate one member of the commission and both parties jointly will designate a third member, the *umpire*. When ending its work, the commission submits a non-binding conciliation-proposal to the parties. Conciliation opens the door towards arbitration, the main difference being that in the latter case the 'arbitral award' will be a binding decision which the parties have an obligation to accept.

Arbitration: Whereas *adjudication* involves the referral of a dispute to an *established* tribunal or court for a binding judicial decision, arbitration implies the referral of a dispute to an *ad hoc* dispute settlement entity or mechanism, perhaps set up by agreement between the parties themselves, for a binding 'arbitral award'. Arbitration is more flexible than adjudication in that it offers the parties control over the selection of the arbiters, the scope of the issues submitted for arbitration and the procedures to be applied. Still, arbitration is a more rigid form of dispute settlement than conciliation and mediation and is generally less appropriate for politically sensitive disputes.

Once a form of third-party engagement has been selected (the 'which'-question) **the modalities of the engagement** by the third party need to be defined (the 'how'-question):

- The **level of engagement**: The third-party must consider at what level to engage with the parties: high-level, senior-level, mid-level, or working staff level. Even in case of nonofficial diplomacy high level leads easily to publicity and risks transforming Track II into Track I diplomacy.
- The **nature of contact**: The third-party will have to decide whether the parties to the conflict will be put in direct face-to-face contact, or indirectly through the intermediary (*shuttle diplomacy*) with obviously the option of transiting, when time is ripe for it, from indirect to direct contact.
- The **appropriate time** for engagement: Does the third party engage at an early stage of the dispute when it is not well-defined, or only after it has crystallised into a well-defined problem or perhaps even later at crisis-point.
- The **location** of the engagement: Where will the third-party meet with the parties to the dispute: a third country, perhaps a country with a strong 'neutrality' reputation (Norway, Sweden, Switzerland) or the headquarters of an international organisation (UN in Geneva, for instance).
- The **periodicity** of engagement: Will the third-party engagement be a one-off exercise, or will contacts be few and occasional, or regular within a certain time frame, or will the process be a continuing open-ended one.
- The **nature of communication**: Will communications with and among the parties be in writing or orally (or both), will the communication be considered secret or merely confidential, quid reporting to the outside world.

In this chapter, we have started addressing questions regarding international peace and security, questions which are at the core of a diplomat's job. International security is a prime concern for diplomacy because it is a precondition for any society to thrive. Economic prosperity, social progress, education, health, justice – all are predicated on security. We introduced the 'conflict cycle' as a useful instrument for conflict analysis. Although actual conflicts are much more messy and unpredictable than the conflict-cycle seems to suggest, as an analytical tool it allows us to identify recurring stages in both the ascending pre-conflict and descending post-conflict phases of an evolving conflict. Each of these stages calls for distinct diplomatic interventions. At the low-end of the pre-conflict phase, recourse may be had to negotiation and mediation, next when a tense situation risks escalating a set of incentives and dis-incentives may be put in place, followed perhaps by limited military measures by way of deterrence. When armed conflict seems unavoidable, a last effort will be made to give peace a last chance. The whole set of measures, actions, and policies that need be taken in the pre-conflict phase can be wrapped up under the label 'preventive diplomacy'. A similar development, obviously with different components, can be made as regards the post-conflict phase of the cycle. Crucial in this phase is the fact that peace needs to be built with the very people who made war and that leads to delicate questions such as those encountered in transitional justice. Throughout the post-conflict stage, a diplomat will need patience and accept that what is expected from them is to manage the conflict rather than to find the perfect solution.

Bibliography

AHTISAARI, Martti & RINTAKOSKI, Kristiina (2015), "Mediation", in: COOPER, 2015, pp. 337–351.

ARNAULD, Valérie (2019a), "Untangling Justice, Peace and Amnesties in the Central African Republic", in: Egmont Policy Papers, No. 23, February 2019.

ARNAULD, Valérie (2019b), "Security Forces' Strategies of Resistance to Transitional Justice", in: Egmont Policy Papers, No. 27, October 2019.

ARNAULD, Valérie (2021), "Developments in the Field of Transitional Justice", in: Egmont Papers, No. 36, June 2021.

AUTESSERRE, Séverine (2020), *The Frontlines of Peace: An Insider's Guide to Changing the World*, Oxford University Press, Oxford.

BERCOVITCH, Jacob & JACKSON, Richard (2009), *Conflict Resolution in the Twenty-First Century*, Michigan University Press, Ann Arbor.

BERRIDGE, G. R. (2010), *Diplomacy. Theory and Practice*, Palgrave, New York, NY.

BROWNING, Christopher S. (2013), *International Security: A Very Short Introduction*, Oxford University Press, Oxford.

CAHILL, Kevin M. (Ed.) (1996), *Preventive Diplomacy: Stopping Wars before They Start*, Basic Books, New York, NY.

CONOIR, Yvan & VERNA, Gérard (Eds.) (2005), *Faire la Paix – Concepts et Pratiques de la Consolidation de la Paix*, Presses de l'Université Laval,Québec.

COOPER, Andrew, HEINE, Jorge & THAKUR, Ramesh (2015), *The Oxford Handbook of Modern Diplomacy*, Oxford University Press, Oxford.

COOPER, Robert (2021), *The Ambassadors*, Weidenfeld & Nicolson, London.

CORNISH, Chloé (2020), "Industry of Peacemakers Capitalises on Global Conflict", *The Economist*, 22 October 2019.

DOBBINS, James, JONES, Seth, CRANE, Keith & DE GRASSE, Beth (2007), *Nation-Building: The Beginner's Guide*, Rand, Santa Monica, CA.

EBAN, Abba (1998), *Diplomacy for the Next Century*, Yale University Press, New Haven, CT/London.

THE ECONOMIST (2021), "Officers and Gentlewomen – Women in War", 24 April 2021.

ESPAS (2019), "Challenges and Choices for Europe – Global Trends to 2030", European Union, Brussels.

GHANI, Ashraf & LOCKHART, Clare (2009), *Fixing Failing States: A Framework for Rebuilding a Fractured World*, Oxford University Press, Oxford.

HANDLER, Scott P. (Ed.) (2013), *International Politics*, CQ Press, Los Angeles, CA.

KISSINGER, Henry (2008), "A World Restored", *Diplomatic History*, 32, pp. 441–469.

8 Use of force

Until some ten years ago, most observers would have considered a clash between the world's great powers very unlikely. But some start having their doubts. They note that long-term shifts in geoeconomics and geopolitics and the proliferation of new technologies are fuelling **great-power rivalry**. Both China and Russia are now revisionist states that challenge the post–Cold War *status quo* of a 'rules-based world order'. They look at their regions as spheres of influence. For China that means East Asia, for Russia, Eastern Europe and Central Asia. Neither China nor Russia seems to *want* a direct military confrontation with the West, which they would surely loose. But they are using their growing hard power in other ways, in particular, by exploiting a 'grey zone' where coercion works just below the level that would risk military confrontation. Years of strategic drift in Washington have played in the hands of China and Russia. George W. Bush's ill-thought second Gulf War was a distraction and sapped support at home for America's global role. Barack Obama pursued a foreign policy of retrenchment and was sceptical of hard power. Donald Trump seemed not more interested in upholding the rules-based system as his Chinese and Russian rivals do. As for the Europeans, they still are not at ease with the idea that, while the soft power of patient and consistent diplomacy is indeed vital, to be credible such power must be backed by hard power, the kind of power that China and Russia only respect.

Not everybody will agree with the specifics of this analysis, but few will deny that our world has indeed become less secure. Even though most countries seldom find themselves directly involved in a war, no war leaves a country indifferent to its potential consequences and implications. That is why any diplomat should be familiar with the logic of the 'use of force' that we will study in the present chapter.

There are two ways to approach the question of the use of force. The first is a *principled, ideology-driven* approach that seems not very helpful for the practising diplomat. The second is a *pragmatic, policy-driven* approach that looks more promising.

Principled approach. Those who approach the question of the use of force *as a matter of principle* divide into two opposing camps.

There are those who claim that, as a rule, recourse to the use of force is prohibited. Advocates of this school rely on the wording of Article 2(4) of the United Nations (UN) Charter stating that 'all members shall refrain in their international relations from the threat or use of force against the territorial integrity or political independence of any state (…)'. But they then add that there are *exceptions* to the prohibition on the use of force, permitted under the UN Charter in case of self-defence (Article 51) and when authorised by the UN Security Council (Chapter VII) (see Box 8.1).

DOI: 10.4324/9781003298182-12

At the opposite end, there are those who deem the recourse to the use of force not to be, in principle, prohibited – that is: permitted. Advocates of this school rely on the wording of the very first paragraph of the first Article of the first Chapter of the Charter on the *Purposes and Principles* of the UN. Article 1(1) of the Charter indeed allows 'effective collective measures' to be taken 'for the prevention and removal of threats to the peace, and for the suppression of acts of aggression or other breaches of the peace (…)'. But then they add that any recourse to the use of force can only occur under the *strict conditions* provided by the UN Charter.

Wrapping up, we have the '*jus contra bellum*' school (recourse to the use of force is prohibited, unless when permitted) opposed to the '*jus ad bellum*' school (recourse to the use of force is permitted, unless prohibited). As was to be expected, with such principled positions we do not get very far. Except for the underlying ideological premises, pacifism and militarism, in the real world both positions amount to pretty much the same.

Box 8.1 To Outlaw War

The most serious attempt ever made in modern history to legislate away conflict was *The General Treaty for Renunciation of War as an Instrument of National Policy*, better known as the **Kellogg-Briand Pact** signed in Paris in 1928 by over 50 nations including the US, the Soviet Union, Germany, Japan, and Great Britain (Franz Kellogg was the US Secretary of State and Aristide Briand his French colleague). The Treaty's effectiveness was, however, short-lived. Only three years after its signing, in 1931, Japan seized Manchuria in what clearly was an aggressive war prohibited by the Paris Treaty. But no one did anything to dislodge the Japanese. Coupled to the disappointing experience with the League of Nations, particularly in the 1930s of last century, and with the devastating political and human experience of yet another world war, world leaders convened in San Francisco in April 1945 and decided to openly recognise that force may be necessary for 'the prevention and removal of threats to the peace, and for the suppression of acts of aggression or other breaches of the peace' (Article 1(1) of the UN Charter).

Pragmatic approach. As of the creation of the UN, states have come to recognise that 'military force (…) is a vital component of any workable system of collective security' and **that the use of force should not only be permitted** *but that such use may, under restrictive conditions, **even be 'necessary'*** for the sake of maintaining or restoring international peace and security. Donald Kagan wrapped it up in five words: '*Peace does not preserve itself*'. The quote given above comes from the *Report of the High-level Panel on Threats, Challenges and Change* (UNITED NATIONS, 2004, pp. 61–69) submitted to the then UN Secretary General Kofi Annan at the eve of the UN Summit of 2005 where a pragmatic, non-ideological approach to security questions led to the adoption of the principle of Responsibility to Protect (R2P) and the creation of the Peacebuilding Commission (PBC).

In approaching questions regarding the use of force, the emphasis today is on both system stability (security in the traditional narrow sense) and human dignity (security more broadly defined). The first, *system stability*, is contained in the recognition of the lawful right of *self-defence* and in the *UN's role in authorising force* to protect international peace and security. Both these functions are consistent with systemic stability as they provide grounds for the use of force necessary to rebalance the international system when faced with aggression. The second concern, **human dignity**, is today reflected in the recognition of the legitimacy of *humanitarian interventions* where force can be used in response to man-made crises caused by failed or murderous states, and which constitute a threat to international peace and security.

In short, military force is a constitutive part of a rules-based order that strives for avoiding war and maintaining peace. *War and peace* are at the core of diplomacy. Which raises the question of the relation between diplomacy and the use of force.

8.1 Diplomacy and use of force

There is a widespread view that diplomacy, with at its core negotiation, and the use of military force, with at its core coercion, are two quite different practices, mutually exclusive, perhaps even contradictory. 'Words' are the weapon of the diplomat, 'swords' that of the military, or so they made us believe. In fact, the opposite is true, as Carl von Clausewitz famously suggested. War should be considered as part of diplomacy – that is, diplomacy by other means. Clausewitz noted that *war is a means of accomplishing political goals* and not an end in itself. War for its own sake has no value, so one would never pursue it without hoping to accomplish some larger political aim (CLAUSEWITZ, 1976, p. 87). A similar point is made by Robert Cooper in his *The Ambassadors*: '*The point of war is peace*: that is where the gains and losses of war are made permanent', as Mazarin did in the Peace of Westphalia (1648) which instituted a new and lasting political order for Europe (COOPER, 2021, p. 41).

War is its own form of negotiation. One of the best examples demonstrating this point today is the war in Yemen. It started in 2015 and since then talking and fighting have been going on in parallel. Most recently, both sides, the Saudi-led coalition and the Houthis, spent most of 2020 in negotiations backed by the UN. In March 2021, the Saudi government offered a ceasefire wrapped in a peace proposal that very much looked like a warmed-up version of a plan that had failed to win agreement during the UN-led negotiations. The Houthis rejected it. They understood that the Saudi offer was nothing but a 'negotiating ploy'. In the meantime, they are pushing for the oil-rich and strategic city of Marib. Although they know that chances for capturing the city are slim, this push for Marib gives them 'leverage'. If the Houthis can be convinced to abandon it, they will expect something in return. In sum, both sides are negotiating with weapons as much as they are fighting with words. *Talking and fighting are just two ways of doing the same thing.*

The mistaken perception about the relation between diplomacy and use of force may be simply due to the association made by many people between diplomacy and *pacific settlement of disputes* on the one hand, and between military force and *coercive* action on the other hand; in UN terms: Chapter VI *versus* Chapter VII of the Charter. The diplomat is the softy, the pacifist who talks, who patiently mediates, and negotiates; the military is the bully, the bellicose who twists your arm and imposes his will. But this is an infantile opposition as George Kennan already remarked in a 1948 memorandum that he wrote in his capacity of Director of the State Department's Policy Planning Staff. In it he invited his colleagues to stop maintaining a watertight separation between war and peace and to start understanding the *continuum* between both:

we have been handicapped…by a popular attachment to the concept of a basic difference between war and peace, by a tendency to view war as outside of all political context, by a tendency to seek for a political cure-all, and by a reluctance to recognize the realities of international relations – the perpetual rhythm of struggle, in and out of war.

(KENNAN, 1948)

This mistaken perception has been the source of some misunderstandings:

• **'There is no military solution'**. In a speech at West Point in May 2014, President Obama said that

when crises push the world in a more dangerous direction but do not directly threaten us – then the threshold for military action should be higher. In such circumstances one should *forgo the use of force for such other tools as diplomacy and development* (my italics).

The sloppy thinking here is that one assumes that diplomacy and use of force are two alternative tools you can appeal to according to the circumstances. Which they are not: one is the complement of the other, not its alternative. The nostrum of 'no military solution' has gained ground lately, not only with President Obama but also with President Trump. Both have said the same, that they were elected to end wars, not to start them. Again, this dictum rests on the mistaken assumption that you can freely choose to start or not start a war, to end or not to end a war. It is true of most modern wars that there is 'no military solution' *in the sense that* they usually end with some kind of diplomatic settlement. But that exactly proves that military action can and should come in support of diplomacy, and *vice versa*. *Diplomatic and military solutions do not contradict each other*, they are intertwined and may be mutually supportive. *Political solutions are often dictated by military conditions* created perhaps by limited, tactical, or indirect action. But if you rule out even such limited actions, then you preordain either a bad political solution or none at all. Obama's refusal to engage in Syria and supply weapons to the moderate secular opposition fighting Assad in 2011–2012 opened the way to the Al-Qaeda-linked al-Nusra Front and, later, the Islamic State (IS).

• **'When diplomacy fails'**. Which brings us to a second, related point. Recourse to the use of force is often said to happen 'when diplomacy fails', again as if both 'use of force' and 'diplomacy' were intrinsically different practices from a political point of view, which they are not. As we have seen in the chapter on the Conflict Cycle, there is a *continuum* going from exploratory talks to negotiation, to incentives and disincentives, deterrence, last effort diplomacy, and then war as the only option left open (last resort), which then prompts to ceasefires and armistices, to negotiation again, to tentative and partial peace-accords, and so on until a durable settlement has been reached. But all these stages of the Conflict Cycle are part of *one single political process*, with the same leaders involved, the same concerns and goals. That political process is a *bargaining process* that relies on both diplomacy (negotiation) and use of force (war). Think about labour strikes. Management and labour negotiate and exchange offers. Labour has the option of calling a strike. But the strike is not an end in itself, but a means for extracting more concessions. The strike itself is thus part of the negotiation process, and negotiation continues during the strike until an agreement is reached that each side prefers over having the strike continue. Similarly, use of force does not mean the breakdown of diplomacy. Use of force is a deliberate political act *complementing diplomacy* as part of the bargaining process. Negotiations continue during war, and war ends when a deal is struck. War as bargaining helps explain why most wars are limited rather than total. Most wars are limited because they are means to a political end, not an end in itself. They leave space for negotiation. That is what Shelling's distinction between using violence as brute force (as in total war) and using it as coercion (as in limited war) points to (see HANDLER, 2013, p. 241).

- **Diplomacy 'backed by force'.** The mistaken opposition between diplomacy and use of force ignores what is key to diplomacy, to wit that its effectiveness is predicated upon its being 'backed by force' as Anthony Lake, Bill Clinton's National Security Adviser in the 1990s of last century, never tired of repeating. One very important consequence of Lake's rule is that you should never make a threat of use of force if you are not fully prepared to actually use that force in case your warning has been ignored. To repeat: it is not as if there were two options out there among which to choose: diplomacy or use of force. Your choice for diplomacy will only work if linked to the threat of use of force. And conversely, your recourse to the use of force will only be legitimate if complemented by a genuine willingness to negotiate. Obama's decision to retreat from enforcing his 'red lines' on the use of chemical weapons in the Syria conflict has damaged the US's diplomatic credibility and caused countries around the world to change their calculations about US resolve. Many are convinced that it helped produce Russia's meddling in Ukraine and that it may have contributed to China's assertiveness in the South China Sea.

8.2 An evolving security landscape – a preliminary warning

Many of us continue to look at war primarily as an inter-state activity that is polarised, decisive, and finite. One side wins, declares victory, and imposes its terms – and narrative – upon the loser. The other side accepts defeat, licks its wounds, and works out how to be smarter next time. But current conflicts, from Afghanistan to Syria, do not conform to this pattern. Who is the enemy? How do you know when you have won? What would victory even look like? In his 1988 Reith Lecture '*War and our World*' John Keegan wrapped it up in one single sentence: 'We are now in an era of long and ragged conflicts, community-based, open-ended, crude and cruel, and beyond the time limitations and technological constraints of much military and diplomatic practice'.

Armed conflicts and wars come in many forms: civil wars, wars of national liberation, world wars, cold wars, counterinsurgencies, a global war on terror, wars of attrition, offensive and defensive wars, proxy wars, nuclear wars, hybrid wars, total and limited wars, just and unjust wars, pre-emptive and preventive wars… .

Before discussing the concept of 'Use of Force', it pays to have a quick look at how the nature, purpose, scope, scale, duration, frequency, ends and means of armed conflict and war have changed over the last decades:

- The most conspicuous change in **the nature** of armed conflict is the transition from **inter-state** conflict (often called 'war') to **intra-state** conflict (often called 'armed conflict'), the latter currently representing over 90 per cent of all conflicts. This development is directly related to the 'End of Bipolarity', which unleashed all kinds of demons (ethnic, religious, sectarian...) which had been kept suppressed under the heavy lid of the bipolar Cold War rivalry. Current conflicts in Yemen, Myanmar, and Ethiopia are intra-state.

- A second change concerns the **number of parties** involved in the conflict. Traditionally an armed conflict occurred between two states, or two coherent groups of states; today we see increasingly a multiple of states (and non-states), each with their own agenda, participating on each of the sides of the conflict (think of Libya with Turkey, the US, Italy and most European countries siding with the UN-backed government, and Russia, Egypt, the United Arab Emirates and France [to some extent] siding with the rebel General Haftar's side).

- Another change concerns **the nature of the parties** to the conflict which are mostly **non-state**. What was formerly the state side today often is some form of multi-national grouping (an *ad hoc* international coalition such as ISAF [Afghanistan] or an intergovernmental international organisation such as NATO [Libya]), while the adversary is often a single or grouping of non-state entities, such as Al Qaeda (Afghanistan), ISIS/Daesh (Syria), Boko Haram (Nigeria), or, most recently, the Houthis, a Shia militant group that seized control of the Yemeni government (and much of the country) in 2015.

- Still another change concerns **the scope** of armed conflict today: from **total** (absolute) war, where the military capacity of the defeated state has been completely exhausted, to **limited** armed conflict, where at the end of the conflict both sides retain at least some ability to fight. As noted earlier, war as a bargaining strategy does not aim at the utter destruction of the enemy, just at enabling the victorious party to advance its political objective (see Box 8.2).

Box 8.2 When the Statistician Looks at War and Armed Conflict

Joseph Siracusa refers to research comparing the scale and intensity of armed conflict with that of war in terms of the annual number of 'battle-related deaths': 25 deaths per year, including civilian casualties, for violence to be categorised as *armed conflict versus* 1,000 combatant and non-combatant deaths per year for violence to be categorised as *war*. Applying these statistical criteria, the research then happily concludes that the incidence of war is declining and that, consequently, the world is becoming a safer place. But this is clearly a *non sequitur* (SIRACUSA, 2010, p. 112).

- Parallel to both these developments, there is the explosion in **the number** of armed conflicts: if we take 1945–2020 as reference period, some 65 per cent of all conflicts occurred in just the last 15 years.

- There is also a change in **the ends** for which there is fighting: from secular warfare (aimed at power, territory, and resources) we have moved to identity conflicts (foremost ethnic, linguistic, sectarian, and religious).

- There is a change in **the definition of victory**: from merely neutralising the enemy through military action ('negative peace') to establishing a more comprehensive security environment through diplomatic action ('positive peace') with a specific concern for 'human security' (see the chapter on 'The Conflict Cycle').

- Total war, where the whole state was at risk, produced clear **winners and losers.** Limited armed conflict produces relative winners and losers; today's lines are not so clearly drawn.
- The **timeline** of today's conflicts has become longer, conflicts and their aftermath last for years (Afghanistan since 2001, Iraq since 2003, Syria since 2011, and Yemen since 2015), sometimes decades (Democratic Republic of Congo – DRC), which has led to a growing weariness with so-called *forever-wars*. That weariness was shared by the three successive US Presidents, Obama, Trump, and Biden.
- There is a change in **the means** with which, and hence in the ways we are fighting: heavy armoury and weaponry (industrial warfare) have been replaced not only by high-tech killer-robots, such as drones (technological warfare), but also by machetes and mass rape as instruments of war (in Rwanda, Uganda, the DRC, and most recently in western Tigray by both Ethiopian and Eritrean soldiers).
- Related to this trend, there is the transition from conventional to **non-conventional** warfare (hybrid wars) involving so-called asymmetrical threats (such as cyber-attacks) not just coming from state but also from non-state actors (such as terrorist groups, crime syndicates, and drugs cartels).

Words are conservative. That is why to operate semantic shifts to keep in tune with evolving realities should be welcomed (think of the new concept of 'hybrid wars'). One must, however, be cautious and keep their imagination in check. Some people invent new words (often pseudo-erudite neologisms) just for intellectual fun. Luckily, the once trendy concept of 'post-modern war' seems to have had its day. The same holds for 'molecular war'. But then new concepts pop up. Recently, I stumbled upon the concept of 'theatrical conflict' as referring to the Russian interference in Eastern Ukraine. It remains a mystery for many how such parlance advances understanding, It rather obscures it. Often this *newspeak* is more misleading than enlightening.

In his *The Utility of Force* (2018), Rupert Smith, a former General in the British Army, tries to make sense of the significant changes in the security landscape and makes an appeal to rethink some of our assumptions in this regard. For Smith, the main reason for the failures of the past 15 years in military action is that we have entered a new paradigm while still operating with the concepts of the old one. He calls this new paradigm the **'War Amongst the People'**, a war that is not one that will be easy to win, especially not solely by military force. Here, follow some of his critical remarks:

- Conflict between States has been replaced by conflict between population groups. Military intervention then means **fighting amongst the people**, literally, figuratively, and virtually, in the new 'theatres of operations': in streets and fields, in hospitals and schools, in airports, on the ground, in the air, and across cyberspace.
- What we have seen for the last 15 years is the repeated phenomenon of **winning the battles but losing the wars**. Western involvement in Afghanistan and Iraq, for example, focused almost exclusively on (military) force rather than on (political) power. The US and its allies used force to great utility in each battle they engaged in and won, but collectively the use of force gained them little enduring power: the underlying *political* confrontation has not been addressed and remained unresolved (see Box 8.3).

Box 8.3 The Soldier and the Diplomat

Let me share with you the following quote drawn from Robert Cooper's *The Ambassadors*: 'The work of the soldier and that of the diplomat should be *complementary*. *Force makes sense only as part of a political strategy*: war should be the pursuit of policy with the addition of other means, as in Clausewitz's definition. The methods of the military and those of the diplomat are directly opposite. The soldier operates by orders and expects obedience. The diplomat's purpose is to accommodate divergent interests through negotiation and to achieve consent since nothing else will last. One of the fundamental choices that political leaders have to make is between negotiation and compulsion. In domestic policy, this is the choice between reaching an understanding and making a law; in foreign policy, it is the choice between negotiation and war (COOPER, 2021, p.68).

- The ends for which we are fighting have become increasingly malleable objectives. **Ends are poorly defined.** Using force has often become a stand-in for just doing something in the face of a problem. Referring to the 2011 Libya intervention, Smith remarks that while this operation was entirely commendable in moral terms, it was somewhere between naïve and untenable in pragmatic – and thus strategic – terms, primarily because none of the three main intervening States (France, the UK, and the US) had any intention of stabilising the outcome with forces on the ground over a period of time, nor of sending a civilian mission to help create a singular national entity in Libya that could assume responsibility for a functioning state. The malignant outcome of this military operation launched for an ill-defined objective is a migration crisis coupled with a failed state.

- In many conflicts, such as the fight against Al Qaeda or ISIS/Daesh, both military and civilian elements are involved, without however disposing over a clear strategy guiding their respective actions and mutual interaction. This itself is the result of a **confusion between defence and security.** For many decision-makers, the solution has been to use the armed forces as an element in the policy 'toolbox' alongside police and other non-military security providers. This has not only confused the purpose of the military action; it has often worsened the security problem these military deployments were meant to alleviate.

- A final weak spot identified by Smith is that 'we fight so as not to lose the force, rather than use the force to achieve the aim'. There is an **obsession with the protection of one's own forces** to the detriment of the success of the operation itself for which these forces were activated in the first place. Even with a defined objective such as the removal of Saddam Hussein in Iraq in 2003, the analysis was primarily focused on the risk to the intervening forces rather than the broader threat posed by the operation to the overall stability of Iraq and the wider region. The much-vaunted 'shock and awe' operation, while minimising the risks to the own forces, was a display of massively superior military force designed to eliminate all opposing forces – the military of the then Iraqi state – but it failed to see that Hussein and his military *were* effectively the state, and that upon eliminating them there would remain only religious leaders, tribes, and rivalry between them all. Thus, the attacking coalition forces did indeed take remarkably few casualties but brought chaos to the state and people of Iraq – for which there was no *military* solution. And it must be repeated, there was no civilian equivalent to *shock and awe*. Summarising: *shock and awe* in Iraq did what military force can do: destroy and kill, but then came the vacuum. A tactical victory, but a strategic catastrophe; *a battle won, but a war lost.*

8.3 Forms of use of force

In order to understand what is involved in armed conflict and war, we need to get acquainted with the basics and a good place to start is by looking at the different ways in which force is being used. We will distinguish three forms of use of force. Note that at this stage we only *describe* these forms. Normative and evaluative questions as regards their legality, legitimacy, or opportunity will be addressed later. There are three contingencies to be studied:

SELF-DEFENCE: The **first** contingency concerns an actual or potential **armed attack** against a state. Self-defence would then seem to be the appropriate response. When aggressed or threatened, a state can defend itself and can do so **individually or collectively** (under which conditions remains to be seen). Self-defence can take three forms:

- (1) It can be **reactive**, as against an actual armed *attack* (for instance, Kuwait being invaded by Iraq in 1990).
- (2) It can be **pre-emptive**, as against an imminent (proximate) *threat* of armed attack (for instance troop concentrations pointing to imminent assault).
- (3) It can be **preventive**, as against a latent (distant) *threat* of armed attack (for example the acquisition, with allegedly hostile intent, of a nuclear weapons capability) (see Box 8.4).

Box 8.4 Anticipatory Self-Defence: Pre-Emption and Prevention

Pre-emption and prevention are each forms of better-now-than-later logic, but they are responses to different threats involving different time-horizons and calling for different strategic responses. Pre-emption involves striking now in the anticipation of an imminent adversary attack with the aim of securing first-mover advantages. Prevention is a response to a future threat rather than an immediate threat. It is driven by the anticipation of an adverse power shift and the fear of the consequences, including the deterioration of one's relative military position and bargaining power and the risk of war – or of extensive concessions necessary to avoid war – under less favourable circumstances later.

(Jack S. Levy, 'Preventive War and Democratic Politics', in: HANDLER, 2013, p. 194)

EXTERNAL THREATS: The **second** contingency contemplates the case of a state posing a **threat** to another state (or states), to people outside its borders, or to the international order more generally, thus upsetting international peace and security. Again, the threatened actions may be actual, imminent, or latent; they may involve the threatening state's own actions or those of non-state actors it harbours or supports. The response to such threats will be **collective** and consist in any kind of **coercive action**, including military action, against the state having thus upset international peace and security. Such external threats would be, for instance, nightmare scenarios combining terrorists, weapons of mass destruction (WMD), and irresponsible states, which may justify the use of force not just reactively, pre-emptively but also preventively and before latent threats become imminent.

INTERNAL THREATS: The **third** contingency to be mentioned is one in which it comes to *saving lives within* countries in so-called man-made catastrophes, particularly in situations of mass atrocity (such as genocide and ethnic cleansing). This form of use of force is known as **humanitarian intervention**. When a sovereign state proves powerless or unwilling to prevent or address such internal threats which upset international peace and security, there arises a **collective** international responsibility justifying a response in terms of **coercive action**, including military action *in* (not necessarily *against*) the State concerned. It is generally agreed that the principle of non-intervention 'in matters which are essentially within the jurisdiction of any State' (Art. 2.7 UN Charter) cannot be, as a rule, opposed to such actions (but again under strict conditions that we will investigate soon).

8.4 Legality of use of force

We now must investigate the tricky normative question under what conditions recourse to the use of force in any of the above-mentioned contingencies can be considered legal. The UN Charter (particularly in its Article 51 and its Chapter VII) as well as customary international law give us partial, but not total guidance in this regard (see Box 8.5).

Box 8.5 Key UN Charter Provisions on Use of Force

Art. 1.7: 'Nothing contained in the present Charter shall authorize the UN to intervene in matters which are *essentially* within the *domestic jurisdiction* of any state (…); but this principle shall not prejudice the application of enforcement measures under Chapter VII'.

Art. 39: 'The Security Council shall *determine* the existence of any threat to the peace, breach of the peace, or act of aggression and shall make recommendations, or *decide what measures* shall be taken in accordance with Art. 41 and 42, to maintain or restore international peace and security'.

Art. 42: '(The Security Council) may *take such action* by air, sea or land *forces as may be necessary* to maintain or restore international peace and security'.

Art. 51: 'Nothing in the present Charter shall impair the *inherent right* of individual or collective *self-defence* if an armed attack occurs against a Member of the UN, until the Security Council has taken measures necessary to maintain international peace and security'.

SELF-DEFENCE (Art. 51 the UN Charter): each of the three forms of self-defence needs to be treated separately:

- **Reactive** self-defence, either individually or collectively, is considered an **inherent right** if an armed attack occurs against a state. No prior authorisation by the Security Council is required, but the state (or states) taking military action against the aggressor must forthwith notify the Security Council and the state's response will stand only until the Security Council has itself taken measures to maintain international peace and security. The first Gulf War of 1991 could have been considered as a collective action of *reactive self-defence* against what clearly constituted aggression. No prior Security Council authorisation would have been needed. The fact, however, that George H. Bush sought and got a prior Security Council authorisation (the famous Res. 678 of 29 November 1990) made it more plausible to qualify the operation 'Desert Storm' as a collective reactive response to an *external threat* (see below).
- **Pre-emptive** self-defence against an imminent and overpowering threatened attack is considered legal only if (1) **no other means** would deflect that threat and (2) the action is **proportionate** to the threat (the crucial concept of proportionality will be analysed further down). Again, the state acting pre-emptively must immediately report to the Security Council. The classic example of a pre-emptive action generally considered legal was the Israeli air strike against the Egyptian air force which initiated the 1967 war. A more recent case that could be considered a pre-emptive attack in self-defence was the targeted air strike in early 2020 killing Qassim Soleimani, the chief of the Iranian Revolutionary Guards' overseas forces. If, as US Secretary of State Mike Pompeo asserted, the Iranian general was indeed planning new imminent attacks against the US troops in Iraq, then the air strike would be consistent with self-defence under international law (see Richard Haas, *America Must Be Ready for Iranian Retaliation*, Financial Times, February 2020). The North Korean case is somewhat more complicated. For quite a number of observers, Trump's unusual advances to Kim Jong Un led to the *de facto* recognition of North Korea's *nuclear* status, which put to rest previous talk of pre-emptive military counter-proliferation strikes. There remains, however, North Korea's *ballistic* programme with regard to which a pre-emptive strike targeting a missile during launch, for example, remains a possibility.
- **Preventive** self-defence against a threat that is claimed to be real but that is not imminent is only allowed upon **prior authorisation** of the Security Council. If the Security Council refuses to grant that authorisation, that can only mean that it deems that other avenues remain available, including persuasion, negotiation, and deterrence after which the military option can be revisited. The bombardment by Israeli air forces of the Osirak nuclear reactor near Bagdad in 1981 is the classic example of a questionable preventive action. The armed intervention against Iraq in 2003, where there was no imminent threat by Saddam Hussein, has been defended by the US and its few allies as a preventive war (the then Defence Secretary Rumsfeld spoke about 'anticipatory self-defence'). No clear prior authorisation had been granted by the Security Council, however. The action therefore must be considered illegal. Currently, some talk is going on and off about the possibility of a preventive action aimed at neutralising the North Korean missile programme as such (not just pre-empting the effects of an imminent missile launch as discussed above).

Use of force as self-defence (reactive, pre-emptive, or preventive) against terrorists and state sponsors of **terrorism** raises specific questions. The very first question is whether terrorist acts constitute an 'armed attack' under Art. 51 of the UN Charter. An agreed definition of terrorism has proven elusive. But it is fair to say that both terrorist acts and state sponsorship of terrorism are now considered unlawful and that **self-defence** against them is legal, provided the action conforms to the legitimacy-requirements of 'necessity' and 'proportionality' (see below). Thus, the *occupation by Israel of Southern Lebanon in 1982* reacting to terrorist attacks emanating from the Palestine Liberation Organisation (PLO) has been condemned as disproportionate, whereas brief *incursions by Turkish forces into Kurdistan in 1995* were accepted as proportionate and necessary to counter terrorist attacks by the Kurdistan Worker's Party (PKK). In October 2001, the *US invaded Afghanistan after the 9/11 terrorist attacks* in New York (Twin Towers) and Washington (Pentagon) that killed 2,800 people. American use of force was directed against Al Qaeda, the terrorist organisation responsible for the 9/11 attacks, and the Taliban regime that was playing host to Al Qaeda. Although the American action was suggestive of armed reprisal (reprisal is lawful only if it does not involve the use of force) it enjoyed broad international support as most states agreed that both necessity and proportionality had been demonstrated.

EXTERNAL THREATS (Arts. 39 and 42 of the UN Charter): the legal scruples with regard to preventive self-defence do not, for good reasons, exist with regard to action decided by the Security Council when at any time, acting on the basis of its Chapter VII powers, it deems that there is a threat to international peace and security. But that action can also be, as we have seen, reactive or pre-emptive. When acting on the basis of Art. 42 of the Charter the Council authorises the use of force typically in the wording: 'authorizes member states to use *all necessary means*'. The Council then effectively proceeds to '*peace enforcement*' (imposition of peace by force). The first peace-enforcement action ever to have been decided by the Council was in 1950 in support of the Republic of Korea against aggression coming from North Korea. Since George Bush senior sought and got a prior Security Council resolution (Res. 678), authorising the operation 'Desert Storm', the first Gulf War is generally considered a case of legal response to an external threat, rather than one of reactive self-defence (see above). External threats need not be clear cases of aggression as in the Korea and Iraq cases. Scenarios combining terrorists, WMD, and irresponsible States, are also increasingly viewed as external threats justifying the use of force not just reactively but also preventively – that is before latent threats become imminent.

INTERNAL THREATS (Arts. 1(7), 39, and 42): The principle of non-intervention does not grant an *immunity* to sovereign governments to do as they wish, including on their home territory. This principle cannot be used to allow governments to condone or remain indifferent as regards genocidal acts, acts of mass murder and rape, ethnic cleansing by forcible expulsion and terror, deliberate starvation, and exposure to disease. Such acts are deemed to constitute a 'threat to international peace and security'. Sovereignty, on which the principle of non-intervention is based, involves not just rights for states but also responsibilities, in particular towards their own people. And while sovereign governments have the primary Responsibility to Protect (R2P) their own citizens from such catastrophes, that responsibility should be taken up by the wider international community when they are unable or unwilling to do so.

Humanitarian interventions are **collective** actions taken on behalf of the wider international community aimed at preventing or redressing catastrophic internal wrongs. Humanitarian interventions are considered legal only if **authorised** by the Security Council establishing that (1) the internal situation constitutes a **threat** to international

peace and security, (2) the government of the state concerned is **unable or unwilling** to protect its own citizens from the catastrophic situation, and (3) the authorised force is deployed only as a **last resort**.

The 1990s saw a dramatic explosion in collective humanitarian interventions. The end of the Cold War broke the veto logjam in the Security Council. Conflicts around the world were no longer viewed as extensions of East-West rivalry which enabled the Security Council to authorise armed interventions in humanitarian crises in Somalia (1992), Bosnia and Herzegovina (1992), Rwanda (1994), Kosovo (1999), East Timor (1999), Darfur (2004), and more recently in Syria, Yemen, and Myanmar. Over the years, there has been a growing recognition that the issue is not '*the right to intervene*' in *any* state but the '*responsibility to protect*' of *every* state when it comes to people suffering from avoidable catastrophe.

This principle of **'Responsibility to Protect' (R2P)** was formally adopted at the UN Summit in 2005. Its first full-blown application happened when in 2011 the Security Council approved Res. 1973 authorising an intervention in Libya and allowing recourse to 'all necessary measures to protect civilians' (in addition to establishing a 'no fly zone', an arms embargo and an asset freeze regime). Soon, however, the action was stretched beyond the scope of protecting civilians. Instead, it became increasingly apparent that the real objective of the operation was the 'departure' of the Gaddafi regime. With it, the R2P-principle was, for all practical purposes, killed *in utero*. When, a few years later, attempts were made to justifiably rely on R2P to intervene in Syria (where the people really deserved to be protected), there was no appetite anymore in the Security Council where Russia and China in particular felt having been deceived by the Libya adventure. We will come back to the analysis of this case in Section 8.6.

8.5 Legitimacy of use of force

Any legal order depends ultimately not only on the legality of decisions made in conformity with that order but also on the common perception of their legitimacy. Legitimacy is a broader concept than legality. You may be legally entitled to have recourse to the use of force, but that does not mean that you should. With legitimacy, the question is not whether force **can** legally be used but whether as a matter of good sense and good conscience it **should** be (what about the converse? – see Box 8.6). In the case of a prospective action, for instance, you may wish to ascertain that the evidence of the reality of the threat against which you consider acting is credible: Does the adversary really have the capability to launch an attack? Does he have the specific intent to do so? There are further questions: is the preventive action you are contemplating the only reasonable one in the circumstances? Or are there alternatives? More generally, is the decision regarding a prospective military action (whether reactive, pre-emptive, or preventive) made for the right reasons, morally as well as legally?

Box 8.6 Legitimacy without Legality

In March 1999, NATO used force (precision bombings) aimed at stopping violent Serb repression of ethnic Albanians in the Yugoslav province of Kosovo. It is generally agreed that NATO's intervention, while legitimate (as it responded to an overwhelming humanitarian need), was not legal since none of the key resolutions on Kosovo (Res. 1160 and Res. 1199) had actually authorised the use of force (although they had recognised that the situation in Kosovo constituted a 'threat to international peace and security'). Actions that strictly speaking are illegal, but which nevertheless seem fully justified are said to be grounded on the *Principle of Necessity* (a principle, we met in Chapter 6 on Concepts and Principles in Diplomatic Thinking).

To judge the legitimacy of the use of force, basic criteria have been advanced which are considered each necessary and jointly sufficient for a war's being considered legitimate. These criteria have been construed by traditional *just war theory* (see Box 8.7) and refer to the so-called ***jus ad bellum***, allowing to evaluate the permissibility of the *recourse to* the use of force generally, and the *launching* of war in particular (as distinct from the *jus in bello* bearing on the rules governing the conduct of war, which we will consider further down).

- **Just Cause** (Seriousness of Threat): The actual injury or threatened harm to the state or human security is of such a kind, and sufficiently clear and serious as to justify the use of military force. We have seen that the kinds of justifications are few: self-defence (either reactive or pre-emptive), safeguarding international peace and security, and averting 'crimes that shock the moral conscience of mankind' (WALZER, 2006, p. 107).
- **Right Intention** (Proper Purpose): Is it clear that the proposed military action is intended to halt or avert the threat, whatever other motives or purposes may be involved; to put it differently, is it clear that the state using force intends to address primarily and specifically the just cause, rather than using that cause as an excuse or pretext for a non-avowable motif or purpose.
- **Necessity** (Last Resort): Has every non-military option for meeting the threat been explored, with reasonable grounds for believing that none of them will succeed? In other words: are there no other less harmful ways to achieve the just cause; is diplomacy (negotiation, mediation) really exhausted? It is this criterion that explains the great reluctance in authorising or otherwise allowing preventive wars.
- **Proportionality** (Proportional Means): The question here is whether the scale, duration, and intensity of the proposed military action is the minimum necessary (and not more) to meet the threat in question. Note that proportionality does not mean that the use of force must be of the same scale or nature as the armed attack, but rather must be of a scale and nature as minimally required to repel the attack.
- **Balance of Consequences** (Reasonable Prospects of Success): Is there a reasonable chance for the military action to achieve its aims, i.e. meeting the threat in question, with the consequences of action not likely to be worse than the consequences of inaction; that the (morally weighted) 'goods' achieved by the use of force outweigh the (morally weighted) 'bads' that it will cause.

Box 8.7 Just War Thinking

The articulation of a fully worked out Just War doctrine is often said to go back to the 13th-century philosopher-theologian Thomas Aquinas. In fact, as John Lewis Gaddis remarks in his magisterial *On Grand Strategy*, Augustine had already worked out a pretty sophisticated view on the matter some nine centuries earlier. Let me quote Gaddis:

> Augustine concluded that war, if necessary to save the state, could be a lesser evil than peace – and that *the procedural requisites for necessity could be stated*. Had provocation occurred? Had competent authority exhausted peaceful alternatives? Would the resort to violence be a means chosen, not an end in itself? Was the expenditure of force proportionate to its purposes, so that it wouldn't destroy what it was meant to defend?
>
> (GADDIS, 2018, p. 101)

Properly understood, all these criteria come down to Proportionality and Necessity which jointly can be considered sufficient conditions for the use of force to be permissible. To get an intuitive grasp on Proportionality and Necessity, note that if someone threatens my life, then killing him would be proportionate (my life is worth no less than his); but if I could stop him by knocking him out, then killing him would be unnecessary, and so impermissible (knocking out is a less harmful alternative to killing). The Proportionality and Necessity constraints have the same root: with few exceptions (perhaps when it is justly deserved as in retaliation), *harm is intrinsically bad*. Harm (and indeed all 'bads') that we cause must therefore be justified by some positive reason that counts in its favour – such as goods achieved or evil averted. Both the Proportionality and Necessity constraints involve comparing the 'bads' caused by an action with the goods that it achieves. Ultimately the only difference between Necessity and Proportionality is that the former involves comparing one's action with a very specific counterfactual, the one in which we do not act to avert the threat, while the latter involves comparing it with all other available options at our disposition (other than the one of not acting) that have some prospect of averting or mitigating the threat.

One can understand that some of these concepts easily get confused. That is particularly true of the criteria 'Balance of Consequences' (use of force should do more good than harm) and 'Proportionality' (no more use of force than necessary) which are often not clearly distinguished. Also note that we have not withheld 'Legitimate Authority' as a criterium for legitimacy. This criterium dates back from a time where wars would only be considered legitimate when formally '*declared*' by an authority entitled to do so (such as, in the past, the Prince, and more recently the state). A relic of this can be found in many constitutions. The US Constitution, for example, provides that only Congress can formally declare war. This provision was meant as an antidote to abuse of power and a check on the executive power of the president, who is also accorded the role of commander-in-chief. In practice, however, this provision has most of the time been ignored, with the willingness of Congress and the courts to put up with it; a notorious exception was George H. Bush who asked and obtained congressional support for the first Gulf war; but most other war-presidents did not seek congressional support: William McKinley (war against Imperial Spain), Woodrow Wilson (war against Wilhelmine Germany), Franklin D. Roosevelt (war against Nazi Germany and Japan), Lyndon Johnson (Vietnam war), and George W. Bush (second Gulf war).

8.6 Legality and legitimacy – so, what?

All these standards of legality and legitimacy look nice and clean on paper but do seldom work out in practice. Very few of the armed conflicts and wars we are familiar with meet these austere criteria. The idea of self-defence has been stretched so broadly as to cover almost any plea of security threat. Below we will look at three cases, a first one presumably related to *anticipatory self-defence*, a second one presumably related to an *external threat*, and a third one presumably related to an *internal threat*.

- **Israeli attacks against Iranian targets in 2018–2021.** In 2018 Mossad, Israel's intelligence service launched an audacious cyber-attack against Teheran uncovering thousands of documents related to Iran's nuclear programme. More impressive still were the 2020 series of attacks and explosions on missile and nuclear sites, including Natanz (a major nuclear facility in Isfahan), and two high-profile assassinations in and around Teheran (one killing Iran's most senior nuclear scientist). Then, in April 2021, the Natanz facility was struck again after part of it had been rebuilt following the 2020 explosion. What is interesting for us to note is that in contrast with previous incidents Israeli officials *did not even make efforts to* somehow frame, that is *justify*, these incidents *in terms of pre-emptive or preventive self-defence*. Indeed, it has been speculated that Prime Minister Netanyahu was guided more by election-related considerations of *political convenience* than *strategic necessity* (see The Economist, 'Explosive Diplomacy', 17 April 2021).
- **The 2003 Iraq war.** Only in 2016 did we get what is considered the definitive account on the Iraq war: the UK 2016 Chilcot-report with its scathing verdict not just on the planning of the war, which is what interests us now, but also on its execution and aftermath. None of the legal and legitimacy standards that we went through have been met in this case.

  Irrespective of how the war was framed, as anticipatory self-defence (not even considering the confusion in the Bush-doctrine between pre-emptive and preventive action), external threat or even internal threat (all three frames have been tried out by the protagonists of the war, the US and UK), this war was *illegal*. For pre-emptive self-defence, there should have been an *imminent threat*, which there was not (see below), and for preventive self-defence as well as action against either an external or internal threat a *Security Council resolution* authorising the use of force should have been obtained, which was not.

  As regards *legitimacy*, the mere fact that the protagonists of this war continually wavered in their justifications and shifted from one to another (WMD, terrorism, and human rights abuses) was on itself a clear indication that no **Just Cause** existed. Regime-change increasingly appeared to be the single real motivation for the intervention, not exactly what one could call a **Right Intention**. Moreover, the military action was not, contrary to claims made by both President Bush and Prime Minister Blair, a **Last Resort**. The enquiry regarding Iraq's putative WMD programme was still going on at the time the attack was launched: indeed, the UN inspection team led by Hans Blix was getting better cooperation from the Iraqis and was pleading for some more time.

- **The 2011 NATO intervention in Libya**. The Libya case started in rather neat circumstances. On 17 March 2011, Resolution 1973 was adopted with ten members of the Security Council voting in favour and five members abstaining (India, Brazil, Germany, China, and Russia, the latter *prophetically* expressing its concern about 'unintended consequences'). Its operative paragraph four authorised member states to 'take all necessary measures...to protect civilians and civilian populated areas under threat of attack'. This was the first (and perhaps last) time ever that a Security Council authorising Resolution was grounded on the R2P-principle. This operation started being conducted by a multinational coalition, the command and control of which was soon taken over by NATO. Shortly after the military operations started, questions arose about NATO's goals and targets, more specifically as regards (1) pressure on the regime to step down (Qaddafi's removal from power), (2) the provision of weapons to the rebels, and (3) offensive actions against the military forces of the regime. Some states, in particular Russia and China, have considered these acts as going beyond the mandate established by Resolution 1973 and infringing the rules regarding **Right intention** (was protecting civilians [also] a pretext for regime change?) and **Proportionality** (were assistance to rebels and offensive actions against the regime necessary to protect civilians?). Questions have also been asked in connection with the **Balance of Consequences** criterion (has the intervention, on balance, done more good than harm and produced an improvement of the situation compared to the *status quo ante*?). Quite a few observers think the Libyan intervention has not passed this first full-blown test of the R2P-principle. They fear that Security Council members will be even more cautious about authorising force under Chapter VII in future cases, particularly when grounded in the R2P-principle. Russia's veto, just one year later, against a Security Council resolution on Syria meant to protect the civilian population, was quite significant in that regard.

Meeting the legality and legitimacy criteria is far from obvious. It was said of the Prussian leader Frederick the Great that when he planned a war, he would convene his generals first and his legal adviser afterwards. Even democratic governments contemplating recourse to the use of force seldom consider questions of legality and legitimacy before they plunge into military action. This does not mean, however, that the legality and legitimacy standards are utterly superfluous. The fact that governments try to show the conformity of their actions with these standards, even if only *ex post factum* and implausibly, proves their normative strength, however much limited that may be (the case of Israel's attacks against Iranian targets discussed above, where even some semblance of legality was not claimed, remains the exception). And what is true of these standards is true of international law generally: unenforceable but nonetheless not totally ineffective (as we will see in the next chapter). For some, this restraining effect helps explaining the transition from total wars to limited wars: wars in which both parties use less than their total force to achieve less than the total destruction of the adversary. If war has any logic at present times it lies in its attempt to create conditions for diplomatic solutions, not in its potential for unlimited slaughter.

8.7 Prudence in use of force

8.7.1 On judgment, wisdom, and prudence

Whatever the importance of legality and legitimacy regarding the use of force may be, ultimately that use is a question of *judgment, wisdom, and prudence*. Even when a prospective use of force may meet the standards of legality and legitimacy, that does not mean launching a war is the smart thing to do. As some have said: having a **casus belli**, which in terms of legitimacy amounts to having a *just cause*, does not amount to having a **casus ad bellum**, a *good case* to actually start a war.

Let us start by giving two examples of decisions, both *prima facie* lawful, where in one case prudence was exercised, in the other it was not:

- When in June 2019 President Trump decided to draw back from a counterattack against Iran after it had downed an American drone (a countermeasure that could have been considered legal) he caused consternation among the hawks of his administration but was praised by many for the self-restraint shown (considerations of proportionality may also have influenced the decision given that some 150 people would have been killed in the operation – see below).
- Conversely, Trump's early 2020 decision to pre-emptively eliminate Iranian general Soleimani, although (again most probably) legally justified, was not considered prudent or wise: first, the operation was quite risky, potentially leading to dangerous escalation if not retaliation, and second, its timing was bad given the US vulnerabilities in the region at the time.

In general, being entitled to do something does not mean there are good reasons for doing it. Let us draw a parallel with the right to free speech. For Timothy Garton Ash, the right to free speech encompasses the *right to offend*. But Garton Ash is quick to add that having the *right* to offend does not imply a *duty* to offend. Interestingly, he makes a call for better education and a bigger role for civil society which should help people become more tolerant and respectful towards each other. Hence, although Garton Ash starts out defending the uncontested right to offend, he ends up suggesting it may not be the best thing to do.

The same goes for the right to use force. Effectively using force is ultimately a question of wisdom and prudence. Historians of war give us long lists of ill-advised and unreasonable wars. In *The March of Folly*, Barbara Tuchman (well known for her one-liner: 'War is the unfolding of miscalculation') gives a most lively but devastating account of the utter irrationality of war in politics 'from Troy to Vietnam'. So does Donald Kagan in his *The Origins of War*, a study of humanity's greatest and most destructive wars from the Peloponnesian War (431–404 BC) and Hannibal's War (the Second Punic War – 218–201 BC) to World War I and World War II. Elsewhere, Kagan notes that

> for the last 2500 years, at least, states (…) have often gone to war for reasons that would not pass the test of "vital national interest" (…). On countless occasions states have acted to defend or foster a collection of beliefs and feelings that ran counter to their practical interests and have placed their security at risk, persisting in their course even when the costs were high, and the danger was evident.
>
> (Kegan in ABRAMS, 2016, p. 1)

We do not need to go back to the Peloponnesian War to see ill-advised wars end in failure. Closer home is President Biden's April 2021 decision to withdraw from Afghanistan. That decision has been rightly criticised but essentially for reasons external to the conflict itself, such as that abandoning Kabul to its fate may undermine other allies' confidence in the US. When it comes to the merits of the Afghan adventure itself, many people would agree with Biden that America's record in Afghanistan could be summed up as a *triumph of wishfulness over prudence*. The war's fuelling costs were predicated on the assumption that well-resourced soldiers and diplomats could *deliver a stable, democratic Afghanistan.* 'But this was a *delusion,* based much less on Afghan reality than American politics, an *overestimation* of American military force and a *desire* to maintain the brief moment of post-9/11 national unity' (see The Economist, 'Retreat from Kabul', 17 April 2021).

Historians look at the past, diplomats look to the future. Some speculate that the next war in the Korean peninsula may well be one of *miscalculation*, others that a next war in the Middle East may be one by *accident*, while still others think the potential for *misunderstanding* is hauntingly present in the current US-China standoff. All three of these factors – miscalculation, accident, and misunderstanding – are feared to be at play in the slow build-up towards what would be a disastrous conflict, a China-Taiwan confrontation.

Miscalculation, accident and misunderstanding – they all point to weaknesses in judgment: overestimating your own capabilities and underestimating those of your enemy, misreading signals and intentions, flawed ideas of the other's red lines, all of them illustrative of the cognitive traps that we studied earlier (recall the 'confirmation', 'overconfidence', and 'optimism' biases). A real risk of military conflict due to miscalculation, accident, or misunderstanding is what seemed in the making in the India-China standoff regarding their long-disputed border. In June 2020, for the first time since 1967, serious clashes erupted between the two armies in the Himalayan Galwan Valley. For some time, both sides had steadily increased their forces in the area, bringing in tanks, artillery, and missile systems to back up tens of thousands of troops. Observers feared that the conflict would spiral out of control with increasing risks of escalation and decreasing opportunities of disengagement. Fortunately, by mid-2021 things calmed down, for reasons as unclear as those which were at the origin of the conflict (see Financial Times, Devesh Kapur, 'India and China Are Edging Towards a Serious Conflict', 14 September 2020).

8.7.2 On Wars of Necessity and Wars of Choice

Richard Haass is well known for the distinction he made between 'War of Necessity' and 'War of Choice' (the title of his book), which he links in his 'Tale of two Wars' (its subtitle) to the first (1991) and second (2003) Gulf Wars, respectively. Haass thus joins Titus Livius who, some 20 centuries ago, said that 'Such war is just that is necessary, and arms are holy where there is no hope but in arms' ('On the Gallic War', Book IX, Chapter I).

Haass contrasts the two Gulf Wars (which we will designate as Iraq I and Iraq II) in the following essentially **legal-political** terms:

- Iraq I was a classical war seeking to reverse aggression and restore the *status quo ante*; Iraq II aimed at regime change, instituting democracy and human rights, and creating the foundations of a new Middle East order.

- Iraq I was a clear case of reactive self-defence; Iraq II was a questionable case of preventive war.
- Iraq I was a multilateral undertaking based on a broad and solid international coalition; Iraq II was essentially a unilateral undertaking.
- Iraq I had strong UN Security Council backing; Iraq II an extremely weak one, most would say none at all.

Note that criteria of legality and legitimacy transpire in these qualifications of both Iraq wars.

To this first list of qualifications of both wars, Haass adds what look more like **cost-benefit** considerations regarding the opportunity to use force: (1) overestimating the political merits of going to war and underestimating the merits of allowing the *status quo* to stand, (2) the presence (Iraq I) or absence (Iraq II) of congressional support and public backing, (3) the financial cost of the military operation (Iraq II costed $1 trillion, that is ten times more than Iraq I), and finally (4) its cost in terms of human lives (Iraq I a few hundreds, Iraq II over four thousand).

Wars of Necessity are those that are essentially unavoidable (former Israeli Prime Minister Menachem Begin called them 'wars of no alternative'). Wars of Choice, on the contrary, are those where a conscious choice has been made while other reasonable options were available but deemed less attractive (see Box 8.8). Examples of the first are World War II, the Korean war, and indeed Iraq I. Examples of the second are the Vietnam war, Iraq II, and more recently the Libya war.

Box 8.8 Maimonides on Obligatory and Optional Wars

The distinction between Wars of Necessity and Choice goes back at least to the great Jewish scholar of the 11th century. Obligatory wars were those waged by the King in **self-defence**, i.e. 'to deliver Israel from the enemy attacking him'. He distinguished these obligatory wars from wars that he termed optional, i.e. discretionary wars undertaken by the King against neighbouring nations 'to extend the borders of Israel and to enhance his **greatness and prestige**'.

Iraq I was a War of Necessity as it was a clear case of collective reactive response to an external threat (it could also have been framed as self-defence, as we saw) with important national and international interests at stake, with no promising alternative to the use of force available, and a considerable price to be paid if the *status quo* were to stand. *Iraq II was a War of Choice* as it was neither a case of self-defence nor one of collective response to an external threat, the national or international interests involved were not very clear (certainly not 'vital'), and viable alternatives to the use of force were available (first and foremost continued diplomacy which on 19 March 2003, the day of the launch of the war, had clearly not yet exhausted its potential). Because a War of Necessity is one which, by definition, could not be avoided, it will be less the object of critical scrutiny than a War of Choice where, given that alternative policies were available, the government of the day will have to carry the burden of proof and demonstrate that the overall results of employing force are positive, that is, that the benefits outweigh the costs. If this test cannot be met, the choice will appear to be ill advised, unwise, and imprudent.

Both concepts of war can also be seen as reflecting **different approaches to foreign affairs**. George H. Bush, assisted by his no-nonsense State Secretary James Baker, launched *Iraq I* on the basis of a cool assessment of which national and international interests were at stake, which basic rules of proper external behaviour had been transgressed, what destabilising precedent Saddam Hussein's behaviour would set in case of non-reaction. In making such assessment, *his concern was with the actions of Saddam Hussein (invading Kuwait), not with the kind of regime he represented (tyranny)*. For father Bush, diplomacy aimed primarily at influencing the external behaviour of states (what they do), not their internal ideology (what they are). What goes on inside other states is not irrelevant, but it is secondary. Iraq I was a success. Its principal war aims were accomplished: the reversal of Iraqi aggression and the restoration to power of the Kuwaiti government. Note that Iraq I was largely consistent with the criteria of Legitimacy mentioned earlier: it was fought for a worthy cause, waged only as a last resort, and was likely to succeed and indeed did succeed. This seems to suggest that while prudence involves more than mere legitimacy, it still does presuppose it.

Iraq II, initiated by Bush's son, reflected a totally different approach to foreign affairs. His concern was not so much with Saddam Hussein's external behaviour as with the *nature of his regime* and the conditions within the country. As a matter of general policy, he believed that American power should be used for moral and ideological purposes, *that democracy and human rights in other countries were a legitimate concern*. But he was reluctant in saying so when it came to justifying an impending war. The official reason for invading Iraq was the presence of WMD. And when nobody could find them, there was a scramble to come up with another justification. And up came terrorism and the supposed links between the Hussein regime and Al Qaeda. But this justification too appeared an empty one. So, the search went on and up came the humanitarian idea of protecting the rights of the Iraqi people. At that point, people started understanding what the real motive was: regime change. This wavering between different successive justifications was symptomatic of the absence of a just cause for this war, or else a very questionable one, and even its advocates could not argue that it was a last resort. As to the likelihood of success, the second Gulf War has turned out to be a debacle and a humiliation for those who thought the invading troops would be greeted as liberators and that the Iraqi people would move smilingly and swiftly to democracy. On the legitimacy criteria, therefore, this war scored badly. But the war was also ill advised for reasons going beyond its lack of legitimacy: the number of lives lost, its huge financial cost, the poor management of the war's aftermath (think of the generalised de-Ba'athification), and above all the geo-political blunders which engendered Iran's enhanced position in the region and made the ISIS/Daesh-terror possible.

Bush junior invaded Iraq, so many Americans told themselves, in the noble cause of planting democracy across the Middle East. In fact, this war of choice plunged much of the Middle East into conflicts that are still raging 20 years later. Making the creation of a *democratic* Iraqi regime that is respectful of *human rights* so central a case for war did seem noble but was not smart. Foreign policy should not be guided by moral fervour, as we will discuss in the chapter on Human Rights and the Rule of Law. In this regard, the so-called **democratic peace theory**, although right as an *empirical* statement that democracies rarely fight each other, can be misleading when one reads it as a *prescriptive* statement – that is, as an invitation or exhortation to export democracy and human rights all over the world. Transiting from the empirical to the prescriptive is exactly what President Clinton did in his 1994 'State of the Union' address when asserting that no two democracies had ever gone to war with each other, *thus explaining why* promoting democracy abroad was a pillar of his foreign policy. Such a tacit transition from fact to norm is misleading for two reasons. *First*, because building mature democracies proves to be extremely difficult if not impossible: it is a long-term enterprise with uncertain results and quite expensive. Countries do not become mature democracies overnight. They usually go through a rocky transition, where mass politics mixes with authoritarian elite politics in a volatile way. *Second*, and more importantly, because we should be aware that our notions of democracy and human rights are neither universal nor inevitable. Some humility is in place here and humility, like patience, are central virtues in diplomacy. As we will suggest when discussing human rights, better than wanting to change the world for the better overnight, just proceed gradually through some sober remedies: improving education, protecting civil society, and promoting the Rule of Law, rather than tackling human rights and democracy head-on.

8.8 The conduct of war

Until now we have been focussing on questions regarding the permissibility of war. These questions are particularly salient when deciding to resort to the actual use of force – that is: to launch the war. Questions concerning the legality, legitimacy, and prudence of **going to war** are known as '**ad bellum**' questions. But once the war has started, new questions arise, this time related to **the conduct of war,** so-called **in bello** questions. Obviously, these are issues that concern the military more than the diplomat. So, our discussion of this aspect of the use of force will be short.

A whole corpus of international law, formerly known as the 'law of war' but currently referred to as **'international humanitarian law',** aims at setting standards for the proper behaviour of combatants and limits to the kind of lethal weapons that they can use. International humanitarian law ranges from:

- the protected status of hospitals and schools (think of the bombardment of hospitals, schools, and other civilian facilities in Idlib [Syria], a city of three million citizens, in the spring of 2020 by regime and Russian forces), over
- the treatment of prisoners of war (which the 'unlawful combatants' presumably implicated in the 'War on Terror' and tortured in Abu Ghraib and Guantanamo were not even considered to be), to
- the outright ban on the use of chemical, biological, and radiological weapons (think of the sarin attack in August 2013 in a suburb of Damascus killing over 1,000 people).

International humanitarian law consists of treaties and conventions dating back to the late 19th and early 20th century with the so-called Hague Treaties of 1899 and 1907, later supplemented by the four 1949 Geneva Conventions (and the two Additional Protocols from 1977) and more specific instruments such as the Ottawa Convention of 1997 banning the use of anti-personnel mines.

It is of no use for us to review the entire corpus of international humanitarian law. Let us just mention some of its basic principles:

- The parties to an armed conflict must at all times make a **distinction** between **combatants and non-combatant civilians**; attacks on civilian targets are prohibited.
- According to the 'principle of limited warfare' the parties' choice of weapons and war tactics is not unlimited; **unnecessary suffering** must be **avoided.**
- **Prisoners of war** are entitled to respect for their life, dignity, and opinions and must be protected against any act of violence or reprisal.
- The **wounded** and the sick must be protected and are entitled to medical care.

Modern warfare raises tricky questions. Just to give the reader a sense of the issues involved in modern warfare, let us mention two of these questions, one related to the proper behaviour of the combatant soldier and the other to the use of technologically advanced lethal weapons:

- In normal circumstances, the '**rules of engagement**' will tell a soldier what to do when facing a certain situation. These rules are supposed to conform to humanitarian law. But not all contingencies can be covered by these rules. A delicate question that emerged in recent years is how to act when confronted with **child soldiers**. International law and most military codes treat underage combatants as innocent victims. These codes offer guidance on their legal rights and on how to interrogate and demobilise them. But they have little to say on the question what to do when a kid points a Kalashnikov at you. Do you shoot him? Such encounters are not rare. Child soldiers fight in many conflicts, in the DRC, the Central African Republic (CAR), and Uganda, as well as in Mali, Iraq, and the Philippines. Soldiers involved in such encounters face one of the worst moral dilemmas imaginable. The Geneva Conventions prohibit attacking schools, abducting children, and other practises that harm them, but say nothing on the contingency just discussed. In 2017, Canada adopted a military doctrine trying to balance between treating children as innocents and recognising them as battlefield threats, ensuring that killing children is a last resort. The UK later considered measures of its own, and other countries may follow. Such is the way international customary law is created, as we will see in the next chapter.
- Traditional humanitarian law, such as the UN Convention on Certain Conventional Weapons (CCWs), originally established in 1980, prohibits or restricts the use of so-called inhumane arms, that is weapons deemed to cause unnecessary suffering. Cluster munitions, landmines, and blinding lasers, among many other weapons, have been banned in the past. A new challenge concerns the so-called LAWs, the **Lethal Autonomous Weapons**, colloquially called '*terminators*'. Such terminators are no science fiction anymore. A UN report of March 2021 of the Panel of Experts on Libya, a body reporting to the UN Security Council, caused quite some consternation when it noted that in a battle around Tripoli in 2020, Libya's government had 'hunted down and remotely engaged' the enemy with drones – and not just any drones: the Kargu-2, of Turkish manufacture, was programmed to attack 'without requiring data connectivity between the operator and the munition'. The implication was that it could pick its own targets.

The critical feature of LAWs is indeed that they are equipped with 'learning programmes' and hence with cognitive skills enabling them to autonomously (hence their name) decide whom, when, and how to fight. They pose daunting ethical, legal, and policy questions (see Box 8.9). Much of the discussion regarding the admissibility of such robotic systems revolves around human's place in the decision-making loop, known as 'observe, orient, decide, act' (OODA). In artificial intelligence (AI) circles, this is called 'the control problem'. There are three types of systems to be considered:

- The first one is called '*in the loop*', as is the case with an operator of a remotely piloted armed drone who decides where it goes and what it does when it gets there.
- An '*on the loop*' system, by contrast, will carry out most of its mission without a human operator, but a human can intercede at any time, for example, by aborting the mission if the target has changed.
- Finally, an '*off the loop*' system would be fully autonomous carrying through every part of the mission, including target selection, the human's role being then limited to merely press the start button (see Box 8.9).

Box 8.9 Killing with Bare Hands or with Unmanned Drones

Imagine trying to kill another person with your bare hands; having to hear, feel, and smell that victim as you attempt to kill him. Most people experience revulsion when they kill, even in a war situation. Scholars have postulated the existence of an inhibitory mechanism that limits aggression in such close-contact scenarios. But now imagine you are able to hit a target person with an unmanned drone as you sit in the control room thousands of kilometres away and use satellite imagery to home in on the target. The person you have targeted will not see or hear anything threatening until it is far too late, and there will be no opportunity for your inhibitory mechanism to get activated. You kill in peace (see D. Grossman, 'On Killing: The Psychological Cost of Learning to Kill in War and Society', New York, NY, 1995).

For now, *western* armed forces *seem* determined to keep humans either in or on the loop. Rules regulating autonomous weapons will be debated in December 2021 in New York at the five-yearly review conference of the UN Convention on CCWs. Not everybody is convinced, however, that limits on autonomous weapons will be agreed. The Great Powers, in particular, the US, China, and Russia, remain wary of ceding advantage to rivals. Verifiability will be at the centre of the debate. Each of the Great Powers suspects that the others will be cheating, a classic case of Prisoner's Dilemma.

As with the 'ad bellum' scenario, beyond questions of **legality**, which the corpus of humanitarian law is supposed to address, there are questions of **legitimacy** involved in the 'in bello' scenario. Beyond the legal rule prescribing the distinction between combatants and non-combatants (see above), considerations of proportionality and necessity also play in the overall assessment of acts of war:

- **Discrimination and Combatant Equality**. Discrimination (the jargon term) involves the distinction (a better term) between combatants (soldiers) and non-combatants (civilians). *Combatant equality* means that there are no restrictions on killing combatants. Non-combatants may, as we have seen, not be killed; they may however *get* killed, but then unintendedly, even when their killing is foreseeable (so-called *collateral damage*), but then the next two criteria have to be respected.

- **Necessity**. Collaterally harming non-combatants, that is, harming them foreseeably but unintendedly, is permissible only if, in the pursuit of one's military objectives, among the alternative actions available the least harmful action is chosen.
- **Proportionality**. Collaterally harming non-combatants is permissible only if the harms occasioned by the action are proportionate to the goals the attack is intended to achieve.

Two examples. One from the past, regarding a large-scale operation: the *indiscriminate bombing of the city of Dresden* in February 1945 as the war in Europe was coming to a close. This bombing operation by the Royal Air Force and the US Army Air Corps has been considered as a flagrant infringement of both the principle of necessity and of proportionality. Just weeks after the operation, Winston Churchill showed regret and dissociated himself from the 'area bombing' when in a memorandum to the British chiefs of staff he wrote (in the typical British style of understatement): 'It seems to me that the moment has come when the question of bombing German cities simply for the sake of increasing the terror…should be reviewed'. The other example, from the present, concerns the small-scale operation that we already met when discussing 'prudence' in the use of force. It happened in June 2019 when, only a few hours before its planned execution, a military *strike by the US against three targets in Iran in retaliation to the downing of an unmanned American drone*, was called off by President Trump on the grounds that some 150 Iranian lives would be lost in the operation, which he deemed *not* to be proportionate to the operation's retaliatory objective. A wise decision inspired by the principle of proportionality: killing 150 people was not worth it.

Before closing this section on the conduct of war, let us briefly look at **Michael Walzer's** influential but **controversial arguments concerning the principle of Discrimination and Combatant Equality**. His starting point is that human beings enjoy fundamental rights to life and liberty, which prohibit others from harming them in certain ways. Since *fighting* obviously involves depriving others of life and liberty, it can be *permissible only if each of the victims has 'through some act of his own…surrendered or lost his rights'*. By *merely posing a threat*, a person alienates himself or herself from the community and its members, and from our common humanity, and so becomes a legitimate target of lethal force. More specifically, by *participating in the armed forces*, a combatant has 'allowed himself to be made into a dangerous man' and has thus surrendered his rights. Walzer's reasoning can be summarised as follows: everyone starts out with a **right to life**, but that right **can be forfeited or lost**, such that one can be killed without that right being violated or infringed. From this it follows that non-combatants, in virtue of not having forfeited their rights, are not legitimate objects of attack while combatants, having lost their rights, are. Note that, in another context, the forfeiture argument has been invoked to justify the death penalty for murder (see Marcel Conche, *Le fondement de la morale*, Presses Universitaires de France, Paris, 1993, pp. 124–127).

8.9　The end of war and its aftermath – just peace

The list of Latin labels that we have been using so far can be further extended. Although slightly obscurantist, they serve as a useful shorthand. Let us recapitulate: '**jus ad bellum**' is concerned with the mere permissibility of war, the *launch of war*; '**jus in bello**' with the permissibility of particular actions that compose the war, the *conduct of war*. '**Jus ex bello**' has been suggested as deserving a separate treatment with a focus on war exit, the *end of war*; however, since ending a war amounts to not continuing it, most scholars would deem this issue as falling under the scope of 'jus ad bellum' as there may indeed be a point in time where the war does not meet any longer the criteria of legitimacy, particularly 'proportionality', 'necessity', and 'balance of consequences' (see Box 8.10).

Box 8.10 Unending and Expanding Wars

There is a growing belief that wars, such as the Syria war and the wars in Yemen and Libya, do not come to an end because of *foreign interference*. Wars have both a *temporal* dimension – how long they last, and they tend to last longer, and a *spatial* dimension – how broad they spread, and they tend to spread out. Both these dimensions are intertwined.

As of spring 2019, we have been witnessing a rising internationalisation of the *Libyan conflict* opposing the rebel general Khalifa Haftar to the UN-backed Government of National Accord. Lined up behind Haftar are the United Arab Emirates, Egypt, and Russia with some political backing by France. On the other side, we have the US, Italy (and most Europeans) with Turkey ramping up its military support for the UN-backed government. Many Libyans believe it will be these *outside powers* that determine whether the fighting will end, amid warnings of diplomats that all the protagonists risk being sucked into a *protracted proxy war* that threatens to reverberate to the Sahel across North Africa and to the Mediterranean region. Turkey is increasingly viewed by Abu Dhabi and Cairo as a destabilising force in the Arab world, supportive of Islamist movements they deem a threat to the region. Libya has become the theatre where these rivalries are playing out. Fathi Bashagha, the Libyan interior Minister is quoted as saying: 'The problem is not Libyan. It is 20 percent Libyan, and we can solve this; 80 percent is from outside countries involved in Libya'.

An older example is the long-standing Arab-Israeli conflict that decades ago sprung the confines of the territory of Israel and Palestine to cover 'new' terrain, in particular Lebanon, and sprouted 'new' conflict actors, such as Hezbollah. Then, Hezbollah participated in the Syrian civil war, which has roots outside the Israel-Arab conflict, and is allied with Iran, the ascendency of which provoked destabilising responses from Gulf states such as Saudi Arabia and the United Arab Emirates, especially in Yemen. In the meantime, Iran-backed Shia militias destabilise Iraq. Then, as noted above, competing political expressions of Sunni Islamism put Gulf states against Turkey in Libya.

These examples show how a single conflict has yielded *secondary conflicts* which suck in, first, regional powers and then, global actors such as Russia and the US, as a result of power and security vacuums created in the chaos of war (see HILTERMANN, 2018).

A recent addition to this list is the '**jus post bellum**', bearing on what should (acts of commission) and should not (omission) be done in the post-war stage. This new concept has emerged in response to the terrible failures to plan ahead in the Afghanistan,

Iraq, and Libya crises where the *aftermath of war* has been neglected and may well have caused more harm than the wars themselves. The underlying idea is that achieving your 'just cause' is not enough. If the war is to be 'proportionate' and 'balanced as regard its consequences', its aftermath must also be sufficiently tolerable. This issue, also known under the label 'just peace' raises quite a lot of difficult questions. To mention just one: how far in the future do we have to look to assess the relevant consequences of conflict?

The message here is that before going to war ('ad bellum') it would be smart to ask the 'post bellum'–question: then what? This is the question that in the early 2010s became Robert Gates' mantra: what happens next? how does this play out? what are the second-order and third-order effects of war, often unintended but nevertheless foresee-able? (Gates was Obama's Defence Secretary). Remember the remarks made by Rupert Smith (which we recalled at the beginning of this chapter) as to either the *bad* post-bellum planning (as in Iraq II with the de-Baathification) or else the *absence* of any post-bellum planning at all (as in Libya). As Gates said in 2012 in the context of the Syria-crisis: 'The hard part is not toppling Assad, it's what comes afterwards'. And even the toppling failed.

Peacebuilding on itself is already a complex undertaking (as we saw in the last chapter on the 'Conflict Cycle'). **'Just peace'**, which is a normative theory in the making, adds to that complexity. 'Just peace' wishes to set forth *standards* that should guide us in ensuring that the peace we build is fair and therefore durable. These standards must be realist in their conception and feasible in their execution. Extremes must be avoided: at the lower end of the peace-continuum, a so-called *deficient peace* (the mere absence of violence) will not do, but neither should one be dreaming of a '*perfect peace*' (ideal, utopian, and celestial) at the upper end of the continuum. The lower end extreme is sometimes associated with a rough political realism, while the upper end extreme is associated with a high-minded moral idealism.

Let us briefly walk through this peace-continuum that stretches from the purely negative peace to the total positive peace:

- **Deficient peace**: This is a peace defined in terms of the mere absence of violence, *negative peace*; it is the peace of the victorious, an imposed, forced, and repressive peace. On 11 November 1918, the French marshal Ferdinand Foch imposed the punitive peace terms of the Armistice upon the Germans. One year later, France repeated its humiliation in the peace talks at Versailles in 1919. This deficient peace may have been a contributing factor to the World War II; the issue remains disputed among the historians.
- **Acceptable peace**: This is the *classic realist* position defended by scholars like Margalit and sometimes expressed as '*just a peace*' rather than a 'just peace'. It is the peace that aims at political stability first, and only secondarily at justice except for the fact that crimes against humanity (such as genocide and ethnic cleansing) and systematic or large-scale infringements of basic human rights will not be tolerated.
- **Decent peace**: This is the *moderate realist* position defended by scholars like John Rawls. In this peace concept, all *basic* human rights (such as the right to life, security, and equality before the law), as well as the right to political participation, should be guaranteed. This moderate realist position stresses the *feasibility constraint*: better an imperfect peace that works than a perfect peace that remains illusory.

- **Honest peace**: This is the peace that genuinely aims at being a *'just peace'*, where both personal *and* 'structural' violence (economic inequality, ethnic or religious discrimination, repression, apartheid, and colonialism) have been effectively eliminated. Such peace rests on the principles of justice, equality, and solidarity; it guarantees the respect of human rights generally (including such rights and freedoms as that of assembly, free speech, privacy…) as well as the right to democratic governance.

- **Perfect peace**: Here we get at the perfect, ideal, and slightly utopian peace, where all people are guaranteed the full panoply of human rights and freedoms (not only political and civil, economic and social, but also the so-called third-generation human rights that we will discuss in the chapter on Human Rights and the Rule of Law). It is the kind of peace the Dalai Lama and some theologians are preaching. Its only weak but fatal spot is that it is perfect and, as we all know, perfection is not of this world.

Now that we have been looking at 'Peace' more closely, there is one tricky question left to be answered. *In matters of war and peace, what is the 'normal', the 'default', what is the 'natural' state of affairs?* Is it peace, as the great 17th century German jurist Pufendorf thought or is it war as his Dutch contemporary Hugo Grotius seemed to suppose (and as Plato thought in his dialogue on *The Laws*)? This controversy coincides broadly with the debate between the New Order of *liberal internationalists* who deem a rules-based international system quite feasible and to be the best guarantee for the preservation of peace and the Old Order of *realists* for whom the anarchic international system, being what it is, lacks rules and for whom there is no security save that provided by power; a successful war is therefore its own justification; if war succeeds, it is just (see Box 8.11).

Box 8.11 A Realist Account of the Origin of War

'Through much of history, war has been the normal part of life: civil wars to establish states and then war between states' (COOPER, 2021, p. 476). Realists explain what historians know: war is normal. The recurrence of war is explained by the structure of the international system. None has expressed this idea better than Kenneth Waltz:

> Competition and conflict stem directly from the twin facts of life under conditions of anarchy: states in an anarchic order must provide for their own security, and threats or seeming threats to their security abound. Preoccupation with identifying dangers and counteracting them becomes a way of life. Relations remain tense; the actors are usually suspicious and often hostile even though by nature they may not be given to suspicion and hostility. (…) The uneasy state of affairs is exacerbated by the familiar 'security dilemma' wherein measures that enhance one state's security typically diminish that of others. In an anarchic system the source of one's own comfort is the source of another's worry.
>
> (see Kenneth Waltz, 'The Origins of War in Neorealist Theory',
> in: HANDLER, 2013, p. 49)

The question is not without importance because according to what your default position is, the *burden of proof* for *explaining* why war occurs or alternatively why peace prevails, shifts shoulders. However, whichever your default position may be, the liberal or the realist, any *particular war* is not explained by such system-level approach but requests its own idiosyncratic explanation in terms of the specific situational factors that prevail at the unit-level of states. That is why in the next section we will reflect on the causes and reasons of particular wars.

8.10 Causes and reasons of war

No doubt many factors enter the analysis of the origins of particular wars. Poverty, economic stagnation, bad governance; ethnic differences and religious zealotry; minerals, competition over scarce water resources or dwindling fertile land. There are structural factors such as demographic pressures, economic inequality, and environmental stress. And there is fear, anger, and hatred, the need for recognition, respect, regard, just due, and prestige.

The analysis of the origins of war dates back to Homer who ascribed the cause of the *Trojan War* to the goddess *Atè* who stands for blind foolishness, disaster, and deceit. Herodotus too sought to explain the 5th-century *Persian (preventive) War* launched by the Greek King Croesus against the Persian Empire of Cyrus; he closes his analysis with this brilliant one-liner that many of us remember: 'No man is so stupid as to prefer war to peace: in times of peace sons bury their fathers, in times of war fathers their sons'. Thucydides, like the modern 'realists', understood international relations as competition for power, and war as the resort to arms in that competition; in his analysis of the origins of the *Peloponnesian War*, he found that people go to war out of 'honour, fear and interest'.

This multiplicity and diversity of factors needs some ordering. This can be done in different ways. Long-term structural trends (desertification – Sahel) can be distinguished from proximate short-term causes (Russian refusal to have former Soviet states join the EU or NATO – Georgia and Ukraine) which in turn can be distinguished from triggers (the downing of Rwandan President Habyarimana's plane – genocide). Material and tangible interests (wealth accumulation) can be distinguished from immaterial and intangible interests (honour and pride). Raymond Aron made the distinction between historic and a-historic (supra-historic) factors. We will distinguish between objective (external) factors, which we will call 'causes' and subjective (internal) factors called 'reasons' (or motivations). Causes and reasons are not always easy to distinguish. Causes engender their effects, and they do so in a lawlike manner. Cause-effect relations pertain to the natural world, out there, and are studied in the sciences. Reasons pertain to the human world, in here, the world of the mind. They originate in man, in their valuations, volitions, intentions, and strivings. And to the extent that states and human beings, that is, persons, are being identified, so will human reasons and motivations come to be attributed to the state as well (see Box 8.12).

Box 8.12 The State as a Person and Use of Force

In his classic *The Great Illusion*, Norman Angell considers the approximation of the state to a person (leading to, I would add, the identification of the state with a person) a false and pernicious analogy. He says:

> Conflicts between nations and international pugnacity generally imply a *conception of the state as* a homogeneous whole, having the *same sort of responsibility* that we attach to *a person* who, hitting us, provokes us to hit back. (…) Yet the fine-spun theories on which are based the necessity for the use of force, as between nations, and the proposition that the relationship between nations can only be determined by force, and that international pugnacity will always be expressed by a physical struggle between nations, all arise from this fatal analogy, which in truth corresponds to very few of the facts (my italics).
>
> (ANGELL, 2012, p. 158)

Three preliminary remarks need to be made: first, objective and subjective factors are *not mutually exclusive*; causes and reasons can overlap and perhaps mutually reinforce or neutralise each other; second, objective and subjective factors can be approached at *different levels of analysis*, some more general and abstract, other particular and concrete; third, causes can be direct or indirect in which case the *causal chain* needs to be closely watched as, for instance, in the case of climate-induced wars where global warming causes environmental degradation which in turn works as a catalyst destabilising regions which in its turn raises the risk of conflict.

8.10.1 *Causes*

- Demographic factors: Population density – according to Jared Diamond, the underlying causes of the Rwandan genocide were population pressure and land degradation (see DIAMOND, 2013, pp. 311–328) (see Box 8.13).

Box 8.13 The Malthusian Cycle

Robert Malthus (1766–1834) is well known for his *Essay on the Principle of Population as it affects the future improvement of Society* (London, 1883) in which he looked at the relationship between population growth and food production. He argued that food production increases arithmetically (1, 2, 3, 4...), while population increase is geometric (2, 4, 8, 16...). This disparity, Malthus argued, results in periodic food shortages and a perpetual cycle: the population increases until food supply is insufficient, with the result that famine and war rage until population growth stagnates and food supply catches up. For a period of time, there is sufficient food to feed the population, but soon the population increases and outstrips food supply again, and the whole 'Malthusian Cycle' begins anew. Thus, human societies are in a *constant state of competition and conflict* for food, water, and other such essential resources.

- Geographic factors: Natural borders (think of the Andes border dispute between Chile and Argentina, the conflict borders between Eritrea-Ethiopia, Ecuador-Peru, and China-India) and rivers (the Blue Nile dispute between Ethiopia, Sudan, and Egypt linked to the construction of a huge dam in Ethiopia); scarce natural resources: water (Blue Nile again), fertile land, oil and gas (South Sudan), and minerals (Eastern Congo – see the studies on 'conflict diamonds' by Paul Collier).

- Environmental factors: Climate change, desertification, deforestation, land degradation, and pollution. The 2006–2010 extreme draught in Syria has been considered an important contributing factor to the crisis that erupted in 2011 (for climate change and its potential economic and social impacts, see Nicholas Stern's alarming report: 'The Stern Review: The Economics of Climate Change', HM Treasury, 2006).

- Economic factors: Economic stagnation, poverty, uneven wealth distribution (inequality), competition, and migration (see COLLIER, 2008).

- Political factors: The nature of the political regime: tyranny, dictatorship, and autocracy; poor or bad governance, corruption; non-respect of basic human rights; aggressive nationalism; imperialism, hegemony; colonialism; and failed and failing states (the latest newcomer being post-coup Myanmar).

- Identity politics: Identities framed along ethnic, racial, sectarian, religious, or linguistic lines polarise people and groups and create fault lines between 'us' and 'them' (see Box 8.14); struggles over identity can quickly become a source of instability within and between states – see 'Human Development Report 2004', UNDP, New York, NY, 2004, p. 10.

Box 8.14 Identity Politics

People crave for an identity. To build an identity, one must belong to a group. A group is created along a criterion. Research has demonstrated that the criterion for group formation can be utterly trivial. What counts is not the criterion itself, but the mere fact that it allows group formation: an in-group and an out-group, 'us' and 'them'. Merely creating groups results in minimisation of within-group differences and exaggeration of between-group differences. That is, the members within each group are seen as more alike than they actually are, and the members of the different groups as more different than they actually are. As groups get constituted, its members start exaggerating the importance in their group life of what originally may have been a trivial criterion, because that is the only basis on which they can create their desired identity. The *trivial becomes important*, not because of any intrinsic revaluation, but only because of its role in group identity formation. Trivial criteria can of course be *manufactured*. And that is where politics comes into play. Consider the Hutu and Tutsi in Ruanda and Burundi, two groups engaged in violent conflicts over many decades, with as climax the Ruanda genocide in the spring of 1994. The trivial criterion of 'height difference' between the two groups has increasingly been emphasised and exaggerated as part of a justification for the superiority of one group over another (see Rom Harré and Fathali Moghaddam, 'Psychology for the Third Millennium', London, 2012, p. 279).

- Cultural factors: Ideological radicalism; religious extremism; divisive nationalism; cultural imperialism, 'the white man's burden', and '*la mission civilisatrice*'.

- Psychological factors: When inherent in human nature itself such as egoism, and envy; the psychology of leaders, in particular, assertiveness (see VOLKAN, 2013).
- Ethological and sociobiological factors: Tribalism, racism and xenophobia; aggressiveness – Konrad Lorenz, in his well-known book *On Aggression* (London, 1961), claims that man is no different from other primates in his innate tendency towards aggression.

8.10.2 Reasons

- Tangible interests: Survival of the state (national security), access to resources, access to the sea sought, for instance, by Bolivia (through Chili), by Ethiopia (through Djibouti, or Somaliland), well-being of the population (prosperity).
- Intangible interests: The search for recognition and respect (post-Yeltsin Russia – Vladimir Putin), for honour, fame, prestige, and glory (Napoleon); pride, vanity, and reputation (Charles de Gaulle's « *une certaine idée de la France* »).
- Power: Power as a means to an end, or as an end in itself, that is: hunger for power, power expansion, and aggrandisement – Clausewitz considered this to be the prime mover towards war; Bertrand Russell remarked that an intrinsic feature of power is that the appetite for it is limitless – see Bertrand Russell, 'Power', London, p. 8: 'To those who have but little of power and glory, it may seem that a little more would satisfy them, but in this they are mistaken: these desires are *insatiable and infinite*' (my italics).
- Fear, anger, and hatred; the desire to escape from disgrace, embarrassment, and shame; the wish to avenge a wrong.
- Identity: Identity can be approached as either an individual or a social construct. Identity politics belongs to the latter category and was therefore mentioned higher up under 'Causes'. But identity is also what individuals crave for – think of the 'strong leader' seeking to build a 'personality cultus' in which case it is better considered as a 'Reason'.

Predicting what will start a war and when, is an unrewarding business. Long-term trends are often clear enough, but less so the short-term causes and least of all the immediate triggers. It would seem that as we move from long-term structural factors towards short-term 'conjunctural' factors, we move from more objective outside (human-independent) 'causes' towards more subjective (human-dependent) 'reasons'. What precipitates a conflict may be a sudden, unforeseen event: an accident, the misreading or miscalculating of a singular event, a temperamental leader's flash of hubris. Take the war in Syria: there were deep-seated long-term root causes that were known by many for decades to be sources of potential instability; but what is striking at how the actual Syria war started is how the participants blundered into it in 2011, responding to each provocation by the adversary with an escalation of their own, so that gradually a *rather insignificant local protest by youngsters* turned into a *full-fledged civil war*, wrapped up in a regional power struggle (Iran–Saudi Arabia), folded in a confrontation between superpowers (the US and Russia).

8.11 Two extremes – nuclear war and hybrid war

We close this chapter on the 'use of force' by focussing on two types of war, both apparently far apart from each other. The first, *nuclear war*, is the paradigm of an all-out open confrontation, while the second, *hybrid war*, operates in the grey zone between war and peace. But as we will see, there is a direct link between both. The aim of hybrid warfare is not to get involved in an open war but to make an intervention by the adversary more risky and costly. Hybrid war is what has increasingly enabled Russia and China to exploit this undefined area between war and peace in their confrontation with the West, the US in particular. Grey-zone operations aim to reap either political or territorial gains normally associated with overt military aggression without tipping over the threshold into open warfare with a powerful adversary. But the main reason why big powers will try to achieve their political objectives short of outright war remains the nuclear threat. The question is then whether the 'balance of terror' which paradoxically brought us stability of some sort will remain as it was in the past.

8.11.1 Nuclear war

8.11.1.1 Deterrence and balance of terror

With the introduction of nuclear weapons, the logic of war as we traditionally knew it has been totally upset. Nuclear warfare does not only kill your enemy, but it kills you too. In nuclear warfare, victory and defeat have no meaning anymore, war has become suicidal. As Robert Oppenheimer put it: 'two scorpions in a bottle'.

The bombings in 1945 of Hiroshima and Nagasaki were atypical and no conclusions regarding the future likelihood of nuclear warfare could be drawn from them: they occurred at a time that the US had atomic monopoly and hence did not have to fear retaliation. It is the lack of any retaliatory capacity at the disposal of Japan that made Truman's decision possible. Things change once you are with two (or more) in the nuclear game. Because then the logic of that game changes fundamentally.

In such duopoly scenario survival depends on effective deterrence, indeed on *symmetrical* deterrence since the need for deterrence by one party also plays for the other party. **The logic of deterrence** is rather paradoxical: deterrence means, analytically, that you have to credibly threaten with the use of force, in order *not* to have to use it. For deterrence to succeed, there must be three conditions fulfilled: (1) you must effectively *have* the nuclear power, (2) you must be effectively *ready to use* it, and (3) your potential adversary must be fully *aware* of these two facts. The second of these three conditions is critical. Deterrence will not work if your threat of use of force is not totally credible (as we too often witness with bland invocations of 'red lines'). Note that given the symmetrical relationship involved it will be, again paradoxically, the countries that possess nuclear weapons that will feel safer than those who do not.

This then is what we have learned to call the '**balance of terror**' resting on the so-called *MAD-doctrine* ('**mutually assured destruction**'). MAD should not be called a 'doctrine' since it is a matter of pure logic. This explains why no strenuous negotiations or written agreements were involved in getting at that 'balance'. That balance came naturally, logically. Not an option, but a necessity. The parties involved readily understood what was at stake: if I kill my adversary, I am assured that he will kill me; so, killing him effectively means killing myself, suicide. The mechanism underlying it is self-fulfilling. It operates through the intrinsic self-interest of the parties. The MAD-logic is often suggested as the primary reason for the Cold War remaining 'cold'. While the Bipolar World might have been intrinsically a rather dangerous place, its MAD-doctrine paradoxically led to stability and predictability. As Ronal Steel put it: 'In its perverted way, the Cold War was a force of stability' (STEEL, 1995, p. 11). Nuclear weapons ended up being viewed as a fundamental source of national security and international stability. Churchill put it in a memorable phrase: 'safety would prove to be the sturdy child of terror' (see Box 8.15). That is why some analysts have suggested that the proliferation of nuclear weapons to India and Pakistan has actually (and again paradoxically) moderated their relationship by raising the cost of all-out war for both parties to unacceptable levels.

The preceding remarks may give the impression that the logic of deterrence only plays with regard to nuclear weapons. That logic, however, applies to any form of deterrence, including with conventional weapons or even sanction regimes. What makes nuclear deterrence special is its 'absolute' nature given the total destruction that would follow in case it would fail.

Box 8.15 Balance of Terror and Morality

In the mid-1980s of last century, there were large demonstrations in quite a few Western European capitals against nuclear weapons installations on their territories. Generally, these movements claimed *the moral high ground* in the nuclear debate. The Soviet authorities were of course totally impervious to such anti-nuclear demonstrations, notably in Brussels, Paris, and London. The abandonment of nuclear arms could only happen in the western democracies. The question then could be asked whether an increased risk of war through the creation of an avoidable imbalance was more moral than the prevention of war by effective balance.

It is quite interesting to note that the MAD-logic was confirmed and indeed guaranteed by the *Anti-Ballistic Missile (ABM) Treaty* of 1972. This was a treaty specifically designed to *ensure the mutual vulnerability* of the Soviet Union and the US by limiting the missile defences they could develop, thus ensuring their continued mutual vulnerability to nuclear attack. The ABM Treaty thus rested on the proposition that the development of effective missile defences by one side would undermine the other side's confidence in the effectiveness of its nuclear deterrent, incentivising it to launch a first strike before it was too late. Significantly, in 2002, the US withdrew from the Treaty in order to be able to pursue the development of its Ballistic Missile Defence system, a move that contradicts the logic behind MAD and thus fragilises the 'balance of terror'.

MAD-logic presupposes that the parties are **rational agents**. But governments do not always behave rationally, which brings us to the questions of No First Use (NFU) and Non-Proliferation (see Box 8.16).

Box 8.16 States as Rational Agents in the Nuclear Age

With the end of the Cold War, it was generally agreed that a nuclear exchange between the recognised nuclear powers was even more unlikely. Attention then increasingly shifted to states whose 'rationality' was questionable or whose hegemonic aspirations posed a threat to global stability. Such states were until recently referred to as 'rogue states'. Listed among them were countries such as Iraq,

Iran, Libya, North Korea, and Syria. The main concern regarding these rogue states is (or was, Iraq, Syria, and Libya are no threat anymore today) the utter *unpredictability and volatility* of their regime's attitudes linked to the hegemonic policies pursued by some of them. Remember Iraq's risky behaviour in sending Scud missiles against Israeli and Saudi Arabian targets during the first Gulf War; or think of Iran, a country with nuclear ambitions, whose current policy seeks regional domination through destabilisation of the Middle Eastern region via a network of proxies stretching from Iraq through Lebanon (Hezbollah) to Yemen. As regards North Korea, doubts persist whether, from a policy point of view, its nuclear ambitions are essentially motivated by defensive considerations or whether they aim at intimidating or even attacking South Korea, but even so the irrationality of a leader like Kim Jong Un is far from reassuring. As regards the so-called unrecognised nuclear states not considered 'rogue', uncertainty remains as to whether India and Pakistan would demonstrate enough rational self-control for avoiding recourse to nuclear force in case of an outbreak of violence.

8.11.1.2 No First Use (NFU)

Not everybody would agree that the logic of deterrence is as compelling as portrayed above. Moreover, as pointed out, the logic presupposes rational agents deciding on the use of nuclear force. **NFU** stands for a doctrine according to which no nuclear weapons would be used against an enemy that has used only conventional weapons. India and China have declared NFU. The US has consciously opted for an ambiguous posture. Proponents of the doctrine think that NFU would make for a safer world. They point out that without NFU, a nuclear state adversary that fears an unexpected nuclear attack is more likely to put its own arsenal on hair-trigger alert, increasing the *risk of accidental launch*. Also, without NFU an adversary might be tempted to pre-empt the would-be attacker by going even faster, engendering a perverse dialectic known as '*reciprocal fear of surprise attack*'.

But many observers are not convinced by these pro-NFU arguments.

From a conceptual perspective NFU opponents point out that the aim should *not* be to diminish the deterrence from nuclear weapons (as would happen with NFU), *but* to minimise the risk that those weapons themselves become the cause of escalation:

- To counter the NFU argument regarding the *risk of accidental launch*, opponents argue that one should not question the overall principle of deterrence but look at formulas to improve the nuclear chain command. One could envisage that the power to decide on a launch should reside in a collective body (a college) rather than a single individual (e.g. the President). Doing so would perhaps not totally avert 'accidental' launches by 'non-rational' actors, but it would at least drastically diminish that risk from happening.
- Also, nuclear powers could make their systems safer. Currently these systems are designed for nuclear forces to be launched within a few minutes, without the possibility of recall (called 'launch on warning'). *Taking weapons off this hair-trigger* by mutual agreement could allow decisions to be made with cooler heads.

- Another way for a first-use policy to be made safer could be that nuclear states make formal *pledges regarding the scope of their first-use* policy. It has been suggested, for instance, that recourse to nuclear weapons should only happen in case the very survival of nations is at stake.

From a political perspective NFU-opponents point out that NFU could make the world a less stable place:

- South Korea, Taiwan, or the Baltic States are countries that face intimidating neighbours; they think (and the NFU-opponents agree) that uncertainty about America's First Use helps deter *conventional* attacks that might threaten their very existence, such as a Russian assault on Estonia or a Chinese invasion of Taiwan.
- Also, were the US to rule out First Use, some of its Asian allies might pursue nuclear weapons of their own. Any such proliferation risks being destabilising and indeed increasing the risks of nuclear war.

8.11.1.3 Non-Proliferation

At the heart of today's security regime is the *nuclear Non-Proliferation Treaty* (NPT). Signed in 1968, the parties to the NPT now include 185 countries: those which have renounced the nuclear path (the non-nuclear-weapon states), as well as five nuclear-weapon states that the treaty 'recognises' as such (the US, Russia, China, France, and the UK). The four non-recognised nuclear-weapon states outside the treaty either never signed it (India, Israel, and Pakistan) or withdrew from it (North Korea). In signing, the non-nuclear-weapon states committed themselves not to develop nuclear weapons and to submit themselves to various monitoring and inspection procedures managed by the Vienna-based *International Atomic Energy Agency* (IAEA). In return, the nuclear-weapon states agreed to help the non-nuclear-weapon states acquire nuclear capabilities for peaceful purposes (e.g. nuclear energy production). They also pledged not to use nuclear weapons to attack them and, most significantly, they agreed to pursue their own nuclear disarmament over the longer term.

In respect of **horizontal** *non-proliferation*, the NPT has generally been successful. Nine nuclear-weapon states (five recognised and four non-recognised) is a long way from Kennedy's nightmare. In 1963 President Kennedy, lamenting his failure to negotiate a ban on nuclear tests, warned that by 1975 there might be 15 or 20 nuclear powers. While some countries, from Brazil over Argentina to Sweden, have flirted with the idea of nuclear weapons at one time or another, few took the next step of actually trying to develop them. Of those, some stopped because the country itself dissolved (Yugoslavia), some because of changes in domestic policy (Brazil), and some because of pressures from allies (South Korea). But the risk for horizontal proliferation is still there. Much will depend on what will happen with the nuclear deal reached with **Iran** in 2015 (the so-called JCPOA – Joint Comprehensive Plan of Action) curtailing its nuclear programme but which President Trump unilaterally resigned. With the arrival of the Biden administration, negotiations have resumed. It remains to be seen whether the revived agreement will effectively foreclose any perspective on Iran going nuclear, not today and not in the future. If not, Saudi Arabia will not want to fall behind and Turkey could well follow. And then others.

Vertical *non-proliferation* is about the nuclear-weapon states' commitment to pursue *nuclear disarmament*. Here, the record is more mixed. Only slowly did the Great Powers come to understand the absurdity of the situation: that the power that has the capacity to destroy the planet ten times over is not 'stronger' than a power that could do so only five times (see Box 8.17). In both cases, there is only one planet to destroy. Still, for too long was there a numerical struggle between the Great Powers in their talk about 'parity', 'superiority', and 'missile gap'. This numerical proliferation in a game in which the stakes are totally fictitious can only be explained in terms of psychology: the psychology of power and prestige.

Box 8.17 Non-Additive Magnitudes

In physics, a distinction is made between additive and non-additive magnitudes. Weight is an additive magnitude. If you add something weighing 20 kilos to something weighing 10 kilos you get something weighing 30 kilos. Temperature is a non-additive magnitude: adding a volume of water of 20 grades Celsius to an identical volume of water of 10 grades Celsius does not result in water of 30 grades Celsius (see Rudolf Carnap, 'Philosophical Foundations of Physics', New York, NY/London, 1966, pp. 70–77).

From the late 1960s onwards, various strategic arms control talks were undertaken and treaties signed. These included restricting the types of nuclear weapons tests which could be undertaken and working towards reducing the overall number of nuclear weapons. The first such treaty, the *Strategic Arms Limitation Treaty* (SALT I) was signed in 1972. Particularly significant was the signing of the *Anti-Ballistic Missile (ABM)* Treaty, also in 1972. As we have seen this treaty was specifically designed to ensure the mutual vulnerability of the US and the Soviet Union by limiting the missile defences they could develop.

More recently, however, accords have been falling apart. The US withdrew from the ABM Treaty in 2002. The INF Treaty (*Intermediate-range Nuclear Forces*) collapsed in August 2019, because of Russian non-compliance. Things went better with the New *Strategic Arms Reduction Treaty* (**New START**), governing intercontinental nuclear missiles. Signed by President Obama in 2010, it brought the level of deployed nuclear warheads down to 1,550. New START was due to expire on 15 February 2021. President Trump was not keen on its extension, mainly because it does not restrain China. On 21 January 2021, however, US President Biden and Russian President Putin agreed on its extension for five years. It is now the only bilateral arms-control agreement that binds the two countries. That is welcome, but prospects for a follow-on are dim.

India, North Korea, and Pakistan are all expanding and modernising their nuclear forces. And so does **China**, which is most worrying. In early 2021, it has been found building over 230 new silos for intercontinental ballistic missiles (ICBMs). As China is reckoned to currently have only 100 or so ICBMs, it is feared that China will rapidly and significantly increase its arsenal. These developments raise two broader questions. One is whether China is deviating from its long-established nuclear strategy. For decades, it has hewed to a policy of 'minimum deterrence', involving the maintenance of a relatively small arsenal that would allow it to hit back aggressors but not wage an elaborate nuclear war. That may change now. The other question is whether these new developments in China will affect nuclear-arms control. As we noted earlier, the only remaining nuclear disarmament pact is the US-Russia New START treaty. If the new silos are seen as confirmation of a rapid Chinese nuclear expansion, one may well conclude that any future arms-control regime will have to involve all three powers, China included.

Progress towards global disarmament, the ultimate aim of NPT, itself the cornerstone of the nuclear order, has been dismal. Frustration led to an attempt to go *beyond NPT* and to push for a world in which nuclear weapons would be illegitimate. This is the goal of the **Treaty on the Prohibition of Nuclear Weapons** (TPNW) which commits its parties to not 'making, using, or hosting nuclear weapons'. Having been ratified by 52 of its 86 signatories, it entered into force on 22 January 2021. This 'nuclear ban' is born as much from frustration as from hope. Sceptics fear it will not change much in the real world. There is something intriguing in the TPNW. Its Article 1 stipulates that 'use' and 'threat of use' should be considered as equivalent notions. But equating 'use' with 'treat of use' undermines the 'logic of deterrence' with which we opened this chapter, thus potentially also upsetting the 'balance of terror' that rested on that logic. This is the major difference with the NPT. The NPT sanctions proliferation but tacitly admits nuclear deterrence. This would explain why the five recognised nuclear-weapons states (the P5) support NPT but not TPNW. So, it is no real surprise that less than two months after the TPNW entered into force, that is on 16 March 2021, the **UK** government published 'Global Britain in a Competitive Age', a strategy paper in which it announced *to raise* the ceiling on its stockpile of warheads to 260, undoing its promise, made in 2010 and reaffirmed in 2015, *to cut* the number of warheads to below 180 by the mid-2020s.

8.11.2 *Hybrid war*

8.11.2.1 *Blurring lines between war and peace*

Many tend to think about conflict in binary terms: you are either at war or in peace; you win, or you lose. This either/or logic is no longer with us, however. Hybrid War, also called New War (see Box 8.18) has blurred the borders between war and peace. Hybrid war refers to a broad range of hostile actions, of which traditional military force is just a small part, and which are executed in concert as part of a flexible strategy with long-term objectives. Characteristic of hybrid warfare is that the exercise of aggression and coercion avoids being exposed to the risks of escalation or severe retaliation. Key to this definition is remaining below or at least **not crossing the threshold of overt warfare**. It is about calibration, leverage, and ambiguity.

Box 8.18 New Wars

Whether the New Wars are really that new is not so sure. George Kennan, in his Long Telegram of February 1946, described the Soviet Union as weak compared to the West and added: 'so its methods will be infiltration, subversion and opportunistic actions rather than a frontal assault' (COOPER, 2021, p. 167), which is not a bad description of what some 60 years later we started calling 'New' Wars. The New Wars, characteristic of the contemporary conflict environment, are sometimes described as post-Westphalian or post-modern, as they are increasingly ambiguous in their nature. These armed conflicts are transnational, dislocated, and decentralised; they defy borders and the boundaries between states and non-state actors. In such circumstances, crime and violence are often indistinguishable from each other (see BERCOVITCH and JACKSON, 2009, p. 6).

It is interesting to note that this new way of warfare has been reinvented by countries such as China, Russia, and Iran. All three countries recognise and to some extent fear superior Western military power, but all of them also see vulnerabilities that they can exploit. They understand, having watched both Gulf Wars (particularly the first one with its precision-strike capabilities), that they would not be able, at least for the time being, to be victorious in war against the US or NATO. Hence, they move away from symmetrical to *asymmetrical* warfare. But there is a paradox here. While it is the comparative weakness of autocratic powers that makes them opt for hybrid warfare, it is comparative strength that results from it. Indeed, the West not only seems to be unable or at least rather embarrassed to effectively respond to this new form of warfare for reasons linked to a continued tendency to think about conflict in binary war-peace terms but also to its deeply entrenched attachment to principles of democratic governance, political accountability and its commitment to a rules-based international system.

The clearest recent cases of hybrid challenges are **Russia**'s continuing interference in Ukraine, **China**'s assertive behaviour in the South and East China Seas and **Iran**'s use of proxy militias to establish an arc of influence from Iraq (Shia militias) through Syria (alliance with the Assad regime) into Lebanon (Hezbollah) and ultimately up to Yemen (Houthis). These actions are part of what could be called a strategy of **'testing and teasing'**, of finding out how far one can go without going too far.

8.11.2.2 Key features of hybrid warfare

Ambiguity: A key aspect of grey-zone challenges is that they should be sufficiently ambiguous to leave targets unsure how to respond. Ambiguity blurs the lines between peace, crisis, and conflict. This blurring of the lines presents a specific challenge when it comes to invoking the collective defence clause of Article 5 of the North Atlantic Treaty, which makes the Central European and Baltic states quite nervous. Hybrid tactics are often shrouded in misinformation and deception; they blur the distinction between civil and military assets and are often conducted in ways that are meant to make proper attribution of the responsible party difficult to nail down.

Calibration: Hybrid threats need to be properly calibrated; much enough but not too much. If states that rely on them do too little, they will face a series of small but cumulatively significant defeats. If they do too much, they risk being responsible for reckless escalation and ultimately retaliation.

Comprehensiveness: Hybrid threats are drawn from a comprehensive toolkit that ranges from cyber-attacks (on power grids, for instance) to propaganda (stirring up local grievances, influencing elections abroad, for instance) and subversion, economic blackmail (such as disruption of gas supplies) and sabotage, sponsorship of proxies (such as the militias in Iraq created by Iran) and creeping military expansionism (through covert or deniable operations, think of the 'little green men' in Eastern Ukraine). Hybrid warfare's success depends on an ability to blend all such instruments of state power in ways that pluralistic, democratic countries find harder to achieve. Robin Niblett, director of Chatham House, a prominent think tank in London, put it thus:

> Any state that is able to bring to bear its full strength rapidly and comprehensively through centrally controlled means – be they economic, military, cultural, informational or social – will be able to create facts on the ground that we, democratic powers, will be weak or unable to respond to.

Graduality: As much as each action of hybrid warfare needs to be carefully calibrated, the process itself needs to unfold gradually and prudently, step by step. Gains are made bit by bit on a slippery slope, using 'salami tactics', the tactics of repeated small '*faits accomplis*' (see Box 8.19). The question here is not: '*how far* can I go without going too far' (calibration), but '*how fast* can I go without going too fast', or to put it in other terms still: how do I make sure that a *difference in degree* does not become a difference *in kind*. China's so-called small-stick diplomacy in the South and East China Seas is a prime example of how to cow neighbours into sulky acquiescence while avoiding a direct confrontation with the US. Things there have been accelerating as of 2010, but still step by step: the creation of artificial islands in 2013 with Xi Jinping stating that he has no intention of militarising them and then, in 2017, doing exactly that with the construction of shelters for missile batteries and military radar installations. What is important to note is that such step-by-step tactical gains end up as a significant strategic gain that cannot later be reversed short of open warfare.

Box 8.19 The Slippery Slope Tactic

The slippery slope tactic is a direct descendant of a paradox with an ancient pedigree, known as the *Sorites paradox* or *paradox of the heap* (which we already discussed in Chapter 5). Its underlying mechanism is disarmingly simple:

- One grain of sand does not constitute a heap. If one grain of sand does not constitute a heap, then two grains of sand do not constitute a heap. Therefore: two grains of sand do not constitute a heap.
- Two grains of sand do not constitute a heap. If two grains of sand do not constitute a heap, then three grains of sand do not constitute a heap. Therefore: three grains of sand do not constitute a heap.
- …
- 999,999 grains of sand do not constitute a heap. If 999,999 grains of sand do not constitute a heap, then 1,000,000 grains of sand do not constitute a heap. Therefore: 1,000,000 grains of sand do not constitute a heap.

(Source: See Louis Demey, *Waarheid*, Lannoo, Tielt, 2019, pp. 156–158)

In this chapter, we started by addressing some key misunderstandings as regards the relation between diplomacy and use of force. When diplomacy is associated with negotiation and the pacific settlement of disputes, then war is obviously seen as diplomacy's failure. But that is a misconception, there is no watertight separation between war and peace. Both are better approached as being part of a continuum. Diplomacy and coercive action do not contradict each other, they are intertwined and may be mutually supportive. Both diplomacy and the use of force are part of *one single political process*, with the same leaders involved and the same concerns and goals. This is, we think, how the question of use of force should be approached. We have distinguished among different forms of the use of force and studied under what circumstances recourse to them can be considered legal. Beyond questions of legality, there are questions of legitimacy to be addressed, with necessity and proportionality among the most prominent criteria. The question then is no longer whether as a matter of law you *can* have recourse to the use of force, but whether as a matter of good sense and good conscience you *should*. And even then, further questions of *prudence, judgment, and wisdom* can be asked: having a just cause to launch a war does not amount to having a good case to actually start it. Criteria regarding necessity and proportionality need also to be respected in the actual conduct of war. And finally, there is the question related to a war's aftermath. What does 'just peace' amount to, mere absence of violence or more? The core idea behind this whole chapter was that the use of force may, under restrictive conditions, not just be permitted but be necessary for the sake of maintaining or restoring international peace.

Bibliography

ABRAMS, Elliott (Ed.) (2016), *Honor among Nations: Intangible Interests and Foreign Policy*, Ethics and Public Policy Center, Washington, DC.

ANGELL, Norman (2012), *The Great Illusion: A Study of the Relation of Military Power to National Advantage*, Bottom of the Hill Publishing, Memphis, TN.

BERCOVITCH, Jacob & JACKSON, Richard (2009), *Conflict Resolution in the Twenty-First Century*, The University of Michigan Press, Ann Arbor, MI.

CLAUSEWITZ, Carl von (1976), *On War*, Princeton University Press, Princeton.

COLLIER, Paul (2008), *The Bottom Billion*, Oxford University Press, Oxford.

COLLIER, Paul (2009), *Wars, Guns & Votes: Democracy in Dangerous Places*, The Bodley Head, London.

COOPER, Robert (2021), *The Ambassadors: Thinking about Diplomacy from Machiavelli to Modern Times*, Weidenfeld & Nicolson, London.

DIAMOND, Jared (2013), *Collapse: How Societies Choose to Fail or Survive*, Viking, New York, NY.

ENZENSBERGER, Hans M. (1994), *Civil Wars*, The New Press, New York, NY.

FIOT, Daniel & PAAS, Roderick (2019), *Protecting Europe: The EU's Response to Hybrid Threats*, EU Commission, Brussels.

GADDIS, John L. (2018), *On Grand Strategy*, Allen Lane, London.

HAASS, Richard N. (2009), *War of Necessity: War of Choice*, Simon & Schuster, New York, NY.

HANDLER, Scott P. (Ed.) (2013), *International Politics*, CQ Press, Los Angeles, CA.

HILTERMANN, Joost (2018), "Tackling the MENA Region's Intersecting Conflicts", International Crisis Group, 22 December 2017.

KAGAN, Donald (1995), *On the Origins of War and the Preservation of Peace*, Doubleday, New York, NY.

KENNAN, George (1948), *The Inauguration of Organized Political Warfare*, New York, NY.

RUYS, Tom, CORTEN, Olivier & HOFER, Alexander (Eds.) (2018), *The Use of Force in International Law*, Oxford University Press, Oxford.

SIRACUSA, Joseph (2010), *Diplomacy: A Very Short Introduction*, Oxford University Press, Oxford.

SMITH, Rupert (2019), *The Utility of Force: The Art of War in the Modern World*, Penguin, London.

STEEL, Ronald (1995), *Temptations of a Superpower*, Harvard University Press.

TUCHMAN, Barbara (1984), *The March of Folly: From Troy to Vietnam*, Alfred A Knopf, New York, NY.

UNITED NATIONS (2004), "A More Secure World: Our Shared Responsibility" in: *Report of the High-level Panel on Threats, Challenges and Change*, New York.

VOLKAN, Vamik D. (2013), *Enemies on the Couch – A Psychopolitical Journey through War and Peace*, Pitchstone Publishing, Durham.

WALZER, Michael (2006), *Just and Unjust Wars: A Moral Argument with Historical Illustrations*, Basic Books, New York, NY.

WOUTERS, Jan (2006), *Internationaal Recht in Kort Bestek*, Intersentia, Antwerpen/Oxford.

Part IV

The normative framework of diplomacy

9 Diplomacy and international law

International law (IL) as a system of rules is unlike any other branch of law. It is the only branch of law of which one can, with a straight face, ask whether it is indeed law at all. The main reason for this uncertainty is due to its decentralised and horizontal character. In the world political system there is no central authority (principle of 'anarchy') given that authority is equally spread over all states (principle of 'sovereign equality'):

No central legislator. The UN General Assembly is not a world legislator; its resolutions are not legally binding. States are their own legislator. States are therefore bound only by the rules they are willing to accept (principle of 'consent').

No central judge. Adjudication by the International Court of Justice (ICJ) is subject to the prior acceptance by states of its jurisdiction. The same holds for international arbitration.

No world police. There is no global enforcement authority. It is up to the states themselves to ensure the maintenance of world 'law and order' (principle of 'self-help').

This rough and admittedly incomplete characterisation allows us to see how the role of 'law' in the 'society of nations' stems largely from the states themselves, from their behaviour in the form of diplomatic claims and counterclaims, and attendant acts and omissions. Without centralised procedures for legislating, adjudicating, and policing its rules, it could be argued that IL, contrary to domestic law, is more in the nature of a vast network of political arrangements (that assume the form of principles and rules) reflecting transient perceptions of national interests. Is IL truly law, or is it floating somewhere between law properly understood and diplomatic practice?

9.1 Law and diplomacy – an ambiguous relation

Lawyers and diplomats do not always see eye to eye. Their worlds both overlap and differ. They overlap because IL is a useful, some would say necessary instrument for diplomacy. A diplomat's idiom is very much that of the international lawyer. Moreover, even though the diplomat may not always be convinced of the 'legally binding' character of IL, he or she too feels what has been called the *'compliance pull'*, the attractive force that makes one act in conformity with the law.

But the lawyer's and diplomat's worlds also differ. IL and diplomatic practise are sometimes at odds with each other. IL is prescriptive, it tells how states should

DOI: 10.4324/9781003298182-14

behave. States' behaviour, however, is often dictated by constraints flowing from prevailing power realities, the 'circumstances' ('la qualità dei tempi') as Machiavelli called them, on which law has only a very limited impact (see Box 9.1). Law is also, by its very nature, principled. There is a strictness to law and much rigour, some would say rigidity, that contrasts with the diplomat's pragmatic search for workable *ad hoc* solutions which require flexibility and a sense of compromise. From a legal point of view a diplomat's solution seldom looks very clean; it is suboptimal, but it is a solution – it works. A diplomat is a fixer, a problem-solver. Theirs is the real world, a nasty world where state interests clash. In the lawyer's world, on the contrary, there is an element of 'ideality' that a diplomat cannot match easily. For the diplomat, IL is an instrument; it should help solve problems, not hinder finding solutions. States have generally preferred to solve their disputes and conflicts by 'talking it over' rather than submit their interests to legal adjudication. Adjudication operates in terms of black and white, whereas diplomatic practice operates in the penumbra zone of one hundred shades of grey. Diplomacy dislikes situations in which a case is either completely won or completely lost.

What all this comes down to is that the role of IL in diplomatic practice is ambiguous. The diplomat is a *disillusioned lawyer* who readily recognises the value of IL but is in his or her daily diplomatic practice often confronted with its limits.

Box 9.1 Law and Politics – An Anecdote

During the Berlin crisis of 1961–1962, President John Kennedy was considering making some concessions to the Soviets with a view of preventing that the situation would deteriorate to the point of conflict. The West German Ambassador at the time, Wilhelm Grewe, an academic authority on IL, repeatedly argued with Kennedy that the American proposals violated the Four Power Agreement of 1945. As Grewe himself recounts, the White House then 'spread the message that the Ambassador was boring the President with professorial juridical advice and that he was treating a highly political matter with legalistic arguments; that it was tactless to remind the US Government of their treaty obligations' (see GREWE, 1999, p. 28).

These introductory remarks may appear dismissive as regards the role of IL in diplomacy. But they are not. I think the international lawyer will readily accept the following two points:

- First, that what is important for the *continuing relevance of IL* is *not* its complete and permanent observance, but rather the fact that what may appear to be violations of the rules will be explained by the parties involved in terms that implicitly affirm, rather than deny, the continuing validity of the rules. Thus, when Israel and its Arab neighbours fought the Six-Day War in 1967, *both* sides claimed to be acting in self-defence and therefore in accordance with Article 51 of the UN Charter. Such parallel claims are obviously contradictory, as two parties to a conflict cannot both simultaneously claim to act in self-defence. But from the point of view of the stability of the international legal order, what matters more than the question whether the claims are valid is the fact that the episode is explained in a way that purports to demonstrate that the states concerned acted within the rules of IL. Hypocrisy tends to have a bad reputation, but it has a vital role in maintaining legal standards alive. As the saying goes: '*Hypocrisy is the tribute that vice pays to virtue*'.

- There is a second point to be made. It is that the appraisal of an action in international politics by reference to the standards of IL is something that we *choose* to do. It is not inevitable. If a dispute among states arises, there is no obvious need, let alone obligation, to turn immediately to the law to resolve it. The diplomat's natural response will be to discuss it, to talk it over, and to reach a practical accommodation which may bear no direct relation to the respective legal rights and duties of the parties. The fact is that the political 'transaction cost' of pursuing *legal remedies* for every wrong may be too high. One chooses which disputes are best handled through formal legal mechanisms and which not. Some disputes are essentially legal, and a solution in line with IL is appropriate. The Iraqi invasion of Kuwait is an example of a clear breach of the norms of IL; recourse to its remedies, including the use of force, was unproblematic. But other conflicts are essentially political. Think of the Arab-Israeli conflict. For decades, negotiations have been couched not in terms of what IL prescribes or forbids but rather in terms of what concessions might reasonably be expected to be made, as was the case with the Track II negotiations in Oslo in 1993.

Prudence, not legalism, is the diplomat's guide in navigating tough political issues. IL does not always provide the good solution. Decisions which are of immaculate legality can become harmful if isolated from the broader context. An historical example of this is the Anglo-French decision early in 1940 to resist the Soviet invasion of Finland. This action, including the expulsion of the Soviet Union from the League of Nations, was legally correct in terms of the League's Covenant. Finland was indeed entitled to receive international support against aggression. But the UK and France nearly found themselves at war with Hitler's Germany *and* the Soviet Union at the same time. Exemplary in legal terms, this action would have been disastrous in political terms. It is possible to be legally correct and politically reckless at one and the same time.

This is not to say that a diplomat can or should ignore IL. A diplomat does well in having a general grasp of IL, of its scope *and* limits. Obviously, the strength of a diplomat's arguments and the soundness of the pragmatic solutions he or she offers in solving problems will gain when supported by IL. Moreover, in cases of compulsory law ('*jus cogens*') the diplomat will not have much choice but to abide by it (see Box 9.2). Hence, the utility of the short overview of IL that is to follow. We will not be insisting that much on the substantive content of different areas of IL, but rather on its formal aspects as they bear on diplomatic practice.

Box 9.2 *Jus Cogens*

Jus Cogens literally means 'compelling law'. It is a controversial notion that has been criticised for its vagueness and potential for abuse. It refers to 'peremptory norms of international law' defined as 'norms accepted and recognised by the international community of states as a whole' (Art. 53 of the 1969 Vienna *Convention on the Law of Treaties* – see below). The notion covers such obvious areas as aggression, genocide, ethnic cleansing, war crimes, slavery, and piracy. In borderline cases, however, the concept risks becoming practically inoperant as not many lawyers seem to know up to where the notion stretches. Unsurprisingly perhaps, the ICJ has never cited *jus cogens* in support of any of its decisions.

9.2 Why international law?

In this section, we will explore the nature of IL, not in an abstract way but in a manner that makes the diplomat understand its peculiarities and some of its underlying paradoxes. We will proceed in this exploration by asking the question: where does IL come from? Who creates it? How is it created? Why do states obey the law? If the rules of IL are made by states in the first place, can they really be regarded as constraints upon them?

Rules of IL come from two main sources: treaties and customary law, both of which are created by states, the former *explicitly* through often arduous and long negotiations conducted by diplomats, the latter *implicitly* through consistent diplomatic practices demonstrating adherence to a rule. States therefore end up being bound by rules which they themselves have chosen to be bound by. This looks slightly paradoxical. We will come back to this issue later. Before that, let us have a closer look at the two main sources of law; customary IL first, which generally is considered as more basic than treaty law in the construction of an international legal order.

9.2.1 Customary international law

Let us start with a simple consideration: governments, *as a matter of fact*, routinely conduct their international relations respecting the rules of IL. This is not a case of rules being *imposed* on states or states feeling *constrained* by rules; it is rather that those rules largely spell out the *normal* way states conduct their relations, rules that are tacitly accepted as the *grammar of diplomacy*. Customary IL concerns the recognition of law as rooted in the regularity of identified diplomatic practices. Some such practices are so ingrained in world society and regarded as so important that a breach of them is considered as particularly serious, attracting not merely opprobrium but exposure to sanctions.

For a practice to become a rule of customary IL, it is not necessary that *every* state subscribe to the practice *all the time*. It is enough that a significant number of states systematically follow the rule, and particularly those having an interest in or being affected by the rule (outer space law, for example, interests and affects states capable of launching rockets in space more than others). Nor is it required that the rule be followed all the time; what is required is that it is followed most of the time; an occasional break of the rule does not mean its end. In sum, what counts for a practice to be considered a rule of international customary law is not so much what states *actually* do but what they *say* they ought to do or what they continue to *pretend* that they do. Remember what we said above about the *virtues of hypocrisy*.

As appears from the preceding paragraphs, customary IL is resilient. Perhaps a little bit too much, one might suspect. Most of its rules are observed by most of the states most of the time. This looks like a mere *tautology*. States normally follow customary IL because it consists of the practices that states normally follow. The circle is round. This logical fallacy is known as 'begging the question' (*'petitio principi'*). The critical point that we must add to break the circle is that states normally follow these practices because they see them as expressions of rules of IL: the *normality* of the behaviour is expressive of the *normativity* of the rule followed by the behaviour. Obviously, not any regular practice acquires the normative strength of a legal rule (think about the rather consistent practice of remitting the intergovernmental debts of poor countries). In order to evidence a rule of customary IL, the international practice must not simply be followed as a matter of fact but must in addition be **regarded as legally binding** by the generality of states. The conviction that the rules are indeed legally binding is known by the Latin name of *'opinio juris'*. It is not so much a case of customary IL *bestowing* binding force on certain rules of conduct, so making them into rules of IL. Rather, customary IL *is* the body of rules with which practices conform out of a sense of legal obligation to comply with them. That is what gives customary IL its normative power.

And that is where international **politics** and diplomacy **meet IL**. States 'make' the rules when they are on their best behaviour, when they are asserting publicly the rules and standards which they believe must be observed, in short when they do politics, when they practice diplomacy. Often the statements are made when states criticise other states for not observing them. But the existence of the rules exerts a real pull towards compliance when states are tempted to fall below the standards that they have themselves adopted. And that is the valuable source of normative pressure within the international system.

Classical examples of customary IL are the rules on sovereign immunity – now usually called **state immunity**. This is the diplomatic immunity granted to foreign Heads of State or Government, members of government, and diplomats from prosecution in local courts. It also concerns the immunity of diplomatic missions prohibiting local police to enter diplomatic premises, unless authorised (recall the case of the London police which was stationed for years outside the Embassy of Ecuador where Wikileaks-founder Julian Assange took refuge in 2012). Another example of customary IL is the recognition in the 1970s of last century of a coastal state's jurisdiction over a 200-mile so-called **Exclusive Economic Zone** (EEZ). This rule emerged from a practice by a handful of Latin American states in the late 1940s and early 1950s which were unhappy with the then prevalent rule regarding the three-mile territorial sea and the one regarding the so-called continental shelf (see Box 9.3).

Box 9.3 Territorial Sea, Continental Shelf, and Exclusive Economic Zone

In 1945, President Truman issued a '*Proclamation*' to the effect that the US affirmed its right to resources on and under its *continental shelf*, which is the seaward extension of the land mass of continents and islands, as distinct from the deep ocean floor. As a sign of good faith, the US said it would recognise comparable assertions of jurisdiction by any other state that was the beneficiary of the same geographical condition. The US lead was soon followed by other states and because of the generality of that practice and the absence of any significant opposition to it, a *new rule of customary IL* swiftly emerged. At the same time the US insisted that this extension did not amount to an extension of the *territorial sea* beyond the three-mile limit embodied in earlier *customary law*. In the view then urged by the US, the three-mile rule was concerned with navigation on the sea and not with resources under it. Good faith or not, a number of Latin American states that did not enjoy such a shelf (which is very narrow in the west coast of South America), much less one believed to contain substantial petroleum resources, but did have rich fishing grounds off their coast, asserted national jurisdiction over the living resources in the seas up to a distance from the coast roughly equivalent to the breadth of the US continental shelf (say 200 miles). Implicitly they were saying that the real issue raised by the new rule regarding continental shelf was control of coastal resources generally. Followed by clear signs of general acceptance in state practice a *new rule of customary law* emerged, that of EEZ (see FARER, in COOPER, 2015, pp. 498–499).

The EEZ example is interesting in two respects. First, it illustrates how *changes* in customary IL may happen and indeed be initiated by a single or small group of states unilaterally applying what they hope will become a new rule of IL. Second, the example shows how rules of customary IL may with time be *codified*. They then change nature: from customary law they become treaty law. This is what happened with the rules regarding the territorial sea, continental shelf, and EEZ which in the 1982 UN *Convention on the Law of the Sea* were codified as part of a new comprehensive legal framework for the use of the sea with a new consensus on the breadth of the territorial sea (12 miles), on the right of countries to assert jurisdiction over their continental shelves and of their rights regarding a 200 miles EEZ adjacent to their coasts (see SOMERS, 2010, pp.118–124).

Rules of customary IL can not only change, but they can also *cease to exist*. This is what happened with state immunity formerly granted not only to states proper but also to their agencies, such as state-trading companies in communist countries which thus benefitted from an unfair competitive advantage compared to private companies of non-communist states. Through the adoption of a new doctrine called the doctrine of '*restricted immunity*', immunity is today accorded only in respect of 'governmental' but not 'commercial' acts of states or their agencies, thus doing away with the immunity formerly granted to state-trading companies.

9.2.2 *Treaty law*

Customary IL was the main source of IL until the middle of the 20th century. It has since been supplemented (but not replaced) by treaty law. Customary law is resilient, as we have seen. But it can be slow in the making. In fact, customary IL is *not made*, it grows, evolves, and emerges out of practices. A practice must first be initiated. One must then wait for it to become settled. Treaty law, on the contrary, is *made*. It is made in a rather straightforward way: new rules of IL are established through a deliberate *negotiation process* followed by the careful *drafting* of texts that must command explicit consensus. A treaty is an agreement between states that is *legally binding*. It can be called by different names (pact, covenant, protocol, 'exchange of notes'); what counts is that the instrument binds its parties. Not all international instruments do, even though they may be of prime political significance. Such was the case with the Atlantic Charter of 1941. The Helsinki Final Act of 1975 offers another example; although negotiated by 35 states in the framework of the Conference on Security and Cooperation (CSCE), it is not considered to be legally binding and does therefore not qualify as a 'treaty'. But not being *legally bound* by an agreement does not mean that the parties are also not *politically bound* by it. In diplomatic practice the latter may be not less relevant than the former.

If states wish to set out their rights and duties in a clear and precise manner (which customary law is not always able to do) they will usually do it by negotiating a *bilateral or multilateral* treaty. Much of that negotiating work is done by diplomats. That is one, but not the only reason why negotiation is so central in diplomatic practice. When negotiating a multilateral treaty there is a *balance* to be struck between maximising participation by states and maximising the scope and precision of the commitments to be made by the parties. One way of addressing the *inverse relationship* between *breadth of participation* and *depth of commitment* is to allow state-parties to make *reservations* (called 'opt-outs' in the EU context). But not any reservation is allowable; only reservations consistent with the object and purpose of the treaty may be made; and even then, each other state-party can choose whether to accept the reservation (in which case the treaty applies between it and the reserving state as modified) or to refuse it, in which case the treaty will not enter into force between it and the reserving state.

Some treaties enter into force immediately upon their *signature*, most however only after *ratification* by all or a specified number of states (or ratio to total signatories) seen as the minimum necessary for the new treaty regime to be viable and effective. Ratification generally involves the consent of the legislature. An example of an important historic treaty that did not get ratified (by the US Congress) is the Strategic Arms Limitation Treaty (SALT II) negotiated by the Carter administration and the Soviet Union in 1979. An example of an important recent treaty setting a specified number of ratifications (50) for it to enter into force three months later is the *Treaty on the Prohibition of Nuclear Weapons*. Negotiations started in 2017 with 122 states participating, out of which there were 86 signatories. The 50th state to ratify the treaty was Honduras, which did so on 22 October 2020. Hence, the treaty entered into force on 22 January 2021.

The rules regarding treaty law are rather straightforward; they have grown out of customary law and have been codified in the 1969 *Vienna Convention on the Law of Treaties* (a treaty which presumably has respected its own rules on treaty-making). As we said earlier, the negotiation of the substantive provisions of a treaty is a diplomat's job, most often carried out in the framework of multilateral organisations or international conferences. The formal aspects of treaty-making are generally being handled by the legal services of the Ministries of Foreign Affairs.

9.2.3 *Other sources*

Customary International and Treaty Law are no doubt the two main sources of IL. But there are some other sources as well. Most important among them are **resolutions** adopted by the UN and other international organisations. Strictly speaking **UN General**

Assembly resolutions are not legally binding and do not therefore make IL. But they have a *moral authority* that, as a matter of politics, one only ignores at its own peril. In some cases, however, such resolutions do have legal significance. A resolution may affirm or restate established rules of customary IL, in which case it somehow *'inherits'* the legal value of the underlying rules and may be considered as an authoritative exposition of the law. An example is the UN General Assembly resolution 2625 of 1970, better known as the *'Declaration on Principles of International Law Concerning Friendly Relations and Cooperation Among States in Accordance with the Charter of the UN'*. As its title suggests it sets out the fundamental principles of IL that were accepted by all states as the basis for relations between them. We will discuss them further down in this subsection. No uncertainties regarding the authoritative force of resolutions exist as far as the **UN Security Council** is concerned. Its resolutions are *legally binding* for *all* member states. As we have seen in the preceding chapter on the 'Use of Force', the Security Council, when acting under Chapter VII of the Charter, has the power to make *binding determinations* of the existence of a breach of, or a threat to international peace and security, and it may order states to implement coercive measures such as sanctions to address such situations.

So-called **specialised organisations** (such as the World Trade Organisation – WTO in Geneva and the International Maritime Organisation – IMO in London) also have powers to take *binding measures* within the limits of their own competences. The IMO, for example, has the power to authorise traffic separation schemes in busy international waterways such as the Strait of Dover. The *conventions* of the **Council of Europe** are also legally binding but only for those countries which choose to ratify them, which they are not obliged to do. As regards the **European Union**, its *recommendations* are not legally binding; in contrast, its *regulations and directives* are.

9.2.4 Soft law

Finally, there is the growing field of non-binding rules that goes by the name of soft law: standards, guidelines, understandings, arrangements, and so on. As new domains stretching from the environment to cyberspace come to be seen as demanding international regulation, states are eager to adopt the necessary rules but may be reluctant to embrace them at once as formally binding. Soft law then offers a way out. It is a convenient option for negotiations that might otherwise stall if legally binding commitments were sought at a time when the parties are not yet ready for it but still wish to negotiate something in good faith in the meantime.

In the past, diplomats and lawyers simply accepted the notion that no law governed a particular subject until a new treaty was concluded or states signalled their consent to a new customary law rule. But things have changed. Today, all but the most doctrinaire of scholars see a role for so-called soft law – precepts emanating from public or private international bodies that conform in some sense to ***expectations of required behaviour*** but that are not binding. Soft law enables states to adjust to the regulation of new areas of international concern without fearing to formally breach the law (and possibly face legal countermeasures) if they fail to comply. In such way *normative expectations* are built *more quickly* than they would through the evolution of customary law, and *more gently* than if a new treaty were foisted on states.

Soft law principles may also represent the starting point for new **hard law**, that is, binding law. As was to be expected in light of the distinction between customary and treaty law, this 'hardening' of soft law may happen in two ways. One is when declarations, recommendations, etc. are the first step towards a treaty-making process, in which reference will be made to the principles already *softly* agreed in the soft law instruments. Another possibility is that soft law understandings may have a direct influence on the practice of states, and to the extent that they are successful in doing so, they may lead to the creation of customary law.

An example of soft law is the *Code of Conduct for Multinational Enterprises* adopted by the OECD (Organisation for Economic Cooperation and Development) in June 2000 as regards labour relations, the environment, consumer protection, and fair competition, among others. Interestingly, the *Code* itself states that, as far as its legal reach is concerned, its *Guidelines* 'provide principles and standards of good practice consistent with applicable laws' adding that their 'observance (...) by enterprises is voluntary and not legally enforceable'. Another well-known example of soft law is the *UN Global Compact*, a declaration of (ten) principles launched at the UN Headquarters in New York in July 2000, in which multinational companies commit themselves to respect international norms regarding human rights, labour, the environment, and anti-corruption without, however, being legally bound by them (see BOSSUYT and WOUTERS, 2005, p. 283).

An interesting but somewhat disputed case of soft law is the set of *Guidelines on the Treatment of Foreign Direct Investment* established by the World Bank in 1992 which, although not legally binding, have been regularly invoked by states and private corporations as the standard for how developing nations should treat foreign capital to encourage investment. But its morphing into hard law was a failure. In 1995, an attempt was made within the OECD to turn this soft law into hard law taking the guidelines as the basis for the negotiation of a *Multilateral Agreement on Investment* that would have been legally binding. As the draft agreement drew widespread criticism from civil society and developing countries, negotiations were interrupted in 1998 and the soft law never became hard.

Soft law needs not originate in states. It can emanate from the private sector directly. Multinational companies can adopt their own *'private codes'*. A well-known example in this regard were the so-called *Sullivan Principles*, a code of conduct that was adopted by over 100 US companies in 1977 with investment interests in apartheid South Africa. The principles called for desegregation in the workplace, equal pay, and equal employment practices. Other examples of private codes are 'The *Body Shop* trading charter' and the '*Nike* Code of Conduct'.

9.2.5 Why do states seek to establish international law?

There are different reasons why states seek to establish IL. Some of them overlap with others; that is particularly the case with the first:

- **Self-interest**. States cooperate wherever the benefits of cooperation outweigh its costs. As Tom Farer notes: 'rules (of international law) embody calculations of self-interest made with great deliberation' (FARER, 2015, p. 506). Pursuing one's self-interest, as John Locke pointed out, amounts to contributing to the common interest.
- **Sheer necessity**. There are matters on which states do not particularly care *what* rule is adopted as long as there is *some* rule that gets adopted, in the way that

within a state it is necessary to reach a decision, however arbitrary, on whether to drive on the right or the left of the road. There are many international agreements on technical standards which illustrate this point: from the precise definition of the metre and the kilogram, over navigation rules and signalling codes for ships and aircraft, to labelling specifications for food and drugs. Historically, the first international organisations were not about grandiose political projects but about down-to-earth technical matters: the International Telecommunications Organisation (ITO, 1865) and the International Postal Union (IPU, 1874); how else would one regulate inter-state telecommunications and postal services but by agreement?

- **Convenience**. And even when states have their own views on what rule should be adopted, they will nonetheless consider it better to have a rule, however imperfect, than none, a free-for-all or a muddle of conflicting rules. In an increasingly inter-dependent world, states need to agree on some basic rules of the game, on world trade, for instance (the WTO with its 'Dispute Settlement Mechanism') or on international finance (the IMF and World Bank and associated bodies such as the Paris and London Clubs for the renegotiation of international debt).

- **Predictability**. There are circumstances not unlike the 'Prisoner's Dilemma' where one state will act only if it knows in advance what steps others will take. Disarmament agreements are an instance of this rule. No country will disarm without being assured that the other relevant player(s) will follow suit. Unilateral disarmament is an invitation for 'free rider' behaviour. The 'free rider' problem is one reason why agreements which only make sense when *all* relevant stakeholders are bound by them, tend to be less strict in the commitments agreed (remember what we said on the inverse relationship between breadth of participation and depth of commitments in treaty-making).

- **Basic Morality**. Most of us are familiar with what has come to be known as the *Golden Rule*: 'Treat others as you would like others to treat you'. This rule of reciprocity is one of the most fundamental rules of ethics. This and other basic rules of morality have shaped natural law which in turn has inspired IL, including its most general principles: the principle of equality of states, of sovereignty, of independence, of non-interference in domestic affairs, of state immunity, the duty to keep your promises, that is, to comply with treaty obligations (*'pacta sunt servanda'*), and many more.

- **International Morality** refers to issues on which all, or practically all, states take the same position as a *matter of principle*. Most of these issues are related to the *fundamental* human rights (or their converse, 'crimes against humanity', of which Article 7 of the Rome Statute of the International Criminal Court gives an exhaustive list). Take torture. Its prohibition in the 1984 *UN Convention against Torture and Other Cruel, Inhuman and Degrading Treatment or Punishment* is described in absolute terms: 'No exceptional circumstances whatsoever, whether a state of war or a threat of war, internal political stability or any other public emergency, may be invoked as a justification of torture'. There may be differences as to what actually amounts to torture (think of the debates regarding waterboarding) and there may even be occasionally a mental reservation that would reluctantly regard torture as permissible in an extreme situation (such as in a 'ticking bomb' scenario), but no state will actually speak out in favour of a right to engage in torture. That is what makes it a matter of principle.

9.2.6 Why do states generally comply with international law?

This question is known as the '*puzzle of compliance*' – unjustly, it seems. After what we said on why states establish IL, there should be no surprises as regards the question why states readily comply with IL. Although other factors such as reputation and reliability may be at play as well, the short answer to the question is that states comply with the rules because they themselves have set them, and they have set them because they suit them. *States are their own legislator.* States have shared interests which naturally draw them into compliance with the law they set for themselves. IL is *not imposed from the outside*, the most you can say is that it is self-imposed.

Compliance by States with IL is an undisputed *empirically verified fact*: most of the states comply most of the time with most of the law. So much is established. It is easy to become mesmerised by occasional breaches of the law and overlook the mass of international relations which proceed smoothly – under the radar, one could say. The main value and practical impact of IL does *not* lie in *enforcement mechanisms* such as international courts and tribunals. It lies in the internalisation of the rules by governmental agencies, ministries, and diplomats, so that compliance becomes second nature. This is not to say that legal enforcement mechanisms to bring transgressors into line are of no use. But we should *not overrate* their importance. To see why, let us ask the following simple question:

9.2.7 What happens when a state breaks a rule of international law?

Having recourse to the judiciary is not the first thing a state will do when facing a breach of law by another state. In international life, law and politics are very much intertwined. Breaches of law are seldom merely a legal affair. Underneath almost any legal dispute there are political interests at stake. And it is this underlying political issue that is the diplomat's concern.

So, how will diplomats address a breach of law by another state? They will use the *same methods and instruments* as when they deal with *political problems* generally. Since most legal problems reduce to a political problem there is no reason for them to look elsewhere than in their usual problem-solving toolbox. That toolbox comprises a *panoply of political and economic means of pressure*. They range from 'Negotiation' over 'Blaming and Shaming', 'Diplomatic Protest', 'Retorsion', and 'Counter-Measures' to full-fledged 'Sanctions Regimes'.

Negotiation. The first avenue a diplomat will explore in solving a political problem is through negotiation. Political problems are not primarily solved through adjudication. As we saw in the introduction to this chapter, adjudication rests on adversarial procedures which risk exacerbating the dispute. It produces winners and losers. And that is what the diplomat will, at least in a first stage, try to avoid. The diplomat is a pragmatist, who looks for workable solutions. Moreover, dispute settlement in an international context has its own idiosyncrasies. Just consider the following two points:

- A first point is that it is often not very clear whether a state *has* broken the law. States are in fact remarkably consistent in conducting themselves in accordance with established rules. Even when a state appears to have violated IL, it is often the case that it considers itself as having acted within its rights. The dispute then concerns a question not *of* law but *about* law. The dispute then turns *not* on *whether* the requirements of IL have been met or not, but on *what* these requirements exactly are.

- A second point concerns the *'de minimis' rule*. At the international level more than in a domestic context, it is neither the intention nor the expectation that IL should be enforced on every occasion when it is violated. Many minor violations are willingly tolerated as the product of occasional failures, or as *not worth* pursuing as this would perhaps occasion *more harm than* whatever *benefit* it may bring.

Given these idiosyncrasies, talking is where one should start when addressing a political problem. Talking is what diplomats are good at. *'Talking it over'* is the essence of negotiation. It is the standard instrument used in diplomacy to find a way out for resolving a dispute. Diplomatic problem solving through negotiation is about convincing and persuading, finding a middle way, a compromise. If negotiation does not resolve the issue, however, the pressure will need to be increased.

Blaming and shaming. Blaming and shaming is when the offended party makes public criticisms via press statements and the social media. It may call upon international bodies or institutions and submit the disputed matter to them for deliberation. Their reports or resolutions may help mobilise shame against violators. Such 'Blame and Shame' actions are by no means insignificant. They can seriously affect the *reputation* and *international standing* of the offending state.

Diplomatic protest. Recourse to diplomatic protest is a standard diplomatic practice in case of disputes. The protest can be brought directly from capital to capital or through diplomatic channels. It can be done in many ways with choices of language, form, author, and addressee signalling with considerable precision the degree of outrage or criticism behind the protest. The diplomatic protest can be carried out by the offended state's ambassador who will transmit a *'note verbale'* or conduct a *'démarche'* at the Ministry of Foreign Affairs of the offending state, or else the latter's resident Ambassador may be called in at the Ministry of Foreign Affairs of the offended state to be delivered the diplomatic protest. A more serious signal of protest consists in the *'recall for consultations'* of the offended state's ambassador to his capital. Diplomatic protests may seem inoffensive, but they are not. They often lead to the cooling of relations between states.

Retorsion. With retorsion we move from 'declarative' to 'action' politics. There are as many ways to make life more difficult for other states and their nationals as there are ways to make it easier. Visa requirements can be tightened (including their cost and the procedures for obtaining them); overflight rights for civil aircraft can be withdrawn; awards of government contracts can be refused. The range of possible measures is very large and the cost to the target state can be very high. The removal of friendly concessions and/or the imposition of unfriendly measures are called 'retorsions' when they involve *no breach of any obligation of IL*. Further examples are the withholding of foreign aid, imposing restrictions on imports and exports (more generally economic boycotts or commercial embargoes), or imposing *travel bans* on named individuals.

Countermeasures (also called *reprisals*). When a state is injured by an unlawful act of another state, it is entitled to suspend its own performance of some obligation owed the offending state, in order to induce the latter to come back into line with its obligations. Such suspensions are known as 'countermeasures' (or reprisals). *As such they are breaches of IL* (which retorsions are not), *but they are justified* and rendered lawful by the prior illegal act of the offending state. Countermeasures must be proportionate to the wrong suffered and may not violate the rules regarding either Human Rights or the Use of Force. An example is the *freezing of foreign assets* by which dealings with deposits in bank accounts belonging to the wrongdoing state or to individuals and companies associated with it are forbidden. *Prima facie*, an asset freeze *is* a violation of IL as it is tantamount to a seizure of foreign property; it is lawful, however, when justified as a countermeasure.

Sanctions. Sanctions, to be legal, need to be either retorsions or countermeasures. So, on themselves, they do not constitute a separate category of political pressure. When organised as a more or less coherent package they constitute a *'sanctions regime'*, such as the one imposed on Russia by both the US and the EU in response to its annexation of Crimea in 2014. More recently, in March 2021, the US and the EU imposed asset freezes and travel bans on several Chinese officials for their role in human rights abuses in Xinjiang. As these examples show, sanctions can be instituted not only by states but also by international (UN) or regional organisations (such as the EU, ASEAN, and the African Union) and can be targeting states as well as individuals (such as members of Putin's inner circle) or private companies. If ordered by the UN Security Council under Chapter VII of the Charter, all UN member states are bound to implement the sanctions. From a means of responding to breaches of law, sanctions have over the last decades evolved into an instrument of foreign policy (see Box 9.4).

Box 9.4 Sanctions and Foreign Policy

Sanctions have become a *central tool of foreign policy* that goes beyond responding to mere breaches of law. Governments increasingly see them as a way to try to change other states' behaviour in situations where *'talking' alone is insufficient* and *military intervention is seen too risky or heavy handed*. Targets of sanctions were once mostly small fry, such as Cuba and North Korea. Now they include much bigger fish, such as China and Russia. Large targets, however, also feel more emboldened to hit back. In 2021, China responded to the Xinjiang sanctions with countermeasures of its own against EU parliamentarians, among others. Its growing economic clout means it can wound when it retaliates. It may also, over a longer period, have a *corrosive effect* on sanctions: the more the large targets respond by seeking to reduce their dependence on European or American finance and technology, the weaker the latter's global economic leverage becomes – and the less potent their sanctions' impact will be. China, for instance, has responded to American technology bans by scaling up plans to invest in producing chips at home. The lesson to be learned is that overuse of sanctions may become *self-defeating*; the more they are used, the less effective they become.

Sanction regimes have attracted criticism. An interesting example is the sanction regime instituted by UN Security Council resolution 1267 in 1999 and targeting individuals suspected of association with the terrorist group 'Al Qaida and Taliban'. Individuals are put on a list by a so-called *Sanctions Committee* (a subordinate body of the Security Council) on the basis of reports from UN member states (particularly Security Council Permanent Members) of which only the sketchiest summaries are made available to the people affected, and which may rely heavily upon untested allegations. The affected individuals cannot challenge the sanctions in the UN itself. This sanctions regime has been criticised as not complying with the basic rule of '*due process*'.

Sanctions are also often criticised as rather blunt instruments that hurt the poor and the weak more than the leaders responsible for the wrongdoing. That is why in recent decades much effort has been put in fashioning so-called '*smart*' *or* '*targeted*' *sanctions* specifically aimed at key institutions and members of the political elite of the state concerned. Another development concerns the so-called extra-territorial effects of sanctions unilaterally decided by a country A (the US, say) aimed at a target country B (Iran) but extended to economic operators in a third country C (the EU member states). That is what indeed happened when in 2018 the US withdrew from the nuclear deal with Iran (the JCPOA), imposing a panoply of new sanctions on Iran which directly affected EU operators in their dealings with that country. *Secondary sanctions*, as they are called, are contested as they turn private actors in a third country, mainly companies and banks, into enforcers of sanctions unilaterally decided elsewhere (see DE RUYT, 2021).

Let us wrap up the discussion so far regarding the way states react to breaches of law by other states. Dispute settlement begins with **talking**, often conducted through the Ministries of Foreign Affairs or diplomatic missions of the states concerned. If the talking (essentially negotiation) does not do the job, one can have recourse to strategies of political and economic **pressure** ranging from 'blaming and shaming' to the imposition of full-fledged 'sanctions regimes'. *Short of the recourse to the use of force* (for which almost inevitably a passage by the UN Security Council will be required) there remains one further option to explore: recourse to the **judiciary**, which happens however to be a more burdensome and often less effective way to settle real-world political differences, disputes, and conflicts.

In recourse to the judiciary, the first reference will be to a **national court** or tribunal. In the US, for example, not only may courts directly apply rules of international customary law, but the US Constitution gives to treaties ratified by Congress a status equivalent to domestic legislation. In other countries, such as the UK, treaty law can only be applied by national courts if it has been incorporated into domestic law by means of national legislation – that is, by enactment in statutes. IL is thus often at work under the surface of national laws in national courts. That is how Karadzic has been sued in a US Federal Court under the *Alien Tort Claims Act*, which allowed foreign nationals to claim recovery for rape and torture during the 'ethnic cleansing' campaign in the former Yugoslavia. And that is how the question regarding the diplomatic immunity of Heads of States was tried in the British courts in the context of the request for extradition of Pinochet from London to Madrid. These matters, if unresolved at the national level, could *in principle* have been brought before an international court or tribunal.

'In principle', because unlike national courts, **international courts** and tribunals have no compulsory jurisdiction. A state is only obliged to appear before an international court or tribunal if it has consented to its jurisdiction. Thus, under the *Statute* of the ICJ a state may sign up to accept the jurisdiction of the court in respect of any *legal* dispute that another state making a similar declaration may bring against it. Fewer than one-third of the UN member states have done that, and many have attached reservations to their acceptances. Also note the restriction of the jurisdiction of the ICJ to '*legal*' disputes, that is, disputes that bear on the interpretation and application of IL as such. Understandable as this restriction is, it thus excludes the large majority of disputes which are, as a matter of fact, political not legal in nature. These remain in the ambit of diplomacy.

9.3 The state as central actor in international politics

States are all around. Their number has increased significantly during the 20th century (see Box 9.5). Traditionally, the state, together with the (intergovernmental) international organisation, has been considered as the main actor on the international scene. In the 1980s of last century, however, under a softly blowing postmodern wind, it became fashionable to undress the state as the prime actor in international relations. In the new *'post-territorial era'*, as times were known then, the state as the central unit of political and economic organisation became considered somewhat *passé*. New actors were seen as playing an important role on the international scene: *non-state actors*, such as transnational corporations (formerly called 'multinationals', Bill Gates' Microsoft, for instance), international NGOs (INGOs such as Human Rights Watch and Transparancy International), the international media (CNN, Al Jazeera), advocacy and interest groups (respectively defending/lobbying for public/private goods), and even political personalities (Bill Clinton) and celebrities (Angelina Jolie); but also *anti-state actors* such as terrorist organisations (Al Qaeda, Daesh, Al Shabab, Boko Harem) and transnational criminal groups (gangs and cartels trafficking in drugs, women, human organs, weapons…).

While there can be no question that these new actors have gained prominence and influence in international affairs, it seems premature to declare the classic state defunct or in bad shape. Not only is the traditional state alive and well, but as of the beginning of this 21st century the state seems to have acquired renewed energies and even some frightening strength in a world where power shifts lead to increasing competition and rivalry, particularly among the Great Powers.

Box 9.5 States in Numbers

There are currently some 200 sovereign states in the world (193 of which are members of the UN). The numbers have been fluctuating in time, sometimes diminishing (as when a state is formed by the federation of former states, such as the United Arab Emirates [UAE]) but most often increasing (as when a state is dismembered into several new states, as happened with the Soviet Union, Yugoslavia, and most recently Sudan). The main reason, however, that the number of sovereign states has more than trebled since 1945 has been decolonisation.

For the international lawyer, the centrality of the state (see Box 9.6) in the international legal system is axiomatic. IL, at its most basic level, aims at securing the 'peaceful coexistence' of sovereign independent states, to put it in somewhat old-fashioned language. Its focus is on the relationships between states. That is why the norms of IL are directly addressed to states. Only indirectly, through the state, do they affect the citizen. *But what is a state from a legal perspective?* Is the Turkish Republic of Northern Cyprus (TRNC) a state? What about the Vatican City? What about the

Islamic Caliphate that Daesh attempted to establish in Syria-Iraq just a few years ago? Quid the 'the facto state' Abkhazia? The territory called Palestine? The former Serbian province Kosovo?

Box 9.6 The State as a Person

Lawyers started it all. They introduced the concept of '*legal personality*' to articulate the idea that states are bearers of rights and duties, can enter into binding agreements with other states and be brought before a court. But they were careful to add that this is a *fiction*. We forgot about the fiction and started to speak of the state as a person, not a legal person, but a person *tout court*.

We thus entered the stage of the '*personification*' of the state. Perhaps as a metaphor first, but soon we forgot about the metaphor as well. The whole vocabulary of human psychology got readily projected upon the state. We came to think and to speak of the state, that non-human entity, in terms of human motivations, characteristics, and actions. Diplomacy inherits of that language: states assume (military) *postures*, *harass*, and *intimidate* each other, *trust* or are *suspicious of* each other. International relations too are strongly modelled on interpersonal relations. We speak about *friendly* nations, *rogue* states, and *good neighbourly* relations. The state, that thing of which we cannot even ask 'where it is', becomes a subject on its own, an autonomous agent with willpower: a '*revanchist*' Russia, an '*assertive*' China.

And then comes the third stage, that of the '*personalisation*' of international politics. States, particularly autocratic states, are increasingly identified with their leaders. We read the Washington Post's headlines: 'Xi prepared to take step back', 'Putin on collision course', and 'Macron faces headwinds'. And with that we get the 'strong leader' because a strong state needs a strong leader. Not just Xi and Putin, but also Erdogan, Modi, Bolsonaro, Duterte, Orban, and the others.

9.3.1 Statehood

As a matter of IL, to be a state, the following **legal conditions** need to be fulfilled:

- **Population**: to be a state, it is necessary for an entity to have a ***permanent*** population. Antarctica may have occasionally visiting scientists or tourists, but has no permanent inhabitants, and therefore is not a state. The concept of population connotes a stable community of people linked to the state by nationality.
- **Territory**: to be a state, an entity must have a ***defined*** territory, that is, a ***physical*** area, however small that may be, over which the state exercises its effective control. Microstates are states (see Box 9.7). That is why the Vatican City is accepted as a state, despite its tiny size (0.44 square km and small population estimated at around 900), and why Cyberspace (a *virtual* territory) is not. A territory is defined by its boundaries. The existence of fully defined frontiers is, however, generally not required for an entity to qualify as a state. The state of Israel exists already since

1949 in spite of the still unresolved issue regarding the precise delimitation of its borders with Palestine.

Box 9.7 Small States and Microstates

The World Bank defines **small states** as those with a population of one-and-half million or less. The smallest among them (the usual criterion is less than 0.5 million people) are called **microstates** (see RANA, 2011, pp. 62–63). Microstates have *nominal* sovereignty but share most of their international competences with their larger partners or neighbours. That is the case with the tiny microstates of Oceania, the Pacific Islands of Melanesia, Polynesia, and Micronesia. In Europe, there are five microstates: Andorra (Spain), Liechtenstein (Switzerland), Monaco (France), San Marino, and Vatican City (Italy). Monaco, San Marino, and Vatican City are 'city states'. Andorra and Liechtenstein are somewhat larger both in terms of population and territory which make them comparable with the post-Soviet separatist territories known as '*de facto* states' (see below).

- **Government**: to be a state an entity must have an ***effective*** government enjoying the monopoly of the use of force and capable of maintaining effective control over its population and territory. Effective government thus implies the power to command the obedience of the people. A *temporary* interruption of the effectiveness of government control (due, for instance, to profound political crises, acute economic instabilities, internal unrest, civil strife, foreign military occupation) is however not considered to affect statehood. That is why 'failing states' are still considered to be states (see Box 9.8).

Box 9.8 Failing States

States where government authority has disintegrated are known as 'failing states', 'failed states', or 'quasi-states' (WILKINSON, 2007, p. 50) but interestingly not as 'non-states'. It thus seems that once an entity has acquired statehood and become part of the international system it automatically retains its status as an independent sovereign country although some of the criteria, particularly the one regarding 'effective control', are no longer (temporarily) satisfied. Many observers consider the latest newcomer in the category of failing states to be Myanmar after the *coup d'état* of 2020.

- **Foreign relations (independence)**: for an entity to be a state it needs to have the ***autonomous*** *capacity* to enter into and manage ***relations with other states***, as well as the capacity to honour its international obligation. Autonomy means that the entity can conduct its own foreign policies as it sees fit and not be subject to control by any other state. That is what makes it an independent state. That is why the TRNC is not considered a state given that it is wholly dependent upon Turkey.

- **Legitimacy**: for an entity to be considered as a state it must have ***achieved*** the requisite independence in a manner ***consistent with IL***. This offers another explanation why the TRNC, being the product of a violation of IL (the 1974-armed invasion of Cyprus by Turkey), does not qualify as a state. The same would obviously have been true if Daesh would have succeeded in establishing the Islamic Caliphate in Syria-Iraq.

More delicate issues are raised by cases of **secession**. The secession of Bangladesh (from Pakistan) and of Kosovo (from Serbia), are generally considered cases where the legitimacy requirement has been fulfilled. They may therefore be considered as independent states. But the same is not true of the secessions operated by the so-called *de facto* states: Abkhazia and South Ossetia (from Georgia), Nagorno-Karabakh (from Azerbaijan), and Transnistria (from Moldova). We will come back to this issue when discussing the principles of Sovereignty, Territorial Integrity, and Self-Determination and their intricate interrelationship below. To overcome the legal subtleties and uncertainties surrounding the legitimacy-requirement, one often has recourse to two *pragmatic criteria* to decide the matter: (1) the formal **recognition** of an entity as a state by a critical mass of existing states (including most major powers); that is what Somaliland is so eagerly aspiring for (see Box 9.9); and (2) the vote by the UN General Assembly acting upon the recommendation of the UN Security Council on the admission of the putative state as a **member of the UN**; that is how Israel got its statehood. '*De facto* states' are territories that have gained *de facto* independence, but no international recognition or support. *Breakaway entities* such as Abkhazia and South-Ossetia (in Georgia), Nagorno-Karabakh (in Azerbaijan), or Transnistria (in Moldova), while upholding effective control over the territories they lay claim on, to the exclusion of the central government, lack legitimacy and therefore fail to secure sovereign and independent statehood.

Box 9.9 Somaliland's Struggle for Recognition

Somaliland is a former British colony, nominally part of Somalia. Located in East Africa it faces Yemen across the Gulf of Aden and has a population of some four million people. In 1991, it adopted a Declaration of Independence when Somalia descended into civil war; it held a constitutional referendum a decade later and conducted three smooth presidential elections since then. Somaliland has done everything to win recognition as an independent state from the international community, but no government has yet formally acknowledged the territory's independence, notwithstanding the fact that there is widespread *de facto* acceptance of Somaliland's *separate status*. For all practical purposes Somaliland fulfils the criteria for statehood, save one: legitimacy (see THE ECONOMIST, 2021).

Laying down neat legal criteria for statehood is one thing, how they work out in the **real world** is quite another thing. When we enter that real world, we see an enormous variation in the degree to which states meet these criteria. Many states struggle to maintain effective control over part of their territory (Colombia with the FARC, Syria with the

Kurds) or face insurgencies (the Taliban in Afghanistan until their takeover in September 2021) or do not have the monopoly of effective control over armed forces within their frontiers (Lebanon where Hezbollah's military is stronger than the Lebanese army). Yet, despite experiencing such fundamental challenges to their sovereignty such states still receive international recognition, enter into agreements with other states, send delegates to the UN in New York, and enjoy the outward (if only symbolic) appearance of full membership of the international community.

9.3.2 Recognition of states

In the preceding paragraphs we have been mentioning the concept of 'recognition' a few times. Recognition of a state by other states attaches certain rights and duties to the entity in question, facilitates its relationship with the other states, brings about legal capacity, and potentially full membership in international organisations. Entities may fulfil the criteria for statehood, but they may not be recognised as a state. Palestine is the most obvious example of an entity that fulfils the criteria for statehood yet remains unrecognised as a state not only by Israel but also by the USA and quite a few other states. *Statehood and recognition as a state are two different things.* Recognition is a purely political act. Contrary to the concept of statehood there are no criteria determining recognition. One state may refuse to recognise another state purely as a matter of *political discretion*. No justification need be given. Which does not mean that non-recognition is arbitrary. States may decide that at a given time political stability is better served by non-recognition, or they may withhold recognition as a means of pressure for a durable political settlement. Such considerations no doubt play a role in the refusal by several states to recognise either Israel or Palestine. Non-recognition may be signalled explicitly by express statements, or implicitly by the refusal to accept the unrecognised state as a party to an international treaty or a member of an international organisation. It should be noted that an unrecognised state is still a state, that is, an entity that fulfils the objective criteria for statehood, and therefore cannot be treated as non-existent. No state is entitled to invade the territory of another state, even when unrecognised, for example. Conversely, recognition does not turn a non-existent state into an existent one. There is a general understanding in IL that *recognition is declarative and not constitutive* of states.

9.3.3 Establishment of diplomatic relations

To be distinguished from both statehood and recognition is the establishment of diplomatic relations. Although a state will obviously not entertain diplomatic relations with an unrecognised state, the reverse is not true; a state may not have diplomatic relations with another state while still recognising it as such. The US, for instance, recognises Iran as a state but does not entertain diplomatic relations with Teheran. Still, to entertain diplomatic relations is the normal condition as between states enjoying mutual recognition; that is why diplomatic relations are often spoken of as *'normal relations'*. In most cases, this condition grows up naturally and is taken for granted. In other cases, however, the *formal 'establishment'* of diplomatic relations – then called the *'normalisation'* of relations – might be the result of a political decision wrapped up in a well-advertised written agreement to this effect (see Box 9.10). As diplomatic relations may be established, they can also be broken off. That is what the US did when the Ayatollahs took over power in Iran and what Argentina did in the context of the conflict with the UK over the Falkland Islands.

Box 9.10 Normalisation of Relations

Normalisation is what happened on 15 September 2020, at a ceremony in Washington when Bahrein and the UAE established formal diplomatic relations with Israel. They are the first Gulf states to do so. Sudan then followed suit. Only two months later, on 10 December 2020, diplomatic relations were established between Israel and Morocco, bringing the number of Arab states (beyond Jordan and Egypt) with which Israel has now official ties to six: Jordan, Egypt, Bahrein, UAE, Sudan, and Morocco. The Arab-Israeli conflict is fading, but that leaves the conflict between Israel and the Palestinians unresolved. The end of an illusion?

Establishing diplomatic relations does not necessarily imply the *opening of an embassy* or the exchange of diplomatic representatives. Microstates, for instance, and many other small states often lack both the financial and human resources to open an embassy in all states with which they entertain diplomatic relations. Diplomatic relations are then managed through other channels of communication, through the UN, through participation in international conferences, or through bilateral meetings.

To summarise, there are four stages separately (and successively) to be considered when speaking about a state: statehood, recognition, establishment of diplomatic relations, and opening of embassies.

9.4 General political principles of international law

There are a few very general and fundamental political principles of IL that constitute the basic framework of the international legal architecture and which act as guidelines for diplomatic action. They would not be called 'principles' if they were not presumed as carrying prescriptive force. Most of them are stated in Article 2 of the UN Charter. We will work through these political principles in two stages: in a first *static 'what'-step* we will briefly discuss each of these principles separately and then, in a second *dynamic 'how'-step*, we will set these principles at work in a case study showing the interrelationships among them. Thus 'applying' relatively abstract legal principles to a specific case will show how *application* in diplomatic practice often amounts to some manipulation of the concepts involved. This again illustrates the somewhat ambiguous relation between the law as it stands and the law as applied in diplomatic practice.

9.4.1 First step: what are the principles?

- **Sovereignty**: Sovereignty is, at its most basic level, **the right of each state to determine its own fate**, both *internally* and *externally*. Internally, as regards its *own citizens* and within its *own territory*, sovereignty gives the state the legal power to do what it chooses, consistently with its own constitutional order. *External* sovereignty bears on a state's relations with other states. Sovereignty then again establishes the right of the state to freely establish its foreign policy, to freely enter in relationships with other states or into binding agreements of its choice, which *third states must respect*. But there are limits to sovereignty. Sovereignty is sacred no more. One of the limits is the result of the normative shift from *sovereignty as authority* to *sovereignty as responsibility* that has emerged in the second part of last century: what a state does within its own borders and towards its own people is indeed its own affair *unless* it threatens international peace or security, a qualification that ultimately has crystallised in the principle of Responsibility to Protect (R2P) formally adopted at the UN Summit of 2005 (see the chapter on the 'Use of Force').

- **Independence**: The Principle of Independence is a direct corollary of the Principle of Sovereignty. Sovereignty amounts to the right of states to determine their own fate and therefore **not to be dictated by** laws or orders from **another state**. The essence of the principle of independence is that the state is subject to the authority of no other state, and that its relations with other states are a matter of its consent and agreement rather than of obligation and direction by some other state. The implications of the principle of independence are worked out in specific rules of IL. The *Vienna Convention on the Law of Treaties*, for example, stipulates that treaties procured by *coercion* are void. More subtly, the independence of states is protected by the basic rule regarding the so-called *exclusive jurisdiction* of states. The exclusive jurisdiction of states encompasses all domains that fall outside the reach of IL. Exclusive jurisdiction thus limits, for example, the extent to which a state can subject people and transactions of another state to its own laws, such as happens when a national law is given extraterritorial reach (as we saw in the preceding section when we discussed the issue of 'secondary sanctions').

- **Equality**: The Principle of Equality of States also follows as a corollary from the basic Principle of Sovereignty. The UN Charter's Article 2 (1) records that the UN 'is based on the principle of the sovereign equality of all its members': the right not to be dictated by other states is a right that **all states** equally share. China (population: 1.3 billion) and Nauru (population: 9,488) are equal sovereign states. That is why each of them has one vote as a member of the UN. In practice of course a state may very well have to defer to the wishes of more powerful states, particularly of Great Powers. But that is a matter of fact, not of law. And it does of course show that law and facts need not and often do not match, but that reduces to the difference between the normative (the 'ought') an the factual (the 'is'). Vast differences in power and wealth do not extinguish the normative principle that in the eyes of the law (if nowhere else) no state can force its will upon another state.

- **Territorial integrity**: Physical territory is not only an essential condition for but also a crucial attribute of statehood. The Principle of Territorial Integrity, referred to in Article 2 (4) of the UN Charter, protects states' territory against *invasion or annexation*. It was essentially to uphold this principled taboo that in 1982 Britain chose to fight Argentina over the Falkland Islands (rather than simply drop it); it explains the easiness with which the US in the first Gulf War of 1991 could assemble a strong international coalition to push back Iraq after its invasion of Kuwait; it is the reason why Russian sovereignty over Crimea after its seizure of the territory from Ukraine in 2014 has been recognised by only a motley crew of countries (including North Korea, Venezuela, and Zimbabwe) or that the Israeli-controlled Palestinian territories continue to be regarded by most countries as 'occupied territories' (see Box 9.11).

Box 9.11 Western Sahara

It all began in 1975, when Morocco *annexed* Western Sahara, after Spain, the colonial power, pulled out. The Polisario Front, a nationalist movement backed by Algeria, which the UN considers the legitimate representative of the Sahrawi people, resisted but was outgunned. With Morocco in control of about two-thirds of the territory, and Polisario controlling the remaining third, the UN brokered a ceasefire deal in 1991 that promised the Sahrawi a referendum on independence. Morocco, though, stood in the way. It has been working hard to transform its *de facto* control over Western Sahara into something more legitimate. In 2020, it succeeded in convincing some 20 African and Arab states to recognise its claim on the territory. But the most significant breakthrough came on 10 December 2020, when the US, under President Trump, recognised Morocco's annexation as part of a deal whereby Morocco established diplomatic relations with Israel (see THE ECONOMIST, 2020).

The Principle of Territorial Integrity also explains the sacrosanct character often attributed to *borders*, which have often been a cause of tension and even open war among states (see Box 9.12).

Box 9.12 Border Disputes and Territorial Claims

The frontiers of states are sometimes arbitrary (particularly those of former colonies). This arbitrariness or the lack of precise delimitation occasionally gives rise to interstate conflicts. Examples are the century-old border dispute between Peru and Ecuador causing regular small-scale armed interventions, last in 1998. More serious was the border dispute culminating in the 1998–2000 war between Ethiopia and Eritrea and finally settled in June 2018, when a border-demarcation agreement was signed allowing diplomatic relations to be resumed. A more recent example is the conflict that erupted in June 2020 between China and India along their long-disputed border in the Himalayan Galwan Valley. Territory is also what was at stake when Chechen separatists fought for an independent Chechnya not part of Russia, or when Tamil Tigers fought for a separate state of Tamil Eelam in the north of Sri Lanka. Territory is what is today at stake when a majority of the people of New Caledonia aspire for it to become an independent state, no longer part of France.

- **Self-determination**: The Principle of Self-Determination refers to the right of all *peoples* to freely determine their own destiny. As such it is enshrined in *Article 1 (2) of the UN Charter* that refers to 'the principle of equal rights and self-determination of peoples'. The essence of the legal principle is that no people should be subject to alien domination, particularly of the colonial variety. Note that the principle of self-determination attaches to a *'people'*. The kinds of characteristics that identify a people are, for example, a shared and distinct ethnicity, language, culture, and history. In this sense the Finns and the Sahrawi, for example, are 'peoples'. Self-determination does not necessarily entail independence. There are two dimensions to the principle. '**Internal self-determination**' refers to the right of a people to participate in the decision-making processes of the state to which it belongs or to the right of a people to pursue its political, economic, social, and cultural development *within the framework of an existing state*. The Falkland Islands and Gibraltar, whose people the UK government regards as having the right of self-determination, remain British territories as a matter of choice, as determined by referenda on the subject. '**External self-determination**' refers to the right of peoples to unilaterally secede from the state (called the *'parent State'*) of which they are part. While some scholars contend that this dimension of self-determination is limited to colonial cases, others assert that it also applies to subjugated peoples outside the colonial context. This remains the subject of much debate to which we will return in the next section.

- **Non-intervention**: The Principle of Non-Intervention too is a corollary of the Principle of Sovereignty. Article 2 (7) of the UN Charter stipulates that nothing in the Charter 'shall authorize *the UN* to intervene in matters which are *essentially* within the domestic *jurisdiction* of any State' (my italics). The clear implication of this provision is that the UN should not interfere in a states' internal affairs. There is a general understanding that, similarly, no UN member *state* should interfere in another states' internal affairs. But there are **limits** to this principle*: first*, and quite obviously, the principle does not affect *action decided by the Security Council under Chapter VII* of the Charter when a state's behaviour endangers the international peace and security; *second*, there is the elastic but carefully chosen word '*essentially*' ('essentially within the domestic jurisdiction of any state'). It is generally accepted that the notion of what amounts to 'internal affairs' (i.e. domestic jurisdiction) has narrowed as a result of the *increasing interdependence of states* which cannot behave without any regard to the consequences of their policies (economic and environmental, for example) for other states, in particular their neighbours; *third*, and most importantly, there is the growing concern, increasingly considered to be legitimate, of states to secure respect of basic human rights in other countries. Until the middle of the 20th century, only the treatment of *foreign nationals* entitled the state of their nationality to intervene in the state of their residence and hold the latter liable for failures to observe the minimal standards of proper treatment of foreign nationals. That rule then changed and made the treatment by a state of its *own nationals* also a matter of IL and the object of the proper concern of other states.

9.4.2 Second step: how do the principles work?

Let us now see how those principles relate dynamically to each other by means of a case study involving Kosovo and the '*de facto* states' Abkhazia and South Ossetia (HAMID and WOUTERS, 2015).

In February 2008, Kosovo formally declared its independence from Serbia. Soon thereafter Kosovo was *recognised* as a state by a large part of the world community which insisted, however, on the 'uniqueness' of the Kosovo case which could therefore not be considered as a 'precedent' for '*de facto* states'. Why? What made the case of Kosovo different from the case of Abkhazia and South Ossetia who also claimed a right to self-determination through unilateral (non-consensual) secession from their parent state Georgia?

As stated above, the question whether external self-determination should be limited to colonial cases or whether it also applies to subjugated peoples outside the colonial context remains the subject of much debate. The core of the problem resides in the fact that the Principle of Self-Determination clashes with the Principle of State Sovereignty generally, as well as with one of its corollaries, the Principle of Territorial Integrity specifically. The Principle of State Sovereignty aims at sanctioning and safeguarding the Westphalian state-centred system. The Principle of Territorial Integrity comes in support of the Principle of Sovereignty; it is a *guarantee against the dismemberment of a state's territory*. It is generally accepted in international legal scholarship that, outside the colonial context, the exercise of the **right to self-determination is limited by the prevailing Principle of Territorial Integrity**. Independent statehood, it seems, is not an entitlement under IL. So far, so good. But matters get more complicated.

As it happens, the **Principle of Territorial Integrity is itself limited by** the rule that **only states conducting themselves in compliance with 'the principle of equal rights and self-determination of peoples' can rely on it** (remember the wording Article 1 of the UN Charter cited above). This means that the right of a state to its territorial integrity is by no means unqualified. As one can see, we turn in circles here: self-determination hurts the wall of territorial integrity, and territorial integrity hurts the wall of self-determination. If we posit both principles as absolute, there is no way out of the contradiction. One can only conclude that either self-determination or territorial integrity or both cannot be considered absolute principles. Arguably then, under the right circumstances, such an approach would leave open the door to unilateral secession. Indeed, if, on the basis of territorial integrity secession were absolutely excluded, the right to self-determination would be rendered illusory. Conversely, the right to territorial integrity would be rendered illusory if, on the basis of self-determination, secession were absolutely admitted.

Secession is the creation of a new and independent entity through separation of part of the territory and population from an existing state, the *parent state*, without the latter's consent. Secession is a unilateral, non-consensual, and hence exceptional act of separation. That is why as an expression of self-determination it can be accepted only in the most extreme cases as a last resort option or *remedy* to the parent state's *persistent denial of internal self-determination* and/or the parent states' *gross human rights violations* (hence the label '**remedial secession**'). Accordingly, if a right to remedial secession exists, it must be qualified. Under what **minimal conditions** is it considered **legitimate**? The doctrine of remedial secession states three conditions:

- First, the group invoking the right must be a 'people' (distinct identity) constituting a numerical minority in relation to the rest of the population of the parent state.
- Second, the parent state must have exposed said people to serious grievances (denial of internal self-determination, massive violations of fundamental human rights).
- Third, no realistic and effective alternative remedies for the peaceful settlement of the dispute are left (last resort, exhaustion of all remedies, all negotiations failed).

The emergence of Bangladesh as a sovereign state, separate from Pakistan (in 1971) and, more recently, the unilateral secession of Kosovo from Serbia (in 2008), are generally cited as examples supportive of the remedial secession doctrine. To a greater or lesser extent, both Bangladesh and Kosovo exhibited the cumulative conditions described above before their leap to independence.

The question remains, however, whether compliance with these conditions can, in and by itself, determine the legitimacy of secessional claims. When looking at international practice (the positive case of Bangladesh and negative case of Quebec), it would seem that a favourable outcome to an attempt at non-consensual secession is highly dependent on **international recognition**. Indeed, as compliance with the doctrine of remedial secession provides political and normative legitimacy on aggrieved secessionist groups, such compliance may encourage other states to proceed to the recognition of their independence. In this regard, it is interesting to note that among the countries that have recognised Kosovo's independence, most have indeed *justified* their response by invoking some, if not all, of the conditions of remedial secession. Unilateral secession, it seems, can only **become effective** through widespread international recognition. But recognition is clearly facilitated by compliance with the doctrine of remedial secession.

Alternatively (and possibly cumulatively) international involvement in the form of a **UN mission** in the secessionist territory would, in all likelihood, also facilitate any attempt at unilateral secession. East Timor is a case in point. It was not until the UN Security Council established a peacekeeping operation and, subsequently, a transitional administration mission (UNTAET), that East Timor became a sovereign and independent state. A similar development took place in Kosovo with the establishment of the UN Mission in Kosovo (UNMIK) which, in the words of Martti Ahtisaari, the Special Envoy of the UN Secretary General, had created an 'irreversible' situation whereby Serbia had ceased to exercise 'any governing authority over Kosovo'. Arguably then, some form of international involvement in entities seeking self-determination may ultimately determine the success or failure of a claim to independence.

Concluding, one could say that for non-consensual secessions to be successful widespread international recognition and/or significant UN involvement are needed in addition to the conditions set out by the doctrine of remedial secession. Otherwise, an entity that claims independence from its parent state, will most likely fail to attain effective *de jure* statehood (due to lack of legitimacy).

The story of the '*de facto* states' Abkhazia and South-Ossetia is a different one. They have not been successful in establishing themselves as independent states. Not only because they were unsuccessful in obtaining recognition by a meaningful number of other states (apart from Russia, they only were recognised by Venezuela, Nicaragua, Vanuatu, Nauru, and Tuvalu), or because they have not been *as such* administered by a UN Mission proper (as the last letter in UNOMIG shows, this was a UN Mission in Georgie although strongly focused on Abkhazia), but simply because they failed to fulfil most, if not all, of the three preconditions for unilateral secession in the first place:

- Prior to the outbreak of the secessionist struggle in the early 1990s of last century, people of Abkhazian and South-Ossetian origin did not constitute a numerical minority of the population in the areas they claimed as their own.
- Even though Georgia's behaviour may not have been impeccable, no serious violations of basic human rights against the peoples of Abkhazia and South-Ossetia took place.
- Intransigence in negotiations made an agreement securing a modicum of internal self-determination very difficult, if not impossible.

In this chapter, we have looked at IL from the outside, rather than the inside. Except for the rules governing statehood, our prime concern was not with the substantive provisions of IL, but with its place and role in diplomatic practice. What do we take home from this chapter on IL? The *first* point is that diplomats and lawyers approach law from different perspectives, simply because of the different nature of their jobs. Strictness and rigour are what you expect from a lawyer. A diplomat, on the contrary, is concerned with finding workable *ad hoc* solutions requiring flexibility. A judge adjudicates, one party is right, the other is wrong. A diplomat compromises, both parties save face. A *second* point concerns the peculiar nature of customary law as a source of IL. The question here is: what is it that makes a mere custom obligatory, legally binding? In customary law there is a silent transition from fact to norm, from the mere *normality* of a certain practice to the *normativity* of the rule underlying that practice. The subtle point here is that to be considered a rule of customary law, the practice must not simply be followed as a *matter of fact* but must in addition be *regarded* as legally binding. The *third* point to be made concerns the question how come that, as an empirical matter of fact, states generally do comply with IL? This is rather surprising given that IL is one of the few branches of law where no enforcement authority exists. The answer is that states comply with IL because that law is of their own making. IL is self-imposed law. But then the question becomes, why do states make law in the first place? And here the answer is: out of self-interest, sheer necessity, and convenience.

Bibliography

AMSTRONG, David, FARRELL, Theo & LAMBERT, Hélène (2012), *International Law and International Relations*, Cambridge University Press, Cambridge.

BISCOP, Sven (2021), "The EU and China: Sanctions, Signals, and Interests", in: Egmont Papers, No. 145, May 2021.

BISHOP, William W. (1971), *International Law: Cases and Materials*, Little, Brown and Company, Boston, MA–Toronto.

BOSSUYT, Marc & WOUTERS, Jan (2005), *Grondlijnen van internationaal recht*, Intersentia, Antwerpen/Oxford.

BROWNLIE, Ian (1979), *Principles of Public International Law*, Oxford University Press, Oxford.

COOPER, Andrew, HEINE, Jorge & THAKUR, Ramesh (2015), *The Oxford Handbook of Modern Diplomacy*, Oxford University Press, Oxford.

DE RUYT, Jean (2021), "Secondary Sanctions and Multilateralism: The Way Ahead", in: Egmont Papers, No. 70, May 2021.

FARER, Tom (2015), "Diplomacy and International Law", in: COOPER, 2015, pp. 493–509.

GREWE, Wilhelm (1999), "The Role of International Law in Diplomatic Practice", *Journal of the History of International Law* 1, pp. 1–22.

HAMID, Linda & WOUTERS, Jan (2015), "We the People: Self-Determination v. Sovereignty in the Case of de facto States", in: Leuven Centre for Global Governance, Working Paper No. 166, November 2015.

LOWE, Vaughan (2015), *International Law: A Very Short Introduction*, Oxford University Press, Oxford.

RANA, Kishan (2011), *21st Century Diplomacy*, Continuum, London/New York, NY.

SOMERS, E. (2010), *Inleiding tot het International Zeerecht*, Kluwer, Mechelen.

THE ECONOMIST (2020), "Heat in the Desert", 19 December 2020, p. 77.

THE ECONOMIST (2021), "Handle with Care", 24 April 2021, pp. 57–59.

WOUTERS, Jan (2006), *Internationaal Recht in Kort Bestek*, Intersentia, Antwerpen/Oxford.

WILKINSON, Paul (2007), *International Relations - A Very Short Introduction*, Oxford University Press, Oxford.

10 Human rights and the Rule of Law

Among the plethora of issues on a diplomat's agenda, few can be considered more important *and* challenging than the protection of human rights (HR for short when used as a class name). We need not insist on the *importance* of HR. Few doubt its relevance, notwithstanding the many complexities which inhere in it.

As was the case in the chapter on International Law, our objective is *not* to review the entire HR field's *substantive* provisions. We are essentially interested in the question why HR pose *challenging* questions for those in charge of foreign affairs. Why is it so difficult to consistently take their defence, let alone run an 'ethical foreign policy' as some have ambitioned at their own expense? For many western politicians and diplomats, defending HR can be an embarrassing experience. Non-western leaders have little truck with finger-wagging westerners: 'Let's talk about democracy – and this *western* democracy!', the steely Rwandan President, Paul Kagame replied to Lionel Barber, editor of the Financial Times, when asked about the HR situation in Rwanda a couple of years ago. This reply points to just one of the questionable issues regarding HR that we will have to address: their pretendedly *universal* character.

Our focus is not on *which* human rights there are, but on *what kind of rights* they are, on what they mean, and *how* you handle them in diplomatic practice. The HR field is beset with conceptual confusions, paradoxes, and inconsistencies, and it is our view that it is these which make a coherent and credible HR policy very difficult. That is why we will look for an alternative policy formula, one based on the concept of the 'Rule of Law' (RoL), less ambitious perhaps than a full-fledged HR policy but with the advantage that, as the Americans like to say, 'it works'.

10.1 Some preliminaries: basic concepts, paradoxes, and inconsistencies

Let us first very briefly recall the basics of HR discourse without feeling obliged to go all the way back to the *Magna Carta* of 1215 or the *English Bill of Rights* of 1689, as traditional approaches do. We also skip the 1778 *American Declaration of Independence* ('We hold these truths to be self-evident, that all men are created equal; that they are endowed by their creator with certain unalienable rights, that among these are life, liberty and the pursuit of happiness'), as well as the revolutionary 1789 French *Declaration of the Rights of Man and the Citizen* ('Men are born and remain free and equal in rights' and 'The aim of any political association is the preservation of the natural and inalienable rights of man: these rights are liberty, property, security, and resistance to oppression') to jump at once to the modern concept of HR as enshrined in the *Universal Declaration of Human Rights* adopted by the UN General Assembly in 1948. Note

DOI: 10.4324/9781003298182-15

that this is a *Declaration* whose provisions are not, as such, legally binding. Legally binding provisions is what we got with the adoption in 1966, again by the UN General Assembly, of two Covenants, the *International Covenant on **Civil and Political Rights*** and the *International Covenant on **Economic, Social and Cultural Rights*** (taken together the Declaration and the two Covenants are referred to as the *International Bill of Rights*). Each Covenant has an *Optional Protocol* which allows individuals to complain to the relevant UN monitoring Committee in case a state has violated the Covenant. A total of 115 states have accepted this procedure for 'civil and political rights' (also in 1966), but *only* 20 states for the 'economic, social, and cultural rights' (and this *only* in 2008). This difference is quite significant and is indicative of the distinct approach that states have towards both categories of rights (we will come back on this point when we will be discussing the problem of the *inflation* of HR). Also note that these Covenants have states as parties bound by them (they are the addressees of the legal obligations contained therein), which gives rise to a *paradox* that we will also take up below.

10.1.1 The nature of human rights

It is not without interest to have a look at **the *nature* of the rights** encompassed in the legally binding HR instruments just cited. Let us start with the **Civil and Political Rights**: there are safeguards and prohibitions. The Covenant *safeguards* rights such as to life, liberty, fair trial, freedom of movement, thought, conscience, peaceful assembly, family, and privacy; it *prohibits* slavery, torture, cruel, inhuman, and degrading treatment and punishment, discrimination, arbitrary arrest, and imprisonment for debt. The rights the state is supposed to safeguard are ***active rights***: they are rights *for us **to do*** things. On the other hand, rights protected by prohibitions are ***passive rights***: they tell what should ***not be done*** *to us*. Both active and passive rights can never be abolished as such. The *exercise* of active rights, however, can be limited or suspended. Not so the passive rights, which are considered ***absolute rights***. They do not allow for limitations, exceptions, qualifications, or balancing against other rights. Take torture, its prohibition is described in absolute terms: 'No exceptional circumstances whatsoever, whether a state of war or a threat of war, internal political instability or any other public emergency, may be invoked as a justification of torture'. Active rights, in contrast, are not absolute, they can be limited, restricted, or suspended. Liberty, for instance, can be restricted in the context of detention of someone following a lawful conviction in a court of law. Freedom of speech is also not an absolute right: shouting 'fire' in a crowded theatre can be punished. As regards the freedom of expression and of press and the related rights to receive and impart information, there can be legal restrictions on communicating, for example, military secrets. However, any such restriction must be justified and be proportionate to the aims pursued by the restriction. How are these limitations applied in practice? The so-called **proportionality test** acts as a guide for the practitioner (lawmaker, judge, politician, or diplomat). The test can be summarised as follows:

*   Is there a *legitimate aim* to the restriction (national security, public order, the rights of others)?
*   Is the restriction *necessary* to attain the aim (is there no less intrusive alternative available)?
*   If necessary, is the restriction *proportionate* to the identified legitimate aim (does the restriction not go further than what is necessary to attain the aim which implies weighing the aim of the restriction against the right itself)?

- Is the restriction *prescribed* by a clear and accessible law applicable to all (to avoid arbitrariness)?
- Is there *protection* against the abusive use of the restriction?

When we move to the **Economic, Social, and Cultural Rights** we enter a totally different world. We are now talking about rights to education, to food, to health care, and housing, as well as the right to work and to fair conditions of work. What is demanded here from the state is the progressive realisation of these socio-economic goods to the full extent of that state's available resources. The difference between the civil-political and socio-economic rights is glaring. What is expected from the state in the first category is: *not to act*, to abstain, and to refrain from interfering with the 'space of liberty' guaranteed by these rights. That is why these rights are sometimes called '**negative rights**'; they can be taxed as '*freedoms from*'. Whereas in the second category of rights it is exactly the reverse that is asked from the state; here the state is expected *to act*, to actively intervene in order to secure, indeed provide these socio-economic goods. That is why these rights are called '**positive rights**'; they are taxed as '*freedoms to*'. The request to simultaneously 'not to act, do less' (not to intervene) in the civil-political area, that is to be the '*minimal State*' and 'to act, do more' (to intervene) in the socio-economic area, that is to be the '*welfare State*', is one of the paradoxes we meet in the field of HR. It has indeed prompted the question *what the 'proper' human rights* are; a queer question as it seems to imply that there are 'improper' human rights as well.

Let us for the sake of clarity summarise what we have said up to this point, this time approaching HR from a slightly different perspective. There are three kinds of rights called HR, and the first kind seems to deserve that label more than the second, and the second more than the third:

- First, there are the so-called **freedom rights**, also called '**protection rights**'. They are negative rights which require the state not to interfere with the freedom that underlies these rights (example: the right to freedom of speech). They constitute **immunities**. Freedom rights belong to the core of HR properly understood, those rights that *men* get by the very fact of *being human*. We call them the 'basic' or 'fundamental' human rights.
- Second, there are the '**political rights**', also called '**participation rights**'. They concern the right of *citizens* to participate in the organisation of public life (example: the active and passive voting rights, that is, the right to vote and be voted for, respectively). Note the shift from rights of 'men' to rights of the 'citizen'. These participatory rights are granted to men as participants in the life of the 'polis', the political community.
- Third, there are the '**socio-economic rights**', also called '**manifesto rights**'. They are positive rights which require the state to provide and guarantee the welfare of the individual (example: the right to education). They constitute '**claims**' or '**entitlements**'. *Most* scholars and practitioners do not consider socio-economic rights as belonging to the *core* of HR. *Many* do not consider them to be *proper* human rights. *Some* do not even consider them to be '*rights*' at all.

After this preliminary exploration of the *nature* of human rights, we may start discussing some conceptual distinctions (and confusions), as well as some legal and political paradoxes (if not outright contradictions), which beset the field of HR. We wish not to be dogmatic in discussing these critical issues. We gladly recognise that most of them remain *open questions*.

10.1.2 The 'legitimacy' question

This controversy concerns the *foundation* of HR. For some, human rights are primarily **moral rights**, rights based on what it is to be a human being. It is by reason of their humanity that human beings are endowed with certain fundamental, inalienable, imprescriptible, and universal rights. As these rights derive from the very *nature* of the human being, they are part of **natural law**. From a strictly legal point of view human rights, thus conceived, are mere *moral claims*, legitimate no doubt within their own domain, that of morality, but not that of law. Although misleadingly *called* rights, these moral claims are not justiciable rights enforceable in courts or other institutions of enforcement.

That is where the distinction between natural and **positive** law (also called *conventional* law) comes in. Natural law is not enforceable, only positive law is. *Pre-legal moral claims* can, of course, become 'legalised' through a process of law making, that is, a process of *positing* these claims as law. They then change nature: from moral claims they become **legal** rights. Legal rights get their legitimacy from the *political will* of the sovereign, the state, and the people (acting as a *conventional* law-maker), not from a foundational story referring to the very *'nature of man'* (see Box 10.1).

The former position is known as the natural law position, the latter as the positivist position.

Box 10.1 The Greeks on Nature (*Physis*) and Convention (*Nomos*)

For Socrates, Plato, and Aristoteles, the inferior status of women as regards men (sexism), of barbarians as regards Hellenes (xenophobia), and of slaves as regards free citizens (slavery) were natural facts, facts of nature, 'givens' not to be questioned. They belonged to the natural state of the world: *physis*. In the later 5th century BC, the sophists vehemently reacted to this, in particular Protagoras for whom 'man (is) the measure of all things' (*anthropon métron*): it is man who determines what is, and how it is. For the sophists then, there is nothing in the 'nature' of women, barbarians, or slaves that dictates their inferior status; such status is not a 'given' at all, but a 'construct', something made up by men either through custom or by law, but in both cases by convention: *nomos*.

Modern rights theorists have sought to **transcend** this old controversy between an open-ended naturalistic and narrow-minded legalistic approach to HR by introducing the concept of **human dignity**. For them, the existence and importance of HR are justified by reference to some overriding values that attach to the dignity of man, such as freedom, fairness, autonomy, agency, equality, and personhood. These are **values** for each of us to see. We do not need a foundational story based on the vague concept of 'human nature' (natural law), nor do we need to become the prisoner of rigid and inevitably somewhat arbitrary legal procedures (positive law). In the human dignity approach, particular emphasis is given to the importance of *individual autonomy and agency*, which is not unrelated to Kant's well-known moral imperatives: first, that each of us has to act according to principles that we wish all other rational beings also to act on, and second, that a person should never be treated as a means to an end but rather as an end in himself (see Box 10.2).

Box 10.2 Kant's Two Moral Imperatives

(1) 'I ought never to act except in such a way that I can also will that my maxim should become a universal law'; (2) 'Act in such a way that you always treat humanity, whether in your own person or in the person of any other, never simply as a means, but always at the same time as an end' (*'Groundwork of the Metaphysics of Morals'*, New York, NY, 1964, pp. 70 and 96).

Whatever position one may take in this foundational controversy, the fact is that when officials (judges, politicians, diplomats) nowadays refer to HR they almost certainly refer to HR recognised or established by (positive) international law. They do not think of human rights as moral rights, without of course denying that moral rights exist along with legal rights. This *shift from natural towards positive law* is characteristic of the modern approach to HR. The foundational questions (the *why* of HR) are left on the side and attention goes to the **actual content** of HR understood by reference to the *legal catalogue* of HR as developed in international legal instruments ranging from the two 1966 Conventions to a panoply of specific Conventions regarding Genocide (1948), Racial Discrimination (1969), Women (1981), Torture (1987), Children (1990), Migrant Workers (2003), Persons with Disabilities (2006), and Enforced Disappearance (2006).

10.1.3 The state paradox

As is the case for international law generally, the parties legally bound by HR law are *states*. It is for states to implement the obligations contained in the HR instruments to which they have agreed, and which are aimed at protecting the individual. Particularly as regards the *freedom rights* (right to life, freedom of assembly, free speech, among others) HR instruments aim at protecting the individual *against the State*; they protect the individual against the states' potential encroachments, its despotism perhaps; they require the state not to hinder or interfere with the free exercise of the individual's rights, not to expand its powers arbitrarily. The **first** paradox to note is thus that the individual must *rely on* **the state to ensure his or her** *protection against* **the state**.

But there is more. In the exercise of his or her human rights the individual must also be protected against infringements by their *fellow members* of society, and for this he or she must *appeal to the state* for effective action and perhaps sanction, which presupposes the existence of a state effectively exercising its monopoly power of coercive action. And here then arises the **second** paradox: ensuring the protection of HR requires on the one hand a *retreating state*, one that passively respects my rights by abstaining to interfere with them, but on the other hand an **assertive state**, one that actively protects my rights by intervening against others infringing them.

For some, these paradoxes are key to understanding the dynamics and complexities of the HR debate. As Costas Douzinas (OXFORD, 2000, p. 12) puts it: '(…) a theory of human rights which places all trust in governments (…) defies their *raison d'être*, which is precisely to defend people from those institutions and powers'. This *double-bind* position of the state is one of the many puzzles that beset HR discourse.

10.1.4 Confusing immunities with entitlements

How have socio-economic rights come to be considered as, or at least associated with the concept of human rights proper, given that, *first*, they do not seem to have their basis in human nature as such, in what it truly means to be human (is the right to a decent job inherent in what it is to be human?), and *second*, the 'rights'-language seems to be inadequate for the articulation of what constitutes the underlying concern of these socio-economic rights (do I become more healthy by having a right to health?).

The answer given to the **first question** may appear rather straightforward (although not without dangers – see Box 10.3). That answer is that, as a *preliminary* for the proper exercise of your fundamental human rights (the civil-political rights), you need to dispose of the *minimum material public goods* that permit you to effectively enjoy them. Does that make the socio-economic rights fundamental? Many observers doubt it. Being straightforward does not make an answer convincing. The doubters make two points: *first*, they think that such reasoning undercuts the very meaning of human rights properly understood and inevitably leads to a *proliferation* of rights, all of which cannot, *by definition*, be considered 'basic' or 'fundamental' (we will come back on this point in the next section); *second*, they stress that the reverse reasoning holds as well: freedom of expression and association are prerequisites for the best *policy* decisions being taken to ensure the rights to food, health, and work. So, the most you can say regarding the relationship between the different types of rights, civil-political and socio-economic, is not that one presupposes the other but that both presuppose each other, that they interact and may be mutually reinforcing.

Box 10.3 Leopold Senghor and the 'Full Belly Thesis'

Leopold Senghor, a former President of Senegal, once said that 'human rights begin with breakfast' which is a slightly more elegant expression than Bertolt Brecht's formula: 'First comes the fretting, and then comes morality' ('Erst kommt das Fressen, dan kommt die Moral'). The underlying idea is straightforward but dangerous at the same time. Straightforward in that the exercise of any right presupposes the fulfilment of its feasibility conditions: the right to food needs to be properly secured before one can turn to the 'luxury' of the right to vote and the right to education is a prerequisite to the 'privilege' of the freedom of expression. But the idea is also dangerous. The problem with this 'Full Belly Thesis' is that by thus prioritising subsistence rights before civil-political rights, governments can be tempted to do without the latter while not able to secure the former, their citizens ending up *with* an authoritarian regime and *without* food.

As regards the **second question** (why have these socio-economic claims been formulated in the language of 'rights'?), the straight answer generally given is that the rights-language is being abused here. Rights talk is precise: to say that A has a right, R, of some specific sort, is to imply that someone else, B, has an obligation, O, of some specific sort relative to A, and that B can be held accountable by some third party, C, vested with the authority to sanction B if necessary. This precision and clarity seldom apply to socio-economic rights. Who are A, B, and C, and what are precisely R and O in these rights? It is hard enough to determine whether such rights have been infringed, let alone who should provide a remedy and how. What we are dealing with here are not 'rights' proper but **calls for policies**; that is why they have been called '**manifesto rights**'. The right to food does not mean that the government must provide food for all. What it means is that it must plan and execute a food policy. The right to health does not mean that we have the right to be healthy. It means that the government must provide for an effective health system. The right to work should not be understood as an absolute and unconditional right to obtain a job. As with the other socio-economic rights, what the right to work does in fact give rise to is a claim, an entitlement. Confusing the rights language, the language of **immunities**, with the language of policy, the language of **entitlements**, is not harmless, and neither is confusing *rights* with what is *desirable* (see Box 10.4). As the legal philosopher Ronald Dworkin has been stressing over and again, rights should be created sparingly and then defended tenaciously. *The misuse of the language of rights undermines the status of all rights.* And that is exactly the main concern of those who refuse to put the civil-political rights in the same bag as the socio-economic rights. We will come back to this issue below when discussing the proliferation of human rights and the banalisation of HR discourse.

Box 10.4 Jean Bethke Elshtain on Immunities and Entitlements

With reference to the American Bill of Rights, which became part of the American Constitution, Elshtain notes that

> these rights revolve around civic freedoms – assembly, press, speech – and around what the government cannot do to you, say, unreasonable search and seizure. Rights were designed primarily as immunities, as a way to protect us from overweening power, not as entitlements. (...) But as time passed, the rights-bearing individual came to stand alone – 'me and my rights' – as if rights were a possession

> (Jean Bethke Elshtain, *'Democracy on Trial'*,
> New York, NY, 1995, p. 15)

10.2 Defending Human Rights – three conceptual vulnerabilities

In this section, and the next, we wish to understand why politicians and diplomats have such a hard time *selling human rights*. Until now we have essentially been pointing to certain inconsistencies and paradoxes inherent in HR discourse. The focus now will be on some core vulnerabilities of that discourse which make a credible and effective defence of HR difficult. We call them **conceptual vulnerabilities** because they inhere in the *concept of human rights* itself. In the next section, we will discuss a specific **legal vulnerability**, one that inheres not in the concept of HR itself but in the politician's or diplomat's *expected role* as defender of HR. We will see that in that role he or she is facing the challenge of reconciling two contradictory legal demands: one to defend HR anytime and anywhere, the other not to intervene in the domestic affairs of other states. All these vulnerabilities constitute arguments which the other party may oppose to your attempt to promote, protect, and defend HR.

The three core conceptual vulnerabilities are:

- The claim that HR are **universal**, that they apply to all peoples, at all times and in all places; all states are bound to respect them.
- The spectacular **proliferation** of HR, their multiplication in all kinds of new areas.
- The growing **banalisation** of HR discourse.

10.2.1 The universality of Human Rights

Are HR really universal? This remains the standard view. There seems to be an impeccable logic to it, at least as far as the 'basic' human rights are concerned. If HR are what they are by virtue of what it is to be a human being, then these rights inhere, by definition, to *all* men, for all times and at all places. In such logic, there is no room for speaking about Western, Asian, Latin-American, or African human rights. But such an essentialist approach does not fly anymore. Increasingly people have come to think that the whole idea of 'universal' human rights is actually – to put it crudely – a fraud where Western imperialist or ex-colonial powers have tried to pass off on others their own, specific and localised idea of which 'rights' should be considered as universal, trampling roughly over everyone else's beliefs and traditions. There is no denying that the mature concept of HR originated in 18th century Enlightenment thinking that led to the American and French revolutions with their respective *Declarations* regarding such rights. From there it is but a small, but not uncontroversial, step to claim that the pretendedly **universalist** HR discourse is in fact but a variant, an extrapolation of a Western cultural tradition that is just one among others, with its **particularistic** set of questions, topics, values, and methodologies that are as **historically contingent** as those of any other (say Asian or African) tradition.

Relying on scientific research ranging from ethnology over anthropology to psycholinguistics, Julian Baggini (see BAGGINI, 2014) has demonstrated how the Western and Eastern minds differ not only in values and worldviews, but also in their thought and logic, in the way they conceptualise time and space, and in the deep structure of their languages. Some of these differences are well known. Think of how Westerners stress the rights of the individual, whereas Asians (particularly in the Far East) prioritize the interests of the community, think of how Westerners stress rationality, autonomy, and freedom, whereas in the East it is hierarchy and obedience that are stressed, of how the Western analytical mind embraces binary either-or thinking, while in the (Far) East it is synthesis and harmony that are embraced. This point needs no further elaboration. There is no denying that there are different logics of HR depending on culture, time, and place. There are European HR stories (as the Kundera story that we will discuss below), as there are African, Asian, and American local, time-bound, culturally determined HR stories, each different. Defenders of *the* HR, unique and universal, will somehow have to address this objection of **cultural determinacy**. Which leads to a risky thought.

If the value-judgements we make ultimately happen to be culturally bound, is it not prudent then (and perhaps just fair) to withhold judgement altogether in respect to those peoples who do not share our culture? Such value-scepticism as regards HR can of course easily lead to the much-feared rights relativism, but then again, are cultures not relative to each other?

10.2.2 The proliferation of Human Rights

The inflation of human rights is the second challenge to address. The central point to be made here is that not only are few rights truly universal, but that letting rights multiply weakens them all. Confusing 'rights' with things that are desirable is not harmless, as we said. The drama of the proliferation of rights from basic human rights to so-called new rights (one of the latest being the 'right to internet access') is that it has led to **the erosion of the traditional fundamental rights themselves**, those for which we really should care.

A useful way to discuss the proliferation of HR is to distinguish between first-, second-, and third-generation HR (see HAARSCHER, 1987). The **first-generation HR** are those that we have qualified as *'freedoms from'*. They constitute the core HR that protect the individual against the state and fellow citizens from interference with his or her untouchable 'space of liberty'. That is why they were called *negative rights*. They constitute *'immunities'*. The **second-generation** HR are those that we have qualified as *'freedoms to'*. They somehow are the inverse of the first-generation HR: instead of requesting the states not to intervene, it is intervention that is now requested through policies and positive action in fields such as health, housing, and education. That is why they were called *positive rights*. With them, we enter the field of *'entitlements'*. At this stage already some start wondering whether confusing second-generation entitlements with first-generation immunities may not damage the distinct status of the basic, fundamental human rights.

Finally, there is the so-called **third generation** of human 'rights', sometimes referred to as the generation of the **'new rights'** which could better be qualified as *'claims'*. While some claims for 'new rights' seem legitimate candidates for recognition as HR, such as the rights of indigenous people for respect of their identity, others are more questionable. There are currently discussions going on among states for the elaboration of a convention on the rights and dignity of older people. 'New rights' campaigns plead for the inclusion of rights of children born of wartime rape, Dalit rights, the rights of LGTBQI+, of people affected by HIV/AIDS, and disability rights. The point is not that these are not legitimate concerns, they certainly are. The point is that one can question whether their defence should be done through the language of human rights, as this risks deflating the value of *all* HR.

Understanding how an issue gets absorbed into the international HR apparatus, tells a lot about the dynamics of HR creation. Clifford Bob explains the process as follows (see CLAPHAM, 2015, p. 59):

- First, politicised groups *frame* long-felt *grievances* as normative claims.
- Second, they place these claims on the *international agenda*.
- Third, *states* and international bodies, often under pressure of *aggrieved* groups, adopt these grievances as *new norms*.
- Finally, the new norms get *implemented*.

Note the word '**grievances**' in the preceding paragraph. The language of international HR has become associated with all kinds of claims, revindications, and disputes. Almost everyone today emphasises their point of view in terms of assertions of rights, which leads, unfortunately, to the banalisation of rights talk. Which is the point we will take up next.

10.2.3 The banalisation of Human Rights discourse

Not only have HR proliferated, but *in the process*, they also have become increasingly devoid of objective meaning. HR discourse gets increasingly framed in the subjective language of human feelings. It is couched in the emotional language of the frustrated, the vindictive language of the aggrieved, or the capricious language of the spoiled. Andrew Clapham (see CLAPHAM, 2015, p. 19 and following) recalls Milan Kundera's parody on rights generally and HR specifically in the story of Brigitte, a rich Parisian girl driving through Paris to buy a bottle of wine from *Fauchon*. Not finding any parking space she simply drives the car onto the pavement, meets with the police, and claims her human 'right to park'. Milan Kundera remarks:

> (…) the more the fight for HR gains in popularity the more it loses any concrete content, becoming a kind of universal stance of everyone towards everything, a kind of energy that turns all human desires into rights. (…) the desire for love (has become) the right to love, the desire to exceed the speed limit the right to exceed the speed limit, the desire for rest the right to rest, the desire for happiness the right to happiness…,

and all these desiring people 'belong to the same army of fighters for human rights' (see Box 10.5).

Box 10.5 The Self-Righteous Activist

One of the targets of economists Paul Collier and John Kay in their recent polemic against the rise of extreme individualism is the self-righteous activist who loudly asserts an ever-expanding set of individual *entitlements* and legal rights – whether to intellectual property, housing, tertiary education, or gender determination. This kind of stridency, they argue, makes it harder to seek a political compromise through reasoned argument. Moreover, the expansion of rights that could only conceivably be met by the state makes it all but inevitable that governments will fail to meet expectations and lose the trust of voters to the benefit of unscrupulous populists (COLLIER and KAY, 2020).

As Chapham rightly states, Kundera's story makes, albeit in an exaggerated manner, a few points about the changing world of HR:

*   First, for some people today HR are simply *obvious*, self-evident, logical *entitlements*. There is often no need for a justification, let alone a foundation of the claimed rights. Feelings are enough.

- Second, HR are claims that automatically occur to one once one *feels* hard done by. In such *victimisation culture*, a mere sense of outrage or injustice can breed a feeling that one has been denied one's rights.
- Third, a *shared* sense of grievance provides powerful succour for those claiming their 'rights'. When those of us who feel aggrieved stand *together in protest*, we find strength through solidarity.

The banalisation of HR talk is a serious concern for many as it voids the very meaning itself of the concept of human rights. If human rights are just a question of subjective feelings and wistful caprices, why then take them seriously?

10.2.4 How to respond?

The three vulnerabilities that inhere in the contemporary concept and discourse on HR obviously make their defence more difficult and will likely be exploited by any party confronted with demands regarding HR. Finding oneself on the defensive is never a pleasant situation. So, what can we do? How to reply to those who point to or exploit these vulnerabilities? Denying the vulnerabilities, being dogmatic, principled, and absolutist about HR, as many unfortunately continue to do, is no option. Recognising the vulnerabilities is a more promising avenue and trying to safeguard what really needs safeguarding is probably the best strategy.

10.2.4.1 Universality

First, HR set standards that should leave some room for different cultures to fill in and thus to choose outcomes which need not be identical. When one moves from the lofty proclamation of HR to their detailed implementation, one should allow that the **local context** (cultural, economic, and political) be taken into account. Providing some **room for manoeuvre** in the interpretation and application of rules is *standard legal practice* (and even more, political and diplomatic practice) and should not be considered as the death knell for the credibility of HR discourse. It is a mistake to imagine that HR can, or should, operate divorced from any local context. And as the 'frozen embryos' case shows, this is not just something the Asians or Africans are insisting on, it is a point made also by Europeans (see Box 10.6).

Box 10.6 Frozen Embryos

In March 2006, the European Court of HR gave a judgement in a case (Evans v. UK) concerning a dispute between the two estranged parents of frozen embryos. The question was whether these could be destroyed. The court held that

> in the absence of any European consensus on the scientific and legal definition of the beginning of life, the issue when the **right to life** begins comes within the range of appreciation which the Court generally considers that states should enjoy in this sphere.

> On the separate question of whether the destruction of the frozen embryos constituted a violation of the mother's **right to privacy**, again the judges considered the matter was better left to national legislators than to a judicial divination of overriding HR principles.

Second, as with *any* legal rule, HR **rules have a core and a penumbra.** The core reflects the underlying rationale of the rule, the 'why' of the rule, its objective. The penumbra bears on modalities, on means to obtain the objective. Making the distinction between core and penumbra, and doing so in good faith, may not always be easy. It is the failure to respect the core content of HR that should concern us, not its periphery.

Third, as we have seen, most HR are not absolute (only the passive rights are). Although the right itself can never be abolished, the **exercise** of an active right can be **modulated**, limited, restricted, conditioned, perhaps even suspended. HR, like any right, should be **balanced with other rights**, which also deserve proper recognition, particularly the rights of others. So here again we see that there is room for manoeuvre.

Fourth, when defending HR in a particular country, it happens that we do so in support of claims that have already been made by the **local** population of that country itself. In such cases, the HR claimed by a country's people may not be that local after all, which makes the authorities' argument regarding their non-universality spurious.

10.2.4.2 Proliferation

Fifth, we must recognise that **not all human rights have equal value**, that the nature of the so-called socio-economic rights ('freedoms to') does differ from that of the core civil-political rights ('freedoms from'). As we already said, it is difficult to conceive of *entitlements* to housing, health, and education as judicially enforceable rights. They reflect legitimate public policy goals but do not constitute rights as such. Defending socio-economic rights is not so much a matter of defending HR as a matter of promoting good and responsible governance. Making the distinction between first- and second-generation 'rights' has the tremendous advantage of safeguarding the full strength of the first, thus avoiding diluting them to some lower common denominator.

10.2.4.3 Banalisation

Sixth, taking the former point one level up, we should make a clear distinction between **HR** 'as they stand' (first-generation rights for sure, second-generation rights plausibly) that merit to be defended and HR as one might, more or less frivolously, **aspire or wish** them to be. That kind of aspirational thinking is what is going on in all kinds of debates and discussions by single issue advocacy groups making revendications for a still 'better world'. Lawyers make a distinction between 'the law as it stands' (called '*de lege lata*') and the law as 'it ideally might have been' (called '*de lege ferenda*'), and they make it clear that it is the first, not the second that they are expected to care for. Diplomats must do the same. Confounding reality with ideality leads to nowhere, except to confusion in HR discourse and dilution of the core human rights, those that really merit being defended.

Whether the six responses that we have suggested as remedies to overcome criticism based on the three vulnerabilities that we have identified are strong enough to ensure the effective defence of HR remains uncertain. Also, because next to these three conceptual vulnerabilities, there is a fourth, this time legal vulnerability, which makes matters even more complicated than they already were (see below).

Before closing this section, one final remark. It has been suggested that a more effective defence of HR would be for foreign ministries to engage in **private** 'human rights dialogues' rather than **public** diplomatic denunciation. I doubt this. I fear that this way of acting is just a subterfuge for not having to face the opposing party frontally, and for having a clean conscience without having dirtied one's hands. The other party will be quick to understand that it is on the winning side in this so-called confrontation. The truth, I think, is that these quiet dialogues serve little purpose other than being a pretext for claiming to have done what in fact has not been done. And if in fact it has not been done, better not pretend and say the reasons why it has not been done. These reasons may be sound and quite defensible. A practice similar to this public/private handling of HR issues has emerged lately. You could call it the **'separation' approach**. It consists in treating HR abuses as a separate item on the foreign policy agenda thus neutralising their 'contaminating effect' on other agenda items. That is what happened on 16 June 2021, when President Biden met for the first time in person with the Russian leader Vladimir Putin. They discussed the Navalny case but, regrettable as HR abuses are, they seemed to agree that they should be treated separately from other issues, such as security. Which again seems a defensible position, why then not say so openly?

10.3 Defending human rights – a legal vulnerability

Although the genuine efforts to defend HR made by states through *démarches* and representations and by institutions (such as the UN HR Council) through their supervision mechanisms are not to be neglected, the fact is that the effective enforcement of these rights remains unsatisfactory. To explain why that is the case, we have already pointed to three vulnerabilities that inhere in the concept of HR itself and that make their effective defence difficult. To these three conceptual vulnerabilities, we now must add a fourth, a legal vulnerability this time.

The idea that governments or institutions can legitimately concern themselves with the way in which another state treats its *own nationals* is a relatively recent and still disputed innovation in international relations. Up to the middle of the 20th century, it was a universally accepted doctrine that how a state treated its own nationals was a matter entirely for its own *sovereign* determination. And it is still not quite clear where exactly on this point we stand today, as the ongoing debate regarding the *scope and limits* of the concept of 'Responsibility to Protect' (R2P) demonstrates. *No two **conflicting** ideas are more difficult to reconcile than the **promotion of HR**,* that is, the duty to defend HR whenever and wherever they are or risk being violated *and **respect for sovereignty**,* that is, the duty to abstain from interfering with another states' domestic affairs. *The former incites the kind of intervention which the latter forbids.* The good faith defender of HR thus finds themselves locked up in a *double bind*.

A careful reading of the UN Charter is instructive as regards this underlying **contradiction**. *Article 2 (7)* of the Charter proclaims with unusual emphasis:

> *Nothing* contained in the present Charter shall authorize the United Nations *to intervene* in matters which are essentially within the *domestic jurisdiction* of any

state or shall require the Members to submit such matters to settlement under the present Charter.

As we saw in the last chapter, it is generally agreed that this principle of non-intervention also applies to states, not only to the UN as such. So far, so good. But then we also have *Article 1 (3)* of that same Charter which states that one of the '*Purposes of the United Nations*' is

> to achieve international cooperation in solving international problems of an economic, social, cultural, or humanitarian character, and in *promoting and encouraging respect for human rights and for fundamental freedoms* for all without distinction as to race, sex, language or religion

(the language in *Article 55 (c)* is slightly different; it speaks of promoting '*universal* respect for, and *observance* of, human rights and fundamental freedoms'.) Just sticking to the language of Articles 1 (3) and 2 (7) of the Charter one clearly gets the impression that its drafters attached more importance to respect for sovereignty than to the promotion of HR. So, what we end up with is one provision inviting active intervention in HR issues, and another stronger injunction saying: 'Keep your noses out of such issues'. What should we do?

10.3.1 On learning to live with ambiguity

This ambiguity, if not outright contradiction, obviously does not help the well-meaning minister or diplomat in his or her efforts to 'promote and encourage respect for human rights and for fundamental freedoms for all'. How to reconcile the opposite branches of the contradiction: intervention (interference) and non-intervention (non-interference)? In the last chapter, we already met some other areas of tension in international law, that between sovereignty as authority and sovereignty as responsibility, that between the right to self-determination and the duty to respect territorial integrity. How can such inconsistencies be overcome? The issue here is not one of logic. Inconsistencies between conflicting values and ideals are part and parcel of international politics and diplomacy, as they are of our lives generally where great virtues too are not always compatible: courage is not always compatible with prudence, liberty with equality, intellectual rigour with free imagination.

Earlier, when opening the chapter on International Law, we already discussed the somewhat ambiguous relation between Law and Diplomacy. Flexible prudence, we concluded, not rigid legalism, is the diplomat's guide in navigating international politics. A diplomat's solution is not one in which one party attains all its objectives, while the other suffers the humiliation of defeat. In a similar way, when facing a conflict between two duties, as between defending HR while respecting a state's sovereignty, the diplomat cannot but search for the right balance between both requirements. He or she usually ends up with a *sliding scale* in which both duties are given no more than partial effect. In diplomacy, you cannot have everything.

But this kind of wisdom may not be shared by all. Obviously when in the process of defending the respect for HR in another country, that country's authorities will wish to slide the scale towards their side, that of non-intervention. As much as you may rely on your duty to defend HR, they will invoke the stronger-worded duty to respect their sovereignty. The legal vulnerability may have been mitigated by your appeal to wisdom, but disappeared it has not.

10.3.2 On ethical foreign policy

Some governments and their Ministers of Foreign Affairs have prided themselves on conducting an ethical foreign policy, one in which HR take centre stage (Jimmy Carter in the late 1970s, Robin Cook in the UK in the late 1990s, Louis Michel in Belgium in the early 2000s, Margot Wallström in Sweden in the mid-2010s) but most of them have come out of the experience (or was it an 'experiment') disillusioned (see Box 10.7). The fact is that an 'ethical foreign policy' is an oxymoron, a self-contradictory concept. *Ethics and diplomacy operate on the basis of discordant premises.* Ethics postulates absolute *values*, noble, neat, and clean. You do not compromise on values. Diplomacy, on the contrary, is about *interests* that clash and that need to be reconciled by way of compromises. Compromises seldom look neat and clean. Diplomacy is the art of the feasible. As Raymond Aron says in his *Introduction* to Machiavelli's *Il Principe* (MACHIAVELLI, 1962, p. 9): 'Men being what they are, the precepts which experience of the world suggests do not coincide with those that the moralists teach us' ('Les Hommes étant ce qu'ils sont, les préceptes que suggère l'expérience du monde ne coincident pas avec ceux que les moralistes enseignent'). Take the question of what happens when the promotion of HR collides with what seems more urgent, more important, or more attainable objectives. Then we see that the proclaimed promotion of HR comes pretty low down the list of a government's priorities. We see this every day around us. In politics first. Upon the death of Chad's leader Idriss Déby in April 2021, the army put in place a military council headed by his son Mahamat, thus ensuring the continuity of a regime known for its systematic violations of HR. The African Union who is supposed to have a 'pro-HR' and 'no coup' policy uttered barely a murmur. France, Chad's main Western ally, turned a blind eye too. The stabilisation of Chad trumped any condemnation of the illegal transfer of power. In economics second. Major commercial contracts worth thousands of jobs take precedence over HR concerns and so does the sale of arms to questionable regimes. Ethical foreign policy then easily collapses. Selling jets to Indonesia was how Robin Cook got the backlash on his ethical foreign policy and being too franc in calling Saudi-Arabia a dictatorship was how Margot Wallströms's HR policy ran in Saudi sands.

Box 10.7 Universal Jurisdiction

In the early years of the 21st century, we witnessed the rise of what came to be called 'universal jurisdiction'. Countries that prided themselves on conducting an ethical foreign policy were particularly sensitive to the idea and started legislating laws empowering their national courts to prosecute perpetrators of genocide, crimes against humanity, and war crimes without requiring there to exist a nexus between the crime and the territory or nationals of the prosecuting country. Belgium was among them and adopted its law on universal jurisdiction in 2003. It received praise from many corners, including the conservative Wall Street Journal: little David dared to take on the nasty Goliaths of this world. No soon was the law on universal jurisdiction promulgated that the first requests for prosecution came in: Israel's Prime Minister Benjamin Netanyahu and US defence secretary Donald Rumsfeld were on the list. Soon Belgium found itself in serious problems. Ostracised and its foreign policy in a shamble, it felt obliged to 'revisit' its law, in fact undoing it of its universalist aspirations. What went wrong? The underlying idea of 'universal jurisdiction' is the belief that justice is best served when it is isolated from politics and power. That belief works at the national level and is realised through the principle of the independence of the judiciary. But does it also work at the international level? Is insulating a legal practice, such as universal jurisdiction, from the bargaining and compromising that characterise diplomatic practice and international politics, a feasible option? As a token of ethical foreign policy, universal jurisdiction has proved self-defeating. Neglecting political *prudence* bears a price. In diplomacy, ideals can be pursued effectively only if considerations of power and national interests are duly taken into account. What universal jurisdiction taught us is that the best can become the enemy of the good. Universal jurisdiction has been, for the Belgians and others, a lesson in *humility*.

Judgements regarding ethical foreign policy do not reduce, as some would have it, to a simple opposition between different schools of thought, one 'idealist', the other 'realist'. Most realists pay sincere attention to ethical values and most idealists acknowledge the overriding claims of national interests. Balancing out conflicting demands is what a politician or a diplomat is being paid for. That is where their job differs from, say, the job of the *UN High Commissioner for Human Rights* (UNHCHR), who has *no other agenda* than the one consisting in defending HR and who therefore can be outspoken in condemning abuses. The UNHCHR has no strategic, military, or economic interests to balance against HR considerations, but governments do have those interests and cannot raise HR issues without taking these interests into account. 'We can't do Mary Robinson' (a former UN High Commissioner), one American diplomat accompanying his Secretary of State on an Africa-trip once said, when they had to balance HR concerns with economic interests (*New York Times*, 15 December 1987, cited in CLAPHAM, 2015, p. 81). A similar remark as the one just made with regard to the UNHCHR applies to *one-issue non-governmental organisations* such as Human Rights Watch.

Concluding, one may say that the politician or diplomat may be excused when, confronted with opposing demands, he or she must somehow find the proper balance between them. There are, however, two situations where that excuse becomes rather thin. The *first* one goes by the name of '*selective indignation*' or '*double standards*'. Washington, for instance, has been fearless in denouncing HR abuses in countries like Cambodia, Paraguay, and Uganda in the past, Myanmar and Venezuela today, countries where the US has negligible strategic and economic interests. Washington has been a good deal less fearless in defending HR when dealing with Turkey, Brazil, Pakistan, and the Philippines, and just circumspect or even silent about Egypt and Saudi-Arabia. Such differential treatment is of course the result of balancing differential interests, but there is no denying that it undercuts the credibility of a country pretending to be an HR defender. The *second* situation occurs when third countries resent being told how to behave by states that themselves have a questionable HR record (see Box 10.8). Let us again take the case of the US. HR criticism by the US is likely to be met with references to the infamous torture programme and network of secret transfers of prisoners that was exposed as part of the 'war on terror'. The same can be said as regards drone strikes for targeted killings used in the fight against ISIS/DAESCH. Taking the moral high ground then becomes a parody. Similarly, it became increasingly difficult for the US to credibly praise the virtues of democracy with third countries while President Trump was openly fooling them at home.

Box 10.8 On Hypocrisy

For a politician to lie can be fatal. We all know some politicians who had to resign because of a lie, even sometimes an anodyne one. But hypocrisy is even worse than lying. And the problem is that people *taking the moral high ground* by defending an ethical foreign policy thus make themselves quite vulnerable to the charge of hypocrisy. Hypocrisy is more than 'saying one thing and doing another'. It is more than mere inconsistency. It is '*failing to practice what you preach*'. Donald Trump has been wildly inconsistent and has been often called a liar, a cheat, a fraud. Accusations of hypocrisy, however, do not tend to stick in his case. That is because Trump did not take the moral high ground; he misled, exaggerated, and bragged shamelessly. But he never pretended to speak the truth. That gave him a protection against the charge. During the 2016 presidential campaign, it was said that he should be taken 'seriously, but not literally'. When you do not have to take someone's words literally, that gives him a lot of latitude.

10.4 An alternative – defending the Rule of Law

As we have seen, both the conceptual and legal vulnerabilities related to HR make their effective defence difficult. The responses that we have suggested as remedies to overcome these vulnerabilities may not convince. Perhaps then we must scale down a little bit our ambitions. Better to be effective on a smaller scale than not being effective at all. Replacing the substantive but ineffective approach to HR with a more formal and procedural approach based on the Rule of Law (RoL) may offer a way out of our predicament. Some may resent such a softening of our approach and consider it too much of a concession. But let's see.

The concept of HR originated in the 18th-century struggle of the Enlightenment movement against the **arbitrariness** of absolute power. The idea was that *substantive* provisions should protect the citizen against such power. And that was how the HR approach got off the ground. But there was also a second idea around at that time to counter arbitrary power. Not by way of debatable substantive provisions, but through a more neutral procedural mechanism. Arbitrariness equals insecurity. Doing away with arbitrariness requires the instauration of **legal security**, which is at the core of the RoL approach. Legal security first and foremost simply means that there *are* rules of the game, laws, so that everybody knows what they can expect from others, including the state (rights), and conversely what others, and the state, can expect from them (duties). The mere *formal* existence of laws, independent of their *substantive* content is where the idea of the RoL gets started. Laws should be *general* and *apply equally*, they should be made *public* so that everybody can know them, and they should only govern behaviour prospectively (towards the future) and *not retroactively* (back into the past). These basic demands and some more, are what constitute the Rule of Law, the *Rechtsstaat* in German, *l'Etat de Droit* in French, meaning 'the law-governed state' (see Box 10.9).

Box 10.9 Friedrich von Hayek on the Rule of Law

In his *The Road to Serfdom* of 1944 Friedrich von Hayek provides one the clearest and most powerful formulations of the ideal of the RoL:

> stripped of all technicalities this means that government in all its actions is bound by rules fixed and announced beforehand – rules which make it possible to foresee with fair certainty how the authority will use its coercive powers in given circumstances, and to plan one's individual affairs on the basis of this knowledge

(cited in RAZ, 2009, p. 181)

Contrary to the **substantive** demands made by HR, the demands made by the RoL are **formal** in nature. Presumably that is their strength and weakness. Their strength because they cannot be questioned on their content (which they have not), their weakness because they lack content. But is lacking content really a weakness? Recalling our discussion of the questionable universality, proliferation, and banalisation of HR, disagreement on content (and underlying values) was exactly what we found to be the weak spot of HR. The demands of the RoL are essentially formal **rules of governance**, they prescribe *how* governments should act (not *what* they should enact) and thus constrain the exercise of power. Another way of expressing this is to say that the demands of the RoL are **procedural**.

The **shift** from **substantive to procedural** approaches, as the one we now suggest, moving from a HR approach to a RoL approach, reflects a general pattern in 20th-century diplomatic practice. Take the question regarding the 'Use of Force' that we discussed in Chapter 8. Instead of asking (and discussing) the substantive question whether war should be prohibited or permitted, and if so under what circumstances (remember the 1928 Kellogg-Briand Pact that went nowhere), the League of Nations Covenant (in its Art. 12) opted for a purely procedural approach to decide the matter (involving arbitration awards, unanimous Council reports, obligatory three months cooling-off periods). Difficult questions of substantive legality or morality were sidestepped. The same approach is the one we find in Chapter VII of the UN Charter. Debates over the propriety of the use of force in contexts such as Iraq (2003) and Libya (2011) frequently focus upon the procedural question whether the necessary *formal authorisation* has been secured from the UN Security Council, rather than upon the substantive moral justification for the use of force (see LOWE, 2015, pp. 66–67).

More generally one could say that it is this shift from substance to procedure that has accompanied and indeed made possible the creation of international organisations. Take any treaty instituting such organisation and you will note that apart from a very few general preambular articles (stating the object and purpose of the organisation), the bulk of the legal provisions of the treaty bears on procedures, on 'how to', not on 'what' questions.

To get a sense of what is involved in the concept of RoL, we will review two models, one elaborated by an American philosopher of law, Leon Fuller and which we will label **minimalist**, and another by the former UK Lord Chief Justice Tom Bingham, which we will label **maximalist**.

10.4.1 *The minimalist model*

Leon Fuller, a lawyer, has formulated eight demands (which I have made nine for the sake of clarity) which capture the concept of RoL, or what he calls the 'inner morality of the law' as distinct from the 'outer morality of the law' which refers to the substantive provisions of the law (see FULLER, 1964, pp. 46–94).

- **Existence of Law**. Law has to do with the governance of human conduct by rules. Therefore, the very first desideratum of any system of law is rather obvious: there must be rules in the first place. Without rules arbitrariness reigns, everything goes.
- **Generality of Law**. The rules must be general, that is they must be impersonal, apply to general classes, apply equally to all individuals belonging to these general classes, not to specific individuals. So-called 'special laws' are not Law.
- **Promulgation of Law**. The rules must be made known. They must be made publicly accessible. In short, they must be published. Nobody can be held liable for not respecting a rule that he or she could not know. Moreover, publishing the rules allows them to be the subject of public criticism.
- **No Retroactivity in Law**. The prohibition of '*ex post factum* laws' simply means that new rules can only apply to the future. The Law should be prospective. To speak of governing or directing conduct today by rules that will be enacted tomorrow is to talk blank prose. Yet retrospective laws (often called '*curative' laws*) can be justified in dealing with mishaps that may exceptionally occur within systems of rules that are generally prospective. But this then is the exception that proves the non-retroactivity principle.
- **Clarity in Law**. This desideratum is one of the most essential ingredients of legality, just as, conversely, obscurity and incoherence make legality unattainable by anyone. Clarity does not mean that such concepts as 'good faith' or 'due care' are to be excluded from the Law's vocabulary. Sometimes the best way to achieve clarity is to rely on common sense standards of judgement that have grown up in ordinary life lived outside legislative halls. Nor can we ever be more exact than the nature of the subject matter with which we are dealing admits. A specious clarity can be more damaging than an honest open-ended vagueness.
- **Consistency of Law**. If the objective of Law is to build a system of rules for the governance of human conduct, then we shall fail in that attempt when we issue contradictory rules which, by definition, cannot coherently be obeyed. Sometimes the concept of contradiction is broadened to that of 'incompatibility' – of rules that, without contradicting each other, do not go together very well. In legal practice, there are numerous interpretative techniques (such as reciprocal adjustment of incompatible rules) and maxims (such as '*lex posterior derogate anterior*' [later law prevails on former law]) to handle inevitable contradictions and incompatibilities in Law.

- **No Law can require the Impossible**. This obvious desideratum (known as the Latin maxim '*Ad impossibile nemo tenetur*') simply aims at ensuring that the requirements of the Law lie within the powers of those subject to it.
- **Constancy of the Law through Time**. This principle demands that the Law should not be changed too frequently. There is a close affinity between the harms done by retroactive laws and those resulting from too frequent changes in the law. Both follow from what may be called '*legislative inconstancy*'. The evil of retroactive law arises because men have acted upon the *previous state of the Law* and the actions thus taken may be frustrated by a backward-looking alteration in their legal effect. But that is exactly what too frequent changes of the law would also result in.
- **Congruence between Official Action and Declared Law**. This principle aims at preventing a discrepancy between the Law as declared and the Law as actually administered (discrepancies that may result from indifference, stupidity, prejudice, bribery, or the drive towards personal power). And it is generally up to the judiciary to act as a bulwark against the lawless administration of the Law (provided the judiciary itself does not impair the requested congruence).

10.4.2 The maximalist model

Tom Bingham, a judge, defends a concept of RoL that is somewhat more elaborated and less purely formal than Fuller's (see BINGHAM, 2010, pp. 37–132). For him, the core of the RoL is 'that all persons and authorities within the State, whether public or private, should be bound by and entitled to the benefit of laws publicly made, taking effect (generally) in the future and publicly administered in the courts' (BINGHAM, 2010, p. 8). The ingredients of the RoL are summarised in eight principles (which I have reduced to six for reasons I will explain below):

- **Accessibility of the Law**. The law must be accessible and so far as possible intelligible, clear, and predictable. All these requirements are captured by the concept of '*legal certainty*' that we mentioned earlier: *it is of more consequence that a rule should be certain, than whether the rule is established one way or the other*, which clearly shows the formal, not substantive character of the requirements involved.
- **Application of Law not Discretion**. Questions of legal rights and liability should be resolved by *application of the law* and not by the exercise of discretion. This requirement states that it is the law, and only the law that needs to be applied and that there can be no discretionary decision-making powers conferred on officials, be they government ministers, public officers, administrators of agencies, judges, and so on. Discretion opens the door to arbitrariness, which is the exact antithesis of the RoL.
- **Equality before the Law**. The laws of the land should apply equally to all, save to the extent that objective differences justify differentiation. In fact, this principle of the RoL is just a replica of what is known as the classic '*Principle of Justice*': all should be treated equally, and differential treatment is allowed only with respect to persons who differ *relevantly* from the others and then only *to the extent* of that difference (see PERELMAN, 1963, pp. 224–233). Non-relevant differentiation is discrimination (as against Jews, Gypsies, and homosexuals, for example). The tricky question is of course how to establish which differences are to be considered relevant and which not (but that is a question of substantive justice, not of formal justice).

- **The Exercise of Power**. Ministers and public officers at all levels must exercise the powers conferred on them in good faith, fairly, for the purpose for which the powers were conferred, without exceeding the limits of such powers and not unreasonably. This principle follows naturally from the two preceding principles, but has the advantage of explicitating some core concepts belonging to the RoL: *good faith* (honesty), *fairness* (no bias or personal interest in the mind of the decision-maker and the 'right to be heard' for anyone liable to have an adverse decision made against them), *proper purpose* (not to advance some other object than the one aimed at by the power conferred), *limits* (not to act beyond the power conferred, that is '*ultra vires*'), *reasonableness* (to act sensibly with due appreciation of one's responsibilities). If any of these rules is not respected, a judge can quash the questionable decision, a process known as *judicial review*.

- **Dispute Resolution**. Means must be provided for resolving *bona fide* civil disputes which the parties themselves are unable to resolve, and this without prohibitive cost or inordinate delay. The idea here is that for the protection of the law to be effective, it must be enforceable. Access to a court often faces two obstacles. The *first* is *expense*. It has been said that justice in the UK is open to all, like the Ritz Hotel. To overcome this obstacle, legal aid should be provided when necessary. The *second* obstacle is *delay*. It is a familiar aphorism that 'justice delayed is justice denied'. But there is no ready remedy for this obstacle which is a structural problem of many legal systems.

- **A Fair Trial**. Adjudicative procedures provided by the state should be fair. The right to a fair trial obviously applies to both criminal and civil trials but also to procedures of a hybrid kind (as when a compulsorily detained mental patient seeks to be discharged from a mental hospital), hence the ponderous language of 'adjudicative procedures'. Fairness in adjudication applies of course to both sides equally (prosecutor or claimant and defendant). Crucial to this principle is the *independence of the judiciary* not only from the government and its ministers, but also from the media, pressure groups, political parties, and others. Next (and close) to independence comes *impartiality* (and, I would add *neutrality*) which requires from the decision-maker (most often a judge) an open mind, free from personal predilections or prejudices, deciding the issues on the legal and factual merits of the case only.

As I said, I have reduced Bingham's eight principles to six. I have dropped what he calls 'The Rule of Law in the International Legal Order' (his eighth principle), because this is not, as such, a distinct principle to be added to the six principles outlined above; it just tells the story of how the six principles play out in the international context. So, dropping this eighth principle is rather innocuous. More critically, I have left out his (fifth) principle of 'Human Rights', because mixing up the RoL with the HR is exactly, I think, what should not be done (incorporating HR in the RoL is what is called a '**thick**' conception of the RoL). The whole point of making the distinction between RoL and HR is that it allows one to separate formal from substantive issues which, as we have argued, is the way out of the problems one faces when trying to defend 'human rights' (such conception of the RoL is called '**thin**'). I realise that by dropping Bingham's fifth principle I have distorted Bingham's conception of the matter.

Before closing, let us stress that the formal 'demands' formulated by Fuller and the 'principles' formulated by Bingham (except for the fifth one), while not being substantive in nature, nevertheless incorporate fundamental *values* such as Order (the mere

Existence of Law), Equality (the demand of the Generality of Law and Equality before the Law), Justice (the request of non-retroactivity of the Law and again Equality before the Law), Certainty (clarity, promulgation, and accessibility of the Law), among others. In Fuller's minimalist model these values remain somewhat below the surface, while in Bingham's maximalist model they occasionally appear above the surface (explicitly in the requirement of Equality before the Law and the one regarding Fair Trial).

Let us wrap up and see what we have learned in this chapter. Here, as in the preceding chapter on IL, our purpose was not to systematically review the corpus of substantive HR. We were interested in studying the place of HR in diplomatic practice. The first thing that we noted was that the concept itself of HR may give rise to inconsistencies and paradoxes. Inconsistencies first, in that the language of rights (as applicable to civil-political rights) got confused with the language of policy (as applicable to so-called socio-economic 'rights'); paradoxes next in (1) that one must simultaneously rely upon the state in order to be protected against the state, and (2) that the protection of HR requires simultaneously a non-interfering, minimal state and an assertive, intervening state according to the rights concerned.

The main concern in this chapter, however, revolved around the difficulty which foreign ministers and diplomats encounter in effectively and credibly defending HR. We have imputed this difficulty to three vulnerabilities which inhere in the concept itself of HR. They already show up in the language of HR once we start speaking of 'basic' or 'fundamental' HR which seems to imply that there are also non-basic or non-fundamental HR, notions that strike us as self-contradictory. Are all HR equally universal? While the right to life or freedom of speech seem indeed to be grounded in what it is to be human or in human dignity, can the same be said of the right to a decent job or to internet access? With this, we touch on the issue of the proliferation of HR (from first- over second- to third-generation rights) which risks diluting *all* of them, as well as on the issue regarding the banalisation of HR discourse that risks turning any human desire into a right. In order to escape these conundrums, we have suggested an alternative approach which consists in defending the RoL instead of HR. Such an approach replaces the substantive but vulnerable demands of HR with formal but no less stringent demands prescribing *how* governments should act rather than *what* they should enact. Procedural demands thus replace substantive demands. They constrain the exercise of power. By defending the RoL we may get further than with defending HR.

Bibliography

BAGGINI, Julian (2018), *How the World Thinks*, Granta, New York, NY.

BINGHAM, Tom (2010), *The Rule of Law*, Penguin, London.

CLAPHAM, Andrew (2015), *Human Rights: A Very Short Introduction*, Oxford University Press, Oxford.

COLLIER, Paul & KAY, John (2020), *Greed Is Dead: Politics after Individualism*, Allen Lane, New York, NY.

DOUZINAS, Costas (2000), *The End of Human Rights*, Hart Publishing, Oxford.

FINNIS, John (2011), *Natural Law and Natural Rights*, Oxford University Press, Oxford.

FULLER, Leon (1964), *The Morality of Law*, Yale University Press, New Haven, CT – London.

HAARSCHER, Guy (1987), *Philosophie des Droits de l'Homme*, Editions de L'Université de Bruxelles, Bruxelles.

KAVANAGH, Aileen & OBERDIEK, John (Eds.) (2009), *Arguing about Law*, Routledge, Abingdon/New York, NY.

LOWE, Vaughan (2015), *International Law: A Very Short Introduction*, Oxford University Press, Oxford.

MACHIAVELLI, Nicolo (1950), *Il Principe*, Hatier, Paris.

PERELMAN, Chaïm (1963), *Justice et Raison*, Presses Universitaires de Bruxelles, Bruxelles.

RAZ, Joseph (2009), "The Rule of Law and Its Virtue", in: KAVANAH & OBERDIEK (2009), pp. 181–192.

WERHANE, Patricia, GINI, A. R. & OZAR, David (1986), *Philosophical Issues in Human Rights*, Random House, New York, NY.

Conclusion
Diplomacy as a way of life

In this book we have approached diplomacy as that 'what diplomats do'. And they do all kinds of things. They analyse situations, report to capitals, advise their Minister, make recommendations, make representations, negotiate, go public, and explain policy, and for all that they need clear thinking, articulate reasoning, persuasive argumentation, and effective communication. What makes a diplomat is not any domain-specific expertise but the whole of his aptitudes, competences, and skills which together constitute his 'practice'. A diplomat is an:

- **Analyst**. Her job starts with a cool political analysis of the world as it stands (Voltaire's 'le monde comme il va'); not just describing that world but deciphering it; not retrospectively but prospectively, sketching trends and tendencies in a reasoned forward-looking account of how the future may unfold, thus allowing the authorities back home to anticipate on future developments and to pro-actively act on them rather than react to them. A diplomat is an early-warning radar for troubles ahead but also a pristine detector of future opportunities.
- **Policy shaper**. A diplomat does not just tell what the problem is, she tries to figure out what to do about it, what the solutions are. She actively contributes to the shaping of the policy response, and that requires smart judgment. She lays down options, devises scenarios, clearly distinguishing between the ideal (in the books) and the feasible (in the facts). A diplomat should never want to get an instruction from her capital that she has not somehow shaped herself.
- **Strategist**. Clarity and certainty of vision are key in diplomatic practice. For that a strategy is needed. Not the big vision thing, but a plan connecting goals to available resources, identifying points of leverage and avoiding overstretch. Effective strategising addresses three questions: what is my starting position, where do I wish to land, and how do I balance my available resources with my goals.
- **Tactician**. Once there is a master plan the next question is, how do I implement it, how do I get from here to there. What are the consecutive short-term steps to be taken? Which means do I put in the execution of the plan, and at what time? How to avoid or to overcome obstacles?
- **Problem solver**: Many issues in a diplomat's life are not about grand politics. Much of his work is about finding swift *ad hoc* solutions to often unexpected, nasty, nitty-gritty problems, none of them very serious but all together upsetting and time consuming. A diplomat is a troubleshooter and problem fixer, no less than an analyst, policy shaper, and strategist.

DOI: 10.4324/9781003298182-16

- **Negotiator**. Negotiation is at the heart of diplomacy. That is where the diplomat can be at its best. Clearly identifying the interests at stake, pre-empting arguments of the adversary, building coalitions, persuading, and always keeping cool.
- **Communicator**. Diplomacy is about influencing the behaviour of others. And that is done through effective communication. Reaching out, telling people what you stand for, explaining and clarifying what your position, what your foreign policy is.

This list of aptitudes, competences, and skills is not unique to the diplomat. A good lawyer, a businessman, a consultant, an academic will most probably have them too; if not all, at least most of them. Let me quote Abba Eban here: 'When all is said and done, *as a profession* diplomacy is not unlike other professions, it becomes less awe-inspiring the more that is known about it' (EBAN, 1998, p. 123, my italics). If there is still some 'mystique' surrounding the profession it is mostly misplaced, often a relic of the past. Demystification then guards the profession against becoming sclerotic.

But focusing on the diplomat's **profession** leaves something important out of the picture. What about a **diplomat's life**, as distinct from his profession? A diplomat's profession may not be unlike other professions, but his life definitely is not like that of others. Compare it with the doctor working for *Doctors Without Borders* (MSF) and the doctor around the corner: same profession, but certainly not same life. *A diplomat is a nomad – physically and mentally*. He has left home, leaving family and friends behind, moves from one country to another (perhaps from one hemisphere to another), meets all kind of 'strange' people, tries to understand *their* culture and how *they* see the world, learns foreign languages, drives left and then right again. All this can be positively challenging: new horizons are discovered, there is adventure all around. But it can also be demanding. A diplomat's life goes through critical moments. He may find himself in a hardship post. Thousands of kilometres from home he may feel estranged. Family life can come under stress. The country he or she lives in and its media may be hostile.

It is sometimes said that diplomacy is no less a choice of a *way of life* than it is of a profession, something like a 'call', a 'vocation'. What seems to be implied by these terms is that diplomacy is something that *absorbs* the *whole of a diplomat's person*. Every aspect of his 'life' (his thinking, feeling, doing) enters in his 'work'. *Life and work are one*. Even though challenging, his profession is *positively absorbing*, because *engaging*. His 'work' is not merely something to be executed; his work is his life: **a diplomat performs himself**. A diplomat has his passion for his job (as Stendahl said: 'c'est un bonheur d'avoir pour métier sa passion'). Diplomacy, for him, is a 'habit', an 'attitude', a 'mode of being', ultimately perhaps a 'way of life' (see DE BLOOIS, 2017, pp. 145–149). 'Living diplomatically' is the expression with which Sharp closes his latest book on diplomacy (SHARP, 2019, p. 126).

There is the old story of a visitor who encounters three stonemasons working on a medieval cathedral and asking each what he is doing. 'I am cutting this stone to perfect shape', says the first. 'I am building a great cathedral' says the second. 'I am working for the glory of God' says the third. These stonemasons were people performing themselves. Diplomacy too is about building something, be it less elevated than a cathedral and more mundane than God's glory: a better world (not a perfect one), simply for man's well-being (not his glory). It was Teddy Roosevelt who said that 'life's greatest good fortune is to work hard at work worth doing'. By that standard, diplomats have reason to feel fortunate.

References

EBAN, Abba (1998), *Diplomacy for the Next Century*, Yale University Press, New Haven, CT – London.

DE BLOOIS, Joost, DE CAUWER, Stijn & MASSCHELEIN, Anneleen (Eds.) (2017), *50 Key Terms in Contemporary Cultural Theory*, Pelckmans Pro, Kalmthout.

SHARP, Paul (2019), *Diplomacy in the 21st Century*, Routledge, London/New York, NY.

Select bibliography

ABRAMS, Elliott & KAGAN, Donald (Eds.) (2016), *Honor among Nations: Intangible Interests and Foreign Policy*, Ethics & Public Policy Center, Washington, DC.

AMSTRONG, David, FARRELL, Theo & LAMBERT, Hélène (2012), *International Law and International Relations*, Cambridge University Press, Cambridge.

BAGGINI, Julian (2018), *How the World Thinks*, Granta, London.

BARSTON, Ronald Peter (2019), *Modern Diplomacy*, Routledge, London/New York, NY.

BERCOVITCH, Jacob & JACKSON, Richard (2009), *Conflict Resolution in the Twenty-First Century*, University of Michigan Press.

BERRIDGE, G. R. (2010), *Diplomacy. Theory and Practice*, Palgrave, New York, NY.

BINGHAM, Tom (2011), *The Rule of Law*, Penguin, London.

BISCOP, Sven (2021), *Grand Strategy in 10 Words – A Guide to Great Power Politics in the 21st Century*, Bristol University Press, Bristol.

BRANDS, Hal (2014), *What Good Is Grand Strategy*, Cornell University Press, Ithaca, NY/ London.

CLAPHAM, Andrew (2015), *Human Rights – A Very Short Introduction*, Oxford University Press, Oxford.

COOPER, Andrew, HEINE, Jorge & THAKUR, Ramesh (2015), *The Oxford Handbook of Modern Diplomacy*, Oxford University Press, Oxford.

COOPER, Robert (2021), *The Ambassadors – Thinking about Diplomacy from Machiavelli to Modern Times*, Weidenfeld & Nicolson, London.

DEMEY, Lorenz & BUEKENS, Filip (2017), *Redeneren en Argumenteren*, Acco, Leuven/ Den Haag.

EBAN, Abba (1998), *Diplomacy for the Next Century*, Yale University Press. New Haven, CT/ London.

ELSTER, Jon (2007), *Explaining Social Behavior*, Cambridge University Press, Cambridge.

FRIEDMAN, Lawrence (1975), *The Legal System – A Social Science Perspective*, Russell Sage Foundation, New York, NY.

GADDIS, John L. (2018), *On Grand Strategy*, Allen Lane, London.

HAASS, Richard N. (2009), *War of Necessity, War of Choice: A Memoir of Two Iraq Wars*, Simon & Shuster, New York, NY.

HANDLER, Scott P. (Ed.) (2013), *International Politics. Classic and Contemporary Readings*, CQ Press, Los Angeles, CA.

HANNAY, David (2013), *Britain's Quest for a Role: A Diplomatic Memoir from Europe to the UN*, I.B. Tauris, London/New York, NY.

KAHNEMAN, Daniel (2011), *Thinking, Fast and Slow*, Allen Lane, New York, NY.

KISSINGER, Henry (2014), *World Order*, Penguin Press, New York, NY.

LOWE, Vaughan (2015), *International Law: A Very Short Introduction*, Oxford University Press, Oxford.

MACHIAVELLI, Nicolo (1950), *Il Principe*, Hatier, Paris.

NYE, Joseph (2015), *Is the American Century Over?*, Polity, Cambridge.

PERELMAN, Chaïm & OLBRECHTS-TYTECA, Lucie (1970), *Traité de l'Argumentation – La Nouvelle Rhétorique*, Editions de l'Université de Bruxelles, Bruxelles.

PETERSEN, Martin (2009), *An Introduction to Decision Theory*, Oxford University Press, Oxford.

POSNER, Richard P. (1995), *Overcoming Law*, Harvard University Press, Cambridge.

POSNER, Richard P. (2001), *Frontiers of Legal Theory*, Harvard University Press, Cambridge.

RANA, Kishan S. (2011), *21st Century Diplomacy – A Practitioner's Guide*, Continuum, London/New York, NY.

SHARP, Paul (2019), *Diplomacy in the 21st Century*, Routledge, London/New York, NY.

SMITH, Rupert (2019), *The Utility of Force – The Art of War in the Modern World*, Penguin, London.

THALER, Richard (2015), *Misbehaving. The Making of Behavioural Economics*, Norton, New York, NY.

WALTON, Douglas (2008), *Informal Logic – A Pragmatic Approach*, Cambridge University Press, Cambridge.

Index